Advance Praise for *Beyond Chinatown: The Metropolitan Water District and the Environment in Southern California*

Steve Erie knocks another one out of the ballpark. Having written a superb book on machine politics in *Rainbow's End* and having brought the state back into urban politics in compelling fashion in *Globalizing L.A.*, Erie does path-breaking work once again in his analysis of water politics in *Beyond Chinatown*, showing us the importance of regionalization and how to study it. The second of a trilogy on infrastructure in southern California, Erie's new book is another fascinating saga in how the west was developed.

> —*Clarence Stone, research professor, George Washington University, and emeritus professor, University of Maryland*

Water history is tough to write, and no one has done it better than Steven P. Erie in this fast-paced narrative based on monumental research. I marvel at the multi-faceted inclusiveness of this story of water, region, politics, engineering, growth, and the environment.

> —*Kevin Starr, professor of history, University of Southern California*

In this path-breaking history of the MWD, Steve Erie brilliantly debunks L.A.'s greatest urban legend and opens bold new perspectives on the secret history of Southern California.

> —*Mike Davis, professor of urban and environmental history, University of California, Irvine*

Perception may be reality in politics, and water politics are no exception, but perception and mythology are hardly enough to support critical public policy decisions on water for people and the environment. Professor Erie lays out for serious students and average readers alike a compelling study of the perception and reality of the MET and the major figures and events that define it. The history of real life intrigue revealed is worthy of the *Chinatown* title, but there is much more here for today's leaders seeking to find a model of success for regional cooperation and accomplishment.

> —*Ron Gastelum, former CEO, Metropolitan Water District of Southern California*

In this sweeping history, Erie gives us not only the people, plans and decisions of a public agency that has allowed a semi arid region to take water for granted but the consequences of those decisions that have assisted in the creation of one of the world's great economies. And then, like a scout at the horizon, he confronts the global challenges facing the future of water for this region—indeed, the future of California. *Beyond Chinatown*, indeed. It's a great read and an important book.

> —*James Flanigan, business and economics columnist,*
> *The Los Angeles Times and The New York Times*

This revisionist history of the Metropolitan Water District transforms its long accepted "black hat" to pale gray. Steve Erie solidifies his reputation as the contemporary authority on Southern California water politics with this highly engaging book. It is a must read for everyone interested in water policy.

> —*Helen Ingram, Warmington endowed chair in social ecology,*
> *University of California, Irvine*

This is an extremely important work. . . . State of the art in terms of its research and findings on one of the most important water agencies in the nation.

> —*Abraham Hoffman, author of Vision or Villainy:*
> *Origins of the Owens Valley-Los Angeles Water Controversy*

This is a first-rate study. It is valuable both for the important story it tells and for the broader lessons it suggests on the role of government in urban development and on the importance of entrepreneurial leadership in meeting complex public needs.

> —*Jameson W. Doig, emeritus professor of politics and public*
> *affairs, Princeton University*

BEYOND *CHINATOWN*

The Metropolitan Water District, Growth,

and the Environment in Southern California

Steven P. Erie
With the Assistance of Harold Brackman

STANFORD UNIVERSITY PRESS
Stanford, California 2006

Stanford University Press
Stanford, California
© 2006 by the Board of Trustees of the Leland
Stanford Junior University. All rights reserved.
Printed in the United States of America
on acid-free, archival-quality paper

Library of Congress Cataloging-in-Publication Data

Erie, Steven P.
   Beyond Chinatown : the Metropolitan Water District, growth, and the
environment in southern California / Steven P. Erie ; with the assistance
of Harold Brackman.
       p. cm.
     Includes bibliographical references and index.
     ISBN 0-8047-5139-0 (cloth : alk. paper)—ISBN 0-8047-5140-4 (pbk. :
   alk. paper)
     1. Sustainable development—California, Southern.   2. Environmental
   policy—California, Southern.   3. Water-supply—California, Southern.
     4. Metropolitan areas—California, Southern.   I. Brackman, Harold David.
   II. Title.
HC107.C23E5585   2006
333.910097949—dc22   2005032772

Typeset by G&S Book Services in 10/13.5 Sabon

Original Printing 2006

Last figure below indicates year of this printing:
15   14   13   12   11   10   09   08   07   06

To Norton E. Long and Robert V. Phillips,
  mentors and friends

Contents

Tables, Figures, and Photos

Tables

Figures

Photos

Abbreviations

AEWSD	Arvin-Edison Water Storage District
AF	acre-feet
AMO	Atlantic Multidecadal Oscillation
Bay-Delta	San Francisco Bay/Sacramento–San Joaquin River Delta
CEQA	California Environmental Quality Act
CFBDA	CALFED Bay-Delta Authority
CVP	Central Valley Project
CVPIA	Central Valley Project Improvement Act
CVWD	Coachella Valley Water District
DBCP	dibromochloropropane
DWR	California Department of Water Resources
Eastside	Eastside or Diamond Valley Lake reservoir project
EDF	Environmental Defense Fund
EIS/EIR	Environmental Impact Statement/Report
EPA	U.S. Environmental Protection Agency
ENSO	El Niño-Southern Oscillation
ESG	Economic Study Group
ESP	Emergency Storage Project
FY	fiscal year
GWRS	Groundwater Replenishment System
IID	Imperial Irrigation District
Inland Empire	San Bernardino/Riverside counties
IRP	Integrated Resources Plan
KCWA	Kern County Water Agency
LADWP	Los Angeles Department of Water and Power
MAF	million acre-feet
Metropolitan	Metropolitan Water District of Southern California
MET	Metropolitan Water District of Southern California
MTBE	methyl tertiary butyl ether
MWD	Metropolitan Water District of Southern California
MWDSC	Metropolitan Water District of Southern California
MWDOC	Municipal Water District of Orange County

NAFTA	North American Free Trade Agreement
NDMA	*n*-Nitrosodimethylamine
NOAA	National Oceanic and Atmospheric Administration
PDO	Pacific Decadal Oscillation
PERC	perchloroethylene
PPB	parts per billion
PVID	Palo Verde Irrigation District
QSA	Quantification Settlement Agreement
SANDAG	San Diego Association of Governments
SCAG	Southern California Association of Governments
SDCWA	San Diego County Water Authority
SDG&E	San Diego Gas & Electric Company
SNWA	Southern Nevada Water Authority
SWP	State Water Project
TCE	trichloroethylene
TVA	Tennessee Valley Authority
UWMP	Urban Water Management Plan
VOC	volatile organic compound
YCWA	Yuba County Water Agency

Preface

In Roman Polanski's celebrated 1974 *noir* movie, Chinatown is more a metaphor for crime and conspiracy than an actual place on the map. Polanski's film—a convoluted tale of secretive, corrupt water politics in Los Angeles—ends with a famous shrug: "Forget it, Jake—it's Chinatown." Challenging the conventional wisdom conveyed by that cynical shrug, this study looks beyond the mythic *Chinatown* to chronicle the remarkable public saga of the Metropolitan Water District of Southern California. Metropolitan (also known as MWD, MWDSC, or MET) is the region's giant water wholesaler and policymaker, now serving over 18 million customers. Its powerful sway radiates far beyond its L.A. headquarters building on Alameda Street—which, ironically, casts its shadow over what was once the historic Chinatown district. Yet *Chinatown*'s seductive mythologies help obscure MWD's authentic, instructive history.

Having lived nearly all of my life in Southern California, I have had a front-row seat for viewing the region's complex water politics. I was born, raised, and educated in Los Angeles and for the past 25 years have lived in San Diego. Los Angeles and San Diego—MWD's two largest member agencies—long have battled for control of this semiarid region's "liquid gold." Early on, Los Angeles dealt itself nearly all the trump cards. Under the visionary leadership of William Mulholland, who brought water to the city in 1913 from the faraway Owens Valley and later played a crucial role in creating MWD, Los Angeles assured itself a reliable water supply into the 21st century.

Not so San Diego, which faces a bleaker water future in part because it never built an aqueduct of its own to deliver its Colorado River water allotment. Urged by the federal government to join Metropolitan at the end of World War II, San Diego still depends on MWD to meet most of its water needs; some fear a lengthy drought could reduce San Diego's water lifeline to a trickle. Impelled by this nightmare scenario as well as by colonial resentment of its seemingly imperious northern neighbor, the San Diego County Water Authority in the early 1990s embarked on what critics saw as a costly and quixotic quest for water independence from MWD and L.A. This and other epic water battles are chronicled here.

This study of Metropolitan's growing and contested water empire has had an unusually long gestation period. In graduate school at UCLA, my interest in the role played by public bureaucracies and infrastructure in Southern California's remarkable growth first surfaced in coursework with Professors Francine Rabinovitz, John C. Bollens, Chuck Ries, and Stephan Thernstrom. Yet not until the early 1990s did I embark on the systematic study of the region's "crown jewels"—the publicly built-and-managed megaprojects that include the L.A. Aqueduct, the Colorado River Aqueduct, State Water Project, the San Pedro Bay ports, Los Angeles International Airport—and their catalytic roles in the region's improbable 20th-century development. *Beyond 'Chinatown'* is the second in a trilogy of "crown jewels" projects. It was preceded by *Globalizing L.A.*, an analysis of regional trade and infrastructure development, and will be followed by *Mulholland's Gift*, a reexamination of L.A.'s storied but still controversial Department of Water and Power.

I wish to thank an able corps of University of California at San Diego graduate students for research and kindred assistance: Craig Burnett, Jim Ingram, Henry Kim, Michael Lloyd, Scott MacKenzie, Susan Shaler, David Shirk, and Tony Smith. Scholars and practitioners kindly read—and improved—earlier drafts of the manuscript. I want to thank Gary Arant, Fred Barker, Carl Boronkay, Lin Burzell, Jim Doig, Paul Engstrand, Tom Erb, Ron Gastelum, Duane Georgeson, Jerry Gewe, Abraham Hoffman, Annette Hubbell, Sam Kernell, LeVal Lund, Dave Oliphant, Marion Orr, Robert V. Phillips, Greg Quist, Jim Wickser, and Howard Williams for their valuable comments and suggestions.

Greg Freeman provided first-rate research help on chapters 1 and 7. My most profound debt is owed to my long-time friend Harold Brackman, who made a vital contribution to this study. I could not have completed this without his invaluable research assistance.

I would like to express my deep appreciation to the Metropolitan Water District of Southern California and its member agencies for their generous cooperation and assistance. MWD's Jennifer Sharpe and Tenille Otero of the San Diego County Water Authority provided invaluable help in locating photographs. I also am grateful to the individuals interviewed, who gave so freely of their time and effort. Further, I wish to express my gratitude for the assistance provided by the MWD, UCLA, and Huntington libraries. I owe a special thanks to the John Randolph Haynes and Dora Haynes Foundation for underwriting much of the research for this book. Project support also was furnished by the University of Southern California's Southern California Studies Center, the James Irvine Foundation, and UC San Diego.

Finally, I want to thank two extraordinary mentors and friends who deepened my appreciation and understanding of public bureaucracy and its role in urban development. One was a preeminent scholar; the other, an extraordinarily able practitioner. The late Norton E. Long was one of the premier students of public administration and bureaucracy. I was privileged to have Norton as an early guide. He encouraged me to undertake studies such as this, though always insisting that the *cui bono* question—who ultimately benefits?—be asked. Much of what I know about the region's water issues was learned from Robert V. Phillips, the gifted former general manager and chief engineer of the Los Angeles Department of Water and Power. A dedication is small reward for the insight and wisdom Norton and Bob so generously imparted.

Steven P. Erie
La Jolla, California
February 2006

BEYOND *CHINATOWN*

I *Overview and Historical Development*

1　Mighty Metropolitan

Water is the life-blood of Southern California.

Metropolitan Water District of Southern California, 1931[1]

If the wars of this century were fought over oil, the wars of the next century will be fought over water.

Ismail Serageldin, World Bank vice president and chair of the Global Water Partnership, 1995[2]

Beyond 'Chinatown' is a study of the complex and contentious politics of water, growth, and the environment in semiarid Southern California. This sprawling megalopolis is now the world's eighth largest economy, encompassing the five-county Los Angeles metropolitan region as well as the San Diego metropolitan area.[3] This is a seemingly inhospitable locale for 20 million-plus inhabitants to live and work, with millions more still coming. Here, annual rainfall resembles the Middle East, averaging 15 inches or less along the coast and 10 inches or fewer inland. Local water supplies can support only a fraction of the current population. For this parched coastal plain to grow into a mighty civilization, it had to imaginatively find and tap—even ruthlessly—new water supplies.

The story of Southern California's quest for needed "lifeblood" is remarkable and still controversial. Starting in the early 20th century, regional leaders embarked on a relentless search for imported water from faraway places—the Owens Valley in the eastern Sierra Nevada, the Colorado River, and Northern California. The saga began with the city of Los Angeles and its still-contested water quest. L.A. water chief William Mulholland pioneered the development of imported water supplies from the distant and rural Owens Valley. Completed in 1913, the 233-mile-long Los Angeles Aqueduct would furnish water sufficient for a city of 2 million residents. In the late 1920s, Los Angeles and neighboring communities such as Pasadena would play crucial leadership roles in a bold experiment in regional cooperation—the Metropolitan Water District of Southern California, also known as MWD or MET—bringing fresh supplies of Colorado River water needed to fuel region-wide growth. Nearly all of urbanizing Southern California would join the "MET family" to secure this essential elixir.[4]

From its inception, Southern California's water quest has been mired in invective and controversy. Early critics of L.A.'s Owens Valley aqueduct charged that it was a nefarious and secretive scheme by L.A.'s greedy land barons and conniving water officials to enrich themselves through secret purchases of San Fernando Valley land (made valuable by water) while supposedly ruining Owens Valley farmers through water diversions to Los Angeles. The conventional wisdom is fictively encapsulated in *Chinatown*—Roman Polanski's famed 1974 *film noir*—depicting an incestuous, developer-driven water conspiracy.

The film *Chinatown* is the fecund offspring, rather than parent, of a long line of L.A. water conspiracy theories dating back to the early 20th century. The film imaginatively encodes the popular understanding of how Los Angeles—and, indeed, Southern California—grew large and mighty. Claiming to draw lessons, policymakers and scholars have creatively used the film to try to shape the water policy debate in California and the West, such as over agriculture-to-urban transfers. Despite accumulating scholarship to the contrary, the *noir* legend stubbornly refuses to die. To this day, Los Angeles's archetypal "rape of the Owens Valley" haunts L.A.'s Department of Water and Power. The specter also haunts the Metropolitan Water District as a *Chinatown*-like shadow conspiracy of L.A. "water imperialism" and its reigning private developers. But is *Chinatown* an appropriate metaphor or adequate explanation for Southern California water development? Regardless of what did or did not transpire in the Owens Valley, has Southern California's search for new water supplies been a tawdry tale of secret backroom deals profiting developers and despoiling communities and the environment?

In these pages we offer an alternative account—based on an extensive analysis of available archives supplemented by interviews—of the Southern California water story, an account that challenges the major themes of the film. We focus on the region's largest and most significant water agency: the Metropolitan Water District of Southern California.

Today, this unheralded organization is arguably the nation's and even the world's biggest and most important public water agency of its kind. We hope to shed new light on this remarkable and little understood public institution, and its strategies and choices aimed at securing a reliable and safe water supply—in an environmentally and economically responsible manner—for one of the world's great regional economies.

Celebrating its 75th anniversary in 2003, MWD remains a dynamic cog in the region's still-prodigious growth machine. But over the years, its roles in the economy and environment have grown more nuanced and balanced. Once castigated as an environmentally despoiling handmaiden of growth and sprawl, Metropolitan is now hailed by many as a global leader in regional resource management and environmental stewardship. MWD also has navigated—albeit with difficulty—the uneasy partnership and rivalry between Los Angeles and San Diego—the nation's second largest and seventh biggest cities—with L.A. historically holding greater political power and water rights.

Not surprisingly, Metropolitan's institutional arrangements, rules, and policies have been hotly contested terrain for competing urban, business, environmental, and agricultural interests. Fierce battles have been fought publicly—in the MWD boardroom, in state and federal legislatures, regulatory agencies, the courts, and at the ballot box. Metropolitan's public history is an epic featuring both cooperation and conflict. In the early years, this extraordinary regional partnership financed and built the Colorado River Aqueduct, annexed most of Southern California into its service territory, and provided vital support for the 1960s-era State Water Project. More recently, with water reliability growing uncertain, conflict has overshadowed cooperation. Since 1990, there have been mounting challenges and battles: San Diego's drive for water independence from MWD and Los Angeles; fierce fights over the Colorado River and fragile Bay-Delta ecosystem in Northern California; and the global rise of water markets and privatization. Regardless of their origins, these contests ultimately have been fought in public forums, inviting public debate, participation, and outcomes.

Today, Metropolitan is faced with burgeoning population growth—adding by 2025 the equivalent of another city of Los Angeles (4 million people) and San Diego (1.3 million residents)—to Southern California in the face of adverse climate changes, a lengthy drought, mounting water-quality challenges, and new post-9/11 security concerns. In response, MWD has devised innovative new formulas for water reliability, quality, financing, safety, and governance—all of which are being closely scrutinized by national and even global observers.

Beyond 'Chinatown' offers a fresh appraisal of Metropolitan's 75-year-plus record and legacy. The MET's supporters deem it a "magnificent institution"[5] providing responsible and reliable water stewardship under challenging circumstances. Its detractors still depict it as a pawn of L.A. "water imperialism" and pro-growth interests, and even threatening to become an inefficient and unreliable water provider. Is MWD an enterprising and effective *public* agency and water guarantor, or merely a *Chinatown*-style "hidden government"—just another, albeit grandiose, special district captured by entrenched interests—with enfeebled ability to meet the region's needs?

These questions have national and international, and not merely regional, import. As the 21st century begins, water conflicts spawned by urban growth and climate change are erupting across North America and on other continents. In a now global search for effective water formulas and institutional arrangements, Southern California's historic experiment in cooperative regional water provision—building an urban civilization in a hostile, semidesert environment and promising to secure its water future—deserves the most careful scrutiny.

"Empire of the West"

Flung out in a thin line across the desert, all the way from the Colorado River to Los Angeles and its twelve sister cities of the [Metropolitan] Water District, this army of workers is engaged in man's latest and greatest battle against his age-old enemy—thirst. It is a battle which has been fought countless times in years gone by—in Babylon, in Carthaginia, in Egypt—in all the great empires that have risen from a semi-desert soil.

Los Angeles Saturday Night, *October 19, 1935*[6]

This ditch [the Colorado River Aqueduct] is water grandeur, California style. Water here is among the most domesticated natural resources on the planet.

Terry McDermott, Los Angeles Times reporter, 1998[7]

The Metropolitan Water District story—indeed the story of modern Southern California—begins with the planning and building of an aqueduct empire. Imported water—from the faraway Colorado River and Northern California—carried by aqueducts hundreds of miles through deserts and mountains has been crucial to building the modern Los Angeles and San Diego metropolises. Figure 1.1 shows the aqueducts serving the region: Los Angeles's Owens River Aqueduct (completed in 1913) and the Second L.A. Aqueduct (1970); MWD's Colorado River Aqueduct (1941); and the State Water Project's Edmund G. Brown California Aqueduct (1972–73).

At the heart of this empire lies the mammoth Metropolitan Water District of Southern California. MWD's accomplishments are global in scale. Starting in the late 1920s, this innovative partnership of Southland cities (later joined by water districts) financed and built the 242-mile Colorado River Aqueduct—an engineering marvel that once was the longest and most expensive aqueduct in the world. To educate local and national audiences about this megaproject, Metropolitan in 1937 produced a widely shown documentary movie, "*Empire of the West.*"[8]

In the 1930s, MWD played midwife to another engineering marvel—Hoover Dam (Lake Mead)—by purchasing a significant share of the project's hydropower.[9] In the postwar era, MWD played a key (albeit belated) supportive role in the State Water Project, which provided critically needed new water for a burgeoning Southland population. Finally, in the 1990s, Metropolitan financed and built the immense Diamond Valley reservoir, providing Southern California with a six-month drinking supply in case of earthquake or drought. As a result, MWD's water and infrastructure have been major contributing factors in Southern California's astonishing 20th-century development.[10]

Today, "Empire of the West" might more aptly describe the Metropolitan Water District itself. MWD was created in 1928 to bring supplemental water from the Colorado River to the city of Los Angeles and 10 other Southland municipalities. Later, its role as regional water policy impresario greatly expanded. In the 1970s, MWD began delivering imported water from Northern California via the State Water Project's aqueduct system. Since the 1980s, as MWD installed more environmentally friendly water policies and rates, Southern California has become a global leader in water resources management and diversification, conservation

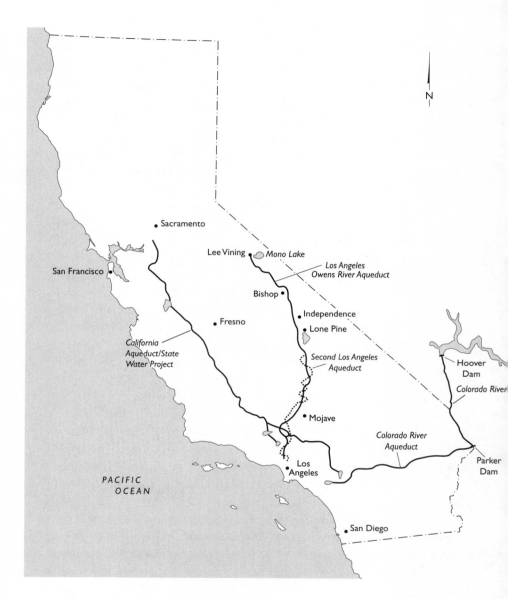

FIGURE **1.1**   Aqueducts serving Southern California

SOURCE: Metropolitan Water District of Southern California (MWDSC).

TABLE 1.1

*The Metropolitan Service Area in Global Perspective:
Countries Ranked by Year 2002 Gross Domestic
Product (in billions of US$)*

Rank	Country	Gross Product
1	United States	$10,417
2	Japan	3,979
3	Germany	1,976
4	United Kingdom	1,552
5	France	1,409
6	China	1,237
7	Italy	1,181
8	**MWD Six-County Service Area***	788
9	Canada	716
10	Spain	650
11	Mexico	637
12	India	515

SOURCE: MWDSC, *2004/05 Proposed Budget* (Los Angeles: MWDSC, 2004), Table 19, "Ranking by Gross Domestic Product," p. 85. The country gross domestic product data are from the World Bank, *World Development Indicators* (July 2003). The MWD six-county gross regional product is an estimate from the UCLA Anderson School Forecast.

*Los Angeles, Orange, Ventura, San Bernardino, Riverside, and San Diego counties.

efforts, and reclamation. Metropolitan now serves as the region's de facto water policymaker, promoting storage and conjunctive use (wet-year storage for dry-year use), as well as providing financial incentives for member-agency local projects such as conservation, reclamation, and de-salination. MWD also functions as the major voice for the region's water interests statewide and nationally.[11]

Supplying nearly 60 percent of the water used in urban Southern California, Metropolitan undergirds one of the world's great regional economies. As Table 1.1 shows, in 2002 the six-county MWD service territory had a gross regional product of $788 billion. The region's economy ranked eighth worldwide, behind China and Italy but ahead of Canada, Spain, Mexico, and India.

Southern California was far from a regional behemoth when MET was created. First delivering Colorado River water in 1941, the water district had a population of only 2 million residents, with a service area encompassing 625 square miles (two thirds of which lay within Los Angeles's city limits). Demonstrating that water is indeed the region's lifeblood,

MWD's customers and service territory have since multiplied over eight-fold, respectively. By 2005, Metropolitan would serve 18 million residents in over 300 cities and communities, representing more than 85 percent of the population of six Southland counties: Los Angeles, Orange, Ventura, Riverside, San Bernardino, and San Diego. MET now serves more than 1 out of every 20 Americans as a customer.[12]

Functioning as a huge regional water cooperative, Metropolitan comprises 26 member agencies—14 cities and 11 municipal water districts in the five-county Los Angeles metropolitan area, and one county-wide water authority serving San Diego. It is governed by a 37-member board of directors, appointed by its member-agency governing bodies.[13] Figure 1.2 shows MWD's member agencies, 5,200-square-mile service territory, and the Colorado River and California aqueducts serving the Southland.

Table 1.2 presents a profile of Metropolitan's 26 member agencies. It shows the year they joined MET, and, for 2003, their population, MWD water deliveries, and MET share of total water supplied. These agencies are a highly diverse lot, ranging from the very small (such as the city of San Marino with a population of just over 13,000), to the very large (such as the city of Los Angeles with a population of nearly 4 million).

They also differ greatly in MWD water deliveries, from San Fernando's mere 383 acre-feet (AF) to San Diego's 613,560 AF. (An acre-foot is equivalent to 326,000 gallons of water, which with conservation meets the yearly needs of 2 average families of 4.) Significantly, they vary greatly in the extent to which they rely on MET for their total water supply. Some members, such as San Diego, Beverly Hills, Torrance, and Las Virgenes, lack adequate local supplies and thus heavily rely on MWD. Other agencies, such as Los Angeles, Anaheim, Santa Ana, and San Marino, have considerable resources of their own, and thus historically have used MWD as a supplemental source.[14]

Despite notable accomplishments, Metropolitan in recent years has been an embattled agency. Environmental critics charge that MET gives lip service to "green" policies and sustainable development but remains overfriendly to development. They contend that MWD's central ethos is still providing water for growth. Public interest advocates claim that MET is an unaccountable "invisible" government, whose insulated, unelected directors are mired in inertia and ineptitude. Conversely,

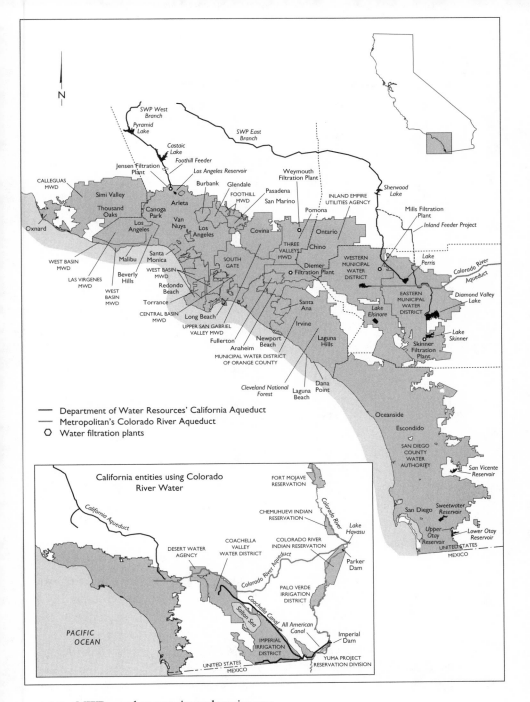

FIGURE **1.2** MWD member agencies and service area

SOURCE: MWDSC, *2004/05 Proposed Budget* (Los Angeles: MWDSC, 2004), p. 90.

TABLE 1.2
Profile of MWD Member Agencies

Member Agency	Year Joined MWD	2003 Population	2003 Water from MWD (acre-feet)	2003 MWD Share of Water (%)
Anaheim	1928	354,295	23,951	25–34
Beverly Hills	1928	41,014	13,577	86
Burbank	1928	105,158	12,470	50
Glendale	1928	187,571	23,049	85
Los Angeles	1928	3,980,333	372,261	35–56
Pasadena	1928	143,968	24,581	60
San Marino	1928	13,470	442	10–15
Santa Ana	1928	323,549	12,227	34
Santa Monica	1928	92,980	13,027	82
Compton	1931	89,362	2,892	53
Fullerton	1931	124,560	12,544	34
Long Beach	1931	462,146	41,987	49
Torrance	1931	131,826	22,690	92
San Diego	1946	2,913,631	626,677	85
West Basin	1948	841,889	171,585	80
Three Valleys	1950	537,922	83,399	60
Eastern	1951	573,104	97,348	80
Inland Empire*	1951	725,676	76,825	30
MWDOC**	1951	2,091,678	340,523	50
Foothill	1953	104,823	12,514	60
Central Basin	1954	1,549,604	86,097	35
Western	1954	679,079	112,969	24
Calleguas	1960	511,398	118,042	76
Las Virgenes	1960	68,840	24,249	100
Upper San Gabriel	1963	882,889	62,325	80
San Fernando	1971	24,380	383	<1
MWD Total		17,555,145	2,388,634	55–60

SOURCES: MWDSC website, www.mwdh2o.com; and MWDSC, Office of Chief Financial Officer.

*Formerly Chino Basin.

**The Municipal Water District of Orange County, which merged with Coastal Municipal Water District in 2001.

aggrieved Northern California, agricultural, and western state interests allege that MWD is an aggressive "water bully" using its substantial political clout to siphon water supplies, vampire-like, from seemingly more rightful and deserving users in California and the Southwest.[15]

Criticism even extends to MWD's boardroom. San Diego water officials charge that the L.A.-headquartered Metropolitan serves Los Angeles water interests at the expense of San Diego—MWD's largest customer—which they claim lies at the end of the pipeline. Although Metropolitan was originally designed to promote regional cooperation and partnership, member agency disputes have grown in recent years. The primary combatants have been the two largest member agencies: the San Diego County Water Authority[16] (SDCWA, or the County Water Authority), in which the city of San Diego is the dominant player, and the city of Los Angeles. Heightened since the early 1990s, sharp conflicts among San Diego, Los Angeles, and other MWD member agencies have erupted over preferential rights (claims to Metropolitan water during shortages), board representation and voting, water transfers and wheeling (conveyance) charges, and MWD water rates and capital financing. As analyzed here, these conflicts may be institutional in nature, rooted in ambiguities in MWD's mission and alleged inequities in agency governance arrangements, rules, and rights.[17]

A Fresh Appraisal

The MWD is not a neutral servant of growth. It is actually the handmaiden of growth.

Pasadena MWD Director Timothy F. Brick, 1991[18]

The mission of Metropolitan, as promulgated by the Board [of Directors] is to provide its service area with adequate and reliable supplies of high quality water to meet present and future needs in an environmentally and economically responsible manner.

MWD Mission Statement, 2004[19]

Given such allegations, what has been MWD's overall track record and performance? And what are its future prospects? How equitable have been MWD's governance arrangements and policies in terms of member agency benefits and burdens? Has Metropolitan merely been a servant of L.A. "water imperialism," as some contend, or have regional interests and needs been addressed and served? Historically, has MWD served as a handmaiden of Southern California's unrelenting growth, suburban sprawl, and ensuing environmental degradation? More recently, has MET lived up to its 1990s-era stated mission of meeting the region's water needs in an environmentally and economically responsible manner? Finally, with ratcheting water needs amid supply constraints and unprecedented environmental challenges, what are the future prospects of this once-innovative water-provision experiment and the semiarid megaregion it serves? These are some of the major questions this study addresses.

In 2003 Metropolitan celebrated its 75th anniversary with considerable fanfare. This powerful but largely invisible public agency has been the *sine qua non* of Southern California's improbable yet explosive 20th-century growth. Yet surprisingly little serious research has been done on what is arguably the world's most important public regional water agency. Most studies of water development in Southern California focus on Los Angeles's Department of Water and Power (LADWP), particularly in relation to the Los Angeles Aqueduct and the Owens Valley. Although there is substantial work on municipal, state, and federal water development in the West, there are only two, now dated, book-length studies of MWD—one an official history and the other a searing environmentally oriented critique—coupled with a few book chapters, theses, and articles.[20]

Beyond 'Chinatown' offers a fresh appraisal of the Metropolitan Water District of Southern California, its leaders, megaprojects, governance arrangements and rules, water policies, and regional impacts—from founders such as William Mulholland, the self-taught civil engineer who brought water to Los Angeles from the Owens Valley; to ambitious megaprojects such as the Colorado River Aqueduct and State Water Project; to a resulting regional landscape of endless sprawl, and calls for greater environmental stewardship; to sharp disputes over MWD's mission, governance system, and policies; to growing conflicts over a scarce and ever more valuable resource; and finally, to an uncertain future as the region searches for new reliability and water-quality formulas. We particularly focus here on relations between the region's dueling urban hegemons and MWD's two largest member agencies—Los Angeles and San Diego.

Mixing history with policy analysis, this study examines and weighs the evidence to tell three interrelated stories about the hydropolitics of Southern California. First, we retell much of the region's 20th-century water and development saga as a innovative public venture rather than a sordid, secretive affair. As noted, the conventional wisdom—depicted in the movie *Chinatown*—holds that unscrupulous developers in league with conniving water officials secretly orchestrated water megaprojects for personal financial gain. In contrast to this tale of private avarice and scheming, we examine the extraordinary *public* decisions and investments that made modern Southern California possible.

Here the *dramatis personae* are the region's public entrepreneurs who created, led, and managed Metropolitan. These include William Mulholland; unsung municipal attorneys such as L.A.'s William Burgess Mathews and Pasadena's James Howard, who together wrote the MWD state enabling legislation; powerful MET directors such as founding board chair W. P. Whitsett, long-serving and imperious L.A. representative and chair Joe Jensen, and San Diego's forceful and irascible Fred Heilbron; and a corps of MWD general managers from early engineers in the Mulholland mold such as Frank Weymouth, Julian Hinds, Robert Diemer, and Robert Skinner to, more recently, lawyers such as John Lauten, Carl Boronkay, and Ron Gastelum.[21]

MET's history also deserves careful study for the critical role played by institutional design, and how this dynamically shapes agency policymaking and performance. MWD is one of the nation's largest special districts—independent, limited-purpose local governments set up to provide services unavailable from general-purpose city and county governments. In the past 50 years, special districts have become a major force in local governance. By the late 1990s, there were nearly 35,000 special districts in the United States, their number having tripled since the early 1950s. Such bureaucracies exemplify the seemingly inevitable tradeoffs between efficiency and accountability. Although supporters claim that special districts such as MET efficiently provide better-quality services at lower prices than do general-purpose governments, critics charge that such "invisible" governments lack accountability. Yet being more shielded from the potentially sharp political and policy swings of state and local general-purpose governments in California (accentuated by term limits), MWD's insulated special-district design may better achieve long-term planning and policy results.[22]

Metropolitan exemplifies the complexities of assessing political accountability. Its 37 directors are generally appointed for fixed four-year terms by the governing bodies of its 26 member agencies and thus are not directly accountable to local voters. However, insulated appointments coupled with a relatively large board may provide needed continuity in terms of long-term water resource and management responsibilities. As a regional agency with local representation, MWD delegates also are torn between service as regional trustees or instructed local delegates. Multiple principals further complicate principal-agent relations and member agency representation. In the city of Los Angeles, for example, water policy is set by three entities: the mayor, city council, and the Department of Water and Power. Whom do L.A.'s MWD directors represent? Finally, there are the complicated dynamics of MET board-staff relations to consider. Early on, long-serving board chairs such as Joe Jensen (1949–1974) reigned supreme. Later, chairs generally were limited to two 4-year terms, enhancing the power of general managers.[23]

How effective is MWD's semiautonomous, special-district institutional design? On the one hand, supporters claim that the mega-agency's success is in large part a function of its delegation of specialized authority and resources insulated from normal electoral politics. This allows MWD to engage in long-term planning, investment, and policymaking, with an eye toward the region's future well-being. MET's success may sober us to the joys of democracy in action and may lead to the conclusion that some salient policy issues such as water are just too important to risk being undone from the outside by vote-seeking elected officials or being diluted through multiple missions on the end side. On the other hand, critics contend that MET's bureaucratic insulation encourages agency capture by well-entrenched interests such as real estate developers. Has MWD been a soulless "Sultan of Sprawl," doing the bidding of private developers and facilitating the region's sprawling development and ensuing environmental degradation? More recently, has MET's insulated structure been responsive to countervailing interests seeking to install more environment-friendly policies?[24]

MET also deserves study as the world's largest and arguably most successful *regional* water agency. Today, there is a strong global movement toward regionalization in water provision. Although the mix between public and private, nonprofit and for-profit, water provision and management differs considerably between countries, the regionalizing trend cuts across national divisions as water agencies are organized not only around geographic "watersheds" but also around water "problem-sheds" at an intermediate regional level. Supporters claim this avoids both overcentralization and excessive fragmentation, fosters cooperation and coordination, and promotes infrastructure investment by encouraging economies of scale. The regional governance model exemplified by

MET has been praised for efficient management, effective coordination, valuable interagency planning, sharing of expertise, and pooling of financial resources. Yet the MET regional approach also should alert us to gnawing questions concerning equitable benefit sharing and burden sharing among constituent agencies.[25]

Second, for the contemporary (post-1990) period we closely examine the institution in action, considering MET's political strategies, policy choices, and outcomes as a now-embattled agency confronted mounting external and internal challenges affecting its viability, water supplies, and Southern California's future. The new water wars centered on plans to reduce California's reliance on surplus water from the Colorado River; proposals to fix the fragile Bay-Delta ecosystem in Northern California; and the evolving role of water markets and transfers. Each featured potentially sharp conflicts among urban water agencies, agricultural, business and community interests, environmentalists, and the federal and state governments.

For the post-1990 era, we also focus on sharp conflicts *within* Metropolitan, particularly between the dueling regional hegemons—Los Angeles and San Diego—over agency policies, benefits, burdens, and even the future of MWD itself. Conflicts between MET's two most powerful members offer a valuable lens into the equity dynamics of institutional design, governance, and policymaking. Thus, although San Diego is MET's largest customer, its preferential right to water during droughts is well below its annual deliveries. In contrast, Los Angeles draws much less MWD water than its preferential claim permits. Given these water rights disparities, many San Diegans believe that Metropolitan remains an L.A.-controlled agency serving L.A. interests first. In the drought-plagued 1990s, this belief helped fuel San Diego's relentless drive for water independence from MWD. Yet, as argued, the *Chinatown* storyline most eerily parallels the hydropolitics of San Diego, where the County Water Authority attempted to secure an independent water supply through secret meetings in the mid-1990s with representatives of the billionaire Texas Bass brothers—who had purchased up to 45,000 acres of farmland in Imperial County for the valuable supposed water rights.

The third story line considers MET's future prospects and the implications for 21st-century Southern California. Already home to more people than all but the very largest states, the region is still growing rapidly. Absent new imported supplies, can MWD meet the water needs created by ever-burgeoning growth without stifling the economy, creating greater environmental degradation, or inciting revolt among residents of water-rich agricultural regions?[26]

Today, adverse climatic conditions threaten the region's water supply. Notwithstanding an unusually wet 2004–05 winter, a five-year drought in the Colorado River Basin has severely depleted Lake Powell and Lake Mead, threatening normal water deliveries to Southern California, Arizona, Nevada, and even Mexico's Baja California. Global warming is another threat, expected to alter precipitation patterns throughout the West and elsewhere. Since September 11, 2001, people have concerns about protecting Southern California's vulnerable water system from terrorist attack. Water-quality concerns are also growing. The Colorado River, a key source of drinking water for Southern California, has become the nation's most threatened waterway. Environmental hazards include radioactive waste from an abandoned uranium mine in an Upper Basin state; chemical contamination from perchlorate, a rocket fuel ingredient; and overburdened sewage systems in fast-growing river communities. Against this somber backdrop, we critically assess Metropolitan's new formulas for 21st-century water reliability, rate refinement, drought management, water quality and security, governance and local agency initiatives.[27]

Water Crises Brewing

Thousands have lived without love, not one without water.
W. H. Auden, "First Things First" (1957)[28]

The only matter that could take Egypt to war again is water.
President Anwar Sadat of Egypt, after signing the historic 1979 peace accord with Israel[29]

As California goes, so goes the rest of the world.
Jim Motavalli, "Down the Drain: The Coming World Water Crisis" (2000)[30]

The MWD saga as a once-innovative and now-challenged regional water agency can offer valuable lessons for audiences everywhere about the dynamics of cooperation and conflict over "liquid gold." In the 21st century, water promises to join oil as a potential flashpoint for global conflicts. Relentless urban growth threatens to overwhelm limited water supplies across the nation and worldwide, leaving citizens and policymakers scrambling to find effective models of conflict resolution and reliable water provision.[31]

Seventy percent of our planet's surface is covered in water, 97 percent of which is salty and thus largely unsuitable for consumption or irrigation. Of the 3 percent that is fresh water, most remains frozen in ice caps at the poles and in glaciers. This leaves just 1 percent of the planet's surface water to sustain a fast-growing global population of more than 6 billion. Yet the demands on the world's fresh water are increasing everywhere, primarily because of inexorable population growth.[32]

In the United States, water resources at the dawn of the 21st century are under intense pressure, particularly in the arid western portion of the country. Prolonged drought has left Lake Powell and Lake Mead at roughly one half of their capacity, and reservoirs are low along the entire Colorado River. New studies suggest that the river's average annual flow is substantially lower than it was during the unusually wet years used as the baseline for allocations under the Colorado River Compact, which was signed in 1922. All the water on the Colorado River has already been claimed. California, relying on its rights to surplus water, has used more than its fixed allocation of 4.4 million acre-feet (MAF) by about 25 percent annually. The seven states that share the river—Arizona, California, Colorado, Nevada, New Mexico, Utah, and Wyoming—are growing rapidly, suggesting that demand will only increase.[33]

These water shortages, once thought to be confined to the arid West, now are rapidly spreading east. Rivers along the eastern seaboard of the United States are being strained by drought, population growth, and increased withdrawals by industrial and domestic users. Maryland and Virginia are battling over the Potomac River; Virginia and North Carolina are fighting over the Roanoke River; and North and South Carolina are arguing over an equitable distribution of the Pee Dee River. Similarly, Atlanta appears to be emulating Los Angeles, both in its rapid growth and in its thirst for its neighbors' water. Consumption in Atlanta has left less of the Chattahoochee River for users downstream in Alabama and Florida. And Atlanta has been casting a covetous eye on the Tennessee and Savannah rivers in Tennessee and South Carolina.[34]

The nation's growing water conflicts are mirrored elsewhere in the world. Spain has had a regional argument about water that resembles the conflicts between Northern and Southern California. Rainfall is more plentiful along Spain's Atlantic coast in the north, whereas most of the south is semiarid. A change in government shelved a $15 billion national hydrological plan that would have built 120 dams and 600 miles of pipeline to transfer over 800,000 AF per year from the Ebro River. Although some of the water would have been diverted north to Barcelona in Catalonia, 80 percent would have been sent south "to drought-prone Valencia, Murcia, and eastern Andalusia."[35] Water transfers to the south were opposed by agricultural interests in the Aragon region (through which the Ebro flows), and its more urbanized northern neighbor, Catalonia. Also opposed were environmentalists worried about the impact on the Ebro Delta.[36] Similarly, in Australia drought and demand from farmers are leading to water shortages along the Murray and Darling rivers. The Murray-Darling basin covers four states in eastern Australia. The two rivers supply almost three quarters of Australia's farm irrigation water, and drinking water for major cities. In July 2003, South Australia farmers had their allocations cut by one fifth.[37]

Groundwater depletion is another simmering issue. Farmers in the central United States face the prospect of even more drastic reductions because of overextended use of groundwater. The Ogallala Aquifer covers 223,880 square miles beneath parts of seven Great Plains states: Texas, Oklahoma, New Mexico, Kansas, Colorado, Nebraska, and South Dakota. Water pumped from the aquifer sustains agriculture on lands decimated by the droughts that cumulated in the Dust Bowl of the 1930s. Yet water unseen beneath the surface appears extremely vulnerable to overuse, and in most areas water is being extracted from the Ogallala far more quickly than it can be replenished. The overdraft, estimated at 14 MAF of water per year, equals the entire annual flow of the Colorado River. The amount of land irrigated by the Ogallala is steadily declining, down 30 percent since 1978, including more than 2 million acres (representing one third of its irrigable land) that have been fallowed in hardest-hit Texas. Smaller aquifers in Tucson, Arizona, Long Island, New York, and elsewhere in the United States are being drained as well.[38]

The pattern of overdrafted groundwater is repeated elsewhere in the world. In Yemen, wells are falling up to 16 feet per year; the capital

Sanaa may be dry within a decade, and the rural economy may disappear entirely. The water's disappearance will be hastened by a rapidly growing population. Bangkok is sinking because industrial users and developers are pumping twice the sustainable level of groundwater. This will expose Bangkok to flooding during the rainy season. In India, drought is exposing water shortages caused by poor water allocation: water is cheap, as is power, making (free) groundwater cheap for farmers to extract. The result has been falling water tables and a water shortage. Less rainfall than usual is the proximate cause of the shortage today; higher demand created by a growing population will make shortages more likely in the future.[39]

Water scarcity—whether natural (drought) or human-made (excessive use)—is likely to be increasingly common in the coming decades. A chief driver is population growth, which creates ever greater demand for additional water to slake people's thirst, to grow food, and to promote economic development. Misallocation and overuse, frequently caused or exacerbated by poor pricing policies, also contribute to shortages. The solution so far has been to embark on ever more ambitious schemes to secure additional water, often diverting it from hundreds of miles away. These water transfers can be effective but often come at a high financial and environmental cost. More ominously, transferring water can create losers as well as winners.[40]

Water is a renewable but still largely finite resource: increasing the amount available for one group necessarily reduces the amount left for others. Damming a river to provide power and irrigate crops may give rise to conflict if it leaves insufficient water flows for the people living downstream. Similarly, transferring water from agricultural areas to cities may require fallowing farmland, which affects not just the farmers but also third-party interests in the rural economy. Balancing these competing interests will be a challenge, particularly when the water involved spills across international boundaries.[41]

In the arid regions of the world, humanity is beginning to bump up against the natural limits of water resources that once seemed inexhaustible. Irrigation has greatly expanded the amount of land under cultivation, and farming accounts for most of the world's consumption of fresh water. In rich nations and in poor ones, agriculture is in too many places consuming water faster than it can be replenished. Rivers are running dry, lakes are disappearing, and underground aquifers are being drained. Urban residents and industrial users place additional burdens on overstretched water resources, and burgeoning population growth will create still more demand. Just as demand is peaking, industrial pollution, agricultural runoff, and sewage are fouling lakes, rivers, and groundwater the world over. And climate change punctuates the looming water crisis with an exclamation mark: shifting rainfall patterns, prolonged droughts, and reduced snowfall may jeopardize the available supplies.[42]

If current usage patterns persist, there will not be enough water to meet the anticipated demand. Conservation and changes such as reduced irrigation of farmland could free up additional water, particularly for urban users. Where water is shared among multiple countries, however, upstream users may be tempted to avoid painful economic dislocations at home by leaving less water for their neighbors downstream. Such choices will be most acute during dry years, when some regions will find there is little enough water for one nation, let alone many. Shared hardship may produce willingness to compromise; but desperation may also lead to conflict and even war.[43]

In watersheds worldwide, nations that rely on shared water resources will need to cooperate in an environment characterized by heightened demand for a limited resource. Thirteen international river basins are shared by five or more countries. Fifteen countries in Europe, the Middle East, and Africa with extremely low per-capita water availability are dependent for 75 percent or more of their water on "international rivers" shared by two or more nations. When there is not enough water to go around, even equitable solutions—such as joint reductions in consumption that spread the attendant hardship fairly—have the potential to leave everyone unhappy. These circumstances will create a powerful incentive to cheat. In shared riparian systems, upstream nations will be tempted to siphon enough water to meet their own needs, regardless of the consequences for people living downstream. In other words, "riparian rights" can translate into sociopolitical wrongs on a global scale.[44]

To date, water has rarely warranted armed conflict. Bloodshed has been confined to isolated incidents such as Mexican peasants dueling over water rights and Yemenis using heavy artillery to settle local water disputes. Nations have had heated arguments over shared water resources: India and Pakistan grudgingly share the waters of the Indus River system; Iraq threatened to bomb a dam in Syria that diminished its share of the

Euphrates; and Syria has had tense words with Turkey over diversions from the same river. Israelis and Arabs also clash over water rights. Some of these disputes ended with treaties governing future allocations of water; yet the potential for conflict along these and other river systems remains.[45]

In Africa, 10 countries and more than 250 million people share the waters of the Nile. Egypt, a desert country located at the mouth of the Nile, is completely dependent on the river. The Egyptians have built multiple dams and undertaken vast irrigation projects, but they remain extremely vulnerable to the growing water needs of their upstream neighbors. If water were diverted before it reached Egypt, it would threaten to disrupt the country's electrical production, irrigation for agriculture, and the very existence of some of its desert settlements.[46]

Burundi, Tanzania, Rwanda, the Democratic Republic of Congo (formerly Zaire), Kenya, Uganda, Sudan, Ethiopia, and Eritrea, however, have an enormous incentive to develop the waters of the Nile River system. They are among the world's poorest nations, and many have been torn in the recent decades by civil unrest, civil war, and genocide. All would welcome additional hydroelectric power and water for irrigation, although poverty, political disarray, and internal conflict have so far kept these countries upriver from Egypt from undertaking large-scale projects to store or divert water. (Dams in Sudan are a notable exception.) In a cruel irony, if the political stability and economic growth so desperately needed in the region ever arrive, they may set the stage for international disputes over water.[47]

In Central Asia, five former Soviet republics—Kazakhstan, Kyrgyzstan, Tajikistan, Turkmenistan, and Uzbekistan—share the waters of the Amu Darya and Syr Darya. Overuse, inefficient irrigation systems, and colossal mismanagement among these nations have already contributed to the virtual disappearance of the Aral Sea. Expanded diversion for irrigation projects planned throughout the region will put additional strain on water resources. And Tajikistan, one of the upstream countries, has suggested that it owns all the water leaving its territory, with the intimation that it could charge its neighbors for water as they charge it for gas. As an Uzbek poet laments, "You cannot fill the Aral with tears."[48]

Closer to home, Mexico and the United States share water along their mutual border based on a 1944 treaty allotting the waters of the Rio Grande, Colorado, and Tijuana rivers. The populations of both countries are rising, particularly in the border region, just as a lengthy drought has strained their interdependent water resources. (One reservoir along the Rio Grande has dropped to less than 10 percent of capacity.) In the West, the United States has assured Mexico it will receive 1.5 MAF of water from the Colorado each year. The treaty, however, says nothing about the quality of the water. Extensive diversions upstream on the Colorado increase the salinity of the remaining water, which the Mexicans complain is almost unsuitable for agriculture. In the east, Mexico is supposed to supply Texas with 350,000 AF per year from its tributaries flowing into the Rio Grande. Although Mexico has reneged on its side of the deal since 1992, unusually heavy rainfall in 2004–2005 in the Rio Grande Basin may allow it to finally pay off its water debt. If these water conflicts aren't resolved, the North American Free Trade Agreement (NAFTA) could even be threatened.[49]

How Metropolitan manages conflict and cooperation over water in California will offer a glimpse into the future for shared riparian systems throughout the world. MWD faces daunting challenges in reconciling competing water interests, beginning with the conflicts among its own members. It must balance environmental protection and economic growth as well as the needs of urban and agricultural users, and satisfy interested parties throughout California and the West. Metropolitan, however, at least enjoys a firmly established legal framework within which to operate. If MWD cannot find workable solutions to Southern California's water needs—where the primary disputants are fellow Californians and other American states, all bound by U.S. law—what hope is there for peaceful resolution in watersheds where the principals are nations and the overarching legal framework is weak or nonexistent?

Organization of This Study

Can Southern California and Metropolitan—its bold regional experiment in cooperative water provision—offer valuable lessons for other regions and nations now experiencing water shortages and conflicts? *Beyond 'Chinatown'* seeks to answer this question. The study consists of three parts and 8 chapters.

Part 1 (chapters 1 through 3) presents an overview and historical development. Chapter 2 ("Ghosts of *Chinatown*: From L.A.'s DWP to

MWD") analyzes critical events in MWD's prehistory, and how they have shaped Metropolitan's subsequent development. We compare the Owens Valley myth versus known history, counterposing the *Chinatown* movie plot to the actual deeds (and alleged misdeeds) of Los Angeles, its land barons, and iconic Department of Water and Power as revealed by recent scholarship. We also examine the long-lasting impact of the *noir* legend that would not die—Los Angeles's supposed "rape" of the Owens Valley—and the haunting to this day not only of L.A.'s Department of Water and Power but also of the Metropolitan Water District by allegations of a *Chinatown*-like shadow conspiracy of L.A. "water imperialism."

Chapter 3 ("Building and Financing an Empire: Balancing Growth and Equity") expands on these themes by examining the historical evolution of MWD, and its role in shaping the region's sprawling development for 75 years. If MET were indeed a *Chinatown*-style metropolitan "shadow government" doing the bidding of Los Angeles and its powerful developers, then these interests should be reflected in MWD's policy decisions. Has Metropolitan historically favored Los Angeles at the expense of other member agencies, particularly later joiners such as San Diego? Or, did the MWD board of directors—including L.A. representatives—actually fashion policies favorable to outlying areas? What have been the effects of MET water policy on regional growth patterns?

Part 2 (chapters 4 through 6) examines mounting challenges to MWD and its water supplies, 1990–2004. Chapter 4 ("David and Goliath? San Diego's Quixotic Quest for Independence") examines San Diego's recent drive for water independence, and sharp conflicts with MET, particularly member agency Los Angeles. We carefully examine the landmark and controversial San Diego–Imperial Valley water transfer deal, from San Diego's secret *Chinatown*-like meetings with the Texan billionaire Bass brothers; to charges of MWD obstructionism; to legal battles over Colorado River Aqueduct "wheeling" (conveyance) charges and the threatened Salton Sea; and to exhaustive federal, state, and regional efforts to reach an agreement. Also explored is San Diego's lawsuit to rewrite preferential rights to MWD water during scarcity. Finally, we explore escalating conflicts *within* the San Diego County Water Authority between a group of inland North County water agencies and the powerful city of San Diego over similar issues of equitable governance, rights, and burden sharing. Does the city of San Diego behave differently in the

MET boardroom relative to the cozy confines of the County Water Authority?

Chapter 5 ("Empire Under Siege: Colorado River and Bay-Delta Battles") explores Metropolitan's involvement in recent water wars over the Colorado River and northern California Bay-Delta ecosystem. We explore the post-1990 political and legal challenges to MWD's imported supplies, and analyze MET's strategies and alliances, the tactics of opponents, and the resulting policy outcomes. In terms of the Colorado River, we consider MET's strategies in interstate and intrastate battles over California's use of surplus Colorado River water, and ambitious plans to limit the state's annual usage to the basic 4.4 MAF allotment allowed under the 1963 U.S. Supreme Court decision in *Arizona v. California*. The chapter also analyzes MWD's strategies, and the resulting bargaining outcomes in efforts to draw up a long-term remedy for the fragile Sacramento–San Joaquin Delta ecosystem, whose water quality, ecology, and habitat are now threatened.

Chapter 6 ("Turbulent Waters? Metropolitan Faces Water Markets") considers water markets and privatization in global, national, and state policy contexts, and analyzes MWD's role in California's evolving water market. From the mid-1980s onward, Metropolitan has been at the very center of agricultural-to-urban water market transactions and controversies in California. Variously hailed as a visionary leader and staunch obstructionist, how has MWD accommodated market forces? We examine MWD's overall track record, and analyze the role that Metropolitan should play in the public policy debate concerning water as a public resource or private commodity.

Part 3 (chapters 7 and 8) considers the future prospects of MWD and of Southern California. Chapter 7 ("MWD Agonistes: 21st-Century Challenges") explores growth in population and water demand in MET's service area, and in competing watersheds in Northern California and the Colorado River Basin. We examine key supply-side challenges—from global warming to the potential impact of long-term drought. Also considered are environmental regulatory impacts on MET and Southern California, ranging from water diversions for species protection and habitat restoration to state laws requiring adequate water for new development. We also weigh looming threats to water supplies, from pollution to terrorism.

Chapter 8 ("Charting a New Course") evaluates how MWD proposes to ensure water reliability and water quality in a challenging environment of still-booming population, diminished imported supplies, and new water-quality and safety threats. We critically examine MET's plans for supply diversification—placing greater reliance on local projects such as conservation, reclamation, and desalination—and methods for coping with water-quality hazards. Can Southern California's future water needs still be met in an environmentally and economically responsible manner? Given MWD's new reliance on member agency initiatives, we examine the status and prospects of major local projects such as Los Angeles's water conservation efforts and San Diego's desalination efforts. We also consider MET's formulas for more equitable governance and rate structures. We conclude by considering the broad lessons of the MWD experience for the nation and worldwide, which now confront the specter of water scarcity and escalating conflicts.

Perhaps owing to the difficulty of the task, much of the retelling of the Southern California water and development story relies on secondary source materials and thus only repackages the conventional *Chinatown* wisdom. In contrast, this study draws on a treasure trove of primary source materials to offer a fresh perspective on Metropolitan and its critical but still largely unsung role in the 20th-century political economy of Southern California. Going beyond regional and water issues, this study tries to address larger questions of institutional design, democracy, bureaucracy, and development. We revisit these broader issues in the final chapter.

Methodologically, I have tapped the MWD archives—annual reports, budgets, planning and project studies. These archival materials, as well as official letters, memos, and consulting reports herein cited, can be difficult to locate. They can be accessed from Metropolitan's archives and website, from public officials' offices, or from the author. Also canvassed are the extensive holdings of the UCLA library (particularly the John Randolph Haynes Collection and its oral histories of former MWD and L.A. Department of Water and Power officials), and the Fletcher Bowron collection and oral histories at the Huntington Library. Current and past Southern California water officials have been interviewed. Newspapers, such as the *Los Angeles Times* and the *San Diego Union-Tribune*, are heavily used. Finally, I have tapped an invaluable regional resource: interviews with regional, state, and federal water and related policymakers published in the *Metro Investment Report*, a monthly newsletter devoted to public investment in the region.

Thus this study explores the complex yet fragile liquid underpinnings of one of the world's great regions and economies. It examines the crucial nexus between private and public interests, powerful but invisible water agencies, and the improbable growth and uncertain future of Southern California. From the alleged scheming of would-be private water barons to the supposedly visionary projects of public entrepreneurs, from fierce urban and rural rivalries to pitched environmental battles, from California's historic north-south conflicts to feuding Western states and fierce San Diego–Los Angeles battles, the MWD story is an epic saga.

2   Ghosts of *Chinatown*: From L.A.'s DWP to MWD

> I originally thought I'd do a detective movie. . . . But then, I didn't want
> to do just any detective movie. . . . [Y]ou start thinking about what
> crime is to you, what it really means, what you think is really a horrible
> crime and what angers you. . . . The destruction of the land and that
> community was something that I thought was really hideous. It was
> doubly significant because it was the way Los Angeles was formed. . . .
> Then, there are some crimes that our society isn't equipped to punish, so
> we reward them. . . . The great crimes in California have been
> committed against the land—and against the people who own it and
> future generations. It was only natural that the script should evolve into
> the story of a man who raped the land and his own daughter.
>
> *Robert Towne, screenwriter of* Chinatown, 2002[1]

The modern Southern California water story—and, indeed, the
very origins of the Metropolitan Water District—begin with the city of
Los Angeles and its still-contested quest for new water supplies in the
early 20th-century. Los Angeles water chief William Mulholland, working closely with former L.A. mayor Fred Eaton, pioneered the development of imported water supplies from the faraway Owens Valley. The
233-mile-long Los Angeles Aqueduct was completed in 1913, ensuring
L.A.'s future territorial and population growth. As noted, from its inception the aqueduct project was mired in controversy. The conventional
wisdom, which dates back into the early 20th century, is imaginatively
encapsulated in the movie *Chinatown* (1974), depicting a secretive and
incestuous L.A. conspiracy between water regulator and developer.

This chapter re-examines these critical events in MWD's prehistory that would so shape future developments. It compares the Owens
Valley myth versus known history, framing the *Chinatown* movie plot
against a backdrop of the deeds (and misdeeds) of Los Angeles, its land
barons, and municipal Department of Water and Power (LADWP) as

revealed by recent scholarship. It also examines the long-lasting impact of the "*noir* legend" that would not die—Los Angeles's supposed "rape of the Owens Valley"—and the haunting to this day not only of L.A.'s DWP but also of the Metropolitan Water District as a *Chinatown*-like shadow conspiracy of L.A. "water imperialism" and its ruling private developers. It concludes by offering an alternative theory of MET as an enterprising *public* agency pursuing *regional* (and not merely Los Angeles) interests. This theory is further explored in subsequent chapters.

"Forget It, Jake—It's Chinatown."

> You steal the water from the valley, ruin the grazing, starve my livestock—who's paying you to do that, Mr. Mulwray, that's what I want to know!
>
>   *Valley Farmer in* Chinatown *(1974)*[2]

Balzac is reputed to have said, "all great fortunes are founded on a crime." So, too, are great cities, at least in the opinion of their detractors. *Chinatown*, the acclaimed Roman Polanski film, told a story of the founding of modern Los Angeles that rolled up into one myth-of-origins Cain's fratricide of Abel, Oedipus's incest, and the sins of the Robber Barons. Set in the Great Depression milieu of Los Angeles's "tough guy" detective fiction, but dramatizing earlier controversies generated by the Los Angeles Aqueduct to the Owens Valley, Robert Towne's screenplay— working title: "Water and Power"—won an Academy Award. Biographical and autobiographical sources describe Towne's variegated inspiration as the reminiscences of a retired Hungarian vice cop and veteran of the Chinatown beat, journalist Carey McWilliams's muckraking exposé of "The Owens Valley Tragedy," and the specters of Sophocles and Shakespeare mediated by Freud.[3]

    Chinatown opens on a hot August day in 1937, with the newspaper headlines screaming and the barber shop conversations murmuring "drought." Detective Jake Gittes ("matrimonial work" his self-described "métier") is approached by an apprehensive Mrs. Evelyn Mulwray, wife of the Los Angeles water czar. No sooner has Gittes undertaken his investigation than he sees embarrassing news of it in the papers, and discovers he's been hired by an impostor. The indignant, alluring real

Mrs. Mulwray relents and retains his services to surveil her husband. Hollis Mulwray (his name a near anagram for William Mulholland) soon turns up drowned in the middle of a water famine. His body is found at the foot of a storm drain in fictional "Alto Vallejo," identified as part of the pastoral northwest Valley not yet incorporated into Los Angeles.[4]

A graduate of the Chinatown-district crime beat, Gittes learns that the tangled web of Los Angeles water and power is even murkier. We follow him to the city council chambers, invaded by a sheepherder with his flock as a water bond issue is being debated; to the offices of the Water Department, with pictures (dated 1905 and 1912) on display in Hollis Mulwray's office of the construction of an historic water project; to the palatial lair of Noah Cross, Mulwray's estranged father-in-law and erstwhile partner in the water business; to Alto Vallejo, where understandably paranoid farmers wrongly accuse Gittes of being part of a water swindle and hired thugs slit his nose; to the County Recorder's Office and the Mar Vista old people's home, where he confirms the sale of vast tracts of soon-to-be-irrigated agricultural land to dummy purchasers; and to the denouement on Alameda Street in Los Angeles's old Chinatown (slated for demolition to make way for Union Station and the neighboring Olvera Street Plaza). There, incest is revealed and Cross's daughter is shot trying to protect her own daughter/sister from the clutches of their molesting father/grandfather.[5]

The story of a larcenous land grab amid Gothic family romance, Towne's script repackaged for a Watergate-era audience the oft-told conspiratorial tale of how the insatiable growth elite of boomtown Los Angeles slaked its thirst for pelf and power by environmental piracy committed against the unoffending farmers of a neighboring valley. Also a Vietnam War–era parable, the film's metaphoric Chinatown is a locale with elastic geographical correlates that magnetically attracts those destined for disaster. It is mysterious and menacing, like the stereotypical Orient—but primarily because the natural harmony of life in Los Angeles has been disrupted by a rapacious Anglo power elite. What is new about the movie is the melodramatic spice added by a detective antihero who unmasks but cannot punish a primordial crime. A modern-day Thebes, Los Angeles is afflicted not by plague but by drought, artificially engineered to further swell his fortune by perverted, perversely named water-and-power magnate Noah Cross. Drunk like the proverbial Noah but with power, Cross is played by the actor-director John Huston, who had previously starred as the Old Testament patriarch in the film *The Bible*.[6]

In *Chinatown*, Noah Cross manufactures his own flood by dumping water into the ocean to cause a contrived shortage. Drought can symbolize spiritual desiccation, but water is not necessarily a cure. Cross jokes that water can make "an instant Eden" but uses it to destroy by turning a saltwater pond into a drowning pool. A Mephistopheles with a cunning smile, Cross also acts out a devilish parody of the biblical Noah's repopulation of the earth. By violating his daughter and coveting his granddaughter, he seeks to impregnate Los Angeles with a future-without-limits. He gets away with it because (in the words of Cole Porter's contemporaneous lyric) "anything goes" in the unbridled metropolis—a Chinatown vice district writ large—over which Cross reigns supreme. And so Cross has nothing to fear because, as he tells Gittes, "Course, I'm respectable. I'm old. Politicians, ugly buildings and whores all get respectable if they last long enough." The future Cross offers is built on his past crimes, both personal and political, as a founding father of Los Angeles.[7]

That water is the West's lifeblood is a hackneyed cliché. But the motto inscribed in Colorado's state capitol—"the land where life is written in water"—is inverted in *Chinatown* into a lesson about Los Angeles's unending search for water as a history supposedly written in lies. Oozing from subterranean cavities, water percolates but does not absolve or cleanse. Instead, it is a malevolent force—the chief water engineer's lungs are pickled by it (his body is moved after he is drowned in salt water)—surfacing only to fructify a system rooted in corruption, fraud, and rapine. Noah Cross is a pioneer individualist—an "American Adam"—who plots evil from the precincts of the elite Albacore Club, mispronounced several times in the film as "apple core" suggesting an association with the Garden of Eden after the Fall. A double-crosser, he crosses the line between exploiting productive resources (land and water) and exploiting reproductive resources (his own offspring).[8]

A hyperpossessive individualist, Cross treats his progeny like property. His incest is as much a crime of selfishness—he refuses to give away his daughter (and granddaughter) to other men—as sexual perversion. Film critics combine Freudian and Marxist analysis to link Cross's personal depravity with the collective amorality of an urban capitalist

marketplace said to make every man into an antisocial wealth accumula-
tor. Jake Gittes also reveals the worst about Los Angeles, but only by violating his own rule: "Stay out of Chinatown." Now all he can do is to
practice forgetting; his erasure of memory will be filled in the audience's
mind by the *Chinatown* myth.[9]

Myth versus History: Los Angeles, LADWP, and the Owens Valley

Jake Gittes: You killed Hollis Mulwray—right here, in this pond, you
drowned him.

Noah Cross: Hollie was always fond of tide pools. You know what
he used to say about them? . . . that's where life begins . . . you know
when he first came out here, he figured that if you dumped water on
desert sand, it would percolate down into the bedrock and stay there,
instead of evaporating, the way it does in most reservoirs. . . . He made
this city.

Gittes: And that's what you are going to do in the Valley?

Cross: No, that's what I am doing with the Valley. The bond issue
passes Tuesday—there'll be ten million to build an aqueduct and
reservoir. . . . Either you bring the water to L.A. or you bring L.A. to
the water.

Exchange from Chinatown[10]

Percussit saxa et duxit flumina ad terram sitientum. ("He broke the
rocks and brought the river to the thirsty land.")

Inscription on William Mulholland's honorary doctorate[11]

Chinatown is a *roman à clef* transposing characters and issues
from a generation earlier into the 1930s. Such dramatic license is not necessarily incompatible with capturing a deeper truth than period details.
By identifying the actual personalities and events reworked in Towne's
screenplay, we can gauge the movie's uses or abuses of history. Yet the
one question of fundamental importance is the accuracy of its underlying
thesis: that the great motor that enabled fledgling, semiarid Los Angeles
to bloom and boom into a global metropolis was the prostitution of the
public good to private greed and ambition, with Los Angeles's Department of Water and Power (formerly known as the Water Department,

1903–1911, and the Department of Public Service, 1911–1925) as prime facilitator and accomplice.[12]

The primary characters making history in *Chinatown* are Noah Cross, the reptilian manipulator who slithers through the plot with ever deadlier effect, and Hollis Mulwray, the public servant whom Cross dispatches early on. The clash of two philosophies and personalities—Cross the monomaniacal businessman possessed by the pursuit of profit and power, and Mulwray the conscientious bureaucrat wedded to expertise in the public interest—results in a premeditated murder linked to the preordained triumph of unfathomable evil. The Luciferian Noah Cross is partly modeled on the *Los Angeles Times*'s combative founder "General" Harrison Gray Otis, a real-estate speculator whose booster enthusiasm was matched only by his unquenchable hatred for business rivals and labor radicals. Hollis Mulwray, in contrast, is rheumy, bespectacled, and intensely diminutive—a puny downsizing of his Promethean analogue in Los Angeles history: the large-framed, visionary founding LADWP "chief" William Mulholland.[13]

Not bound at the hip Cross-Mulwray fashion, Otis and Mulholland were explosive personalities who kept each other at a safe distance. An Irish immigrant success story and the highest-paid government employee in California, Mulholland admired accomplishment, but did not equate wealth with moral rectitude and had no veneration for millionaires. He agreed with Otis about using water to leverage San Fernando Valley annexation, which Mulholland viewed as essential to increase the city's tax base and bonding capacity for future public-works projects. They disagreed, however, over public distribution of aqueduct-generated electric power, which Mulholland favored as a source of revenue for more infrastructure.[14]

In the movie, Gittes asks: "Noah Cross worked for the Water Department?" He is told: "Yes and No. . . . He owned it."[15] He owned it jointly with Hollis Mulwray, who prevailed on him to sell it to the city, ostensibly transforming a private asset into a public trust and resource. This victory—Mulwray's only one related by the movie—imperfectly corresponds to an actual stormy transition in Los Angeles water history. At the turn of the 20th century, the 30-year franchise granted the Los Angeles City Water Company ended in an acrimonious lawsuit. In 1902, the city of Los Angeles bought out the private company with a successful municipal bond issue, and created a Board of Water Commissioners. The latter was the precursor of the Board of Commissioners of the Department of Water and Power, authorized under the 1925 City Charter and destined to become the largest and most powerful municipally owned utility in the United States. In *Chinatown*, this municipal triumph is deceptive and fleeting. We learn that Cross, who previously forced Mulwray to construct an unsound dam, is now pressing him to build with a new bond issue a second dubious dam as part of a conspiracy to corner and then develop the farm lands of Alto Vallejo.[16]

In important instances, Towne's spin on history results in serious distortions. First, the movie makes it look like the shift from private to public control of the municipal water supply changed little in terms of who wielded the power. In fact, the buyout of the Los Angeles City Water Company and end of the reign of "the water ring" marked the emergence of a newly energized "local state" committed to accelerated urban and regional development by public means and resources. It also went hand in hand with Los Angeles's success in convincing California courts, on the basis of the seeming precedent of Spanish and Mexican water law, that the city possessed an absolute and exclusive "pueblo right" to the water of the Los Angeles River. Second, the repeated—and now discredited— charges in *Chinatown* (borrowed from Carey McWilliams) that the Water Department engaged in dumping water to create an artificial water famine derive from Los Angeles's conspiratorial folklore—not from known history. Such charges whizzed back and forth during the bond elections of 1905 and 1907 when aqueduct opponents interpreted breakdowns of the antiquated municipal water system, causing significant water loss, as a part of a calculated plot by project backers.[17]

Third, rife real-estate speculation was the result, not the cause, of the Owens Valley aqueduct project. The San Fernando Mission Land Company was incorporated in November 1904 by Otis, his publishing rival Edwin T. Earl, transportation and real estate magnate Henry E. Huntington, and other Los Angeles business luminaries. The syndicate used privileged information about the city's successful negotiations with the United States Reclamation Service (renamed the Bureau of Reclamation in 1923) over the aqueduct project to buy up irrigable land. A follow-on syndicate, the Suburban Homes Company, was formed in 1909. Land purchased for $35 per acre was resold in a few years for $250 to $500 per acre. But there was no government plot to aggrandize San Fernando Valley speculators. As William Kahrl—not an admirer of the Los Angeles growth machine—puts it, "no conspiracy was necessary," because the "objectives were the same" of business and bureaucrats who acted independently but out of a common booster mind set. As the aqueduct project was taking shape, the real estate syndicate positioned itself to make a speculative windfall when the water flowed. It exploited insider knowledge, most likely provided by water commissioner Moses H. Sherman in an egregious breach of public trust by Sherman for personal gain.[18]

Yet the real impetus to build the aqueduct came from three men who did not belong to or benefit financially from the San Fernando Valley land syndicate. Two were civil engineers. Water chief William Mulholland viewed the aqueduct as his personal and professional gift to building a greater Los Angeles. His vision was shared by federal Reclamation Service official Joseph B. Lippincott. "Though an enthusiastic reclamationist," wrote Remi Nadeau of Lippincott, "he was first of all a citizen of the ambitious city of Los Angeles." Lippincott was reviled as "Judas B." by Owens Valleyites as soon as they learned of his engineering and economic reports favoring Los Angeles. A third prime mover was engineer-politician Fred Eaton—formerly chief engineer for L.A.'s private water company, and later L.A. city engineer, and then mayor. He was the first to envisage an aqueduct as a lifeline for Los Angeles at a time when the noted geologist Arthur Powell Davis was of the opinion that such a project "is as likely as the City of Washington tapping the Ohio River." Without Eaton there might have been no aqueduct at all. Yet his attempts to parlay the project into a personal fortune were largely unsuccessful and focused on real estate speculation in Long Valley (now Crowley Lake) neighboring the Owens Valley, not in the San Fernando Valley.[19]

In 1906, President Theodore Roosevelt bestowed the ultimate blessing on the aqueduct by declaring, "It is a hundredfold or a thousandfold more important . . . if [this water is used] by the people of the City than if used by the people of the Owens Valley."[20] However, the federal government insisted on full municipal ownership of any aqueduct project in order to qualify for a blanket easement through federal lands. This made it impossible for Eaton to convince Mulholland or the L.A. Water Commissioners to join him in a public-private partnership to market Owens Valley water.[21]

Returning to the Owens Valley in 1905, Eaton used the cover of his professional consultancy with the Reclamation Service to buy additional options on land and water rights. Many of his purchases were made directly for the city of Los Angeles. The city also bought most of Eaton's own holdings when Los Angeles voters in 1905 resoundingly approved a $1.5-million bond issue that was a preliminary to the $23-million aqueduct bond decisively passed in 1907. Eaton retained, however, a large cattle ranch in the upper reaches of the Owens River. The gorge leading from this valley provided an ideal site for a reservoir. He hoped eventually to sell this site to the city of Los Angeles for at least $1 million. But Eaton's dreams of millionaire status were dashed because of Mulholland's aversion to what he called "capitalists who were stealing the unearned increment" from the aqueduct project. Eaton boycotted the aqueduct's completion ceremony in 1913 as part of a running feud with his former friend and protégé. Mulholland chose to meet water storage needs by bypassing Eaton's Long Valley property rather than accede to his demands.[22]

A fourth serious distortion in *Chinatown* relates to the St. Francis Dam disaster of 1928, which cost at least 400 lives and fatally wounded the career of LADWP chief William Mulholland. In the movie, Hollis Mulwray regrets having succumbed to political pressure to build the flawed Van der Lip Dam. In reality, Mulholland overly relied on the fatally defective St. Francis Dam as part of a strategy to store emergency water south of the San Andreas earthquake fault line in the face of rampant population growth and drought conditions in the early 1920s. Less convincingly, some critics have argued that Mulholland championed the dam to avoid aggrandizing Fred Eaton, the owner of the ideal Owens Valley reservoir site. For these critics, the dam supposedly was built, at least partly, to avoid making a corrupt bargain rather than to consummate one. The city of Los Angeles bought, for only $650,000, Eaton's Long Valley property at long last in 1933, five years after the St. Francis Dam collapse. Both broken men nearing death, Eaton and Mulholland finally reconciled.[23]

The historical picture—in contrast to movie fiction—is that of real-estate speculators in the San Fernando Valley exploiting their connections to make money, but only after the Los Angeles Aqueduct project had been midwived by public servants such as William Mulholland, acting from professional and public-regarding motives. Fred Eaton's frustration in translating his precocious vision into dramatic private gain from the aqueduct project is the lone exception among the real historical actors who were the aqueduct's true founding fathers. But there was at least one "public man" who peddled influence, most probably Los Angeles water commissioner Moses H. Sherman.[24] More typical of the ethical norm was the attitude of fellow water board member J. M. Elliott, who declared,

> I had a perfect right to buy land anywhere but I didn't want any question to come up afterward whether I did or did not, and I determined that I wouldn't and I didn't. . . . I took that attitude because I would know earlier than anybody else of the possibility of that water coming down through there, and I knew that its coming down there would make that land very much more valuable.[25]

During and after the aqueduct was built, Mulholland and members of his circle, including Lippincott, Harvey Van Norman, Ezra Scattergood, Roderick McKay, and Phil Wintz (all engineers), joined many other Angelenos in buying San Fernando real estate, but did so without exploiting insider knowledge. Of humble origins himself, Mulholland clearly identified more with the San Fernando Valley farmers than with the real-estate speculators. The major conflicts over the aqueduct project involved differing conceptions of public good and professional responsibility advanced by public decision makers whose vantage point was government service—not private wealth or corporate power.[26]

Fred Eaton used his Reclamation Service connections to mislead Owens Valley residents into believing he was purchasing options for the federal government to build a reclamation project in the northern portion of the valley that would benefit their community; yet his covert purchases were mostly on behalf of the citizens of Los Angeles. Because of L.A.'s then-limited bonding capacity, project supporters claimed that secrecy was needed to prevent valley land speculation, which might have doomed the project by making it too expensive. Yet before resigning his federal position in 1906, Lippincott appeared to serve two masters—the Reclamation Service and the city of Los Angeles—and critics claimed that the supposed impropriety was becoming increasingly obvious even to those with only a rudimentary notion of "conflict of interest."[27]

William Mulholland, in contrast, had no master except himself and his moral compass. "I am the authority," he said of his role in LADWP policymaking. The St. Francis Dam disaster was the tragedy of a self-taught engineer, seemingly oblivious to the danger of professional hubris. The frequent likening of Mulholland to a Moses leading Angelenos out of the desert carried with it a dark side. Moses also struck rock to bring forth water, but did so without divine permission, with the result that he died after seeing, but not being permitted to enter, the Promised Land. Even at his most overreaching, Mulholland viewed himself as subordinate to a greater good embodied in growing Los Angeles. To his critics, Mulholland sinned—if he sinned at all—in ostensibly exaggerating in the early 1900s the city's real water shortage—relative to its explosive population growth—into a water crisis to reinforce public opinion in favor of the aqueduct project. Yet there is growing evidence that L.A.'s drought-induced water shortage was indeed real. In true booster fashion, Mulholland believed in Los Angeles's heroic future, although he applied restraint by introducing water meters and other conservation measures and also half joked that overheated population growth could be "cured" by killing off Frank Wiggins, the L.A. Chamber of Commerce's tireless secretary-publicist.[28]

As Los Angeles's water authorities after World War I began buying up more farmland in the Owens Valley to tap the water supply, critics charged that Mulholland—as President Theodore Roosevelt had appeared earlier—seemed callous to the plight of Owens Valley people. Yet recent research suggests that this was not necessarily the case. In all, Los Angeles spent over $24 million (or over $275 million in 2004 dollars) through 1934 to purchase Owens Valley agricultural and town properties. Compared to farmers and ranchers in neighboring Great Basin agricultural counties, Owens Valley landowners did substantially better in selling their land and water rights to the city than if they had stayed in agriculture and ranching. These were voluntary transactions; no land was purchased under threat of eminent domain. Further, most lands were leased back to their original owners for farming or livestock grazing. Later, Los Angeles, although a tax-exempt municipality, agreed to voluntarily pay property taxes in Inyo and Mono counties.[29]

Despite these apparent economic benefits, some in the Owens Valley felt aggrieved. Seemingly losers in a zero-sum competition with

Los Angeles, and envious of far greater land-value appreciation in the now-fertile San Fernando Valley, these Owens Valleyites responded with symbolic protests punctuated occasionally by sabotage and dynamite. L.A.'s equivalent of Rome's *Curator Aquarum*, or water czar, Mulholland came to view Owens Valley "dynamiters" as the equivalent of the Goths who disrupted imperial Rome's aqueducts in the year A.D. 537.[30]

Yet Mulholland's public-regarding conception of Los Angeles's destiny remained worlds apart from the all-devouring, solipsistic future coveted by *Chinatown*'s Noah Cross. Mulholland—not the fictional Noah Cross or actual real-estate speculators—created and guided L.A.'s Department of Water and Power during its formative era. Mulholland's famous cryptic declaration at the opening ceremony dedicating the aqueduct in 1913—"There it is. Take it"—hid the thoughtful side of a visionary man of action. Mulholland traced his personal and professional ethic back to a sacred site predating modern marketplace society. Noting that King Hezekiah had channeled water to the City of David, Mulholland pointed to the absence in the biblical account of "any mentions of dividends. . . . we may infer that the works were public, for public officials are guiltless of paying dividends—except in the indirect way of good service—if it so happens that they are good servants." It should be remembered, even in *Chinatown*, that Noah Cross admits that it was his son-in-law the engineer who really "made this town." So in actuality did William Mulholland.[31]

Yet if anyone else deserved credit or blame for the aqueduct project, it was a collective actor—Los Angeles's impatient, Progressive-era citizenry. Unwilling to brook opposition to their vision of future greatness, they rendered overwhelming majorities at the ballot box—14 to 1 in 1905 and 10 to 1 in 1907—for aqueduct bond issues that mortgaged themselves and their posterity to the promise of water for unlimited growth. In all, L.A. voters approved 12 of 16 water bond issues, 1904 to 1931, worth over $4 billion in 2003 dollars, by an average favorable majority of 76 percent. They were the LADWP's ultimate godfather. Whereas the movie *Chinatown* centers on a ruthless campaign to secure a fictional $10-million bond issue, LADWP quickly recovered from the 1928 St. Francis Dam debacle. With the overwhelming backing of the Los Angeles electorate, it scored two great general-obligation bond election victories—$38.8 million in 1930 for the Mono Basin extension, and

$220 million in 1931 to finance construction of MWD's Colorado River Aqueduct—during the Great Depression.[32]

Los Angeles's creation of a water-and-power political/bureaucratic machine to propel its megaprojects and growth was distinctive, although not unique. San Francisco's building of a municipal water-and-power project as well as the Hetch Hetchy Dam in Yosemite National Park proceeded in parallel fashion—with former mayor James H. Phelan playing the role of Fred Eaton, Irish-American water engineer Michael M. ("More Money") O'Shaughnessy that of William Mulholland, and J. B. Lippincott performing the same advisory and facilitating functions in both cities. Among the differences, though, was that, first, private water and electric companies were far more entrenched in San Francisco than ever was the case in L.A. Second, the political culture of Boss Abe Ruef's San Francisco was more susceptible to corporate bribery of public officials making water policy decisions. Third, the San Francisco electorate never quite matched Los Angeles's audacious, consistent embrace of "ballot-box growth" in the form of comprehensive rather than piecemeal approval of financing for expensive infrastructure projects. In Los Angeles, what historian Mike Davis has called "the Bismarckian will" to seize metropolitan greatness was the common property, not solely of the elite, but of the Progressive-era citizenry. The Department of Water and Power was the efficient conduit for that municipal public will.[33]

The *Noir* Legend That Would Not Die

In conclusion, it may be said that Los Angeles gets its water by reason of one of the costliest, crookedest, most unscrupulous deals ever perpetrated, plus one of the great pieces of engineering folly ever heard of. . . . The City of Angels moved through the Valley like a devastating plague. It was ruthless, stupid, cruel, and crooked. . . . It was an obscene enterprise from beginning to end. Today there is a saying in California about this funeral ground, which may well remain as its epitaph: "The Federal Government of the United States held Owens Valley while Los Angeles raped it."

Morrow Mayo, 1933[34]

Hole's third album, "Celebrity Skin," is dedicated to "all the stolen water of Los Angeles . . . and to anyone who ever drowned." The record is an L.A. story, and L.A. stories, from Roman Polanski's "Chinatown" to Mike Davis' "City of Quartz," usually begin and end with water, piped down from Northern California, stolen and somehow symbolically poisoned.

Alex Pappademas, 1998 [35]

Contrary to the truism that "the winners write the history," Los Angeles won the aqueduct war but has seemingly lost the ongoing battle over popular perceptions of the Owens Valley project. Even humorist Will Rogers, who claimed that he never met a man he didn't like, poured scorn on the "heartless" Los Angeles water seekers who seemingly savaged the Owens Valley.[36]

The water conspiracy theory encapsulated in *Chinatown* has a lengthy history. The seeds of Los Angeles's and the Department of Water and Power's public-relations Dunkirk began before World War I with the politically unsuccessful but poisonous opposition to "the water swindle" by minor newspaper publisher Samuel T. Clover, failed water capitalist W. T. Spilman, and the local Socialists—all of whom pilloried "Aqua Duck Bill" and derided "Saint Mulholland." The protest gathered momentum as the Owens Valley found voice for its grievances in Mary Austin's 1917 novel, *The Ford*, and in W. A. Chalfant's *The Story of Inyo* (1922 and 1933 editions). And just as the Owens Valley and the city reached an uneasy truce in the late 1920s, it exploded like a minefield in the nonstop polemics against "the rape of the Owens Valley" unleashed by publicist Andrae B. Nordskog and the muckraking writers, including Morrow Mayo and Carey McWilliams, whom he influenced.[37]

For over a decade after the construction of the Los Angeles Aqueduct, L.A.'s so-called water-and-power machine dominated the local media, holding "Aqueduct Days" with promotions ranging from prayer services to jazz bands to bond campaign commercials on the "Amos 'n' Andy" radio show. In the 1920s, William Mulholland—announcing himself "a sort of Bill Hart [an early cowboy actor] of the aqueduct"— even appeared in a LADWP promotional film, *Into the Future*. A few years later, the Metropolitan Water District tried the same approach by producing a talking picture entitled *Thirst*. Yet even though the Los Angeles electorate continued to be loyal to municipal water and power during the 1920s, the aqueduct's history was highly polarizing, with opponents harping on it, in conspiratorial fashion, to explain whatever ills they perceived in the Jazz Age metropolis. Prohibition-era Los Angeles was also punished in Sacramento for the statewide unpopularity of its water-and-power machine. During the administration of conservative California governor Friend W. Richardson, retribution against those responsible for "the broken hearts of the Owens Valley" was the major rationalization for the 1924 defeat of a state legislative redistricting plan friendly to Los Angeles County. In 1925, the state Reparations Law was enacted (and then reenacted in tougher form in 1945), making cities that tapped a watershed liable for damages.[38]

Given only grudging credit for the success of the Boulder (now Hoover) Dam project, Los Angeles and the Department of Water and Power were inundated by a flood of Owens Valley–related unfavorable media coverage in the 1930s and 1940s. Morrow Mayo's New York–centric book, *Los Angeles* (1933), excoriated the West Coast metropolis; Cedric Belfarge's novel, *Promised Land* (1938), fictionalized Mayo's account. In a 1935 Republic Pictures "B" movie entitled *New Frontier*, a young John Wayne comes to the rescue of the farmers of New Hope Valley, threatened by Metropole City's archdeveloper, Murdoch Mac-Quarrie. And in the 1950 novel, *Golden Valley*, a Mulholland clone again appears, this time as hulking Angus MacAndrew. Mulholland was a fading memory even in LADWP's offices (where his picture hung obscurely in the commissioners' meeting room) in the 1970s when the completion of a second L.A. aqueduct to the Owens Valley stung Inyo County to renew its historic fight with Los Angeles, but this time on fresh legal terrain created by new, stringent federal and state environmental protection laws. About the same time, LADWP supposedly agreed to a request by Roman Polanski, director of *Chinatown*, to be allowed to film his detective story on its historic Owens Valley sites.[39]

Red-faced when the film came out, Los Angeles officials lamely explained that they had granted permission because the filmmakers had told them that they "were doing a detective story set many years ago, so . . . [we] had no idea what was going on." After the film was released to a storm of controversy, a Department of Water and Power official is said to have attended a dinner party where he lamented that "It's all wrong. It's totally inaccurate!" Asked to elaborate, the best he could do was to exclaim, "There was never any incest involved." Mulholland remained more alive in the consciousness of the residents of Los Angeles's supposed water colony of the Owens Valley than he did in minds of citizens of the imperial metropolis. When Mulholland's statue in a Los Angeles park was shot in 1978 with an arrow tied to sticks of dynamite, the suspicion was that the explosion was the handiwork of marauding Owens Valleyites.[40]

When scriptwriter Robert Towne lectured on his film, the questions were invariably predicated on the assumption that it was a literal transcription of Los Angeles's past. Fiction had indeed triumphed over fact—and myth over history. The divergent reactions to two books published within a year of each other—Abraham Hoffman's *Vision or Villainy* (1981) and William Kahrl's *Water and Power* (1982)—were in part a reflection of the Owens Valley's ideological triumph. Hoffman's impressive and energetic demolition of conspiracy theories surrounding the formative decades of the LADWP—and the closely overlapping early years of MWD—was largely ignored except by specialists. Kahrl was no conspiracy monger, but his widely read book struck the perfect cynical tone for a generation disillusioned with both business and government. Quoting praise for Los Angeles's belated attempts to repair the Owens Valley ecology, Kahrl snickered, "so might Genghis Khan be admired today as an early advocate of open space preservation for his work in obliterating the cities of Central Asia."[41]

In 1924, six hooded men from the Owens Valley seized the control center at the Alabama Gate spillway north of Lone Pine, and diverted aqueduct waters into Owens Lake. Half a century later, the stir caused by *Chinatown* may have served as inspiration when the Alabama Gate was again the target, this time of alleged "ecoterrorism."[42] Writing in the 1990s, historian John Walton credited the film, despite inaccuracies, with capturing "the deeper truth" of the new rebellion attempting to rebuke "the vile association of money and power" that had built the aqueduct to the seemingly great detriment of the Owens Valley. Whether or not one agrees with Walton's defense of antiaqueduct populism, the rhetorical question he asked is still relevant: "Owens Valley symbolism threatens serious political repercussions. Why else did L.A.'s DWP, the nation's largest public utility, worry about the movie *Chinatown*?" For LADWP staff and supporters, the worry was that fiction posing as seeming fact had captured the popular imagination.[43]

Certainly the Owens Valley symbolism still remained powerful in 2000 when a Northern California member of Congress accused CALFED proposals to reduce California's dependence on Colorado River water as a plot by LADWP, MWD, and San Francisco to make "rural Northern California [into] a virtual water faucet for the Bay Area and Southern California—just like the Owens Valley."[44] A few years earlier, journalist Robert Jones surveyed in the *Los Angeles Times* Mono Lake's phoenix-like comeback after a decade of historic environmental compromises between Los Angeles and the Mono Lake Committee. His article's title: "Death of 'Chinatown.'" In the opening years of the 21st century, the coroner's jury was still out about whether that obituary for Los Angeles's seeming and much-maligned "water imperialism" was premature.[45]

MWD as *Chinatown*-Style Shadow Conspiracy

The City of Los Angeles cannot be trusted with the privilege of diverting a single gallon of water from the Colorado River; there is the tragic lesson of Owens Valley.

Sacramento Union *editorial, April 5, 1927*[46]

Not addressing the issues of the [Salton] Sea will ensure that future generations will have to do so, as well as suffer the environmental and economic consequences, much like the people of the Owens Valley have had to endure from metropolitan California's first big "water transfer" from a rural valley.

Tom Kirk, executive director, Salton Sea Authority, 2002[47]

In *Chinatown*-style mythology, the Los Angeles Department of Water and Power committed "original sin" in the Owens Valley, with the Metropolitan Water District of Southern California inheriting the crime and re-enacting it on a wider regional scale. Indeed, even before the 1930s—the decade in which the film's Jake Gittes learns the legendary dark secrets of LADWP's history—a companion conspiracy theory was crystallizing about MET as a new metropolitan "shadow government" doing the bidding of Los Angeles's "water imperialism" and its powerful private developers.

The headquarters' office space, engineering and budgetary support, and staff expertise that L.A.'s Department of Water and Power provided MWD during its first few years were plausible grounds for "guilt by association." In 1925, Los Angeles's supposed "rape of the Owens Valley" was invoked in Sacramento as reason enough to vote against an enabling act to create a Metropolitan Water District of Southern California. Echoes of the Owens Valley controversy were again heard in 1931 when the state legislature passed the County of Origin Law prohibiting export of water needed in one area to develop another. Receiving belated legislative authorization in 1927, MET was incorporated in 1928 to finance, build, and operate the Colorado River Aqueduct. But in part, MWD was also meant to forge a regional water consensus in Southern California that would counter the statewide political isolation of Los Angeles resulting in large measure from its reputation as the villain in the seeming Owens Valley tragedy.[48]

Yet such so-called keepers of Owens Valley history as publisher Andrae B. Nordskog saw to it that MET was too busy defending itself to provide much of a shield for Los Angeles and its Department of Water and Power. A singing teacher turned publicist for the Owens Valley cause, Nordskog wrote a massive polemic exposing "Boulder Dam in light of the Owens Valley Fraud." At the root of all evil was "the Mulholland political crowd" that also "is in control of the Boulder Dam situation." In other words, the seeming past crimes of LADWP and current sins of MWD were two sides of the same coin. Nordskog's exposé was read in manuscript by muckraking writer Carey McWilliams, who called it "the most sickening yarn I have ever read . . . of conspiracy, double-dealing, rotten politics, greed, avarice, amusing chicanery, etc." Yet because it was written "like a bond salesman with a yen to be a poet," no publisher would touch the manuscript.[49]

Deficient as a poet laureate, Nordskog was a potent lobbyist. He used the radio station of conservative L.A. evangelist Robert Shuler to broadcast his broadsides, and also organized the Southwest Water League to criticize the Colorado River Aqueduct project as a Los Angeles power grab. In 1931, when the California State Senate adopted a resolution creating a special committee to investigate the Owens Valley affair, Nordskog prevailed on Assembly Speaker Edgar C. Levey of San Francisco to have printed in the *Assembly Journal* as an "official document" a

28-page précis of his conspiracy theory linking L.A.'s DWP and MWD, 1,500 copies of which were run off and distributed widely by the California State Printing Office.[50]

In subsequent decades, whenever MET was buffeted by political controversy, its critics could be relied on to link it negatively to Los Angeles's alleged victimization of the Owens Valley. In 1927, the *Sacramento Union* opposed MWD's creation because

> There is a warning to be heeded. Here is a case where political ownership of public utilities had full sway for demonstration. The city concerned reverted to ruthlessness, savage disregard for moral and economic equations, to chicanery and faith breaking. . . . The municipality became a destroyer, deliberately, unconscionably, boastfully.[51]

In 1948, when MET initially refused to annex Pomona and Ontario, proponents of annexation again invoked the specter of the Owens Valley for Metropolitan not acting to benefit outlying agricultural areas. The Owens Valley analogy also was common currency used by critics of MWD during the debates over the State Water Project in 1960 and the Peripheral Canal in 1982. Some urban water agencies refused to even consider water transfer proposals "due to fears of resurrecting the 'Owens Valley syndrome.'"[52]

When water market transfers or swaps were first proposed in the 1980s between MET and the Imperial Irrigation District, a former director of the California Department of Water Resources invoked the Owens Valley and pointedly asked, "What would be the public reaction if the 11 million people who are served by the Metropolitan Water District should take the water away from one of the most productive agricultural areas of the state, the Imperial Valley?"[53] Then, when negotiation of such a deal actually commenced in 1985, the *Los Angeles Times* reported that some opponents were calling it "the Chinatown syndrome," whereas others cried, "Owens Valley. Look out, Los Angeles will steal your water. . . . You let them have one drop and they soon will have it all. Imperial Valley will become a desert waste again." When MWD General Manager Carl Boronkay spoke at meetings in Imperial County to explain MWD's proposal as one funding local conservation improvements with no loss of farm water, he faced hostile questions regarding "his stealing water from the Owens Valley." Boronkay had to spend considerable time distinguishing MET from Los Angeles and the latter's activities in the Owens Valley.[54]

In 1987, a newspaper in the Palo Verde Valley, Imperial Valley's neighbor, opposed a deal with MET involving land fallowing. The paper invoked the Owens Valley precedent and editorialized, "MWD: Drop Dead." In 1991, rural lawmakers in Sacramento again drew an "analogy with the Owens Valley" in opposing an MWD-supported water-transfer proposal that, they insisted, would "destroy California agriculture." Two years later, when the MET proposed purchasing water from San Joaquin Valley farmers, a local water district described the attempted purchase as "the same old 'divide-and-conquer' campaign used 90 years ago in Owens Valley." That same year in a scathing critique of Southern California water development, David Getches gave as his opinion that "The story of L.A.'s raid on the Owens Valley water . . . [was] exaggerated only slightly in the movie 'Chinatown.'"[55]

When MWD in the early 1990s crossed swords with the San Diego County Water Authority over drought-related cutbacks and water transfers, MET was berated for denying San Diego "water independence" and treating it as a colonial dependent—much as Los Angeles allegedly treated the Owens Valley. In contrast, when San Diego's water inner clique tried to secretly negotiate water purchases with the Bass brothers, the Texas billionaires who aspired to become Imperial Valley water farmers, the deal was castigated as "a modern-day version of 'Chinatown.'" According to Coachella Valley Water District general manager Tom Levy, "What the Bass brothers are doing in the Imperial Valley is the same as what Los Angeles did in the Owens Valley." San Diego was warned against disastrous environmental consequences "much like the people of the Owens Valley have had to endure from metropolitan California's first big 'water transfer' from a rural valley." Rick Mealey—farmer, rancher, and Imperial Valley's unofficial poet whose family came from the Owens Valley—intoned that Imperial County could become another "valley that died too soon."[56]

In heated response, the *San Diego Union-Tribune* castigated those who "vilified [the Bass brothers] with 'Chinatown' allegations" and who accused San Diego of "a 'Chinatown' takeover of Imperial Valley water," when the real hypocrite, if not culprit, was MWD, which "has recently engaged in exactly what it accused San Diego of doing" by buying land for water rights in the Mojave Desert. Advocates of the Imperial Valley–San Diego water transfer warned that, if MET succeeded in blocking it, Southern California would turn elsewhere to slake its thirst and "ravage the north," *Chinatown*-fashion. With water rights attorney Arthur L. Littleworth lamenting that the "Owens thing comes to haunt every water transfer that comes up," MWD and San Diego County Water Authority partisans busily hurled the *Chinatown* accusation at each other.[57]

MET's haunting by the *Chinatown* legend continues unabated. William Fulton prefaced his 1997 account of the building of MWD's huge Diamond Valley Lake reservoir project (generally lauded by environmentalists) with the observation "There aren't very many places left in Southern California where you can stand on top of a mountain and feel like you're in a scene from the movie *Chinatown*—where you can look across a vast, barren landscape and imagine the power brokers of the growth machine conspiring to transform it into money."[58] And in a supercilious 2003 travelogue, the London *Financial Times* pontificated for the benefit of its readers that "the rape of the Owens Valley" and "feudalistic struggles portrayed in *Chinatown* were the start of the reputation, still plaguing the Metropolitan Water District, of "Southern Californians . . . [as] alien, unmanageable, unfathomable, untrustworthy."[59]

In recent decades, Robert Gottlieb, a water maverick appointed in 1980 by Santa Monica to the MWD board of directors has been the most influential popularizer of the picture of MET as a *Chinatown*-style "shadow government." In *A Life of Its Own*, Gottlieb emphasized the growth-machine nexus between "the urban development complex" and MWD, which, although "dominated" by representatives of the city of Los Angeles, "immediately established policies that were more favorable to newly developing areas rather than the city itself." According to Gottlieb, Southern California land developers in relation to water were a variation on Willie Sutton, who explained that he robbed banks "because that's where the money is."[60]

A seeming case in point for Gottlieb was MET board chair (1983–1986) E. Thornton Ibbetson, who represented L.A. County's Central Basin Municipal Water District, but who had real-estate interests stretching from Lakewood and Long Beach to the Imperial Valley. As Gottlieb explains quoting "Ibby," he couldn't subdivide his land without water, "So I joined the water board to get to the water."[61] Then there was MWD's first chairman (1928–1946), W. P. Whitsett, a founder of Van Nuys and developer of the early bedroom suburb of Burbank. And not the least was MET's "grand old man," Board Chair (1949–1974) Joseph Jensen, a Standard Oil executive (actually, a geologist and mining engineer by training) who is reputed to have said, "Land is just land until water gets on it." Jensen was preeminent among the so-called old-guard water buffaloes that developed MWD's watering holes.[62]

In Gottlieb's second book, coauthored with Margaret Fitz-Simmons, *Thirst for Growth: Water Agencies as Hidden Government in California* (1991), the great real-estate subdividers are still prominent, but their hold over MWD's "hidden government" is circumscribed by Los Angeles's imperial will to dominate its smaller neighbors. Hence, Gottlieb and FitzSimmons explain, "Even the prominent role assumed by the City of Pasadena in the formation of the District was designed to disguise the fact that the District was indeed dominated by Los Angeles."[63]

How close is the fit between the actual history and politics of MET and Gottlieb's thesis characterizing Metropolitan as a well-camouflaged pecuniary vehicle for the great regional real-estate developers, limited only by the countervailing force of Los Angeles's hierarchical ambitions to sit atop the metropolitan empire? To preview the next several chapters, they are not very close at all. First, as to MWD's origins, rather than being hidden they were acted out in explosive public fashion as part of the water-and-power battles between public and private power lobbies that were pivotal conflicts in local, regional, state, and even federal politics involving California during the 1920s. The Los Angeles Chamber of Commerce encouraged the drafting of the original MET blueprint, but the conflict over the project soon exceeded the boundaries of polite debate within such elite confines. Opposing the initial 1925 MWD enabling act (called "little Swing Johnson" in contrast with the "big Swing Johnson" bill in Washington that authorized the Boulder Dam Project), the *Los Angeles Times* denounced it as "one of the most radical and Socialistic proposals ever submitted to the State Legislature." In the June election of the same year, three of the five Southern California Republican assemblymen who sided with the *Times* and against the MET proposal were purged from office by the victorious pro–public water-and-power "machine" of then L.A. mayor George E. Cryer.[64]

Then in 1926, Progressive Republican Clement C. Young was elected governor as a strong supporter of both the Colorado River Aqueduct and MWD enabling legislation. In this changed atmosphere, the

Los Angeles Times grudgingly supported passage of a new MWD bill, granting the agency somewhat narrower powers. However, the *Times*'s editorial line—usually an accurate barometer of the interests of Harry Chandler's diverse real-estate empire, running from Santa Barbara to Baja California—continued to be extremely wary of the new Metropolitan Water District. The *Times* believed that MWD was beholden to "John R. Haynes, W. B. Mathews, and others in the [LADWP] Power Bureau Clique" who "are actuated by political motives and have sought to coerce and intimidate other communities in Southern California."[65] This is why the *Times* rejoiced in 1930 when conservative mayor John C. Porter forced John Randolph Haynes, Los Angeles's most prominent public-ownership advocate, to choose between his positions on the LADWP and MET boards (he resigned from the latter).[66]

Second, although Gottlieb is of course aware of the differences between the engineering mentality of most of MWD's early general managers and the entrepreneurial agendas of many of its board directors, he underemphasizes at least until the rise of Carl Boronkay, a lawyer turned MET general manager (1984–1993), the decisive importance of the professional and technical staff in shaping the agency's mission.[67] MWD's first general manager was engineer Frank Weymouth, who came to the agency from the federal Bureau of Reclamation and L.A.'s DWP. While overseeing construction of the Colorado River Aqueduct, Weymouth submitted a comprehensive report to the board in October 1930 that arguably was the most influential document in the agency's formative history. Laying out straight-line projections until 1980 from Los Angeles's 1920s-era population boom and accompanying drought, Weymouth justified the aqueduct as vital to meeting future regional water needs.[68]

In 1941, when the first Colorado River water reached metropolitan Los Angeles—in the wake of the Great Depression that severely stunted regional growth—the need had not yet materialized, and there were virtually no takers. This temporary embarrassment hardly fazed the aqueduct's master builders, whose measure of success was constructing a mighty infrastructure empire that would underwrite for generations to come, not only a growing population but a diversified economy that by the time of the 1941 Pearl Harbor attack boasted major rubber, tire, steel, auto, aircraft, and other manufacturing facilities whose continued development necessitated the ready availability of water as well as hydroelectric power. Shaped by engineers such as Frank Weymouth, MET no more appeared to pursue policies narrowly designed to aggrandize real-estate developers than the pharaohs built pyramids to provide their stone masons with lucrative careers. The pyramid and aqueduct builders were both products of "hydraulic societies," yet (to borrow Kevin Starr's phrase) their "material dreams" differed profoundly in the kinds of social order they created in semiarid environments.[69]

Third, and as later argued, Los Angeles was not always the monolithic, dominating force in MWD councils as portrayed by Gottlieb. There were divisions within Los Angeles city government and its representatives on the MET board between those who considered the Colorado River Aqueduct as a taxpayer burden versus an infrastructure-and-growth bonanza. This internal fissure ran from before World War II, when L.A.'s Municipal Research Bureau questioned the economics of importing Colorado River water; to the 1970s, when L.A. councilman Ernani Bernardi led the forces that threatened a class-action lawsuit or even a pullout from MWD over the alleged excessive charges paid by L.A. taxpayers; and later to when Ellen Stern Harris from Beverly Hills carried an economic critique of MET's rate structure into its own boardrooms. The conflict continues to this day.[70]

Furthermore, on the MWD board, where Los Angeles representatives long enjoyed veto power with the unit rule (bloc vote) and control of 50 percent of the board vote, the city delegation on numerous critical occasions was either unwilling or unable to dictate policy over regional opposition. In 1948, Los Angeles members on the MET board actually vetoed annexation requests of relatively undeveloped Pomona and Ontario, which lacked even San Diego's tax base to contribute to MWD levies. Anti–Los Angeles grumblings on the board, together with the threat of hostile legislation from Sacramento, forced the L.A. city board directors to back down. In 1952, MET adopted, over doubts voiced by some Los Angeles directors, the Laguna Declaration extending its commitment to develop water resources to meet the needs even of low-assessment agricultural areas. In 1960 the Los Angeles board delegation, led by imperious MWD chairman Joseph Jensen, bitterly opposed the State Water Project on the ballot that year as financially unfair to their city until just days before the election when both internal and external political pressures caused them to capitulate and endorse the historic water bonds. Later, Jensen would criticize San Diego's supposed "free ride" at the expense of Los Angeles, but with no discernible effect on MET policy.[71]

Although many of these conflicts might seem examples of regional developer interests trumping Los Angeles and triumphing at the expense of its taxpayers, the picture of MWD's relationship with powerful businesses and landowners was much more complicated than that. Just as MET in its formative era was opposed by the formidable Chandler family media-and-real-estate empire, MWD's support of the Peripheral Canal in 1982 set it at loggerheads with traditional allies among Kern County agribusinesses such as the J.G. Boswell and Salyer Land companies that bankrolled the successful anti-Canal campaign. In the 1980s, MWD broke the historic urban-agricultural water agency alliance, and began to cooperate with the environmental community. MET entered into an alliance with the Environmental Defense Fund (now Environmental Defense) to study how to improve water quality and protect groundwater supplies. MWD's environmentalism put it at odds with some former business-developer allies during the successful 1996 campaign for Proposition 204, "The Safe, Clean, Reliable Water Supply Act," and the 2000 campaign for Proposition 13, "The Safe Drinking Water, Clean Water, Watershed Protection, and Flood Protection Bond Act."[72]

As argued in subsequent chapters, the Metropolitan Water District of Southern California over its long history has not been a *Chinatown*-style "hidden government" simply beholden to the interests of Los Angeles and private developers. From its inception, MWD was an enterprising regional public agency tasked with a mandate to lead—not follow—in the application of Progressive-style expertise to the development of water resources for a dynamic, diverse region. Hannah Arendt traced the root of the word "authority" to the Latin *augure*, meaning the legitimate augmentation of the founding purposes of a state. MWD's leaders have sought to augment the promise and potential of Southern California. When Metropolitan has failed to measure up, the reasons may sometimes have been fundamental defects in the California Dream—but were not the result of overplotted conspiracies mistakenly accepted by fans of films such as *Chinatown* as accurately capturing real history.[73]

3   **Building and Financing an Empire: Balancing Growth and Equity**

> You have been a material part in building an empire. You could have at the inception sat tight and played a strictly selfish Los Angeles City game. That is, the City made it possible to finance the Colorado River program at Hoover Dam. It had the controlling interest of Metropolitan. Under your leadership, Metropolitan water was made available from Ventura County to the border. Without water these communities would have had very slow growth.
>
> *Frank P. Doherty letter to Joe Jensen, long-serving MWD board chair and L.A. director, 1967*[1]

> When the first rush of Owens Valley water moved swiftly down a spillway into the San Fernando Valley in 1913, Mulholland uttered a now-famous phrase that aptly sums up L.A.'s approach to water: "There it is. Take it." . . . As the fictionalized retelling of this story in the 1970s film *Chinatown* suggests, L.A.'s growth brokers had learned the most basic lesson. . . . Whoever controls the water, controls the future, and Los Angeles boosters proved willing to be as muscular, imperial, and ruthless as necessary to secure enough water to ensure unlimited future growth.
>
> *William Fulton,* The Reluctant Metropolis *(1997)*[2]

From inauspicious beginnings, Metropolitan has grown into a mighty empire. In 1941, with little fanfare the Colorado River Aqueduct was opened. Soon MWD was being vilified as an ill-conceived "white elephant" saddled with huge debt payments and few customers. In the postwar era, Metropolitan overcame its troubled debut and began casting an ever-lengthening and more powerful shadow over Southern California. Armed with liberal annexation policies and initially low water rates, it mushroomed in size. Between 1928 and 2003, Metropolitan's service territory and customers multiplied eightfold, to 5,200 square miles and 18 million customers, respectively. Its mission also blossomed, from supplemental water supplier to 11 cities to Southern California's chief water resources planner, manager, and lobbyist.

Yet nagging questions remained concerning the regional water empire being built: who ruled, who paid, and who benefited? Despite contrary evidence, as noted in chapter 2, many claim that MWD was—and remains—a metropolitan "shadow government" doing the bidding of the city of Los Angeles. As Norris Hundley Jr. argues,

> Not surprisingly, Los Angeles emerged as the preeminent, though not absolute, power in the MWD, largely through possession of the largest bloc of votes on the board of directors. . . . MWD also obtained what Mulholland and other city leaders had provided for the Los Angeles Department of Water and Power commissioners: insulation of the board of directors from politics and popular control. . . . [Los Angeles was] armed with an efficient and powerful new vehicle for acquiring water.[3]

Insulated from direct popular control, how has the Metropolitan board used its discretion? Have MWD's policies indeed favored Los Angeles? Or, as critic Robert Gottlieb contends, did the MWD board of directors—including the powerful L.A. city delegation—actually create policies favoring the suburbanizing periphery such as southern Orange County and San Diego? If so, what might explain this seeming anomaly? Could MET's insulated design have furnished Los Angeles directors and other board members the freedom to pursue agency and regional long-term interests with little fear of ratepayer and taxpayer reprisal for the near-term burdens imposed? Claims of member agency subsidies and inequitable burden-and-benefit sharing have been recurring sources of dispute within the MET family.[4]

This chapter examines the growth, financing, and equity dynamics of the water empire being constructed. It considers major MWD policies—annexation, capital financing, water rates, voting and water rights from 1928—MWD's inception—through 2003—the last fiscal year (FY) for which complete data were available. The 1928–2003 period examined here covers nearly the entire MWD life span through two very different fiscal regimes (pre-1970, based on taxes versus post-1970, based on water charges). In 2003, MET implemented a new water rate structure unbundling various service costs.

Unraveling the Water-Growth Nexus

Land is just land until it gets water on it. When it gets water, its assessed value and its sale value increase materially. . . . That is the best evidence of the benefit that the MWD creates for an area.

Joe Jensen, MWD board chair, 1970[5]

To bring Colorado River water to Los Angeles, the growth machine created what may have been its most brilliant organizational achievement: . . . the Metropolitan Water District of Southern California. . . . The Met grew to become the leading instrument for rapid and expansive urban development in metropolitan L.A. This agency has always insisted that its job was not to stimulate growth but merely to provide water wherever growth occurred. But in fact, the Met's goal was, and continues to be, to acquire such vast amounts that water would not be an issue in planning Southern California's future. In this task, the Met succeeded.

William Fulton, The Reluctant Metropolis *(1997)*[6]

Since the creation of Metropolitan, what has been Southern California's pattern of development? Between 1928 and 2003, the population of metropolitan Southern California increased 10-fold, from less than 2 million to over 20 million residents. The city of Los Angeles, the original urban core, grew from 1 million to nearly 4 million residents—a 300 percent increase. But the rest of Southern California experienced far more prodigious growth—1,500 percent, from 1 million residents to a population of 16 million. Although the city of Los Angeles was the pre–Depression era growth leader, in the immediate post–World War II era the rest of Los Angeles County witnessed fast-paced suburbanization. By the 1960s, the fastest-growing areas were Orange and San Diego counties. Recently, the Inland Empire (San Bernardino and Riverside counties) has emerged as the region's growth leader. Future population-growth estimates for the region suggest little slackening in the fervid growth pace. As noted, Southern California is forecast to grow by over 5 million residents by 2025. The fastest-growing areas are predicted to be the exurban periphery: western Riverside County, San Bernardino County, northern Los Angeles County, southern Orange County, and San Diego County.[7]

The region's post-1928 growth pattern has been—and continues to be—one of massive and unrelenting suburban development. Recently, though, the prospect of ever-more suburban sprawl and attendant threats to the region's environment, quality of life, public services, and infrastructure have pushed "smart growth" or sustainable development to the forefront of policy discussions—ranging from land use planning to transportation and water—in the Southland and California. Yet, the policy dynamics—and potential leverage points—shaping metropolitan growth patterns are complex and multifaceted. Transportation technology (for example, the streetcar and automobile), cultural values, and federal highway and housing policies have been major contributory factors. State and local policies also have played a crucial role. These include zoning and land use controls, municipal incorporation and taxation policies, and, in the case of Southern California, the provision of county public services to newly incorporated suburbs.[8]

In the semiarid West, there is widespread recognition that water has played an essential role in regional development. Without the massive infrastructure that was put in place over the last century to supply water to both urban and agricultural areas, most western states would have been unable to sustain the rapid population growth they have experienced. Yet there are few studies of how water policy may be an important contributory factor to development *within* regions such as Southern California. In one of the few intraregional analyses, Robert Gottlieb argues that, driven by growth imperatives and developer influence, MET policymakers established water policies favoring the suburban periphery at the expense of the city of Los Angeles. Was this indeed the case? If so, why did L.A. public officials acquiesce?[9]

As considered later, Los Angeles's relentless drive for secure water supplies may have led it to miscalculate the benefits and costs of MWD membership. Starting in the 1930s, L.A. secured greater amounts of less expensive water from the Owens Valley and Mono Basin (which supplies later would be reduced by lawsuits and regulatory decisions). As a result, L.A. did not fully claim its anticipated share of MWD water, even while fully paying its large share for the infrastructure that supplied it. Los Angeles also acquiesced in MET's liberal annexation policies, which greatly expanded its service territory. By its actions, L.A. underwrote Metropolitan's early infrastructure and growth, and also freed up surplus MET water for fast-growing outlying areas in Southern California.[10]

Very little of Southern California's staggering population growth and economic development to date could have occurred without an adequate supply of affordable imported water. As noted, the city of Los Angeles pioneered the development of imported water supplies, completing its aqueduct from the Owens Valley in 1913. This would allow L.A. to grow from one-half million to 2 million residents.[11] In 1928, Los Angeles and its suburbs joined in creating the Metropolitan Water District to bring fresh supplies of imported water from the Colorado River. In effect, MWD created a "water wall" around Los Angeles, breaking up the city's water monopoly, which had been used as a potent force for territorial expansion. Los Angeles's boundaries in 2004 (469 square miles) are roughly the same as they were in 1930 (442 square miles). Although L.A. aggressively annexed neighboring areas to capture nearly half of the five-county metropolitan area's pre-1930 population growth, since Metropolitan's creation fully 80 percent of regional growth has occurred outside L.A. city limits. In this fashion, MWD made possible the postwar suburbanization of Los Angeles County (as over 50 new cities soon were incorporated) and of neighboring Orange County. The new cities formed municipal water districts that were annexed to MET.[12]

From the 1940s onward, as Colorado River water became available, outlying areas such as San Diego applied for annexation to Metropolitan. Annexation would become a contentious policy issue within MWD. The agency had started as a confederation of cities seeking supplemental water supplies. With heavy rains in the 1930s and L.A.'s decision to extend its municipal supplies to the Mono Basin, MET was left with few customers and heavy debt payments. As a result, it pragmatically accepted annexations involving municipal water districts needing primary water supplies. Thus, Coastal Municipal Water District (now part of the Municipal Water District of Orange County) joined MWD in 1942, and the San Diego County Water Authority joined in 1946. In the late 1940s, with member agency fears of stretched water supplies and diminished rights, MET's board debated the wisdom of bringing in other outlying water-intensive agricultural areas with few local supplies.

The annexation debate soon ended. In the early 1950s, MWD pledged itself to guaranteed water supplies and further territorial expansion. In 1952, it established a new policy, known as the Laguna Declaration, which pledged the agency to find a permanent water supply for the region, and to provide water to anyone who requested it in its service territory. This proved a potent catalyst for further annexations to Metropolitan. The annexation debate refocused on the magnitude of membership fees. In 1960, under the leadership of Governor G. (Pat) Edmund Brown, the State Water Project was approved, bringing new imported water (albeit representing only half of the California Aqueduct's planned capacity) from Northern California for distribution by MET to its member agencies. As a result, MWD's service area grew to encompass most of urban Southern California.[13]

Financing MWD: From Taxes to Water Charges

> The hardest shaping of policy, as far as I'm concerned, has been raising the price of water. In the future for the protection of the assessed valuation and the industries of Los Angeles, we simply cannot afford to continually overload them. . . . And so I think the time is coming soon on our problem—to face the issue of proper pricing of water. In the past, taxes were justified because the aqueduct was not running at full capacity. Now, however, the aqueduct will be running at full capacity and should in the future earn a substantial profit.
>
> *MWD Board Chair Joe Jensen, 1970*[14]

How has Metropolitan financed its water, infrastructure, and growth? Initially, some supporters believed that the agency might be able to pay most everything—operations, maintenance, and capital projects—out of water charges. However, taxes would be needed to build an aqueduct before revenue-bearing water could flow. Thus, MWD initially relied on property taxes and annexation fees rather than water charges. In the early years of its existence, property taxes provided the bulk of MET's revenues. Although Colorado River water did not make its way to Southern California until 1941, when the aqueduct finally was completed, Metropolitan began collecting property taxes early on to finance the mammoth $220-million aqueduct—which, with bond interest repayment, would cost $2.7 billion in 2003 dollars. L.A. had by far the greatest assessed valuation in the district, and its taxpayers would shoulder a significant share of the burden. Property taxes remained the principal means of financing MWD operations through the 1960s because capital projects could not generate revenue until they were completed, and early water sales were paltry.

By the mid-1940s, Metropolitan was awash in water but not customers, forcing the agency to sell water at below cost in order to encourage greater purchases by member agencies as well as possible annexations. Thus, in 1947 MET only charged $15 per acre-foot (AF) for treated domestic water, a price that only slowly rose to $49/AF in 1970. The agency was in serious danger of becoming a "white elephant"—a costly facility with too few customers.[15] Early low water rates were designed to induce outlying areas to join MWD and stop over-drafting groundwater. After most of urban Southern California was annexed, MWD then could raise rates to pay much of its operating and capital expenses. By 2005, the Tier 1 rate (recovering the cost of maintaining reliable supplies) for treated water was to be $443/AF.[16]

Los Angeles, whose taxpayers paid 42 percent of the real (inflation-adjusted) costs of the Colorado River Aqueduct, drew little initial MET water—less than 10 percent of total Metropolitan deliveries—because the city continued to develop its own water supplies. In the 1930s, Los Angeles extended its system to the Mono Basin. Later, in 1970, the city completed a second aqueduct to the Owens Valley. Owens Valley water was much cheaper, because it featured a gravity-flow system, whereas MWD needed costly pumping plants to move its Colorado River water over desert mountains.[17]

Starting in the early 1960s, Metropolitan began shifting its capital financing from taxes to water sales.[18] By then, nearly all of the urban coastal plain had been annexed to Metropolitan. Now it was easier for MET to raise water prices to recover capital and operating costs. The State Water Project, begun in 1960 and completed in 1972–1973, served as a major catalyst for capital finance restructuring. Los Angeles demanded that the State Water Project, with its more expensive water, be financed by water sales rather than taxes. San Diego, however, resisted. The San Diego County Water Authority, MWD's largest customer, drew one quarter of Metropolitan water deliveries but had only paid 13 percent of MWD annexation fees (representing back taxes) and property taxes since joining Metropolitan in 1946.[19]

Los Angeles increased its pressure for MET to shift much of its capital financing from property taxes to water rates. In 1960, the MWD

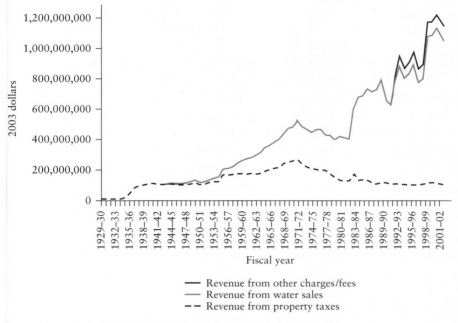

FIGURE **3.1**   MWD revenue contributions (in 2003 dollars), 1929–2003

SOURCE: MWDSC, Office of Chief Financial Officer.

board of directors adopted a new policy (Resolution 5821) which required that at least half of all capital expenses plus all operating and maintenance costs be borne by water sales revenues.[20] This partially allayed Los Angeles's concern that Metropolitan would continue to rely heavily on tax revenues. A subsequent Los Angeles lawsuit and a new proportionate-use formula (Resolution 7746) in 1979 furthered the shift in MET capital financing to water sales.[21]

As a result, there are two distinct MWD fiscal regimes, pre- and post-1970, reflecting these dynamics. Figure 3.1 shows Metropolitan's changing revenue sources (in constant 2003 dollars), 1929–2003. Before 1970, property taxes constituted the major source of agency revenues. Taxes paid for virtually all MET capital projects; they even underwrote water sales and operating expenses. By the 1970s, water sales had become the primary revenue source. As State Project water flowed into Southern California, Metropolitan's uniform or postage-stamp water rates (in which member agencies paid the same amount for similar kinds of water) were raised to include most capital, operating, and maintenance charges.

By the mid-1990s, yet another fiscal regime was emerging as new capital-financing policies were installed. In response to reduced water deliveries and lessened revenues produced by a lengthy drought coupled with the sizable financing needs of an ambitious capital-improvement program, MWD adopted a new rate structure designed to shift capital costs away from variable water sales toward new, more stable charges. These included a readiness-to-serve charge to meet debt service needs, water reliability, and quality under normal demand; a standby charge for unimproved land benefiting from legal access to MET water; and a new demand charge (later suspended) to recover capital costs associated with meeting new demands. In 2003, after lengthy strategic planning, MWD implemented a new two-tier rate structure, partially unbundling MWD's historic postage-stamp water rate while still guaranteeing a fixed revenue stream. Tier 1 provides a basic supply and finances system maintenance, whereas Tier 2 is a more expensive supplementary option for member agencies needing additional supplies to accommodate growth or improve water quality. The new rate structure is examined in chapter 8.[22]

Figure 3.2 compares the components of total MWD revenue for the two regimes, 1929–1970 and 1971–2003. In the pre-1970 period property taxes and annexation fees accounted for 75 percent of MET's total revenue, whereas water sales only amounted to one quarter. Taxes not only were the main source of early capital financing, they also paid a significant share of operating costs. Even as late as 1960, one third of MWD's *ad valorem* tax rate was devoted to general outlays rather than to debt service. MET kept water prices artificially low to make its water financially attractive relative to groundwater usage, and thus encourage annexations. (Outlying cities or water districts had to request annexation, which needed MWD board approval.) This strategy of low-priced water forced continued reliance on property taxes as the agency's principal revenue source. The original 13 member agencies, which had joined MET between 1928 and 1931, later were joined by 13 more agencies annexed to Metropolitan between 1942 and 1963; San Fernando joined in 1971.[23]

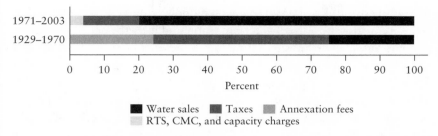

FIGURE **3.2**   Components of total MWD revenue collected (in current nonadjusted dollars), 1929–1970 and 1971–2003

SOURCE: MWDSC, Office of Chief Financial Officer.

For the post-1970 period, the relative magnitude of the two revenue streams was reversed. Water sales now accounted for over 75 percent of total agency revenue. In contrast, taxes, fees, and other charges generated less than one quarter of MWD revenue. Increased water sales revenues reflected both the shift in capital financing and MET's willingness to raise water rates for full cost recovery as annexation was completed.

Has L.A. "Subsidized" Water Provision for San Diego and Outlying Areas?

The City of Los Angeles had to pay a whole lot of [MWD] taxes and they got very little [MWD] water. . . . But San Diego got a free ride. They paid very little taxes, and as long as the water rates were low they were riding on Los Angeles's water, really. And where it became bitter was between San Diego and Los Angeles.

> *Robert V. Phillips, former LADWP general manager and chief engineer (1971–1975), 1995*[24]

Subsidy—"a direct financial aid furnished by a government"—is a misnomer here. As required by its organic Act, MWD applies the same tax rates to every taxpayer and uniform water rates to all water users. Disparities in comparative contributions to MET's revenues are not the result of subsidies, but are due to the different assessed land valuations in each member agency and the different amounts of water purchased.

> *Paul Engstrand, former SDCWA General Counsel (1970–1990), 2005*[25]

Given the dynamics of MWD's financing polices, has the city of Los Angeles indirectly subsidized water provision and growth for outlying areas such as San Diego? Subsidies remain a bone of contention between Los Angeles and San Diego water officials. L.A. officials claim that the city's large early Metropolitan capital investments, coupled with limited water deliveries until recently, constitute a major subsidy to other member agencies. However, San Diego officials counter that these are "fictitious costs." They argue that not only are cost-of-service disparities between member agencies a result of the application of uniform MET rules, but also that Los Angeles has derived substantial economic benefit from Metropolitan, ranging from an augmented water supply to its rise as the region's premier financial and service center.[26]

San Diego County Water Authority consultants hired in 1999 to examine the subsidy issue concluded that Los Angeles had indeed historically subsidized water provision to other MWD member agencies such as San Diego, although on a smaller scale than proffered in these pages. Unfortunately, the SDCWA consultants selectively included only those "adjustments"—involving option value (drought insurance), agricultural water, and water quality—which subtracted from (but didn't add to) L.A.'s historical subsidy for San Diego water provision.[27] A subsequent study questioned such adjustments (such as for discounted but interruptible agricultural water) and included counterbalancing offsets—such as L.A.'s MWD surplus water benefiting San Diego and L.A.'s own water-quality mitigation outlays—which were ignored in the SDCWA consulting report. The reanalysis confirms the overall magnitude of Los Angeles subsidies for San Diego water provision presented here.[28]

Calculating Cost-of-Service Disparities

There are substantial cost-of-service disparities between Metropolitan member agencies, particularly Los Angeles and San Diego. These can be calculated in terms of MET member agencies' total real (inflation-adjusted) financial contributions (water charges, property taxes, annexation charges, and other charges or fees) relative to the amount of MWD water they have received. This approach—average real unit cost per acre-foot—is quite sensible in a cooperative structure such as Metropolitan, as it provides a direct link between financial contributions and tangible benefits to member agencies. In general, water deliveries to the original 13 member agencies have not matched their early, substantial capital outlays for the Colorado River Aqueduct. In contrast, many later-joining agencies have drawn a greater share of MET water relative to their financial contributions. Such benefit-burden disparities give credence to the argument that MWD policies have resulted in subsidies between member agencies.[29]

This appears to be especially true of Metropolitan's two largest member agencies—founding member Los Angeles and later-joining San Diego. From 1928 to 2003, the city of Los Angeles in real terms paid over twice its share of MWD financial contributions (17 percent) relative to the share of MET water received (8 percent). In contrast, San Diego received over a one third greater share of Metropolitan water (26 percent) than its proportion of total financial contributions in real terms (19 percent). As a result, San Diego has received more than three times the MWD water deliveries as Los Angeles has received while paying in real terms only 12 percent more in total MWD revenues. San Diego water officials counter by calculating Metropolitan financial contributions in nominal (current) dollars, thereby magnifying newer customer payments at the expense of older customer contributions. By their calculations, San Diegans have paid to MET nearly twice as much as Los Angelenos—$3 billion versus $1.6 billion.[30]

The inflation-adjusted cost-of-service disparities can largely be traced to the city of Los Angeles underwriting much of Metropolitan's early capital costs for the Colorado River Aqueduct, and then drawing far less MET water than planned. Figure 3.3 displays the Los Angeles Department of Water and Power's (L.A. taxpayers' and ratepayers') share of total MWD revenues relative to MWD capital project expenditures, 1933–2003, expressed in 2003 dollars. It graphically shows the enormous early financial contributions of L.A.'s citizenry to Metropolitan as the Colorado River Aqueduct was being constructed.

Figure 3.4 displays the real unit costs of MWD water deliveries for the city of Los Angeles, the rest of Los Angeles County, and the other five counties served by Metropolitan, 1929–2003. The real unit cost represents the total MWD financial contribution (in 2003 dollars) per AF of water delivered to each jurisdiction. I have chosen counties as the primary unit of analysis because counties and their political subdivisions, not

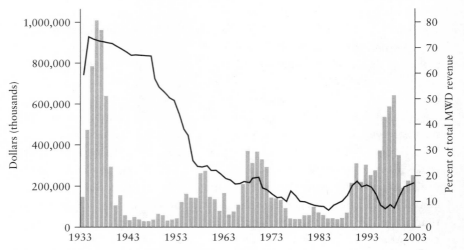

FIGURE **3.3**   LADWP share of total MWD revenue versus capital projects expenditures, FY 1933–FY 2003

SOURCE: LADWP Water Resources Business Unit; and MWDSC, Office of Chief Financial Officer, 2004.

NOTE: Capital projects expenditures (left scale) are in 2003 dollars.

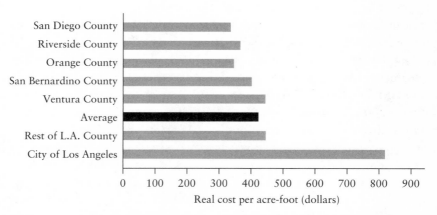

FIGURE **3.4**   Unit cost (in 2003 dollars) per acre-foot of MWD water delivered, by counties and the city of Los Angeles, 1929–2003

SOURCE: MWDSC, Office of Chief Financial Officer.

water agencies, make land use decisions and thus shape patterns of growth and development. MET member agencies have been aggregated to the county level. Given the major historical financing role played by the city of Los Angeles, the figure shows data for the city separately. Note the substantial differences in unit water costs for the city of Los Angeles relative to the rest of Southern California. Los Angeles has paid $833/AF of water, nearly double the $431 average. In contrast, outlying and suburbanizing San Diego, Riverside, and Orange counties only paid $338, $371, and $350 per AF, respectively.

What explains these substantial unit-cost disparities? Figure 3.5 disaggregates MWD financial contributions by jurisdiction into four components: water sales, property taxes, annexation fees, and other charges such as standby, readiness-to-serve, and connection maintenance charges. Thus, 62 percent of L.A. City's total contribution has been from taxes, compared to 36 percent from water sales. In sharp contrast, only 21 percent of San Diego's total financial contribution has come from taxes and annexation fees, whereas three quarters have come from water sales. Similarly, less than one third of Orange and Riverside counties' contributions to Metropolitan have come from taxes and annexation charges, compared to two thirds from water sales.[31]

Changing Cost-of-Service Patterns: Pre- and Post-1970

The pronounced shift in MET capital financing and revenue sources circa 1970 suggests that there may be different cost-of-service patterns in the pre- and post-1970 eras. Figure 3.6 shows that this indeed is the case. Here we measure the magnitude of the financial overpayment or underpayment to Metropolitan (in 2003 dollars) relative to actual water deliveries for the city of Los Angeles, the rest of L.A. County, and the other counties served by MWD, for 1929–1970 and 1971–2003.

Figure 3.6 shows that most of the "subsidies" between member agencies occurred in the early era under a tax-based fiscal regime that heavily relied on the region's urban core. In the 1929–1970 period, the city of Los Angeles overpaid $1.7 billion and the rest of L.A. County $70 million in MET contributions relative to their water deliveries. In sharp contrast, the San Diego County Water Authority underpaid $838 million relative to MWD water deliveries whereas Orange County

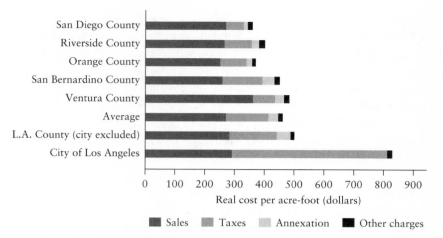

FIGURE **3.5**   Types of MWD financial contributions (in 2003 dollars) per acre-foot of MWD water delivered, by counties and the city of Los Angeles, 1929–2003

SOURCE: MWDSC, Office of Chief Financial Officer.

member agencies—primarily the Municipal Water District of Orange County (MWDOC)—underpaid $754 million. Riverside County's pre-1970 subsidy was smaller ($207 million), reflecting its limited MET purchases given ample groundwater supplies. Riverside joined to ensure future growth. Few early subsidies involved San Bernardino and Ventura County water agencies.

After 1970, with the postage-stamp (or uniform) water rate rising to reflect most MWD expenses (including much capital financing), interagency subsidies were reduced, but hardly eliminated. Los Angeles continued to significantly overpay—the city by $683 million and the county by $494 million—and San Diego to heavily underpay (by $780 million), whereas Orange County's subsidy was nearly halved (to $432 million).

Overall, between 1929 and 2003, urbanized Los Angeles City and County appeared to heavily underwrite water provision to the suburbanizing periphery in Orange and San Diego counties. Los Angeles City overpaid nearly $2.4 billion and the rest of L.A. County over $500 million relative to water deliveries. In stark contrast, Orange County water agencies underpaid $1.2 billion, whereas the San Diego County Water Authority underpaid $1.6 billion relative to water deliveries.

Figure 3.7 compares for these jurisdictions the real unit cost per acre-foot of water delivered, 1929–1970 and 1971–2003. There were

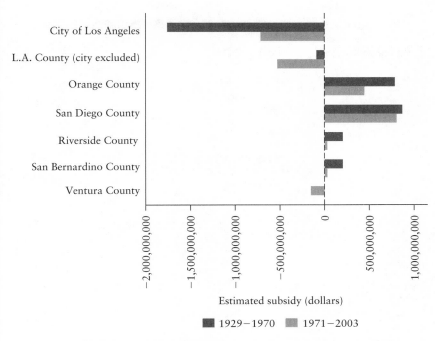

FIGURE **3.6**   **Estimated subsidies (in 2003 dollars), by counties and the city of Los Angeles, 1929–1970 and 1971–2003**

SOURCE: MWDSC, Office of Chief Financial Officer.

early and substantial unit-cost disparities between the city of Los Angeles and all other subregions. For 1929–1970, the city of Los Angeles paid $1,996/AF for MET water deliveries (in 2003 dollars). No other jurisdiction paid even half as much.[32] The high pre-1970 unit cost makes the city of Los Angeles appear a fiscal profligate. Yet, as noted, L.A. early on primarily relied on its own water supplies, taking few MWD deliveries before the advent of the State Water Project. Hence, the retail cost of water to Los Angeles customers remained relatively low and did not represent an inhibitor to development. Also of note is the high early unit cost for the remainder of Los Angeles County—$541. From 1928 to 1931, 12 of L.A.'s suburbs also joined MET, fully contributing to the financing of the Colorado River Aqueduct and later drawing water from Metropolitan, which began deliveries in 1941.

In dramatic contrast, in the pre-1970 era San Diego, Orange, and Riverside County water agencies only paid $253, $274, and $238 per AF,

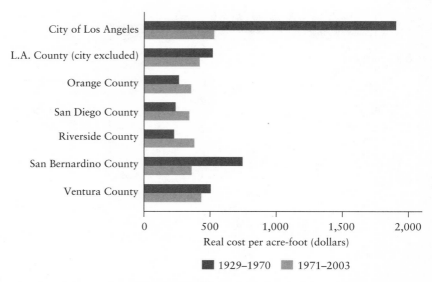

FIGURE **3.7**   Unit cost (in 2003 dollars) per acre-foot of MWD water delivered, by counties and the city of Los Angeles, 1929–1970 and 1971–2003

SOURCE: MWDSC, Office of Chief Financial Officer.

respectively. As noted, their low unit costs were driven by small assessed valuations (and thus low annexation fees) coupled with discounted agricultural water deliveries. For example, SDCWA and MWDOC paid $34 million and $32 million in annexation charges, respectively, which represented small, 10 percent shares of total MWD annexation charges. After 1970, though, as Metropolitan's water rates were raised substantially, unit cost disparities among member agencies were reduced.

Los Angeles's Large, Early Outlays: Calculus or Miscalculation?

Though the city of Los Angeles's representatives dominated the new MET [Metropolitan] board and management, they immediately established policies that were favorable to newly developing areas rather than the city itself. They did so in part as developers in their own right, and as participants and leaders in the urban-development complex that transcended the boundaries of particular municipalities. These policies were designed to draw on the tax base of the developed areas while creating pricing incentives for water use and development of the new areas. . . . The key to such policies was annexation, this time not to the city, but to the water district.

Robert Gottlieb, A Life of Its Own *(1988)*[33]

The large unit-cost disparities between urban Los Angeles and suburban San Diego and Orange counties raise the inevitable question of why the city of Los Angeles so heavily contributed to early MET capital financing, in effect indirectly subsidizing water provision to suburbanizing outlying areas. Why would the members of MWD's board of directors—initially dominated by the city of Los Angeles—allow such cost-of-service disparities to be created, and later to persist? Assuming the board members were rational actors, there are several possible explanations. Here we explore two in some detail: (1) board members used their positions to promote subsidies that encouraged growth because it enhanced their own profit opportunities; and (2) policymakers made good-faith decisions that seemed reasonable at the time but that helped create the described member-agency unit-cost disparities.

Robert Gottlieb's provocative theory suggests that L.A.'s MWD directors were actually acting in their capacity as regional developers and investors. Thus, by supplying plentiful, affordable water to undeveloped areas, Metropolitan supposedly oiled the region's growth machine that would turn desert land into profitable real-estate investments. Although MET ultimately did play an important part in making Southern California's suburban growth possible, Gottlieb's explanation appears to conflate the eventual outcome with the alleged motives of the original policymakers. Undoubtedly, some of the early MWD board members had strong personal economic motives to promote full-throttle growth in Southern California. However, the 1928 Metropolitan enabling legislation was written several years before there was even a board to be filled with development-oriented directors. The bill's chief drafters were two local government attorneys: William Burgess Mathews, L.A. city attorney, LADWP attorney and later first MWD general counsel, and James H. Howard, Pasadena city attorney and later Mathews's successor as MWD general counsel. As Don J. Kinsey, a former MWD official, recalled, "The Metropolitan Water District Act was very largely a conception of Mr. Mathews and Mr. Howard."[34]

L.A. water officials such as William Mulholland supported MET's creation because of the need for new reliable water supplies for Los Angeles. In the 1920s, L.A. had experienced both explosive population growth and drought. Armed with Panglossian projections, the L.A. Chamber of Commerce—the ultimate booster machine—estimated that, at current growth rates, the city's population would reach 4.2 million by 1960 and 5.1 million in 1970. The chamber would lend its powerful support to creating the Metropolitan Water District. Given apparently stratospheric demand, Los Angeles water officials frenetically searched for new supplies. The city of Los Angeles could not build the Colorado River Aqueduct on its own, as Mulholland initially had wanted, because the project's $220 million price tag (in 1931 dollars) would far exceed, in conjunction with existing municipal debt, the city's bonding capacity of 15 percent of assessed valuation. Mulholland also realized that if the city built the aqueduct, it would have to annex the rest of L.A. County, making the city unmanageable in size.[35] Public power considerations also played a critical (and under-recognized) role in early L.A. support for Metropolitan. MET and the aqueduct would help pave the way for the Boulder Canyon Project Act (Hoover Dam), whose enormous hydroelectric power capacity was desperately needed by L.A.'s Department of Water and Power in its fierce battles with archrival private utilities Southern California Edison and Los Angeles Gas and Electric Company.[36]

In 1931, notwithstanding a horrific economy, L.A.-area voters overwhelmingly approved (84 percent in favor) the $220-million aqueduct project—the nation's largest voter-approved bond measure to that date. They thereby saddled themselves with new property tax burdens representing over 10 percent of assessed valuation. Today this would be equivalent to adding over ten Proposition 13's to their tax burdens. (In 1978, voter-approved Proposition 13 capped California's *ad valorem* real property tax rate at 1 percent of assessed valuation). The bond campaign swayed economy-sensitive voters with promises of 10,000 construction jobs (reserved for U.S. citizens and residents of the MWD cities) and of low interest and amortization charges rather than high capital costs. Full bond redemption would only begin in 1946, seven years after the anticipated project completion date. With the expected doubling of the district's population in 20 years, per capita bond-redemption costs would be substantially reduced.[37]

In effect, MWD functioned as a colossal debt-pyramiding scheme for Los Angeles and its suburbs. It provided an additional 15 percent bonding capacity (above existing municipal debt ceilings) and, importantly, reduced the voter-approval threshold from two thirds (for example, for L.A. municipal bonds) to a simple majority (for MWD special district bonds). For Metropolitan's bill drafters and LADWP officials, these startup costs seemed reasonable. Given presumed robust future demand, policymakers assumed that Los Angeles would draw a substantial portion of MET water deliveries, greatly reducing if not eliminating the city's water delivery-revenue contribution disparity. Future growth would increase the tax base, thus reducing the relative burden on individual taxpayers.[38]

Yet, although appearing to act reasonably, L.A. water officials seemingly made two critical miscalculations. First, they overestimated city population and water demand growth, which were flattened by the Great Depression. Second, they appeared to overgauge the reliability of their new water supplies. In the 1930s, Arizona sought congressional redress and began filing federal lawsuits against California to establish Lower Basin Colorado River allotments. As a result, L.A. policymakers realized their Colorado River priority rights were less secure than originally thought and turned back to developing their own more secure municipal water supplies in the eastern Sierra Nevada. Additional water from the Owens Valley and Mono Basin allowed the city of Los Angeles to draw far less in deliveries from MET than it had originally planned, despite its heavy initial infrastructure investment.

The question remains, however, as to why these apparent tax-based capital subsidies persisted until the 1970s and beyond. Although some MWD directors may have pursued self-interested development agendas, as Gottlieb suggests, powerful institutional and policy forces were at work. One credible explanation is that as MET board directors were installed, they primarily acted as guardians of Metropolitan's fiduciary interests. As Gottlieb himself admits, "[A]fter Colorado River water arrived in the Basin in 1941, so much surplus water was available at first that MET practically offered to give it away for free in order to establish a more substantial revenue base."[39] Below-cost water charges and low annexation fees encouraged the rest of Southern California to join MWD. This enhanced the agency's long-term revenue stream and would allow for later readjustments in the relative financial burdens of older and newer member agencies. And although L.A.'s MET directors early on may have agreed to subsidies out of necessity, some observers believe that L.A. later acquiesced out of a sense of community. Service on the MET board encouraged directors to think in terms of regional, not merely member agency, well-being, and beyond the short term. MWD's communitarian organizational culture encourages a long-term regional perspective and should not be overlooked.[40]

Another, more self-interested policy explanation is that Los Angeles acquiesced because it continued to derive substantial benefit from MWD. In exchange for financing most of the Colorado River Aqueduct and bestowing its substantial Colorado River water entitlement on MET, the city was offered substantial inducements.[41] The Metropolitan Water District Act conferred preferential rights to water, such as during times of scarcity, on the basis of property taxes and other financial contributions for MWD capital and operating costs, exclusive of water sales. In 2004 Los Angeles had a preferential claim to 22 percent of MWD water (while historically drawing only 8 percent of MET deliveries) compared to SDCWA's 16 percent claim (while drawing 26 percent of MWD's deliveries).[42]

In effect, Los Angeles appeared to treat MET as an expensive drought insurance policy should its Owens Valley supplies prove insufficient. Los Angeles also was assured a major role in MWD policy-making when assessed valuation, the basis for property taxes levied, became the basis of board representation and voting. To protect smaller member agencies, however, Los Angeles only was given 50 percent of the initial weighted vote—in effect guaranteeing it a veto—even though, on the basis of assessed valuation, the city was entitled to 75 percent. By 1960, though, with the State Water Project offering additional secure MET supplies, Los Angeles's MWD directors pressed for a shift in capital financing from property taxes to water charges. As noted, heavy MWD water users such as San Diego fought, but could only delay, this financing shift.

Did Los Angeles Indirectly "Subsidize" Suburban Growth?

L.A. County, where taxes are heavy and assessed valuation high, feels that a service of great value has already been rendered for Southern California, and that the time has come when areas that are annexed should contribute more toward the cost of getting the water. . . . They will never contribute what the real cost of their development is. The tax burden falls most heavily on developed areas—as annexed areas grow, so the burden should be distributed.

Joe Jensen, MWD board chair, 1970[43]

Untangling the empirical relationship between MET capital financing and water rate policies, and resulting member-agency cost-of-service disparities, on the one hand, and the region's suburban sprawl, on the other, is complicated by both conceptual and data issues. Regional growth is a complex, multifaceted phenomenon and is not driven solely by any single variable. In addition to secure, affordable water supplies, key growth determinants include land availability and price, zoning and land use controls, local taxes, and infrastructure (such as transportation), education and amenities. Our ability to undertake a multivariate analysis is also hindered by the fact that data for many demographic, economic, and policy variables are available at the county and city levels but not for MWD member agencies that are not coterminous with county or city boundaries. Such agencies can span both incorporated and unincorporated areas, making data comparability and analysis difficult. Further, a multivariate analysis would ideally employ a lag variable so that population growth in a given period is regressed over water unit costs in a previous period, a difficult task given the long aggregate periods used here.

Even using simple bivariate correlations, one needs to approach the subsidy-growth relationship with caution. Cost-of-service disparities arose from the early tax-based capital financing structure of MET, and (except for interruptible agricultural and other water discounts) not through differential incremental water prices for member agencies. Because developers and investors in the city of Los Angeles and in the capital-subsidized, later-joining areas faced similar uniform prices for water (the so-called postage stamp rate), the relationship between cost-of-service disparities and urban growth is obviously not as simple as a bivariate analysis suggests. Nonetheless, using only one independent variable (unit cost-of-service) to determine how this factor correlates with a dependent variable (population growth) is valuable as a first cut. The exploratory nature of these results is emphasized, as well as the need for further research.

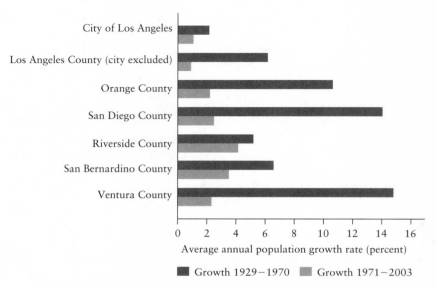

FIGURE **3.8**   Average annual population growth rate, by counties and the city of Los Angeles, 1929–1970 and 1971–2003

s o u r c e s : Southern California Association of Governments (SCAG) and San Diego Association of Governments (SANDAG) population data; MWDSC, Water Resources Management Group.

We have performed a correlation analysis between the cost-of-service scores for 27 MWD member agencies, expressed as their real cost per acre-foot of MWD water delivered, and their average annual population growth rates since joining Metropolitan.[44] As Figure 3.8 shows, there are wide variations in average annual growth rates for the city of Los Angeles, the remainder of Los Angeles County, and the other counties served by Metropolitan, in 1929–1970 and 1971–2003. Because of the smaller population base in the pre-1970 period, early growth rates are much higher and show greater variation. Los Angeles City and County, because they already were settled, experienced lower annual growth rates than sparsely settled Orange, San Diego, and Ventura counties. Differences persisted after 1970, with annual population increases in the Inland Empire nearly four times as great as the city and the county of Los Angeles.

Figure 3.9 compares unit water costs and average annual growth rates for the three leading cases of cost-of-service disparities between central city and suburbs: the city of Los Angeles, and Orange and San Diego

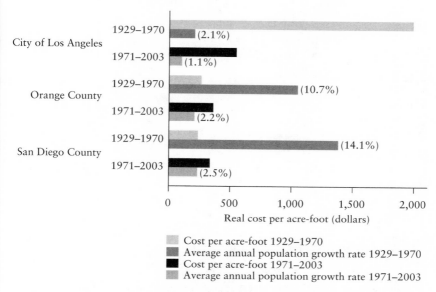

FIGURE **3.9**   Unit cost (in 2003 dollars) per acre-foot and population growth rate, city of Los Angeles, Orange and San Diego counties, 1929–1970 and 1971–2003

s o u r c e s : MWDSC, Office of Chief Financial Officer, and Water Resources Management Group; and SCAG and SANDAG population data.

counties, 1929–1970 and 1971–2003. It graphically illustrates the early water-unit cost-growth relationship. Prior to 1970, L.A. paid dearly for its MET hookup but only grew at a modest growth rate. In contrast, San Diego and Orange counties paid little to MWD early on and had robust growth rates. However, the water-growth relationship substantially weakens after 1970.

The early unit cost-growth relationship also appears to hold for all 27 MET member agencies (reduced by a merger to 26 in 2001). Figure 3.10 displays the correlation between member agency real unit costs per acre-foot of water delivered and average annual population growth rates, 1929–1970. The relationship is quite robust, with $R^2 = .4338$. Thus, over 40 percent of the variance in early growth rates for MWD agencies is accounted for by the cost-of-service "subsidy" index. As noted, the San Diego County Water Authority and the Municipal Water District of Orange County represent the two agencies with the highest "subsidy" index scores and some of the highest annual population

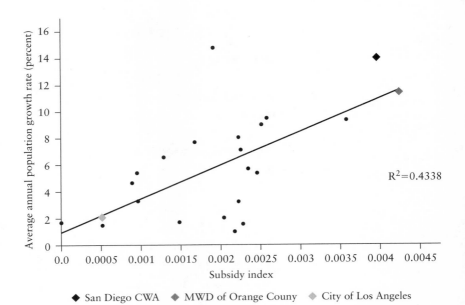

FIGURE **3.10**   Correlation between water subsidy index and population growth rate by MWD member agency, 1929–1970

SOURCES: MWDSC, Office of Chief Financial Officer, and Water Resources Management Group; and SCAG and SANDAG population data.

growth rates. This contrasts sharply with the city of Los Angeles, with slower growth rates and a low index score.

Finally, Figure 3.11 displays the correlation for the member agency relationship between cost-of-service and growth for 1971–2003. As expected, for the later period the correlation is much weaker, with an $R^2 = .1796$. Here, less than 20 percent of member agency growth is accounted for by the subsidy index. Thus, MWD capital financing and water pricing after 1970 appear much less growth inducing.

Our results suggest that the subsidy-growth relationship for MET member agencies was robust for the pre-1970 period—when MWD primarily relied on property taxes for revenue—and the early water-growth nexus should be further researched. In the interim, our tentative findings are consistent with the historical record and common sense. Had Los Angeles not gone ahead and invested $4.5 billion to develop its Owens Valley and Mono Basin supplies, and instead shifted its demand to MET to deliver an additional 200,000 acre-feet per year, it would have

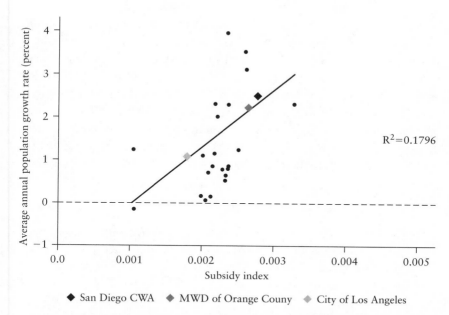

FIGURE **3.11** Correlation between water subsidy index and population growth rate by MWD member agency, 1971–2003

SOURCES: MWDSC, Office of Financial Officer, and Water Resources Management Group; and SCAG and SANDAG population data.

left substantially less water for everyone else in Southern California. Potential shortages could have affected other MWD customers, with predictably dire consequences for regional growth. Thus, by developing its own water sources L.A. significantly reduced its early demand on Metropolitan's supplies, relieved MWD of having to then develop additional supplies, and provided a form of free drought insurance for other member agencies such as the San Diego County Water Authority.

By limiting its use of MET water deliveries, Los Angeles seemingly allowed its early and large MWD capital investment to serve as an indirect subsidy and inducement for later-joining agencies. Another L.A. contribution to suburban growth involved the MWD water that the city did not use when it chose to develop its more secure municipal supplies. By making Colorado River water readily available for others, Los Angeles in effect made the water supply of all other MET agencies that much more secure. This also relieved upward pressure on the price of water. Plentiful, inexpensive MET water sent strong signals to developers, businesses, agriculture, and potential home buyers that the suburban periphery could support extensive development. This was the *sine qua non* for regional development and concomitant suburban sprawl. Consider which of these two possibilities was more likely: (1) the existence of MWD without a growing periphery to buy its water; or (2) a growing periphery without MWD to supply water? Only the first is plausible. Thus, San Diego's meager and low-priority Colorado River water appropriation (the city of San Diego filed in 1926 for 112,000 AF), and limited local groundwater would have left it with insufficient water supplies to grow without MWD.

Assessing MWD's Track Record

However, it was those citizens with a broader vision and who recognized the advantage to the City of Los Angeles by having an active, strong and growing area within the City's sphere of influence that prevailed and made possible the approval of the [1931 MWD Colorado River Aqueduct] bond issue. This outside area needs the support of the City, and the City needs the outside area in order to establish and maintain its identity as a regional financial and service center. Therefore the creation of an adequate water supply for the outside area was of mutual benefit.

Harry Griffen, former MWD and SDCWA director[45]

We suggest a complex relationship between regional water policy and suburban development, and between the city of Los Angeles, its older suburbs, and the rest of Southern California. The Metropolitan Water District, ostensibly the creature of imperial Los Angeles, for the first 40 years heavily underwrote suburban sprawl and development of the then-regional periphery, particularly San Diego and Orange counties. Post-1970 policy shifts reduced L.A.'s apparent subsidy for suburban water provision but did not end the intraregional conflicts over who benefits and pays for water.

MET's pre-1970 policy of relying on *ad valorem* property taxes for capital financing and many operating expenses produced substantial cost-of-service disparities between member agencies—particularly between founders such as Los Angeles and later joiners such as San Diego—and favored new suburban development. How fair was this early tax-based financing system? Should new suburban areas have been subsidized by established urban centers such as Los Angeles in the same way that a nation might protect infant industries or parents might indulge a child until maturity? An argument can be made that MWD's founders and later directors consistently pursued a policy of enlightened self-interest, creating a suburban hinterland and thus greater economic opportunities for the core urban center.

As noted, a strong case also can be made that when faced with a possible stranded asset such as the Colorado River Aqueduct, MWD officials pursued a rational long-term strategy of encouraging low-cost annexations and subsidized water sales so that rates could be raised at a later date. One wonders what the founding cities' MWD costs would have been if outlying areas had not been encouraged to join the MET family. And what would be the costs to areas such as San Diego of not joining MWD, and of having to develop to the extent possible their own water supplies and infrastructure?

Yet there is growing evidence that subsidies have unwanted consequences. Because beneficiaries fight ferociously to maintain their privileged status, cost-of-service disparities can become self-perpetuating. The protracted battle over shifting MET capital financing from property taxes to water rates offers vivid testimony in this regard. In recent years, with central city decline and rampant suburban sprawl, it has become clear that urban centers can no longer be called on to subsidize the suburban periphery. Indeed, there is growing realization that the fate of metropolitan areas fundamentally depends on the prosperity of the central city. Advocates of smart growth now call for the elimination of subsidies encouraging suburban sprawl. Because newly developed areas require greater capital investments, a cost-of-service logic suggests they should pay additional, not reduced, charges for vital services such as water provision. This is at the center of current metropolitan development policy debates.[46]

MET's post-1970 shift from tax-based financing to a water charge–based system featuring substantial cost recovery has resulted in a more equitable and less growth-inducing fiscal policy. The new rate system reduced cost-of-service disparities among member agencies and resulting subsidies. Yet, Los Angeles's apparent subsidy of water provision to other member agencies—particularly San Diego—continued, although at lower levels. As noted, since 1970 the city of Los Angeles has overpaid $683 million and other L.A. County water agencies have overspent $494 million, whereas

San Diego has underpaid $780 million relative to their respective water deliveries. Although a portion of San Diego's lower water costs are due to agricultural discounts (which initially came with reduced water reliability), MET's continued reliance on property taxes for up to one quarter of its capital investment plan (designed to generate a stable, dedicated revenue stream and thus lower borrowing costs) saddles Los Angeles, which has a large tax base, with a disproportionate share of MWD costs.[47]

Overall, between 1929 and 2003 the taxpayers and ratepayers of the city of Los Angeles have overpaid nearly $2.4 billion and L.A. County residents over $500 million relative to their MET water usage. As a result, the Los Angeles metropolitan core appears to have indirectly subsidized water provision to the suburbanizing periphery by nearly $3 billion. In contrast, San Diego County residents have underpaid $1.6 billion, and Orange County residents $1.2 billion, relative to their Metropolitan water deliveries.

But MWD's strategy of piggybacking much of its costs onto water charges has not been without risks. It has made most of its capital financing dependent on water sales and revenues. In the early 1990s, as MET embarked on an ambitious capital program while suffering drought-induced declines in water sales and revenues, the limitations of this rate structure became evident. Hence, MWD adopted new charges—readiness-to-serve, standby, and new demand rates—to firm up capital financing and create greater equity between established and rapidly growing areas for financing the capital projects needed to accommodate new growth.

The postage stamp rate and new-growth charges created incentives for major customers such as the San Diego County Water Authority to reduce their large and growing MWD capital-financing burdens by purchasing non-MWD water—for example, through a large-scale water transfer deal with the Imperial Valley (discussed in the next chapter). With MET capital costs firmly embedded in water charges, San Diego could extend its heretofore successful strategy of limiting payment for use of Metropolitan infrastructure by garnering non-MWD supplies. Ironically, by the 1990s Los Angeles also felt MWD's capital-financing burdens as it too took large MET water deliveries. But rather than following San Diego's lead and buying non-MWD water, Los Angeles saw the clear advantages of MET membership and opposed San Diego–style cost shifting.

It once was said of Queen Victoria's empire that the British acquired it "in a fit of absence of mind."[48] Not so MWD's sprawling regional empire. Contrary to belated provincial gripes, MWD's so-called regional imperialism heavily taxed the urban Metropole for infrastructure and growth, and thus indirectly subsidized the periphery's accelerated development. Without such subsidies, growth south of L.A. and north of Tijuana would have been stunted if not stillborn.[49]

In return for early fiscal burdens, Los Angeles and its citizenry gained three key presumed long-term benefits. First, they believed they had received an important "insurance policy"—albeit expensive and (as it turned out) of dubious enforceability—to cover city water shortages in the event of severe drought, reduction in Owens Valley supplies, or to meet the demands of future growth. Second, L.A. business interests could share in the profits of region-wide growth. Third, Los Angeles could boast of its status as the region's capital. As Rome taught all later imperialists, the political and psychological gratifications to the Imperium are not only tempting but tangible. As architects of a new regional Imperium on the Pacific Rim, Metropolitan's founders (to paraphrase Ralph Waldo Emerson) may have "builded better than they knew."[50]

William Mulholland, first general manager, Los Angeles Department of Water and Power

First MWD board of directors

Photo courtesy of the Metropolitan Water District of Southern California

Joe Jensen, Los Angeles MWD director and long-serving MWD board chair

Photo courtesy of the Metropolitan Water District of Southern California

Fred Heilbron, San Diego MWD director and long-serving San Diego County Water Authority board chair

Photo courtesy of the San Diego County Water Authority

Building the Colorado River Aqueduct

Photo courtesy of the Metropolitan Water District of Southern California

Colorado River Aqueduct

Photo courtesy of the Metropolitan Water District of Southern California

Hoover Dam

Photo courtesy of the Metropolitan Water District of Southern California

Parker Dam

Photo courtesy of the Metropolitan Water District of Southern California

Parker intake plant

Photo courtesy of the Metropolitan Water District of Southern California

California Aqueduct/State Water Project

Photo courtesy of the Metropolitan Water District of Southern California

The Bay Delta

Photo courtesy of the Metropolitan Water District of Southern California

Diamond Valley Lake Reservoir
Photo courtesy of the Metropolitan Water District of Southern California

II *Mounting Challenges, 1990–2004*

4   David and Goliath? San Diego's Quixotic Quest for Independence

We were more MET than MET.

> *Former San Diego County Water Authority General Manager Linden Burzell (1964–1984)*[1]

I would rather pay 10 times what I pay now for water than get down on my knees and bow to Los Angeles.

> *Fred Thompson, city of San Diego delegate, San Diego County Water Authority Board of Directors, 1998*[2]

We [San Diego County residents] are facing dramatically increasing water rates and a treated-water shortage for the next three years because the County Water Authority has been more focused on battling MWD and gaining more "independence" for San Diego from L.A. than on taking care of its primary responsibility as a regional utility for reliably and affordably meeting our imported water-supply needs.

> *Anonymous San Diego County water official, 2005*[3]

The next three chapters examine mounting challenges and conflicts regarding Metropolitan and its water supplies, 1990 to 2004. This chapter considers internecine battles within MWD, analyzing San Diego's confrontational drive for water independence. Subsequent chapters explore recent conflicts over Colorado River and Northern California water supplies, and controversies over MET's role in evolving water markets and transfers.

Here we examine the San Diego County Water Authority (SDCWA, or the County Water Authority)—MWD's largest customer but with less voting strength and water rights—and its growing battles over MET governance arrangements, rules, and policies, particularly with member agency Los Angeles, early on a dominant force at Metropolitan. San Diego now characterizes itself as "David" in its battles for independence from the allegedly dictatorial MWD "Goliath" headquartered in—and ostensibly controlled by—Los Angeles. Yet earlier on San Diego appeared to be using a loyalist strategy that the late economist Albert O. Hirschman called "voice" to amass influence within MET to achieve a reliable, low-cost water supply. This was not always easy, given Los Angeles's superior position with respect to voting strength and preferential rights.[4]

Starting in the early 1990s, with newer, highly assertive San Diego MWD directors installed and regional water supplies dwindling, San Diego shifted to a more confrontational "exit" strategy of seeking new water supplies outside of Metropolitan, and of influencing MET externally rather than internally, through state legislative action and lawsuits. San Diego even considered breaking up or breaking away from the giant L.A.-based water wholesaler. The lengthy drought of 1987–1992, severely threatening the region's water supplies, served as a key catalyst for heightened hostilities.[5]

In this chapter we examine San Diego's strategic shift from regionalism to local independence, and tactically from cooperation to confrontation within MWD's boardroom. Analyzed here are allegations of San Diego's so-called shotgun marriage to MET in 1946; the dynamics of early Los Angeles and San Diego influence within Metropolitan; and, since the early 1990s, San Diego's relentless drive for water independence, featuring epic battles within MWD and at the regional, state, and federal levels over water transfers, preferential rights, water policy, governance, and even the future of MET itself. The San Diego case illuminates two distinct water-reliability strategies: regional cooperation versus independence, and their associated benefits and costs. We consider whether resource and infrastructure independence for member agencies such as San Diego is possible, given growing regional water interdependence.

Also explored are the politics of San Diego's controversial water-transfer agreement with the Imperial Valley—the centerpiece of its quixotic independence drive. Considered too is a key San Diego complaint—limited preferential rights to MWD water during shortages—and dialogues with Los Angeles and MET to change seemingly archaic entitlement formulas. This led to San Diego's 2001 lawsuit to overturn preferential rights. At the same time, eerily similar "David-and-Goliath" battles were being fought within the San Diego County Water Authority itself, with a group of rebellious North County agencies seeking greater freedom of action and influence apart from the now-dominant city of San Diego. Critics claimed to see sharp inconsistencies between the behavior of San Diego water officials in MWD's downtown L.A. boardroom compared to the cozy confines of the County Water Authority. We conclude with an analysis of conflicts occurring within the San Diego water agency.

San Diego and MWD: The Gathering Storm

The relationship between the two agencies [Metropolitan and the Water Authority] had from the beginning elements of a "shotgun marriage," and it soon became clear that, to use the phrase of water authority Philip Pryde, it was an "unhappy marriage where divorce was impossible."

Dan Walker, Thirst for Independence *(2004)* [6]

Although there were some diehards in San Diego who believed the Authority made a grave error in deciding to annex to MWD . . . the majority of San Diegans felt differently and recognized some of the advantages by looking at the broader picture.

Former SDCWA and MWD Director Harry Griffen [7]

A Shotgun Marriage?

In the drought-plagued early 1990s, when MET was forced to cut back water deliveries to its member agencies, San Diego's insurgent water leaders rewrote history with respect to both Metropolitan and Los Angeles. In the newly received wisdom, San Diego was a victim of a federally ordered "shotgun marriage" to Metropolitan. Seemingly forced to join MWD in 1946, the County Water Authority paid its annexation fees (back taxes) in full, relinquished its Colorado River water entitlement, paid half the cost of the connecting San Diego Aqueduct, and rescued MET from impending financial ruin by becoming its biggest and best customer. [8]

San Diego supposedly received little comparable in return. Regularly drawing one quarter or more of MET water deliveries, San Diego's MWD voting strength and preferential rights were only half or less of that amount. In contrast, L.A. held much greater voting strength and water rights, despite taking little Metropolitan water. Thus, in 1960 San Diego drew 32 percent of total MWD water deliveries yet had only 10 percent of the vote entitlement. That year L.A. drew 17 percent of MET deliveries yet had 34 percent of board voting strength. Based on cumulative property taxes and annexation fees, the preferential rights disparity between San Diego and L.A. was even greater.[9]

Understandably, San Diego grew nervous about Metropolitan's reliability given that 90 percent of its total water supplies (as of 1960) came from MWD, compared with less than 20 percent for Los Angeles, which had ample municipal supplies at that time. In the revisionist story, Los Angeles energetically defended its "anomalous" preferments and drought insurance policy, deploying its sizable influence within the Metropolitan boardroom to resist changing seemingly inequitable and archaic formulas for voting entitlements and water rights. Thus, the seeds of San Diego's later drive for independence were planted early on by a seemingly forced merger, unfair MET rules, and L.A.'s overbearing influence and intransigence. According to San Diego general manager Maureen Stapleton, Los Angeles added insult to injury in the early 1990s by invoking its preferential rights—in a supposed phone call to Metropolitan—to guarantee its water supply at the expense of San Diego. L.A. water officials categorically deny the allegation. Then MWD general manager Carl Boronkay has no recollection of such a phone call, and claims the MET board deliberately avoided preferential rights issues with a uniform drought-induced cut in water deliveries to all its member agencies.[10]

San Diego's reconstructed "David-and-Goliath" account of its early dealings with Metropolitan and Los Angeles seriously distorts the historical record. The "shotgun marriage" tale relates that San Diego was on the verge of building its own aqueduct to the Colorado River when the federal government forced it to join Metropolitan as a wartime emergency measure. In 1926, San Diego filed for 112,000 acre-feet (AF) of lower-priority water from the Colorado River. In anticipation of a future aqueduct, San Diego contributed support for the construction and ongoing operation of the All-American Canal in Imperial County. In the 1930s there were sharp local debates about how best to get that water to the region. Some favored the construction of an aqueduct eastward through the mountains to the west end of the All-American Canal. Others favored joining the fledgling MWD, and tying into the Colorado River Aqueduct then under construction.

President Roosevelt's wartime executive order ended the debate. It directed the Navy Department to construct an aqueduct linking San Diego's water system (42 percent of which by 1944 was for defense-related uses) to MET's Colorado River Aqueduct. Yet with the approach of peacetime, construction was deferred. Faced with labor and material shortages, the federal government no longer viewed the project as a key priority. Foreseeing a postwar population boom, San Diego's civic leaders became the aqueduct's champions, successfully lobbying Washington to keep the project alive and funded. In 1944, the San Diego County Water Authority was created as a vehicle to fund and operate an aqueduct to bring imported Colorado River water to the region. The creation of the SDCWA temporarily ended years of local strife between urban and agricultural water interests. Imitation being the sincerest form of flattery, the SDCWA Act was modeled after the 1928 Metropolitan Water District Act, complete with preferential water rights for local member agencies (finally abolished in 1989). In the 1930s San Diego water officials inquired whether MWD could charge a fee to deliver San Diego's Colorado River water via MWD's aqueduct system. For MET, annexation was required, because the MWD Act didn't allow water delivery to nonmembers.[11]

By no means was San Diego dragged kicking and screaming into MET. By more than 14 to 1, San Diego voters overwhelmingly approved the merger. The County Water Authority board unanimously agreed to join Metropolitan. San Diego also willingly gave up its small, lower-priority Colorado River entitlement in exchange for access to MWD's larger, firmer Colorado River water rights and fiscal base. With few customers and large fixed capital costs, Metropolitan needed San Diego's revenue so that its taxes would not be raised. So eager was MET for San Diego's business that it agreed to demands that San Diego annexation fees be paid without interest over 30 years rather than the customary 20 years. As a further inducement, MWD generously split the San Diego Aqueduct's cost with the SDCWA, building its facilities six miles south into San Diego County, from where the County Water Authority paid for the remaining portion. Despite some grumblings in San Diego and L.A., San Diego's joining of MET more resembled a marriage between willing and even eager partners. At the very least, it was a mutually convenient arrangement benefiting both parties.[12]

Los Angeles and San Diego: Dueling Hegemons?

Once installed in Metropolitan's boardroom, San Diego's MWD delegates faced Los Angeles's formidable influence. In 1950, with 50 percent of the board vote and the unit rule (bloc voting) in effect (until 1968), L.A. still possessed veto power over board decisions. With L.A.'s share of total assessed valuation declining as MET annexed fast-growing outlying areas, so did its vote entitlement, dropping to 20 percent by 2000. Although its voting strength ebbed, Los Angeles still remained powerful. For almost 50 years, L.A. city directors held a near monopoly on the coveted MWD board chairmanship: W. P. Whitsett (1928–1946), V. H. Rossetti (1946–1947), and Joseph Jensen (1949–1974). Los Angeles's early directors (those appointed between 1928 and 1972) enjoyed lengthy 13-year average tenures, accumulating expertise, seniority, and influence.[13]

Yet Los Angeles was not always a monolithic, dominating force within MET's boardroom. For starters, there were three separate governing bodies on water policy within L.A. municipal government—the mayor, city council, and Department of Water and Power—who did not always agree. Their mixed messages created quandaries for Los Angeles's MWD directors. Although fixed terms of appointment gave L.A. delegates some measure of independence, they frequently were either unwilling or unable to dictate policy over regional opposition. Thus, early Metropolitan board chair W. P. Whitsett—an Angeleno and pioneering San Fernando Valley real-estate developer—was a consensus builder, seeking board unanimity even at the expense of L.A. city interests.[14]

Later, powerful MWD board chair and fellow Angeleno Joe Jensen took a different, more L.A.-centric tack. As noted, Jensen's hand was forced on key occasions. Given anti–Los Angeles animus in the state legislature, Jensen and other L.A. directors were loath to have the Pandora's box of the MWD Act pried open. When faced in the late 1940s with the threat of hostile state legislation to do away with the unit rule, Jensen and other L.A. directors reluctantly dropped their opposition to MET annexation of the Pomona and Ontario areas. In 1960, Chairman Jensen, who opposed the State Water Project, would again be overruled on a crucial vote. As a result, the MWD board—and the L.A. delegation—provided essential support for the massive state undertaking.

San Diego skillfully countered L.A. hegemony. On paper, San Diego's influence appeared limited. With only an 11 percent vote entitlement in 1950, San Diego's voting strength slowly rose to 16 percent by 2000. Able leadership amplified San Diego's voice. Long-serving San Diego directors—Fred Heilbron (1947–1973), Hans H. Doe (1959–1986), and Harry Griffen (1963–1997)—effectively advanced San Diego interests while often displaying regional statesmanship and stewardship. San Diegans soon ascended to MET leadership posts, serving as board vice chairs and secretary (but not chair). Early San Diego directors (those appointed before 1972) averaged a 13-year tenure, thus matching their L.A. counterparts in seniority and influence. Despite persistent conflicts within the County Water Authority among urban, suburban, and agricultural interests, San Diego's MET delegation spoke with a unified voice. In Fred Heilbron's long reign, this was made easier by the fact that he was both San Diego's MWD director and County Water Authority board chair. Although a San Diego city director, Heilbron chaired the SDCWA board for nearly 30 years as a forceful advocate of regional interests.[15]

San Diego's early MET directors proved adept at coalition building, further thwarting Los Angeles—which long rested on its early veto power and did little to build coalitions, even among L.A. County member agencies. Starting in the 1950s, L.A.'s influence was challenged by newly annexed MWD member agencies with large local groundwater supplies such as West Basin (1948), Central Basin (1954), and the Municipal Water District of Orange County (1951). San Diego supported the latter's demands for low water replenishment charges in exchange for their support in San Diego's fight with L.A. over water rates and capital project financing. As MET expanded into outlying rural areas, San Diego also anchored "an active and effective" agricultural coalition—consisting of then-agricultural San Diego, Orange, and Riverside county member agencies—to counter a core urban coalition of Los Angeles city and suburbs. Agricultural water rates and policies, not preferential rights, were the key issues. Later, in the early 1990s, San Diego director Mike Madigan and L.A. director and board chair Mike Gage would enter into a short-lived *entente cordiale* between the two competing metropolises. Summing up his 20-year tenure (1964–1984) as general manager of the San Diego County Water Authority, Lin Burzell concluded that "the end result at MWD was that San Diego got every significant thing it asked for."[16]

Yet storm clouds were brewing. L. A.'s Jensen and San Diego's Heilbron, the imperious leaders of their delegations and representatives of their respective cities from the late 1940s into the early 1970s, often clashed. The conflict was political as well as personal. As William H. Jennings, former general counsel of the San Diego County Water Authority observed, "Los Angeles [MWD] directors began to be critical of the fact that San Diego, a Johnny-come-lately to the organization, was taking so much of the water available by building up a rival economy, a competitive economy, to that of Los Angeles with water that Los Angeles had made available and was selling to San Diego at an exceedingly low rate."[17]

The Los Angeles and San Diego MET leaders and their delegations squabbled over equitable burden sharing involving water rates, capital financing, the State Water Project, and preferential rights. Preferential rights would become San Diego's *cause celebre*, and a seeming catalyst for water independence. Yet, in the early years this conflict remained muted. The Laguna Declaration (1952), guaranteeing MWD water for all, appeared to render preferential rights superfluous. Later, in the 1960s, the State Water Project—expanding MET's imported supplies—allayed San Diego's shortage fears. In the 1970s, the completion of the second L.A. aqueduct to the Owens Valley reduced L.A.'s dependence on Metropolitan, freeing up water for San Diego and other agencies. However, in the 1980s preferential rights moved to the forefront of conflict. The defeat of the Peripheral Canal (1982) was a sharp wakeup call to San Diego and other fast-growing Southern California communities that imported supplies were limited. Later, San Diego's shortage fears were heightened by the prolonged drought, MWD's cutbacks, and allegations of L.A. invoking preferential rights.

By the 1980s, Los Angeles's influence within Metropolitan was ebbing relative to San Diego's. L.A. seemingly abdicated its historic leadership role. After monopolizing the board chairmanship from 1928 to 1974, L.A. directors held the chairmanship for less than one year between 1975 and 2005. Under L.A. mayors Tom Bradley (1973–1993) and Richard Riordan (1993–2001), the city's MET delegation experienced politically induced high turnover. As average board tenure fell to six years, L.A.'s influence declined. In the early 1990s, Los Angeles was a deeply troubled city, preoccupied with recovery from a severe recession, civil unrest, earthquake, and fires. For L.A. policymakers, water was a secondary concern. Things were quite different in San Diego, where long MWD board tenure still ruled, and a new breed of aggressive directors—such as Francesca Krauel and Chris Frahm, both lawyers—came to power. In the drought's wake, the newcomers were eager to diversify San Diego's water supplies and contest L.A.'s preferments—a task made easier by L.A.'s apparent vulnerability.[18]

Regionalism or Local Independence?

By the early 1990s, the San Diego County Water Authority's leadership and MET delegates were recalculating the benefits and costs of regionalism (continued reliance on and support for MWD) versus greater local independence, and of cooperative versus more confrontational tactics. Even with the lengthy drought, a strong case could be made for the value of continued regional cooperation—or interdependence—over independence. San Diego had an enormous stake in a strong and successful MET, since the fast-growing region would always need a large core supply—at least 400,000 to 500,000 annual AF—supplied by Metropolitan. MWD provided great economies of scale, and thus lower costs to member agencies. It had the operational flexibility needed to cope with shortfalls and periodic interruptions in the various sources supplying the region. Finally, MWD had the political muscle to influence state and federal policy, and to successfully compete with other regions for water resources and project funding.

Regionalism also posed seeming risks and costs. With limits on its impact on MET policymaking, San Diego had less control over water resources and how they might be allocated in times of shortage. By the 1990s, San Diego was footing a large share of MWD's capital investment bill (now largely included in water charges) with arguably limited local returns on investment. Compared with locally initiated and targeted projects, the benefits of MET's region-wide investments appeared diluted, potentially offering less San Diego benefit. There also were growing fears in San Diego business circles that rival Metropolitan member agencies would use its water resources to economically benefit Los Angeles and Orange counties at San Diego's expense.[19]

What County Water Authority leaders sought was greater independence of water supplies. Independence, though, could prove to be an expensive and even quixotic undertaking. Given the cost-effectiveness of resource and infrastructure investments spread out over the entire MWD service area, anything that San Diego did on its own would likely be more expensive. Thus, the seemingly best way for San Diego to make new "independent" water supplies—such as agricultural-to-urban transfers or desalination—cost competitive was to secure external subsidies, either from MET, or the state and federal governments. Yet "subsidized independence" also had long-term risks and costs. Further, if independence reduced access to MWD's regional resources and infrastructure, San Diego could even lose local reliability and operational flexibility in the process.[20]

Although the 1987–1992 drought catalyzed San Diego's independence drive, there were deeper roots. Many San Diego civic and business leaders believed that San Diego could never be a real metropolis as long as it depended on Los Angeles for its water supply. They felt at a competitive economic disadvantage if L.A. seemingly controlled the region's water supply and San Diego relied heavily on MWD. This led to keen interest at the County Water Authority in identifying and developing independent water supplies. In the mid-1980s, after the Peripheral Canal defeat, this involved the Galloway Plan for an interstate water transfer from the Upper Colorado Basin to San Diego. Legally flawed and politically doomed, the plan never was implemented. In the 1990s, the centerpiece was the controversial water-transfer agreement with the Imperial Irrigation District (IID). In the early 21st century, the new panacea became desalination.

Significantly, the city of San Diego, not the region as a whole, was the major force behind the drive for independence. With the potential leverage of the weighted vote (based on assessed valuation—the same as MWD), the city could greatly influence the County Water Authority's governance process. City support would be crucial for SDCWA approval of the Imperial Valley water deal. Given its heft in local water governance, the city of San Diego also could craft local rate structures and other policies to minimize its own burden relative to others paying a larger share.

To justify the higher expense of independent water projects and supplies, the County Water Authority inner clique in the 1990s launched a vituperative anti-MWD campaign, vilifying Metropolitan as both unreliable and unresponsive to San Diego's needs. In the process, history was rewritten to highlight the unfairness of San Diego's so-called shotgun marriage to MET. As firebrand San Diego MWD delegate Francesca

Krauel put it, "I can say it in two words: involuntary servitude. We are completely dependent on another metropolis for our future. . . . We were pulled kicking and screaming into MWD and we brought water with us."[21] Influenced by Krauel and other leaders of the local water rebellion, the editorial page of the *San Diego Union-Tribune*, the metropolis's major newspaper, unleashed a fusillade of anti-MWD broadsides. Chris Frahm, then chair of the SDCWA board of directors and a leader in secret talks with the billionaire Bass brothers in the Imperial Valley, praised the "special relationship" between the newspaper and the County Water Authority. San Diegans were led to believe that they could no longer rely on MET and must support more expensive supplies—whether water transfers from the Imperial Valley, a new joint aqueduct with Mexico, or desalination projects.[22]

What the County Water Authority leaders and local media failed to tell San Diegans was that by embarking on this course they could wind up with the most expensive water in California. Yet the apparent plan all along was to make others help pay the steep price of independence. Rarely mentioned was the irony that San Diego's independence would still be heavily dependent on Metropolitan, because it either supplied the necessary aqueduct system and other infrastructure for transferring water or offered hundreds of millions of dollars to encourage local projects such as desalination. Such was the paradox of ineluctable interdependence.[23]

Declaring Independence: The San Diego–Imperial Valley Water Transfer

Some pundits have gone so far as to call this deal another "Chinatown," comparing it to the trickery once employed by Los Angeles barons to seize water from the Owens Valley. This is pure literary fancy. . . .
The San Diego County-Imperial Valley transfer would be an honorable deal, enriching both regions and benefiting all of Southern California. Why should anyone oppose it?

San Diego Union-Tribune *editorial, 1996*[24]

In essence, [San Diego is] asking the rest of Southern California to subsidize its "independence" like a teenager who moves out to be free of parental rules but needs help from Mom and Dad to pay the rent.

Ventura County Star *editorial, 1998*[25]

At the center of San Diego's independence drive was the celebrated and controversial water-transfer deal with the Imperial Valley. San Diego County—with nearly 3 million people and an economy worth over $125 billion annually—had lived in the shadow of an even more populous and powerful Los Angeles for well over a century. Facing by 2015 an increase of 1 million new residents—adding another 20 percent to its water needs—San Diego's heightened desire for water independence from Los Angeles–based MWD appeared understandable. The serious drought of 1987–1992 caused both MET and the County Water Authority to develop drought plans to meet impending shortages. Although MWD's plans never involved preferential rights, some SDCWA officials used the fear of preferential rights in the early 1990s to support a quest for independent water supplies.[26]

In 1991, San Diego claimed to get a bitter taste of vulnerability when the MWD Board voted to impose sizable water-delivery reductions—20 percent on "non-interruptible" municipal and industrial supplies and 50 percent on "interruptible" agricultural and groundwater replenishment deliveries—on all its member agencies. These across-the-board reductions for all member agencies did not rely on preferential rights. According to SDCWA director Mike Madigan, "San Diego County was at great risk, and MWD essentially walked away from the Laguna Declaration."[27] The County Water Authority then voluntarily chose to cut all its deliveries by a weighted-average 31 percent, protecting local agricultural deliveries at the expense of urban supplies, and making the MET reductions appear even worse for the region. Supporters argued the importance of agriculture to the local economy. Critics claimed that the uniform cutback was designed to galvanize local support for the SDCWA in looming battles with Metropolitan. In the event of more severe future drought, the County Water Authority direly warned that consumption might be reduced by 50 percent. Just as the County Water Authority made the supposedly draconian cutbacks mandatory, heavy spring rains began and the order was soon rescinded.[28]

The April 1998 "conceptual" agreement between the SDCWA and the IID for the purchase of up to 200,000 AF per year promised to make it possible for San Diego to serve the water needs of one third of its population, possibly reducing its dependence on MWD water from 90 percent to less than 60 percent, by importing water from the Imperial

Valley. The apparent overriding goal for San Diego's embrace of the water market option was not economic but political—achieving regional water independence from Metropolitan and Los Angeles and exerting a greater degree of local control. Yet this was the same Colorado River water delivered through the same MET infrastructure, only the SDCWA would be paying IID rather than MWD for the same service.[29]

San Diego could not claim that it originated the idea of water purchases from the Imperial Valley. In 1989, after the State Water Resources Control Board found that IID was wasting water and should partner with other agencies to fund conservation and transfer agreements, IID concluded such a deal with Metropolitan—after the County Water Authority had spurned a similar offer as too expensive. The 1990s drought and threatened MET cutbacks dramatically changed the minds of many SDCWA board members as well as the local public. Once again, however, the initiative for a water purchase did not come from San Diego.

The Bass Brothers and San Diego: Another Covert Chinatown?

In 1993, the Texas billionaire Bass brothers (Sid and Lee) completed their acquisition (by purchase or lease option) of up to 45,000 acres in the Imperial Valley—representing about 10 percent of the area's total irrigated land—making their Western Farms subsidiary the largest private landowner in the county. The local newspaper, the *Imperial Valley Press*, subsequently denounced them as "carpetbaggers." The charge was that they had entered the valley under the camouflage of a cattle-ranching operation but with the real intention of a water deal that would leave their substantial landholdings fallow and turn the valley into a new "Dust Bowl." Suspicions of "another *Chinatown*" inevitably were rife. "What the Bass brothers are doing in the Imperial Valley is the same as what Los Angeles did in the Owens Valley," fumed Tom Levy, general manager of IID's neighbor and sometime bitter rival, the Coachella Valley Water District.[30]

In fact, as early as 1994 Western Farms offered to sell to MET, at the exorbitant rate of $600/AF, Colorado River water that Western Farms would acquire for a mere $12.50/AF. This offer was rejected by MWD. A subsequent 1995 suggestion from the Bass interests that San Diego outmaneuver both MWD and IID by itself becoming a "water farmer" through purchase of an ownership interest in Western Farms was rejected by the SDCWA. The Bass brothers bragged to San Diego water officials that there was no need to worry about resistance because they had "done a thorough job politically" to neutralize the "inefficient, overstaffed, bureaucratic MWD." Perhaps they did too good a job—politically. In 1996, an Imperial County Grand Jury found evidence of "undue influence by outside parties" (Western Farms) after a former Bass functionary became general manger of the IID. Amid a rising tide of criticism, the publicity-shy and highly secretive Bass brothers in August 1997 exchanged their Western Farms properties for more than $250 million in U.S. Filter Corporation stock, making them the firm's largest shareholders. Subsequently acquired by the European water giant Vivendi, U.S. Filter announced its aspiration to become "the General Motors" of the water conservation and reclamation industry.[31]

Walking away from the Bass brothers as politically radioactive, the County Water Authority flirted with the possibility of playing U.S. Filter as a trump card against MET. However, San Diego's prime strategy became direct negotiations for a water purchase agreement directly with IID; after a 3-year roller coaster ride, these negotiations eventually bore fruit in April 1998. Initially, San Diego hoped to purchase as much as 500,000 AF annually over a 75-year contract period. Under pressure from angry local constituents, IID was unable to be that accommodating. Even so, the bug of windfall profits had bitten deeply in Imperial Valley. Dissident IID board member Don Cox lamented, "Some of our farmers . . . have been mesmerized by the thought of getting rich quick for doing nothing, and are not thinking this through."[32]

The final IID-SDCWA contract guaranteed San Diego less than 200,000 AF per year, only 140,000 AF of which would come from on-farm sources. The contract term was for 45 years, with a possible 30-year option. Cost estimates suggested that Imperial Valley farmers could make a handsome profit by selling water to San Diego at around $200/AF. Instead, the contract set the initial price—guaranteed for only 10 years—at approximately $250/AF; but transportation costs would have to be added. In SDCWA-MWD negotiations over wheeling (or conveyance) charges, transportation costs for the IID water initially were set at a discounted $97/AF. This would make the transfer water only slightly more expensive than direct MET deliveries. However, the SDCWA later offered to pay Metropolitan's full $253/AF cost for transporting water in exchange for an additional 77,000 AF conserved from the lining of Imperial Valley canals.[33]

As a result, IID transfer water would cost San Diegans nearly 50 percent more per acre-foot than MET deliveries. Later, the deal's hefty local price tag would be driven even higher by $64 million in present-value environmental mitigation costs and $20 million in third-party economic impact costs. This would push the acre-foot cost of IID transfer water to almost $600/AF—the Bass brothers' initial asking price. In contrast, SDCWA then only paid MWD $350/AF for delivering a blend of untreated Colorado River and State Water Project water that was superior in quality to Imperial Valley water from the lower Colorado River. Ironically, the County Water Authority early on had pledged that it would kill the deal if the price of transfer water exceeded the cost of MET deliveries. Needless to say, SDCWA ignored its deal-killing pledge when MWD thwarted its drive to force either MWD or the state of California to subsidize its IID deal. MWD's transfer of the canal water was particularly shrewd because it left the County Water Authority, not Metropolitan, vulnerable to criticism of depriving Mexico of the seepage water resulting from the unlined canals.[34]

Did the IID-SDCWA deal resemble the fictional plot of *Chinatown*? There were obvious parallels in San Diego's secretive dealings with the Bass brothers. On the San Diego side, after the Bass brothers approached County Water Authority insiders, true due diligence was never performed. Angry at MWD and desperately seeking water independence, San Diego's inner clique made no serious attempt to compare the benefits and costs of competing transfer proposals such as from Central Valley water agencies. Very real concerns about potential environmental harm to the Salton Sea or economic harm to the Imperial Valley were brusquely dismissed as well. To avoid public disclosure (and pressures for due diligence), discussions between the Bass brothers and the County Water Authority's inner clique were conducted in strictest secrecy, producing long-lasting mistrust of San Diego's motives and actions among Imperial Valley residents and the IID board.[35]

As discussions moved from private law offices to the seemingly public confines of the County Water Authority, the pretense was made that this was a "real estate" deal, and thus could legally be discussed in closed session—outside of public view and participation—when in fact no real estate was involved. The potential transfer never even appeared on the SDCWA's agenda as required under the Brown Act, the state's open-meeting law. The negotiations were reported on in closed session under a generic water-rights discussion item. Further, as later argued, when the closed-session deal finally went public in late 1995, the County Water Authority insiders changed the SDCWA's customary voting procedures to ram it through the board of directors despite vocal dissent and growing environmental concerns. Tellingly, the SDCWA board approved the deal before a required environmental review was even completed.[36]

On the Imperial Valley side, it seemed as if local residents and decision makers had learned the seeming lessons of the Owens Valley. In the IID-SDCWA transfer, water rights and lands were not sold (even though the Owens Valley transactions were strictly voluntary with willing seller-buyer purchases). The water yield from conservation and fallowing was essentially leased for a specified period of time, with opportunities to subsequently adjust the price to more closely reflect the future economic value of transferred water. Environmental impact costs, not considered in the early Owens Valley experience, finally were identified and estimated in the 1998 IID-SDCWA transfer agreement, and seemingly included in the overall transaction costs. Yet who ultimately would pay the mitigation costs remained unclear, purportedly reflecting the parties' desire to shift these costs elsewhere. Rather than dealing with individual property owners or groups of owners, as was the case in the Owens Valley, all IID-SDCWA transfer transactions ultimately were funneled through the Imperial Irrigation District, whose board was elected by voters (not just landowners) and who held the water rights in trust.

It can be argued that the now-folkloric Owens Valley experience made once-hidden transaction costs part of a more upfront and public bargaining process in the Imperial Valley, but not necessarily in San Diego. Economic and environmental factors affecting the long-term yield, security, and acceptance of transfers were better identified, sorted through, and reasonably resolved prior to the transaction being completed. As a result, water transfer transactions in the early 21st century promise to be more open, complex, and expensive than they were a century ago.

But in other key respects the IID-SDCWA transfer may not be a superior transaction to what happened in the Owens Valley. L.A. water czar William Mulholland exercised due diligence, surveying all possible new water sources, including those in Southern California, before picking the Owens Valley as the most promising site. San Diego never seriously looked beyond the Imperial Valley, such as to the Central Valley. According to critics, SDCWA single-mindedly pursued the Imperial Valley deal in order to spite MET, because of bruised civic and personal egos and because of frustrations over a seeming inability to change MWD policies. Thus, the IID-SDCWA deal was a sole-source transaction, with no competitive marketplace pressures to moderate price and terms.[37]

Although the Owens Valley transaction actually brought new water to Los Angeles, the IID-SDCWA deal does not bring one single drop of new water to Southern California. This was the same water, but with a SDCWA tag rather than an MET tag on it. As Paul Engstrand, former County Water Authority general counsel, noted, "The transfer does not diversify the water portfolio; it is simply a change of brokers with significantly higher transaction costs."[38] Any value added only comes from the lining of the All-American and Coachella Canals. Although MWD had planned to do this, San Diego took over the lining project and the additional 77,000 AF of water in exchange for paying Metropolitan's full wheeling rate. L.A. made large early infrastructure investments to deliver the new supplies to the city, but the IID-SDCWA deal resulted in no new direct investment in water infrastructure. Instead, it depended on prior investments made by MET (such as in the Colorado River Aqueduct) and essentially displaced aqueduct capacity that MWD could have used for its own water deliveries. Here too there appeared to be little regional value added.

The Wheeling Charge Controversy

The IID-SDCWA deal appeared to hinge on keeping down transaction costs, particularly the cost for wheeling (or transporting) the water through MET's aqueduct empire. As noted, the SDCWA initially had pledged to keep the deal's total per acre-foot cost below MWD's treated-water rate. Metropolitan's system remained the only conveyance option for San Diego unless and until it built its own aqueduct. Unfazed by the deal's questionable, uncertain economics, the SDCWA board chair argued that the only alternative was for San Diego to remain "an appendix of

Los Angeles and Metropolitan." Decrying this "anti-L.A." fixation, Gregory Quist, a skeptical SDCWA board member from northern San Diego County, complained that "Here we are not even close to knowing all the facts—without the facts we don't even have the luxury of making an informed bad decision."[39]

Such reservations were shared by the nearly one third of the County Water Authority's 23-member agencies, mostly from the North County and representing agricultural and suburban districts, who voted against the purchase agreement that was ramrodded through the County Water Authority—in much the same secretive, high-handed fashion that San Diego accused so-called imperial Los Angeles of using to dominate the MET board. Support for the deal in metropolitan San Diego would have evaporated entirely had the SDCWA board not given up for the foreseeable future its plan for San Diegans to pay the $2- to $3-billion price of building a new aqueduct to transport Imperial Valley water purchases. Even if such a new aqueduct were affordable, it would have "put another straw" in the Colorado River—a political nonstarter with the other Western states. They need not have worried, however, because the County Water Authority board at the time was unwilling to approve even the modest $122 million needed for a sixth pipeline connecting it to MWD's aqueduct system. Instead, the County Water Authority demanded that Metropolitan convey at a significantly discounted rate the IID transfer water through MET's own Colorado River Aqueduct. MWD countered that this would subsidize San Diego and force its other 26-member agencies to absorb a 10 to 20 percent rate hike and make them more vulnerable to shortages.[40]

The issue of wheeling charges was one (though not the sole) controversy between San Diego and MWD. Robert V. Phillips, a former LADWP general manager–chief engineer, accused San Diego of demanding "a special, Quebec-like relationship with the MET." One MWD official direly prophesied that the deal "could be the end of the MET as we know it." Another MWD official mused more philosophically about "a parent-kid, haves and have-nots, big L.A.-little San Diego, sibling rivalry" that had "always been the same" during his 25-year tenure. Pressured by a broad cross-section of its membership not to give San Diego "a free ride," MET initially demanded that SDCWA pay the standard charge of $262/AF for making space available to wheel water. Unable to resolve their differences, the feuding water agencies ended up in court.[41]

In January 1998, a California Superior Court judge held that MWD maintenance and capital costs could not be included in wheeling charges—an apparent vindication of the San Diego position. However, the victory was a Pyrrhic one—the decision was unambiguously reversed in May 2000 by the California Second Appellate Court. Later, the California Supreme Court refused to review the case, thus closing the issue legally. This would only be the first in a long line of fruitless lawsuits brought by SDCWA against Metropolitan. Even before the adverse 1998 decision, MET had offered to reduce its asking price for wheeling IID-SDCWA water to $70/AF (half its usual space-available rate)—provided that San Diego store unused water with Metropolitan that could be used to meet the needs of other members in the event of shortages. In the event of a drought—and if one sixth of the Colorado River Aqueduct's capacity were reserved exclusively to move San Diego's Imperial Valley purchases—Los Angeles County cities highly dependent on the aqueduct (such as Long Beach, Cerritos, and Norwalk) could face unprecedented and severe water rationing. Thus, the core disputes involved San Diego's demand that its Imperial Valley water receive dedicated capacity in the Colorado River Aqueduct, and MWD's insistence on water storage for equitable distribution to meet system-wide drought conditions.[42]

In the MWD-SDCWA dispute, wheeling charges and dedicated-supply issues were ultimately finessed by a two-tier, compromise solution suggested by State Water Resources director David Kennedy in January 1998. San Diego would be able to move its Imperial Valley water purchases through the Colorado River Aqueduct for $80/AF when space was available, but would be charged $110/AF when it was not. The compromise did not specify the cutoff point for determining when space was available. Nor did it address MET's concerns about the storage of Imperial Valley water purchased but not used by San Diego.[43]

MWD had difficulty defending its position during the controversy, because of the serious deterioration of its political standing in Sacramento. Critics alleged that MET's officialdom, in an uncharacteristic display of ineptitude, had channeled $12,000 of a public relations budget amounting to more than $400,000 into what was deemed opposition research on its critics such as San Diego water and state elected officials, and the Bass brothers. Whereas the IID had paid its dream-team lawyers over $2.2 million to consummate the water deal, MET's comparatively paltry public-relations expenditure was enough to ignite a political firestorm. MWD officials were accused of felony violations (for faulty public records on campaign contributions); critics clamored for the dissolution of the $8-billion district; and the *San Diego Union-Tribune* editorialized—no doubt metaphorically—that MWD ought to be "dynamited" out of the way for its obstruction of the Imperial Valley water purchase.[44]

Desperate to recoup politically, MET swallowed the broad contours of the IID-SDCWA water purchase in May 1998. It even offered a $1-billion package for new storage, including facilities to store San Diego water. Skeptical San Diego water policy makers preferred instead a new suggestion from State Water Resources Director Kennedy that $100 to $125 million of the governor's proposed water bond issue be earmarked for new facilities to store San Diego's IID water purchases. Governor Wilson had suggested that "if it was only money that separated the two agencies, the state might be willing to close the gap." In San Diego's eyes, money from Sacramento rather than MWD would come, presumably, with fewer L.A. strings attached.[45]

Proposition 13, the state water bond, passed in March 2000 with no funding for building new storage reservoirs. But it did contain a $3-million allocation to study a new aqueduct to ship water directly from the Colorado River to San Diego and Mexico. There was also money that could be used to line Imperial Valley's All-American Canal and its Coachella Branch as well as meet the demands of the San Luis Rey Mission Indians who had their own claim on Colorado River water. Yet most monies for lining the All-American and Coachella canals came from an earlier state general-fund commitment of $230 million designed to seal the deal. This figure represented MET's calculation of its cost for giving the SDCWA a low $97/AF wheeling rate, rather than the $250/AF rate that Metropolitan was charging others. Ultimately, MWD transferred the $230 million to the SDCWA, which took on the canal-lining projects that would secure an additional 77,000 AF of net annual yield. This was done even though the SDCWA's own analysis showed that the actual cost of the canal linings likely would exceed $300 million.[46]

MWD's enemies in both Northern and Southern California kept the agency on the defensive in Sacramento where legislation was floated in consecutive sessions by state senator Steve Peace (D-San Diego), L.A. assemblyman Richard Katz, and others to transfer from MET to the

Public Utilities Commission or the little-known State Water Resources Control Board the power to determine fair compensation for shipping water.[47]

Metropolitan continued to try to walk a tightrope. "Deregulation in the water industry would be a disaster," said MWD CEO Ron Gastelum. "But I think most would agree that at least some form of water transfers and marketing would be necessary in California's future." MET—perhaps self-servingly but not necessarily inaccurately—warned that losing authority to set rates high enough to pay for essential infrastructure and storage would have the same disastrous effect on water availability and prices that electricity deregulation—another of Senator Peace's pet projects—had on the California power market. In 1997, when the bloom was still on the rose of energy deregulation, SDCWA general manager Maureen Stapleton invoked precisely that analogy in explaining her hope to transform MWD into "a transmission company, with local water agencies responsible for finding their own water supplies." In seeming lockstep, the *San Diego Union-Tribune* editorialized, "Just as California has deregulated energy, it should deregulate water."[48]

MET's position was reflected in a report prepared for the State Senate's Agriculture and Water Resources Committee that warned the committee to investigate whether anti-MWD bills were motivated by a desire to enhance water policy or private companies' profits. The report was referring to lobbying by the Western Water Company, the private water marketer, on behalf of anti-MET legislation that might lower Western Water's wheeling bills. The San Diego County Water Authority also continued to be an active member of the anti-MWD lobby in Sacramento but also looked to Washington for relief. In November 1998, Congress approved the IID-SDCWA deal. Then in August 2001, Congressmember Duncan Hunter (R-El Cajon) introduced House Resolution 24, a bill that would federally subsidize environmental mitigation for the San Diego–Imperial water deal and streamline its environmental review.[49]

Unanticipated Consequences

The IID-SDCWA transfer agreement was a classic example of how policy can produce a myriad of unintended and unanticipated consequences. The Bass brothers made a handsome profit from their land-stock swap, but had their hopes frustrated that their Western Farms investment would become the building block of a gigantic California "water farming" empire. In 2004, ironically the Imperial Irrigation District bought the 42,000 acres of farmland that had once been owned by the Bass brothers, who had started the entire process. The IID board ultimately brokered a San Diego deal but lost much local goodwill and alienated the neighboring Coachella Valley Water District—which had its own beneficial-use claim to the water. Clinton administration Interior Secretary Bruce Babbitt complained that Imperial Valley typified wasteful California water practices that other Colorado River water users would no longer tolerate.[50]

For San Diego, the purchase secured less water at a higher price over a shorter assured delivery period than it wanted. Ironically, the water independence that San Diego so desperately sought could have been secured much earlier—and at lower cost—if it had been willing to pay for it. As noted, in the 1920s the city of San Diego had filed for an independent (albeit lower-priority) claim to 112,000 AF a year of Colorado River water. However, it never built its own aqueduct to convey this water. After joining MWD in 1946, San Diego surrendered its Colorado water rights to Metropolitan. In the postwar era, SDCWA board chair Fred Heilbron—San Diego's version of MET's imperious Joseph Jensen—presided over a "growth bloc" that involved a common stance on many issues with Riverside and Orange County water officials and made the SDCWA "more Met than Met," increasing San Diego's dependence on MWD. Not until the early 1980s—after the Peripheral Canal defeat and MET's shift of much capital financing from taxes to water sales—did San Diego water officials show the first unmistakable restive stirrings for alternative water sources that caused MWD general manager Carl Boronkay to muse jokingly whether they "actually smoked a [controlled substance] before meetings."[51]

Belatedly, San Diego in the 1990s revived in earnest its pre–World War II crusade for water independence, and in the process severely strained its relations with MWD and most other local water agencies from Orange County to Ventura County. Despite tough talk about water independence, San Diego still refused to seriously consider making a major commitment to building the expensive new aqueduct to deliver Imperial Valley water that would give substance to its aspirations. Instead—to escape dependence on Metropolitan—San Diego preferred to base its aspirations for independence on the chimerical prospect of a joint Colorado River aqueduct with Mexico—hopefully to be subsidized by Washington or Sacramento—notwithstanding the strenuous objections of the Imperial Valley, the other Colorado River Basin states, many local water officials, and even San Diego residents. When such prospects dimmed, San Diego embraced desalination—again to be subsidized by MET to the tune of $250/AF, and by possible state and federal outlays. San Diego's quixotic and expensive dream of water independence could eventually turn into a nightmare if bond-rating agencies—by vigorously applying market-oriented criteria—began to downgrade SDCWA's credit rating. If truth be told, in Southern California water *interdependence* is inescapable.[52]

The County Water Authority leadership also bore major responsibility for the federal government's decision in 2003 to abruptly turn off the Colorado River spigot, leading at least temporarily to a more insecure and expensive water future not only for San Diego but for all of Southern California. At the end of 2002, last-minute talks among Southern California urban and agricultural water agencies concerning the Imperial Valley–San Diego water-transfer deal—the lynchpin of a broader Colorado River Quantification Settlement Agreement (QSA)—collapsed. The federal government then ushered in 2003 by swiftly cutting off 700,000 AF of surplus Colorado River water for Southern California. The blame game for this debacle began in earnest. Not surprisingly, San Diego's leaders and media pointed the finger at the usual list of culprits: the Imperial Irrigation District, Coachella Valley, and, of course, the MWD. Nary a word of local criticism was directed at the seemingly sacrosanct County Water Authority.[53]

Yet the San Diego water insiders played a major role in lobbying to make the IID-SDCWA water transfer and enabling QSA the very centerpiece of the California 4.4 Plan, allowing Southern California water agencies to receive surplus Colorado River water for 15 years. This linkage would force MET and other local agencies to support the transfer or risk losing surplus water themselves. Although politically advantageous to San Diego, tying the transfer to a continued surplus allotment was risky business because it was done before the deal's environmental effects were fully assessed, particularly the adverse impacts on the fragile Salton Sea ecosystem. In lockstep, the *San Diego Union-Tribune* now castigated this "dying sea," for which fixes were "just too costly."[54]

As those impacts and the responsibility and massive expense of mitigation finally were raised, the plan abruptly shifted at the 11th hour from on-farm conservation to the taboo topic of land fallowing, which the County Water Authority originally had pledged would not occur. With neither the federal and state governments nor MWD willing to subsidize billions of dollars of mitigation, the responsibility fell squarely on the shoulders of the Imperial Irrigation District and San Diego. Justifiably concerned, the IID board balked. When the IID directors barely approved a last-minute revised plan shifting mitigation responsibility to Coachella and MWD, the latter agencies understandably balked as well. Later, a revised QSA agreement would be approved, with the state of California assuming a large measure of mitigation responsibility. But by then, with the worst drought in 500 years occurring in the Colorado River Basin, there would be no surplus Colorado River water for thirsty Southern Californians for the foreseeable future.

Nor could Metropolitan escape responsibility for failing to anticipate the consequences of its actions. Having concluded its own conservation-transfer deal in 1989 with Imperial Valley, it might have foreseen the inevitable upshot and cut its losses sooner. A more proactive, positive stance by MET might have allowed it to shape a less objectionable IID-SDCWA agreement. Instead in 1995, MWD acted promptly— but negatively—when it caught wind of the deal. Goaded by San Diego's delegates, MWD ordered its engineers to stop work on a new pipeline connecting San Diego to the Colorado River Aqueduct. This proved ineffective and counterproductive when San Diego officials, who had argued the project was not needed, then claimed the stoppage was proof of MET intimidation.[55]

The IID-SDCWA deal also proved a mixed blessing for its sponsors in Sacramento. In the 1990s, the state water bureaucracy moved from criticism to praise of Imperial Valley agriculture's water utilization practices, despite the fact that conservation efforts failed to prevent an increase in water usage. The IID-SDCWA agreement was even ballyhooed by legislators as the cornerstone of the California 4.4 Plan for reducing the state's Colorado River use. Yet by drawing critical attention from the U.S. Interior Department to California's failure to measure—much less control—the voracious thirst of its great agricultural water users, the deal jeopardized the California 4.4 Plan and invited the Bush Administration's cutoff of surplus Colorado River water to California.[56]

San Diego's Puzzling Preferential Rights Lawsuit

And we have lived in San Diego County upon water that the City of Los Angeles was entitled to take but did not for the reason that they had their own supplies.

> William H. Jennings, former general counsel, San Diego County Water Authority, 1967[57]

When asked about the appropriateness of the skewed preferential rights formula, Los Angeles representatives generally adopt a paternalistic air and insist they would never use that formula against San Diego. However, the equivalent of preferential rights were invoked during the last drought, when the MWD voted for a cut in San Diego's water deliveries that would have amounted to 50 percent, while the city of Los Angeles was actually increasing its MWD purchases.

> San Diego Union-Tribune editorial, 2004[58]

In early 2001, the San Diego County Water Authority opened another battlefront in its drive for water reliability. It sued the Metropolitan Water District, the city of Los Angeles, and, later, the other MET member agencies over preferential rights to water during droughts. San Diego's suit seemed understandable in the middle of yet another drought and with dire predictions that global warming might leave California with serious water problems over the next 50 years. The antiquated 1928 allocation formula, based on property taxes and other contributions exclusive of water sales, in 2001 gave the city of Los Angeles rights to 22 percent of MWD's water during scarcity compared to San Diego's 15 percent. As MET's largest customer, San Diego took one quarter or more of its water deliveries, a large and risky overdraw if shortages occurred.[59] As SDCWA director Mike Madigan observed, "Water rights are the closest thing to royalty in the United States, and San Diegans are the serfs."[60]

Yet, given the political unenforceability of the preferential rights formula as well as readily available alternative remedies, critics claimed that San Diego's lawsuit was but another quixotic action in its all-but-declared war against MWD. By a host of contentious and inconsistent actions, San Diego's water agency risked becoming the pariah of the Southern California water community. San Diego's lawsuit over so-called paper rights seemed unnecessary. Many legal experts (including some MET general counsels) believed preferential rights were unenforceable under the State Water Code's sections 350 et seq. MWD policy, going back to the 1952 Laguna Declaration, pledged adequate supplies to meet member agencies' growing needs.

Although leading San Diego water officials claimed that preferential rights were used during the early 1990s drought, it is clear from the record that Los Angeles never called for them and MWD never invoked them. In 1981, San Diego had supported MET's interruptible water program in exchange for agricultural price discounts. In the event of shortages, agriculture would be among the first to be cut off—after being given a year's notice. With one quarter or so of its MWD purchases representing interruptible agricultural water, San Diego gambled and, with the 1990s drought, seemingly lost. Responding to pleas from San Diego and other heavy interruptible users, the MET board in 1990 revised the interruptible program to provide for only a 50 percent agricultural cutback, and an "equitable" 20 percent cutback in non-interruptible residential and business deliveries. All MET member agencies were treated equally.[61]

As a result, San Diego took an overall 31 percent reduction. Unexpectedly heavy rains in March 1991 softened the effects of the cutbacks. For its part, L.A. supported a "share the pain equally" approach during shortages. In the early 1990s, L.A. took more MWD water as its Owens Valley supplies were scaled back, but still absorbed MWD's cutbacks. Although the city of Los Angeles imposed mandatory rationing during the drought, the city of San Diego's rationing was voluntary. As a result, and with little complaint, L.A. absorbed about the same reduction in water usage that San Diego claimed was so dire.

Many believed that San Diego might have bargained rather than sued. Although San Diego officials claimed that Los Angeles had walked out of previous discussions, the blame was shared equally. In the mid-1980s, Los Angeles agreed to essentially abolish preferential rights, with the symbolic proviso that it would be guaranteed the first 50,000 AF of MET deliveries. But L.A. mayor Bradley balked, claiming that San Diego gave nothing in return. San Diego then got MWD's board to go to

Sacramento to try to change the MWD Act, but was blocked by L.A.'s strong state legislative clout. At the time an MWD director, San Diego's Mike Madigan, claimed to have "found no L.A. receptivity to changing preferential rights."[62] In the early 1990s, Los Angeles and San Diego were back at the bargaining table. L.A. offered to revise the formula to include all capital contributions (including from water sales) adjusted for inflation. Under this plan, San Diego's paper rights would grow while L.A.'s substantial historical investment in MET would be recognized. This time, San Diego walked away. Critics claimed that, with the Imperial Valley deal looming, to rally local support for a highly contentious deal San Diego needed a wound to scratch.[63]

Even with the antiquated preferential-rights formula, San Diego's entitlement was growing while L.A.'s was shrinking due to continued growth in San Diego County whereas L.A. City was essentially built out. As Figure 4.1 shows, around 2015, San Diego and L.A. both could claim about 19 percent of MET's deliveries.[64] Thereafter, San Diego's water rights would increasingly exceed Los Angeles's. Regardless, San Diego pressed a lawsuit in 2001, but found the state courts quite unsympathetic. The trial court sustained MWD's demurrer. The appellate court also ruled in MWD's favor, finding that the appropriate remedy was legislative— amending the Metropolitan Act—and not judicial. The California Supreme Court refused to hear the appeal. San Diego was forced to claim a Pyrrhic victory, arguing that its preferential rights were now secure. According to SDCWA director Mike Madigan, "Any decision was more important than no decision. It clarified matters, and allowed us to make plans."[65] To critics, San Diego had spent over $1 million in legal fees for outside counsel to achieve essentially nothing.[66]

San Diego's preferential rights flip-flops and puzzling lawsuit were part of a growing pattern of County Water Authority inconsistencies that raised serious questions about what it *really* wanted from MWD. San Diego also demanded firm take-or-pay water delivery contracts for all MET member agencies. Heavily dependent on imported water, San Diego claimed this would assure that its future needs were met. Yet San Diego wanted the contracts structured so that L.A. would either have to pay for more than it took (thus reducing San Diego's bills), or pay a penalty for exceeding the contract amount on those occasions when

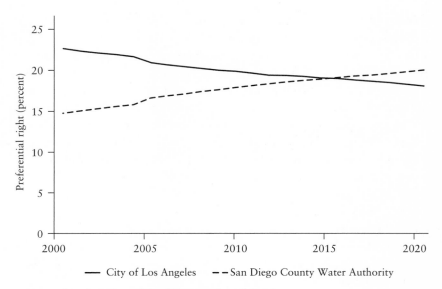

FIGURE **4.1**   Los Angeles and San Diego preferential rights

SOURCE: MWDSC, Office of Chief Financial Officer.

required to by hydrology. The key issue was that Los Angeles has variability in MWD needs, whereas San Diego's needs are relatively uniform. L.A. water officials charged that San Diego wanted to shift contract costs onto Los Angeles, although L.A. paid for a very large share of the MET infrastructure making peak deliveries possible, and thus would be paying twice. When MWD finally offered modified contracts, San Diego water officials quickly turned into its most vocal critics. All MWD member agencies except San Diego signed an initial framework.[67]

Further, San Diego long had sought a blend involving more high-quality State Project water. At that time most San Diego imports were high-salinity Colorado River water because there were limited ways to ship state water there. In response, MET started building the Inland Feeder Pipeline, helping to better connect the State Water Project to distant agencies such as San Diego. Although this was the only realistic way to secure a better blend, San Diego fought the Inland Feeder for years, apparently looking to sue MWD and halt construction. The SDCWA claimed that its opposition was merely one of timing, route, and design.

Critics discerned a darker motive: it was not politically advantageous for San Diego to improve MET's water quality and reliability.[68]

This combative, inconsistent behavior took its toll. Within the County Water Authority, dissident North County water officials expressed concern about the agency's all-consuming determination to fight MWD, which they contended produced contention, litigation, discord, and unnecessary costs rather than compromise and consensus. Within MET, all the other member agencies routinely voted against an intransigent San Diego delegation. In Sacramento, San Diego's influence was waning despite its having spent a small fortune on lawyers, lobbyists, and public relations firms.[69]

What did San Diego hope to gain by its actions? County Water Authority officials claimed they were seeking a reliable supply for their region while protecting their ratepayers from needless and wasteful MWD expenses. In contrast, critics contended that San Diego was trying to sabotage MET, or at least embarrass and purge its leaders, in its quixotic quest for independence. An ineffective MWD invited deregulation, and could turn the once-mighty water wholesaler into a mere set of pipes for private water transfers. This might explain San Diego's contradictory opposition to expanding MET's system through the Inland Feeder, which would enhance regional reliability and water quality, while claiming that MWD could not be counted on during droughts. Critics also claimed that San Diego's rancorous behavior distracted and weakened the Southern California water community during critical discussions on the future of Colorado River and Northern California water imports.

Another theory is that, much as estranged couples escalate hostilities to trigger a divorce, San Diego was building a case for separation from MWD. Independence long had been a rallying cry for some directors at the County Water Authority. Despite clear opposition from many SDCWA member agencies and the public, the SDCWA soon began planning for a new binational aqueduct to the Colorado River bringing Mexican treaty water to Tijuana as well as San Diego's Imperial Valley deliveries. Fearful that San Diego would permanently take more than 200,000 annual acre-feet of its water, the IID board voted unanimously to oppose a new Colorado River aqueduct. Other western states also expressed deep concern about a new straw in the river.

David and Goliath, San Diego–Style

The brewing turmoil in the San Diego County Water Authority bubbled over Thursday as 11 agency directors walked out of a board meeting, calling it "a waste of time." The directors protested a call for a change in voting procedures that gives [city of] San Diego members considerably more weight in all future decisions.

Kim Peterson, San Diego Daily Transcript reporter, 1996[70]

The recent walkout over voting procedures and the formation of a new splinter water group . . . is in fact harming the ability of the County Water Authority to focus on constructing positive solutions for our water future.

Mark Watton, former chair, SDCWA, 1997[71]

The history of the present San Diego County Water Authority board of directors, under the control and leadership of the City of San Diego, is a history of repeated actions designed to continue a system of control which is not in the best interests of the members of the Economic Study Group (ESG), the people who depend upon ESG water agencies for their water, and even the people of San Diego County as a whole.

Economic Study Group, "The Case for Withdrawal"[72]

Since the late 1990s, the San Diego County Water Authority has experienced internally its own fierce David-and-Goliath governance battles, pitting a group of North County suburban and agricultural member agencies against the mammoth city of San Diego. The dissidents claimed that there were serious local governance inequities, resulting in questionable decision making and major inconsistencies between San Diego's behavior at Metropolitan compared to its behavior at the County Water Authority.

Coup d'État

In San Diego, water governance concerns dated back to the IID-SDCWA deal. In late 1996, San Diego city water officials pushing the transfer realized that they would need firm control of the SDCWA board of directors in order to secure needed approval. Who better to have in control than brassy Chris Frahm—a city director, leader in the secret dealings with the Bass brothers, and a lawyer to boot? However, there was a problem. Frahm was not in line for the SDCWA chair position; she was not even a board officer. Mild-mannered Dr. Joe Parker was the vice chair and next in line for the chairmanship. With Frahm apparently lacking the votes needed to be elected chair under the traditional voting method—one director, one vote (all 23 member agencies having at least one director, with the city of San Diego having 10 directors)—her supporters realized that the rarely used weighted vote (based on assessed valuation) would be needed. After Frahm was nominated from the floor, there was a call for the weighted vote for the election of chair and for all board votes in the future. Frahm then was elected chair by the weighted vote. In protest, 11 County Water Authority directors walked out of the meeting, claiming that their participation and vote had been rendered meaningless. The SDCWA leadership responded that, by law, all board actions were to be by weighted vote. Yet the operational practice for many years had been one director, one vote—as shown by the SDCWA board minutes.[73]

Reacting to the *coup d'état*, a group of protesting North County member agencies banded together and geared up for action. Subsequent negotiations produced several changes in the SDCWA voting laws, which were approved in 1997. First, the weighted vote was changed from member agency assessed valuation to all financial contributions to the SDCWA, less monies paid to MWD. This somewhat shifted the voting strength of member agencies, and reduced the city of San Diego's weighted vote from 48 percent to 41 percent. Second, to further reduce the power of the city of San Diego, the needed winning vote threshold was raised from 50 percent to 55 percent (until the city's weighted vote dropped below 38 percent). These turned out to be cosmetic changes, and did little to loosen the city of San Diego's tight grip on SDCWA governance.[74]

Beginning with the installation of Chris Frahm as board chair, the city of San Diego commandeered the SDCWA governance process. Voting as a bloc and armed with the weighted vote, the city's 10 delegates drove questionable decision-making practices. Thus, a few County Water Authority insiders secretly negotiated the Imperial Valley deal's initial terms and conditions, months before it was presented to the full SDCWA board of directors. City delegates then successfully pressed the full board to enter into an exclusive transfer agreement prior to completing an environmental review, which could have revealed the Salton Sea impacts—potentially fatal flaws. Later, city insiders inserted the IID deal into the California 4.4 Plan in a risky attempt to force approval from MWD and other agencies. City directors also led the campaign to vilify and discredit MET, even though the IID transfer's ultimate success depended on MWD's cooperation.

The seemingly imperious city delegation was active on other fronts as well. It secured passage of a new SDCWA rate structure benefiting the city at the expense of outlying areas. Eerily reminiscent of the city of San Diego's failed oversight of its burgeoning pension-fund deficit, the SDCWA permitted massive cost overruns on capital improvement projects. A flagrant example was the much-ballyhooed Emergency Storage Project (ESP), whose cost ballooned 55 percent—from an estimated $534 million to $826 million. At the same time, the SDCWA excoriated MET for a modest 5 percent (or less) cost overrun on the $2.1-billion Diamond Valley Lake Reservoir project. The city's SDCWA board delegates also secured the purchase of city-owned mitigation bank properties for the ESP, even though properties costing only half as much were available.

Later, the city delegates doggedly pursued the controversial binational pipeline project through northern Mexico, despite the opposition of many SDCWA directors, the Imperial Valley, other Colorado River Basin states, and even the federal government. Belatedly, the SDCWA's Regional Facility Master Plan conceded that this project provided a low level of supply reliability, and, in a post-9/11 world, exposed San Diego water users to safety and security risks.[75]

Many observers grew concerned about questionable County Water Authority governance and policymaking. The weighted vote system allowed the city of San Diego and a few other agencies to implement policies without reaching consensus—or even considering—the perspectives and needs of smaller member agencies. Decisions were made secretly by a few insiders, in a vacuum, without consideration of other viewpoints. Smaller agencies soon realized that their participation in the SDCWA boardroom was inconsequential. They were forced to "go public" with their concerns outside the SDCWA governance process, either in the media, the state legislature, or the courts.

North County Rebels: The Struggle for Reform

In response to the bloodless coup, seven inland North County member agencies (Fallbrook Public Utility District, Vallecitos Water District, Vista Irrigation District, and Rainbow, Rincon del Diablo, Valley Center, and Yuima municipal water districts)—all effectively disenfranchised by the new voting rules—organized themselves in mid-1998 as the Economic Study Group (ESG). Together, these agencies contributed nearly one fifth of the SDCWA's total revenues. The ESG initially sought to reform inequities in the County Water Authority's water-rate structure and later moved to change SDCWA's governance rules and decision making. For their actions, the dissidents were sharply attacked. State Senator Steve Peace labeled them "Benedict Arnolds," while former County Water Authority board chair Mark Watton accused them of giving aid and comfort to archenemy Los Angeles.[76]

Much as in the County Water Authority's challenge to MWD's uniform wheeling rates (featuring inclusion of system-wide costs), the ESG attacked the SDCWA's similar "postage stamp" conveyance charges, which allegedly resulted in large subsidies by northern agencies to southern agencies. With strong city of San Diego and southern agency opposition, the North County rebels achieved little in the way of serious rate reforms and the desired "point-to-point" wheeling charges. With this major setback, the ESG members turned to more drastic action. They explored how to detach themselves from the County Water Authority, in possible preparation for joining the Metropolitan Water District. Because the San Diego County Water Authority Act, like the MWD Act, is state legislation, the ESG turned to Sacramento. The rebellious agencies had legislation introduced—AB 1385 (Haynes, R–San Diego)—which would facilitate the division of SDCWA aqueduct capacity and other assets in the case of member agencies departing SDCWA.[77]

Armed with AB 1385, which aroused considerable interest, the ESG proposed a new governance system for the County Water Authority modeled after the new system for San Diego Association of Governments (SANDAG). In the SANDAG scheme, a measure needed both a majority of the weighted population vote as well as a majority of the member city vote for passage. As Gary Gallegos, SANDAG's executive director, argued, the new system encouraged a "focus on consensus" and kept everyone at the table participating. Responding to the concerns of large agencies, Gallegos noted, "If you can't get a majority of the members to go along with you, then you are probably proposing something you ought not to be proposing." With a slight modification (substituting the weighted all-financial vote for the weighted population vote), the ESG championed the SANDAG system as a more-equitable governance model for the County Water Authority that could improve regional water decision making. For leverage, the ESG included this new governance model in AB 1385.[78]

The ESG governance reform effort ultimately failed in the legislative process, because the County Water Authority and the City of San Diego marshaled strong opposition. The ESG members then looked to other approaches for a more balanced, inclusive SDCWA governance process, short of changing the way the board voted. One such idea would be to reinvigorate the County Water Authority's ineffectual committee system. All committee decisions automatically go to the full board, which frequently overrides their recommendations. The ESG suggested that proposals failing in committee would die unless a majority of member agencies resurrected them. The city and its allies still could override committee inaction, but might be reluctant in the face of strong opposition.

Although the governance reforms proposed by the ESG would benefit 22 out of the 23 County Water Authority member agencies—all except the city of San Diego—few member agencies besides the rebellious seven seriously enlisted in the reform cause. Only five other agencies offered even modest support. Why did member agencies fail to endorse reforms that would benefit them? Using a variety of stratagems, the County Water Authority leadership and lead city directors successfully defused dissent. First, the inner clique rewarded friends and punished enemies. Ambitious SDCWA directors aspiring to be an MWD delegate, board officer or committee chair learned to toe the party line. Rebels were punished. With one exception, no ESG director served as an MWD delegate, board officer, or committee chair. ESG director Dale Mason, after 12 years of loyal and effective service as a MWD delegate, was stripped of his Metropolitan post.[79]

Second, the city of San Diego used its power over other regional agencies to quell water rebellion. Regarding the Metro sewer system, many County Water Authority member agencies represented areas dependent on the city of San Diego's sewer system. Any support for reducing the city of San Diego's power at the SDCWA could negatively impact them in terms of future negotiations over sewer capacity and treatment costs. Regarding SANDAG, the agency possessed power to allocate regional transportation projects and funds. Even under the agency's new governance system, the city of San Diego played a key role with the largest population vote. SANDAG cities with County Water Authority membership, such as Oceanside, Escondido, and National City, had to carefully balance any gains they might achieve in water governance reform against what they might lose in the SANDAG boardroom.

One notable accomplishment for the ESG dissidents involved bringing into sharp relief the inconsistencies between San Diego's behavior vis-à-vis Metropolitan, and what transpired within the County Water Authority. While the SDCWA constantly complained about ill treatment at MWD, it rode roughshod over its own dissident member agencies. A major San Diego grievance at Metropolitan involved the seeming recent paucity of San Diego MWD directors appointed to board officer or key committee chair positions. At the County Water Authority, dissident directors were shut out from any leadership or committee chair positions. At MET, San Diego constantly pressed for governance reform to diminish the power of Los Angeles. At home, the city of San Diego quashed meaningful governance reform efforts threatening to diminish the city's power. Finally, vis-à-vis Metropolitan, the County Water Authority championed point-to-point wheeling (or conveyance) rates for transferred water, and opposed MWD's inclusion of a pro-rated share of system-wide costs. Yet at home the County Water Authority favored inclusion of system-wide costs and rejected an ESG proposal to allocate costs to local member agencies based on the amount of the SDCWA system used to deliver water to each agency.[80]

For many observers, such blatant inconsistencies made the County Water Authority's behavior seem even more bizarre and puzzling. Embracing independence at MWD, San Diego's water leadership quashed dissent at home. At Metropolitan, San Diego fiercely battled for expensive independent water supplies—for example, the Imperial Valley water transfer and desalination projects—while consistently seeking to avoid paying their full price. Other MET member agencies or the state and federal governments were always asked to pay the extra expense. Small wonder that Metropolitan began striking back. In late 2004, the MWD board approved a rate integrity plan that would withdraw hefty MWD subsidies for local projects, such as for desalination, from rebellious member agencies such as San Diego that sued or lobbied the state legislature to challenge MWD's rate structure. San Diego and other member agencies later tried to get this provision overturned, but failed.[81]

San Diego was given renewed hope in the fall of 2004 with the selection (with San Diego support) of Orange County director Wes Bannister as Metropolitan board chair coupled with the long-planned retirement of MWD chief executive officer Ron Gastelum, whom some San Diegans believed favored L.A. Not surprisingly, because L.A.'s MWD delegates did not support Bannister, no committee chairmanships were bestowed on L.A. directors. On the water planning committee, arguably one of MET's most important postings, the new chair appointed three of the four San Diego directors, two Orange County directors, and no Los Angeles director. With MWD leadership appearing to tilt southward and away from Los Angeles, San Diego now appeared to have incentive to relearn the once-effective strategy of responsible voice rather than threatened exit, and to extol regionalism and interdependence rather than go-it-alone independence.[82]

5   Empire Under Siege: Colorado River and Bay-Delta Battles

> In the West, whiskey is for drinking; water is for fighting over.
> *Mark Twain*[1]

> This morning, I came, I saw and I was conquered.
> *President Franklin D. Roosevelt, dedicating Boulder (Hoover) Dam, 1935*[2]

Growing up in the aftermath of L.A.'s Progressive-era construction of the Los Angeles Aqueduct, the Metropolitan Water District of Southern California was at the center of the subsequent half century of California "water wars"—from the creation of the Colorado River Aqueduct and the Central Valley Project in the 1930s and 1940s, to the evolution of the State Water Project in the 1950s and 1960s, to the unsuccessful Peripheral Canal campaign of the 1970s and 1980s. In the 1990s, MWD remained at the vortex of California's continuing struggles to control and manage water resources—a prize that has contributed much more than gold ever did to the Golden State's development and growth.

This chapter explores MET's involvement in California's contemporary "water wars" over the Colorado River and Northern California Bay-Delta ecosystem. It considers the post-1990 political and legal challenges to MWD's imported supplies, and analyze MET's strategies, alliances, and opponents' tactics in interstate and intrastate water conflicts. California needed secure, reliable, quality water supplies for a population projected to rise from 34 million in 2000 to 48 million by 2020—a difficult task made even more challenging by a political environment that demanded unprecedented sensitivity to ecological concerns, cost effectiveness, and consensus building. Discerning regional and state policymakers drew parallels between the California energy crisis of 1999–2001 and its growing water woes. Without corrective action to ensure a dependable water supply, the state might trade an energy crisis for a water crisis. Whether the Golden State succeeded or failed depended in significant measure on the efforts of Metropolitan. MET was at the center of the state's new water conflicts because it must draw imported water from the Colorado River and Northern California to meet the needs of millions of Southern Californians. Indeed, MWD's sprawling aqueduct empire interwove seemingly unrelated water conflicts, because reductions from one source forced greater reliance on others.[3]

The Sword of Damocles—*Arizona v. California*

We're all downstream.

Ecologist's motto[4]

Southern California has lived for over four decades under the threat of sharply reduced Colorado River water supplies. In 1963, the U.S. Supreme Court in *Arizona v. California* upheld the interstate allocation of water under the Boulder Canyon Project Act of 1928. The decision limited California to an annual entitlement of 4.4 million acre-feet (MAF) of Colorado River water, plus half of any surplus. The key was the projected surplus. California's water agencies had built sufficient aqueduct and canal capacity to carry over 5.2 MAF of Colorado River water. Yet, by the 1960s stream flow studies of the Colorado River had cut earlier annual estimates from 16.4 to 13.5 MAF, reducing the likely size of future surpluses. With Upper Basin states and Mexico using more of their entitlements to Colorado River water, and Arizona assured 2.8 MAF under the 1963 decision, California was indeed under a Damocles sword. Use of other states' unused apportionment and declarations of surplus by the U.S. Interior Department provided a reprieve for California, allowing the state to consistently take roughly 20 percent more than its basic river allotment.[5]

But it was only a matter of time before the declarations of surplus would end, as unused water from Arizona and Nevada disappeared. Unprecedented Colorado River basin drought conditions starting in 2000 set the stage for an end to surplus declarations. The prospect of losing 800,000 annual acre-feet of water had particularly dire implications for Southern California, which heavily relied on the Colorado River. And the

brunt of any loss was sure to fall on MET, owner of the 1.3-million annual acre-feet capacity Colorado River Aqueduct, but with only fourth-
and fifth-priority claims among California users of the Colorado River—
each for just 550,000 annual acre-feet of water.[6]

The U.S. Supreme Court decision in *Arizona v. California* had a
long-acting "ripple effect" on water resource management in Southern
California. MWD quickly contracted with the California Department of
Water Resources for an extra half-million acre-feet of Northern California
water from the State Water Project, bringing its total entitlement to
2 MAF. According to some L.A. city water officials, MWD then encouraged LADWP to import more water from the Owens Valley and Mono
Basin, thus reducing pressure on MWD's more precarious supplies. This
proved fruitless, as MET could only offer limited political support for
Los Angeles, then under sharp assault by a highly effective environmental
lobby—the Mono Lake Committee. Forced on the defensive, L.A.
ultimately could import less water from the eastern Sierra Nevada, and
thus was forced to take more—not less—water from Metropolitan.
Los Angeles's water diversions from four of seven streams in the Mono
Basin were successfully challenged in a 1983 California Supreme Court
decision that Mono Lake was "a navigable waterway" to be protected in
accordance with "the public trust doctrine." In 1994, the California State
Water Resources Control Board ordered LADWP to stop its stream
diversions until the lake water level reached specified elevations. MWD
responded that it could adjust to the loss of L.A.'s Mono Basin supplies,
but that it would need a functional San Joaquin River Delta to allow
adjustment, in part, through voluntary water transfers.[7]

In parallel with this result was the prolonged battle, not settled
until 1997, between Los Angeles and the Concerned Citizens of Owens
Valley and Owens Valley's Great Basin Unified Air Pollution Control
District demanding that L.A. divert up to 13 percent of its Owens Valley
water supply to mitigate environmental damage, particularly dust clouds.
To date, the LADWP has spent $400 million for mitigation—with the
amount of diverted water estimated at 40,000 AF or more annually and
with an accompanying loss of hydroelectric power. The final result,
imposing unprecedented dust-mitigation requirements on Los Angeles
and agreed to by then L.A. mayor Richard Riordan and then LADWP
general manager S. David Freeman, was approved by the federal

Environmental Protection Agency (EPA). In an intergenerational retort to William Mulholland's 1913 declaration on completion of the Los Angeles Aqueduct—"There it is. Take it."—EPA Regional Administrator Felicia Marcus declared, "The dust stops here."[8]

Thus, the day of reckoning was at hand when Los Angeles would become more dependent on MWD for imported water from both the Colorado River and the State Water Project. MET's worst fears came to pass as Los Angeles's dependence on MWD for water—as low as 3 percent of the city's water needs in the early 1970s (with completion of the second L.A. Aqueduct to the Owens Valley) and just 10 percent in the middle 1980s—increased to 65 percent during the drought year 1991, and only dropped to 34 percent during subsequent nondrought years. Thus the California Department of Water Resources gradually began reallocating water supplies to urban users from San Joaquin farmers, who responded by seeking allies among urban agencies such as MET for support of a second phase of the State Water Project that became the Peripheral Canal project. Decisively defeated by voters in 1982, the Peripheral Canal plan was refloated by MWD in 1990 in the middle of the statewide drought.[9]

Yet MWD general manager Carl Boronkay had serious doubts about the political viability of such an option. A lawyer rather than an engineer by training, Boronkay recognized that after the defeat of the Peripheral Canal, it was a political survival imperative for MET to move beyond the mentality of the so-called water buffaloes, such as Joe Jensen and Earle Blais, who had once dominated the Metropolitan board. "The Met had a one-track mind—to go forward with the State Water Project," Boronkay recalled. "But after the Canal vote it became clear that the State Water Project wasn't going to be completed in any reasonably foreseeable period. . . . We got nervous about the future [and] didn't see any major projects coming on line." During a period when the MWD board experienced a 70 percent turnover, with the new members younger, more diverse in gender and race, more liberal, and more questioning of the "MWD pro-development ethos," the new board majority proved receptive to innovative initiatives from MWD staff. This staff also was being revamped as part of a reform process begun under Boronkay, who won the respect even of strong MET critic Assemblyman Richard Katz. Reforms continued under his successors as MET general manager, John Wodraska and Ron Gastelum.[10]

In MWD's new "A.C. (After Carl)" era, the agency's traditional alliance with agribusiness began to look like a liability. Abandoning the alliance would make it possible to target for reduction and redirection the over 80 percent of California water consumed by agriculture. Boronkay signaled a shift in priorities in 1991 when he convinced the MET board to oppose the traditional veto that rural water agencies maintained over water sales beyond their jurisdiction. In 1992, he supported the federal Central Valley Improvement Act, including a provision for water markets, even though its environmental provisions were vehemently opposed by California agribusiness. According to Congressman George Miller's chief of staff, MWD was critical to the bill's passage: "The Metropolitan Water District is fundamental in water politics in California. You've got to have the Met on your side." At a critical Senate hearing, U.S. Senator Bill Bradley created a stir by leaning his 6-foot 7-inch, frame over the first row of environmental witnesses to greet Boronkay warmly.[11]

Looking for new allies in Sacramento, Boronkay had decided that water transfers to urban users were necessary whether rural interests liked it or not: "We all like farmers, we grow up drawing crayon pictures of farmers. But there is no way . . . people are going to be denied water while farmers plant [water-intensive] alfalfa and rice. . . . Because if we don't get moving, we could be in real jeopardy."[12] Boronkay claimed that "MWD's historic political alignment changed from water users, and urban and agricultural agencies versus nonusers and environmentalists, to water use reallocation, generally from farm to city involving water marketing."[13] By the late 1990s, MET was directly challenging the Seven Party Agreement of 1931 guaranteeing California agriculture the lion's share of Colorado River water. Urban Southern California's "need to sustain and develop its economy," MWD officials told Interior Secretary Bruce Babbitt, "will inevitably require an assessment of whether the intra-California allocations, made by your predecessor in 1931, meet the changes that have occurred in the public's need."[14]

Entering into an unprecedented alliance with the Environmental Defense Fund (EDF, now called Environmental Defense) to eliminate toxins from aquifers that could be a source of reclaimed, relatively inexpensive groundwater, MET sought ever-more diverse water supplies to lessen the impact of the salinity of imported Colorado River water. Colorado River water safety was even more ominously threatened by leaks of radioactive mill waste from Moab, Utah, although the radioactive level of Colorado River water imported into Southern California was still only one third of federally acceptable limits.[15]

Thus, MWD blended its Colorado supplies with less saline Northern California imports, although the blend cost more as MET purchased greater amounts of State Project water, which featured high electricity costs for pumping the water south over the Tehachapi Mountains. The blend tradeoff involved higher organic content, higher-cost, but less-saline State Water Project supplies versus lower organic content, lower-cost, but higher-saline Colorado River supplies. Higher organics also created more trihalomethanes—carcinogens—when chlorine disinfection was used. Yet MWD's ability to take deliveries from the State Water Project was becoming more problematic. In 1986, the California Court of Appeals in *United States v. State Water Board* invoked the "public trust" doctrine to limit State Water Project purchases by state contractors such as Metropolitan. Critics charged that a proposal to cut back MWD's SWP purchases would effectively "institutionalize drought" and would constitute "a dagger plunged into the heart of the Southland."[16]

By the 1990s, the thread holding the Damocles sword hanging over California's dependence on Colorado River water was frayed to the breaking point by a combination of factors. The population of the six-county Los Angeles metropolitan region grew from 7.8 million to 14.7 million between 1960 and 1990—an increase of 88 percent, with a whopping 6 million people added during the 1980s. In the next decade the region's population grew by a modest 12 percent, to 16.5 million by 2000. Droughts in 1976–1977 and 1987–1992 in western state watersheds stressed regional and statewide water delivery systems in unprecedented fashion.[17]

In 1989, the three Lower Basin states—California, Arizona, and Nevada—had for the first time fully used their combined Colorado entitlement of 7.5 MAF. In 1993, the Central Arizona Project delivering water from the Colorado River to Phoenix, Tucson, and Central Arizona farmers was completed. Then, in 1996, the Arizona Water Banking Authority was established to facilitate Arizona's storage of Colorado River water both to replenish its aquifers and for possible interstate sales, such as to Nevada. Some observers also claimed that the Water Banking Authority was a response to the machinations of the billionaire Bass brothers Sid and Lee, allegedly trying to "dry up" MWD's Colorado River Aqueduct to create unused conveyance capacity for Imperial Valley water going to San Diego, or to the lamentations of San Diego water officials of looming regional water shortages, or to both.[18]

As Clinton administration interior secretary Bruce Babbitt repeatedly warned, even while he regularly postponed the event with his yearly declarations of Colorado water "surplus," a day of reckoning was coming for California. Projections for the opening decades of the 21st century were for annual statewide water shortfalls of 2.4 MAF in normal rainfall years to 6.2 MAF in drought years. With 1 acre-foot of water (roughly 326,000 gallons) sustaining two average families for a year, this suggested that California faced looming shortfalls equivalent to the annual water consumption of between 4.8 million and 12.4 million families. Roughly two thirds of these families lived in Southern California and were served by Metropolitan.[19]

Tensions among MWD's then-27 member agencies about how to manage these prospective crises gradually boiled over. The greatest friction point was between MET's largest and most powerful customers— Los Angeles and San Diego. In the early 1990s drought, San Diego water officials claimed to have learned that, in water politics, power ultimately flowed to money. Over the decades, Los Angeles ostensibly had purchased an expensive "drought insurance policy" from MWD that might be cashed in sometime (if preferential rights were indeed enforceable) at San Diego's expense. General manager Maureen Stapleton of the San Diego County Water Authority defined a drought as "when you find out who has the water rights and who does not." Supremely confident that it had right (if not water rights) on its side, in the late 1990s San Diego sued to change MET's preferential rights policies. As noted, the courts ultimately decided that state law was in MWD's favor and that the appropriate remedy for aggrieved San Diego was the state legislature, not the judiciary. Other critical fissures were opening within MET's once-solid member-agency ranks. Older member agencies such as Pasadena and Santa Monica wanted to end the lower "blended rate" that subsidized newer growing areas. Another division was between those members with groundwater they could tap as an alternative to purchases from MWD and those such as San Diego that lacked such supplies.[20]

The California 4.4 Plan

[The California 4.4 Plan is a] peace treaty between the four water agencies and the promise for lasting peace among the seven states that share the Colorado River.

San Diego County Water Authority, "Quantification Settlement Agreement," 2003 [21]

The California 4.4 Plan, as the name suggests, was an effort to reduce California's dependence on the Colorado River to its basic annual entitlement of 4.4 MAF. Responsibility for shaping the plan during the 1990s was shared between the director of the California Department of Water Resources—David Kennedy during Governor Pete Wilson's administration and Thomas Hannigan under Governor Gray Davis—and California's Colorado River Board. The board was an advisory body whose membership included Southern California's six major water agencies: the Palo Verde Irrigation District, the Coachella Valley Water District, the Imperial Irrigation District, the San Diego County Water Authority, the Los Angeles Department of Water and Power, and Metropolitan.[22]

The evolving 4.4 Plan envisaged agricultural seepage recovery by concreting unlined sections of the All-American and Coachella canals. It also addressed the Federal Bureau of Reclamation's demand for "quantification," namely, that the Imperial Irrigation District and Coachella Water District quantify their respective shares for third-priority rights. Beyond quantifying water use—an issue addressed by a 1999 agreement between California water agencies and the U.S. Department of Interior—the even harder issue of imposing usage reductions was put off until a later, second stage. The plan also promoted the transfer and banking of surplus water through the development of water markets both within California, where MWD and the SDCWA favored competing approaches, and interstate with Arizona and other Colorado Basin states. Also looking beyond California's borders, the plan proposed improved reservoir operation on the Colorado River to allow more flexible standards for maintaining water levels. This would make it easier for California to continue to take surplus Colorado River water while gradually reducing consumption down to its basic 4.4 MAF entitlement.[23]

Before the 4.4 Plan, MET had secretly pursued what were called "dream team" negotiations with Las Vegas's Southern Nevada Water Authority (SNWA) involving joint cooperation toward development of water resources. The negotiations or the secrecy or both outraged Arizona's governor Fife Symington but were defended by Nevada governor George Miller: "Arizona's been kicking sand in our face for a long time. And now with the political might of Southern California, it's like we've got a big brother to stand behind us."[24] In 1995, MWD general manager John R. "Woody" Wodraska had announced that his agency had forged an alliance with the SNWA. The alliance remained in place even after California governor Pete Wilson rejected a water-sharing deal between the two different state agencies as a violation of the state government's sovereign prerogative. But then there was a falling out over how to manage surplus water, and the dream turned to nightmare. In March 1996, Wodraska announced to a California General Assembly hearing that the MWD-SNWA deal was "off the table." Years later, SNWA's general manager Pat Mulroy denounced MWD as a "rogue water agency" obsessed with "protecting its stranglehold over California water supplies."[25]

To succeed, the 4.4 Plan faced the formidable dual task of forging a California consensus behind a plan that would also win the approval of the other Colorado Basin States and the federal authorities. To mediate intrastate differences, particularly between MET and SDCWA, seasoned Middle East peace negotiator Abraham D. Sofaer was retained in 1996; he gave up in less than a year. The interstate negotiations, sometimes called "the 7/10 process" because the original Colorado River Compact proceedings (1922) involved seven states and 10 Indian tribes, dragged on throughout most of the 1990s, with the non-California parties agreeing only that California was a chronic water guzzler and must be made to consume less.[26]

Inside California, regional divisions and partisan differences interacted to cause problems. For example, a group of prominent Bay Area Congressional Democrats was joined by a scattering of Southern Californians in June 1998 in a letter assailing CALFED for emphasizing new construction projects rather than conservation measures. Despite such obstacles, momentum in the late 1990s slowly built behind the California 4.4 Plan. In December 1997, Interior Secretary Babbitt increased pressure on the Golden State to live within its 4.4-MAF entitlement, and drew attention to profligate water use by California agriculture. Two months earlier, Governor Wilson signed legislation giving State Department of Water Resources director David Kennedy authority to mediate the MWD-SDCWA dispute over using the Colorado River Aqueduct to carry San Diego's purchase of water from the Imperial Valley.[27]

Despite or perhaps because of its dispute with San Diego, MET not only further embraced the concept of water markets but also advanced water transfers and storage through its massive Eastside (Diamond Valley Lake) Reservoir. Built for $2.1 billion in the Domenigoni and Diamond valleys, near Hemet in southwestern Riverside County, the reservoir when completed in 1999 had a storage capacity of 800,000 acre-feet— nearly double that of all other Southern California reservoirs combined and equal in size to 1,700 Rose Bowls. At a time when Interior Secretary Babbitt was declaring that "dams are not like the pyramids of Egypt that stand for all eternity," the Diamond Valley Reservoir was an environmental trendsetter, built without sacrificing any river flows and surrounded by a 9,000-acre nature preserve. In a gesture of what William Fulton described as "environmental penance," MWD's Carl Boronkay won Riverside County's goodwill, solving its problem with the U.S. Fish and Wildlife Service by making much of the land around the reservoir into a kangaroo rat preserve. Notwithstanding its huge size, Diamond Valley was only one facet of MET's ambitious Integrated Water Resources Plan, unveiled in 1996, that shifted the agency's priorities from water importation to management through a combination of contaminated groundwater retrieval and recovery of wastewater and agricultural water. By 1999, MWD was saving 700,000 AF a year, allowing it to support 3 million more customers with the same volume of water it provided in 1986.[28]

Yet even as the California 4.4 Plan won the support of Metropolitan and other major stakeholders, a storm was brewing. The plan failed to address fundamental questions, putting off until a vague Stage 2 tough decisions between building new surplus-water storage facilities or cutting back on consumption to get California down from 5.3 million to 4.4 MAF of Colorado River water use. Moreover, it proposed "solutions" that were visionary but highly implausible. For example, Arizona residents might eventually sell to Californians stored Colorado River water at premium prices. But it was hard to imagine them ever looking favorably on California's proposals for more flexible definitions of the water level in Lake Mead (the Hoover Dam reservoir) that would make it easier for California to claim extra Colorado River water in normal, nonsurplus years. California continued to be widely distrusted. Such proposals ran the risk of reinforcing skepticism in the other western states and in the nation's capital about whether California had truly reconciled itself to living within the limits of the 4.4 plan. A potpourri of approaches was no substitute for clear-cut priorities and the political will to make hard choices.[29]

In May 2000, California issued its Colorado River Water Use Plan. In July 2000, all seven Colorado Basin states and the Interior Department, agreed in general terms to a plan to "wean California" over 15 years down to 4.4 MAF, with MET slated for 850,000 AF—more than its basic entitlement of 550,000 AF but far below its recent annual draws of 1.2 MAF—during the transition period or so-called soft landing. Interior Secretary Babbitt had spent years trying to instill a sense of urgency by telling Californians that "it is past time for California . . . to get suited up, out of the locker room, and into the game." In January 2001, just as new management was about to arrive, the weary water warrior changed metaphors and made a Camp David–style declaration of "peace on the river," while the Interior Department issued guidelines giving California two years to finalize its blueprint for learning to live within its basic 4.4-MAF Colorado River water entitlement. Many issues were left unsettled, including complaints by treaty partner Mexico that conservation of the Colorado River delta might adversely impact the parched reaches at the northern end of the Gulf of Mexico. As in the Middle East, the pursuit of peace proved elusive, with the devil in the details.[30]

Quantification Quandaries

Negotiations were like the movie "Groundhog Day," in which the hero keeps reliving the same day—trying to "get it right."

MWD General Manager John R. "Woody" Wodraska, 1997[31]

To achieve enforceable, permanent reductions in Colorado River water use, California had to "quantify" the joint entitlement to 3.85 MAF of water of the Imperial Valley, Coachella Valley, and Palo Verde irrigation districts. Without first quantifying each district's individual allotment, enforcing usage limits would be nearly impossible and water transfers would be difficult. Under pressure from both the State Department of Water Resources and the Reclamation Bureau for wasteful water practices, the Imperial Irrigation District entered into a tentative Quantitative Settlement Agreement (QSA) with the Coachella Valley Water District (CVWD), and MWD, the next largest entitlement holder, in October 1999. The QSA was expanded in December 2000 to include the Imperial Valley's water transfer deal with San Diego. Earlier, MET general manager Wodraska had lamented that Southern California water negotiations were like the movie *Groundhog Day*. Now, the negotiations to finalize the details of the QSA—a precondition to the federal government's willingness to continue to provide the Golden State with surplus Colorado River water during a 15-year transition period—also proved a Yogi Berra–like case of "déjà vu all over again."[32]

The obstacle that loomed ever larger during 2001 and 2002 was the Salton Sea. Created in 1905 when Colorado River floods broke through farmland irrigation levees and submerged what had been a great salt flat and prehistoric sea, the Salton Sea was a 360-square-mile inland lake (California's largest) about 80 miles northeast of San Diego in Imperial and Riverside counties. Although replenished by agricultural runoff primarily from Imperial County farms, it was increasingly brackish because it lacked freshwater inflows while suffering intense evaporation that made it 25 percent saltier than the Pacific Ocean. Ironically, because of the loss of historic natural wetland habitats to extensive farming in the Central Valley of California, the sea emerged as an important stopover point for 2 million migratory birds along the Pacific flyway and as a sports fishing area. It also became the special cause of Palm Springs members of Congress Sonny Bono and, later, his widow, Mary Bono, whose congressional district included parts of the bordering Coachella Valley.[33]

In 1998, Congress passed the "Sonny Bono Memorial Salton Sea Remediation Act" mandating action by the federal Bureau of Reclamation, which, however, failed to meet a January 2000 deadline for producing a recommendation for saving the sea. Instead, the Interior Department joined with the U.S. Fish and Wildlife Service in the summer of 2000 to place interested California parties on notice that they would be expected to meet as yet undefined federal standards for protecting the Salton Sea and requesting that they postpone any potential damaging action for three years.[34]

Mary Bono blocked congressional approval of a proposal by Congressmember Duncan Hunter (R-El Cajon) and state legislator David Kelley (R-Palm Springs) that would have allowed the California 4.4 Plan to proceed, including the water transfer to San Diego from Imperial County, despite the possible negative impact on the Salton Sea of reduced agricultural runoff. Congressman Ken Calvert (R-Riverside), who called the Salton Sea "a rotten apple in an otherwise healthy transfer deal," joined Congressman Jim Hansen (R-Utah) in attempting to write the California 4.4 Plan into federal law. In late 2002, Mary Bono joined 22 California elected officials, including Senator Dianne Feinstein, in signing a letter to the Department of the Interior demanding prompt action on its overdue Salton Sea report. The department then offered a series of possible solutions without recommending any, provoking the director of California's Salton Sea Authority to accuse it of having "chosen to punt." Earlier, Bush administration assistant secretary of the interior Bennett Raley had declared that "the California 4.4 Plan cannot and should not be held hostage to the larger issues presented by the Salton Sea." Having decoupled the two issues, he now wondered out loud "whether an investment [in the Salton Sea] of $1 billion would be prudent in light of other national priorities."[35]

The expensive Salton Sea restoration plan that Mary Bono and others favored to break the impasse was put forward by U.S. Filter, the nation's largest water and wastewater treatment firm. The $1.8-billion project involved construction of a huge dike (shaped like a doughnut) that would create a low-saline "river" for birds and fish, separated from a highly salty pond. U.S. Filter would build and operate a desalination plant to produce 500,000 AF per year that would be conveyed to thirsty cities via the Coachella Canal and the Colorado River Aqueduct. Congresswoman Bono continued to lobby the Bush administration (albeit unsuccessfully) for a massive environmental mitigation program for the Salton Sea, even holding January 2004 hearings of the House Energy and Air Quality Subcommittee where advocates urged swift action, comparing "what could happen at the Salton Sea to what has already happened in Central California at Owens Lake."[36]

In parallel with these developments, California Assembly Speaker Emeritus Robert Hertzberg was given the task of ramrodding through an agreement among state and local agencies. Hertzberg's leverage increased dramatically when the California Assembly passed Concurrent Resolution 251, declaring that signing the QSA by December 31, 2002, was of "utmost importance to the people of California." This was the deadline that would avert the threatened January 1, 2003, cutoff by the Interior Department of the Golden State's allocation of surplus Colorado River water.[37]

Demanding that the parties agree by October 15, 2002, Hertzberg hammered out an apparent compromise that included the generally acceptable caps of 3.1 MAF of Colorado River water for IID, 330,000 AF for CVWD, and 550,000 AF for MWD, which also would have a priority claim to any additional surplus water. In addition, MWD would receive 110,000 AF annually from its 1989 transfer deal with the IID. The state of California agreed to pay for the lining of the All-American Canal, with approximately 77,000 AF of conserved water going to MWD. Also incorporated was a proposal by environmental groups and MWD that Imperial County fallow land make up at least part of the water to be transferred to San Diego, and thereby reduce the impact on the Salton Sea. Despite its initial vehement opposition to anything that might imperil Imperial County's farming culture and economy, the IID negotiators grudgingly accepted a five-year, 50,000 annual AF land-fallowing program in return for a Christmas wish list of concessions including "no surprise" assurances that would protect it from liability for environmental mitigation or possible federal punitive action reducing water entitlement because of wasteful agricultural practices. In particular, the QSA draft contained a "condition subsequent" that a federally approved Habitat Conservation Plan for the Salton Sea would be completed by the end of 2003 "acceptable in form, substance and coverage to IID . . . in its sole, complete and absolute discretion."[38]

Other conditions subsequently gave Metropolitan and the San Diego County Water Authority the right to bail out of the agreement if environmental mitigation costs became unacceptably high. MWD signed on despite its unabated unhappiness about the absence of an ironclad guarantee that it would receive surplus water during the 15-year transition period gradually reducing California's annual usage to 4.4 MAF.

After several days of around-the-clock negotiations, a ceremony was held on October 15, 2002, unveiling a QSA Framework that negotiator Hertzberg hailed as the dawn of "lasting peace on the river."[39]

But almost immediately the QSA Framework began to fall apart. None of the parties would take responsibility, yet the manifest cause was the inability of the IID "to sell" the agreement to its deeply divided Imperial Valley constituency. On December 31, 2002, the IID board vetoed the Hertzberg deal, and instead voted three-to-two in favor of a sham "agreement." The IID-approved version of the QSA was festooned with provisions allowing Imperial Valley to back out of the deal, and also demanding an additional $200 million in loan guarantees and grants to IID for mitigation. The IID's agreement was meaningless, because the CVWD and MWD had already rejected its unilaterally imposed provisions. To critics, a one-man majority on a water board representing 100,000 Imperial Valleyites had imperiled the water future of the more than 18 million Southern Californians dependent on Metropolitan.[40]

The Spigot Is Closed

So we beat on, boats against the current, borne back ceaselessly into the past.

The Great Gatsby, *quoted by Assistant Interior Secretary Bennett Raley*[41]

That same day, Assistant Interior Secretary Raley announced that the Interior Department would implement its long-threatened "nondiscretionary obligation" to limit California's Colorado River water supply to 4.4. MAF. Washing her hands of California, Interior Secretary Gale Norton declared that the state's QSA quagmire was now a local matter and not her business "from a philosophical and legal perspective." MWD's allotment would be reduced to 550,000 AF, but IID was singled out for a reduction below the 3.1 MAF it would have received under the QSA to 2.8 MAF. Ironically, Nevada was also penalized under the suspension of "surplus" water deliveries, a perceived injustice that helped explain Southern Nevada Water Agency general manager Pat Mulroy's outburst against the better-positioned MWD as a "rogue water agency."[42]

Theoretically, there still was an opening for California's surplus allotments to Colorado River water to be resumed. The spigot could be turned on again—provided that there was a binding agreement to the QSA Framework imposing specific, permanent caps. Practically, however, the onset of a new drought cycle beginning in 2000 had ended the period of relatively full reservoir conditions in the Colorado River Basin. Absent the intervention of a rainmaker, there would likely be little surplus to share for the indefinite future. The failure of marathon negotiations to achieve a viable agreement produced a lament of frustration from Assistant Secretary Raley, quoting from *The Great Gatsby*. The diverse reactions of major California players to the cutoff of surplus Colorado River water were telling. IID sued the Interior Department in federal court and, on March 18, 2003, obtained a temporary injunction. Its Colorado River allotment was restored to 3.1 MAF, but the district would have to run the gauntlet of future environmental hearings in which it would have to prove to the Interior Department—"the River Master" of the Lower Colorado—that its water uses were "reasonable and beneficial" rather than wasteful.[43]

MET had a more ambivalent reaction to the cutoff. Although ideally it would have liked to "firm up" its Colorado River supplies, it recognized as a practical matter that this might not be possible in what was being called "a new era of limits." Whether or not the QSA was implemented, the likelihood was for less surplus water. In August 2003, a Caltech Jet Propulsion Laboratory researcher issued a report, commissioned by MWD, arguing that drier years were ahead for the West, with dire implications for California. MET was not enthusiastic about a deal requiring it to pay tens of millions of dollars in subsidies for what MWD spokesman Adan Ortega called "fictional water" that the drought-stricken Colorado River might not be able to deliver in coming years.[44]

The implications for MET were that it should go full speed ahead with its strategic shift from water importation to conservation, storage, conjunctive use, and even desalination. Initially, MWD feared that it could afford to go only two years without surplus Colorado River water before facing a crisis. But soon it upped its estimate to 20 years. There also was the consideration that, if the deal fell through and the Interior Department punished Imperial Valley farmers for their profligate ways, MET would be next in line for whatever extra Colorado River water was freed up. Did MWD really want to give up its right to legally challenge water guzzling in the Imperial Valley and doubly subsidize profligate farmers whose wasteful ways were already underwritten by the federal government? In contrast, IID board chair Lloyd Allen smelled "subterfuge and political intrigue" by the "regionally dominant" MWD, which "has long coveted the Imperial Valley's water," and, now in cahoots with the Interior Department, "has designed, as nearly as we can tell, to separate the Imperial County from its water."[45]

From the perspective of many in MWD's management, the agency was the victim of "water torture" during 2003 by other parties that wanted to revive the California 4.4 Plan and QSA much more than MWD did. At a March 2003 meeting of the Colorado Basin states, the state of California pressured its feuding Southern California water agencies to present a united front behind a "new and final" QSA. Although lacking Neville Chamberlain's umbrella and bowler hat, Governor Davis hailed this yet again as a definitive "peace treaty."[46] Actually, the revised document was an "iffy affair" that promised no more than that the signatories would recommend that their agencies sign on when a series of conditions were met. Among the conditions: that the IID lawsuit against the Interior Department would be settled; that the Interior Department would reinstate the Surplus Guidelines; that the California legislature would pass environmental regulatory relief; and that there would be no Habitat Protection Plan for the Salton Sea imposed that was unacceptable to the Imperial Valley. In addition, the revised QSA was predicated on the Imperial Valley meeting its obligations with temporary land fallowing during the 15-year transition period. In contrast to conservation reducing water consumption, fallowing was, as water analyst James S. Lochhead put it, "a measure that can be quickly implemented, but also quickly reversed. . . . As a result, the permanence of the program to reduce California's reliance on surplus Colorado River water is again brought into question."[47]

By the summer of 2003, the controversy surrounding the revised QSA was more toxic than the Salton Sea. Denying that it had ever definitively agreed to "the definitive" deal, the MET board passed a resolution— calling for all involved parties to fund their share of program costs—that the other parties deemed a declaration of war. In 1998, MWD had been threatened with dissolution by California legislators if it failed to accept the water-marketing deal between San Diego and the Imperial Valley that had been negotiated in secret without its participation. Now the gambit was repeated, with the San Diego, Imperial Valley, and Coachella Valley water agencies threatening to exclude MWD from the QSA negotiations, and the governor's representative Richard Katz, a long-time MWD critic, "jokingly" suggesting that the state might approve an end run around the agency. Working with San Diego and IID, the Davis administration proposed to raid up to $250 million from Proposition 50 funds to pay for the environmental mitigation costs of the IID-SDCWA transfer. Coupled with the $235 million from the state's general fund that was approved to cover the costs of canal-lining projects, this would amount to nearly a half billion dollar state subsidy for the deal. The proposal was made while the state was in the middle of a severe budget crisis that would lead to the Davis recall campaign. Among the negotiators, only MWD opposed the proposal. But once MET made the proposal public, environmental groups also voiced opposition. Under pressure from key state senators, an embarrassed Davis administration dropped the raid on Proposition 50 funds but was furious at MWD.[48]

Fearful that Metropolitan would "ravage" Northern California in seeming "Owens Valley fashion" if the Imperial Valley deal fell through, Assemblyman Joe Canciamilla, chair of the Assembly Water, Parks, and Wildlife Committee, seriously proposed introducing two-barreled legislation forcing MWD to open its aqueduct to water purchased by San Diego from the IID, and blocking transfers from the north of any water to make up what MWD lost because of the failure of the QSA. "I don't want to reopen the north-south water wars but at the same time I'm not just prepared to sit idly by and see California's water supply jeopardized by the failure to get this agreement because of one water agency's intransigence," Canciamilla said. "There's going to be a price to pay." Closer to home, IID board chair Allen exclaimed, "If Metropolitan wants to be left out in the cold, so be it."[49] MWD negotiators called the bluff and refused to budge. In response, the SDCWA, IID, and CVWD met with the Davis administration to craft a QSA without Metropolitan's participation. In the new "sans MWD" scheme, state legislation would override MWD's ownership and operation of the Colorado River Aqueduct, and the federal government would ignore MWD's Colorado River rights. When this was presented to representatives of the Colorado River basin states and the federal government, the reaction was swift: this was unworkable, and MWD had to be part of any real QSA.

Cooler heads eventually prevailed. In August, the California legislature passed a three-bill package needed to implement the QSA, including State Senator Sheila Kuehl's bill (SB 317) easing endangered species protections to facilitate Imperial Valley conservation, the provision of Proposition 50 money to line leaky canals, and the promise of $330 million to restore the Salton Sea to be raised by the state government playing in the water market. Governor Davis in language reminiscent of previous hyperbolic declarations, called the legislation "a historic shift in water policy" that would "end decades of confrontation and replace it with unprecedented cooperation."[50] Joining the San Diego County Water Authority, MWD signed on to the deal, with MWD board chair Phillip Pace declaring, "For the first time everybody's really ready to put this thing to bed." The IID also began gravitating toward approval because, in the words of Imperial board director Bruce Kuhn, it "gives us the opportunity for peace and stability in water delivery. . . . All the dirt in the world isn't worth a dime without water."[51]

Yet Andy Horne, another IID board member, still demanded "iron-clad assurances" from the Bush administration, which the Interior Department claimed it could not legally give, guaranteeing that Imperial Valley would never be subjected to cutbacks for wasting water: "We need something that tells us that as long as we're helping the rest of California that they're going to leave us alone. We don't have that yet. . . . A partial peace treaty doesn't work any better here than it does in the Middle East." For their own reasons, San Diego environmental groups, including Southern Californians for Sustainable Water Use and San Diegans for the Salton Sea, also opposed the QSA, although statewide environmental groups and the National Audubon Society supported it as a means of reducing pressure to import water from Northern California.[52]

In October 2003, IID finally agreed to a package that purported to be "the final-final solution" to the quantification quagmire. The deal featured the Imperial–San Diego water transfer of up to 200,000 AF of water annually for from 45 to 75 years at approximately $50 million per year. IID also agreed to potentially sell an additional 1.6 MAF of water over 15 years to the state, which would then resell the water at a higher price to MET or others, with the estimated $300-million profit to be used to fund a state-operated fund to rehabilitate the Salton Sea. A final lubricant for the deal was a commitment to pay an additional $133 million for environmental mitigation by IID jointly with San Diego and Coachella Valley.[53] IID director Horne, who still voted no, complained, "We have compromised and compromised, and struck bottom line after bottom line. This is a clear example of the type of deal you get when your bottom line is 'where do we sign.'" Director Rudy Maldonado, who voted yes, pictured the result as a rural David versus urban Goliath struggle won by the Goliath of the all-powerful state government and the region's big water agencies: "They're not here for the asking. They're here for the taking."[54]

Now the question was whether and when the federal government would again turn on California's surplus Colorado River water spigot. Given the long-term drought affecting the Colorado River Basin states and the resulting receding water level in Lake Mead (only a little over half filled in 2004), this was not likely to happen for years. The 2003 update of the California Water Plan, known as Bulletin 160, followed up on the 4.4 Plan by proposing to reduce Colorado River water usage using a multilayered strategy, on the local, state, and interstate levels, that used market incentives as well as regulatory strategies. Eschewing the search for a single "magic bullet," the state water plan favored a combination of approaches including heightened conservation, more groundwater extraction, water transfers, water storage banking, new storage and conveyance facilities, desalination plants, and improved reservoir operations. By and large, the bulletin echoed MWD's Integrated Resources Plan and plans for management of Colorado River water. The state plan also proposed a two-tier strategy, starting with an emphasis on conservation and water transfers within California.[55]

The CALFED Bay-Delta Program

> In water wars, when Californians organize a firing squad, they form a circle facing inwards.
>
> *Interior Secretary Bruce Babbitt*[56]

The threat of reduced supplies of Colorado River water heightened MET's focus and reliance on local water supplies, conservation, reclamation, desalination, and on water projects in the more verdant northern half of the state. Voter sentiment in the Golden State toward water projects, however, shifted dramatically in the years following approval in 1960 of the nearly $1.8-billion State Water Project. In 1982, California voters approved a state ballot referendum to cease funding the $1.3 billion Peripheral Canal. The project had called for the annual diversion to the California Aqueduct of Sacramento–San Joaquin Delta water that would otherwise run off into the San Francisco Bay. Despite the support of most of agribusiness, major water districts in Central as well as Southern California, and the California Departments of Water Resources and Fish and Game, the Peripheral Canal was defeated decisively—the first rejection of a California water project since the 1920s. At the time, *Los Angeles Times* cartoonist Paul Conrad showed a hulking, cigar-chomping figure, labeled "Northern California," standing on a state map and urinating toward Los Angeles. The Northerners more than reciprocated such felicities.[57]

The "no" campaign mobilized a crazy-quilt coalition of environmental critics, large agribusiness corporations, such as the J. G. Boswell and Salyer Land companies, that wanted no environmental restrictions, and Northern Californians who simply didn't like the Southland. A representative of a Northern California water board expressed a regional consensus: "We don't want to give the Metropolitan Water District the plumbing to suck us dry in a drought year." Reflecting widespread skepticism that the project would be managed so as not to damage Northern California, State Senator Peter Behr of Marin County announced, "You can't contain a thirsty beast in a paper cage."[58]

Just as the statewide drought of 1976–1977 gave impetus to the ill-fated Peripheral Canal proposal (which actually originated as early as the 1960s), the drought of the early 1990s, together with the prospective reduction in California's share of Colorado River water and the deterioration of the delta's water resource environment, spurred a new project. The CALFED Bay-Delta Program was meant to coordinate and complete the unfinished links in California's interconnected empire of major water projects. In December 1994, a consortium of 14 state and federal agencies signed the Bay-Delta Accord. Although the accord was initiated and largely driven by public stakeholders, including MWD, it ultimately was signed by urban, agricultural, business, and environmental organizations as well. This was a three-year stopgap measure, meant to be finalized by

1997 but subsequently extended, that sought to stabilize—pending the engineering of a long-term solution—the water quality, ecology, and habitat of the Sacramento–San Joaquin Delta. Finding a solution was critical because the delta provided drinking water for 22 million Californians (over 18 million in Southern California) and irrigated 5 million acres of the Golden State's 28 million acres of farmland.[59]

The federal Central Valley Improvement Act of 1992, together with federal regulatory rulings under the Endangered Species Act, had created conflicts with the State Water Resources Board. CALFED emerged as a cooperative attempt by the California Water Policy Council and the Federal Ecosystem Directorate to end federal-state friction over water policy. Yet though the signatories were governmental entities, the accord also signaled a truce among California's triad of water policy stakeholders. Urban water districts had concerns about reliability and the potability of brackish water with high bromide content. Agribusiness desired more water storage capacity while eschewing environmental and endangered species mandates that reduced irrigation flows. And environmentalists were less insistent on new regulations and more responsive to using market incentives to encourage conservation in the wake of conservative Republican victories in the state capitol and the U.S. Congress in November 1994. All three stakeholder groups struck a more conciliatory pose toward the new campaign to "save the Delta."[60]

In May 1995, the accord evolved into a formal planning mechanism—the CALFED Bay-Delta Program—that also incorporated public and interest group participation through a 32-member Bay-Delta Advisory Council. CALFED began with four prime objectives—ecosystem restoration, efficient water use, improved water quality, and safer levees—but soon added watershed management and water transfer policy design. CALFED also announced six "solution principles": (1) reduced conflict among beneficial uses (such as fisheries, irrigation, and water quality); (2) equitable distribution of benefits and burdens; (3) affordability; (4) broad political support; (5) durable implementation; and (6) no hidden consequences or "redirected impacts" inside or outside the delta.[61]

Not surprisingly, CALFED's interest-group advisers began persuading and even pressuring to shape policy in their favor. Central Valley farmers acting through the Wilson administration in Sacramento convinced CALFED that an early proposal to permanently retire 800,000 acres of farmland would cause a "redirected impact" in violation of the solution principles. But environmentalists, acting through the Interior Department, attempted to override an interim understanding that no more than 1.1 MAF annually would be diverted to protect fisheries. Ironically, officials from San Francisco, an environmental hotbed, did not want to relinquish their city's pristine Hetch Hetchy municipal supplies to replenish dwindling salmon runs. (As of 2005, San Francisco had not dedicated a single drop of water to the protection of the Bay-Delta watershed.) A compromise was ultimately reached whereby farmers would be compensated for any additional water diversions that benefited salmon at their expense. In a similar vein, environmentalist opposition to the inclusion of $300 million for planning and construction of reservoirs and off-stream storage led to the withdrawal from the June 1998 state ballot of a $1.3-billion general-obligation water management bond favored by the governor. The issue was resolved in March 2000 under Governor Gray Davis when a $1.97-billion bond measure—the Safe Drinking Water, Clean Water, Watershed Protection and Flood Protection Bond Act—was approved by California voters.[62]

Conflict and tumult were regular features of CALFED's existence. The contentious policy battles contributed to CALFED's decision to abandon in 1998 its original strategy and schedule for issuing a specific, detailed blueprint. Instead, CALFED punted the issue back to the public by releasing a 2,200-page environmental impact statement-report (EIS-EIR) offering broad programmatic alternatives for restoring the delta—one of which would be chosen as the basis for drawing up "a preferred alternative." The 75-day EIS-EIR public comment period was marked by an escalation of the rhetorical sparring among interest groups that was already a regular feature of the CALFED process. Environmentalists were divided. Some, especially from the Central Valley, were willing to consider a comprehensive plan emphasizing environmental enhancement and conservation measures. Others, especially those based in the San Francisco Bay area, were outraged. Environmental Defense attorney Tom Graff, for example, called the EIS-EIR "a document stuck in reverse, a wishful throwback to the era of big dams, sterile channels, and lifeless canals." Amid the mounting controversy, Governor Wilson met with Interior Secretary Babbitt to issue a joint declaration recommitting state and federal governments to the issuance of a final draft plan for the delta by year's end.[63]

CALFED's first restoration blueprint was issued in 1996, the year California voters approved a $995-million water bond issue with two thirds earmarked for restoration of the delta. The revised draft document, released in December 1998, featured three prosaically named alternatives. The first or "Alternative System Conveyance" option involved minor structural changes to improve fish and flow control barriers in the South Delta. The second or "Modified Through Delta Conveyance" alternative proposed dredging a shallow new channel or canal to improve water flows from north to south. The third—the "Open Channel Isolated Facility" or "Dual System Conveyance"—alternative proposed construction of a new canal bringing better-quality Sacramento River water around the delta to the aqueducts pumping it to the south. With total capital cost estimates ranging from $9 billion (Alternative 1) to $10.5 billion (Alternative 3) spread over 20 to 30 years, all three alternatives envisaged $1 billion for restoring the delta ecosystem and Central Valley river habitat. Other common elements included substantial expenditures to shore up delta levees, reduce polluted runoff from farms and mines, encourage greater water efficiency, and enlarge water storage capacity and foster a market for water transfers. Each alternative would have also increased diversion through a new connection to State Water Project and Central Valley Project pumps in the South Delta.[64]

Alternative 1—quickly dubbed "CALFED Lite"—was least objectionable to environmentalists because of its emphasis on conservation rather than construction. Alternative 3—also called "Son of the Peripheral Canal"—was the most controversial option because its "isolated conveyance facility" was a CALFED euphemism for a new canal. The conveyance facility was similar to the Peripheral Canal rejected by voters in 1982 but would have had half the planned carrying capacity. All three alternatives offered more ecosystem protection than the 1982 proposal and also included plans for increased water reliability through above- and below-ground storage facilities that would equal the storage capacity of the Shasta Dam.[65]

A statewide business coalition including 28 California CEOs endorsed decisive action, but its supportive letter to President Clinton and Governor Wilson focused on lobbying for "an expanded voluntary water

transfer market [that] is essential to any successful long-term solution."
Southern California's big agricultural interests approved of increased
water transfers, although Delta Valley farmers did not always concur.
Yet Richard Pombo (R-Tracy), the congressman representing the delta,
threatened to scuttle CALFED in the House Appropriations Committee
despite the prominent inclusion of features universally favored by agricultural interests, such as increased water storage capacity. Congressmember
Pombo was reacting to local agriculture's dislike of another element
shared by the three proposals, the Ecosystem Restoration Program Plan.
This plan anticipated converting between 138,000 and 191,000 acres of
the delta to wildlife habitat or "wildlife friendly agricultural land."
(Later, Pombo was instrumental in the passage of HR 2828, which authorized a balanced plan, including some ecosystem restoration.[66])

MWD weighed in and reiterated its commitment to play "a leadership role" in CALFED. A new canal carrying fresh water around the
brackish Delta would resolve MWD's water quality concerns, and increased diversionary capacity might make it easier for the agency to conclude water acquisition deals with delta suppliers such as the Arvin-
Edison and Semitropic water storage districts. The failure of CALFED,
warned MET's "Woody" Wodraska after a visit to Wall Street, could
imperil MWD's future credit worthiness. MET asked for more "local assurances" that Southern California growth projections would be taken
into account and that Southern California would not be expected to provide "approximately three-quarters of total conservation and reclamation
for the State." The San Diego County Water Authority—angered by
MWD's criticism of San Diego's plan to buy Colorado River water from
Imperial County—threatened the otherwise universal support for
CALFED among Southern California water agencies. SDCWA demanded
its own "local assurance package" from MWD before agreeing to any
CALFED alternative.[67]

"Hide the children and the faint of heart," declared the *Los Angeles
Times* in a March 1998 editorial, "the peripheral canal debate has
officially begun." Agribusiness, which had been divided over the Peripheral Canal in 1982, was unified behind CALFED in 1998. Environmentalists, previously unified against the Peripheral Canal, were now split, with
Bay Delta Advisory co-chair Sunne McPeak and activist Marc Reisner
supportive of CALFED. But Northern California still bristled with

regional resentment against "dams and ditches" that would benefit Southern California. Bay Area representatives in Congress voiced skepticism about cost and efficiency, and one candid critic explained, "If you don't water it, it won't grow."[68]

Responding to an editorial in the *Oakland Tribune* condemning the CALFED proposals for "smelling like a plain old water grab," MWD deputy general manager Timothy Quinn pleaded, "This is not a Southern California water grab. The system will not go out of control." He urged proponents to work "to eliminate the fear factor. That's the engine that has driven the controversy: fear of Southern California." Yet MWD rejected Northern California demands that MWD unilaterally reduce its entitlement from the State Water Project as "a sign of good faith."[69] Given the manifold obstacles to achieving consensus, CALFED took the path of least resistance. In 1998, it substituted for a single proposal a Preferred Program Alternative—the first, least controversial package of Bay-Delta improvements, with other steps to follow only when they became necessary. This new approach produced an angry backlash by MWD, warning that "Southern California's $500 billion economy, quality of life, and environment will be threatened." Yet MWD finally acceded to the decision by Governor Wilson, a Peripheral Canal supporter, to put off consideration of any such project for at least seven years. Then CALFED prolonged the process of public review—and policy refinement—into 1999, in hopes that a new governor might be willing and able to invest fresh political capital in CALFED and delta restoration.[70]

In early 1999, Governor Gray Davis inherited CALFED's contentious history. In many respects, the first year of his term proved a reprise of the last year of Wilson's, with new rounds of public hearings and federal-state summits. CALFED went back to the drawing board and forged a revised "Stage 1" Plan that demoted the development of dams— "groundwater and/or surface water storage"—from a proposal to a possibility, to be subjected to further study by experts evaluating "CALFED's progress toward these measurable water quality goals" of "50 ppb [parts per billion] bromide and three ppm TOC [total organic carbon]." Environmentalists rejected even the study of "subsidized, damaging projects," whereas MWD announced that its new top priority was improved "drinking-water quality . . . that meets the minimum health standards" for Southern California where the salt content of water is "four to six times higher . . . than the national average," posing "critical . . . public health risks" while costing hundreds of millions because of "additional water treatment [costs] and accelerated corrosion of not only manufacturing facilities but residential hot water heaters and home plumbing systems."[71]

Adjusting to new realities, MWD announced that it was willing to settle for an annual average of 1.5 MAF from the State Water Project (less than its 2-MAF entitlement) by 2020 if water quality were improved. After considerable controversy had arisen over Alternative 3 (the infamous "dual facility"), Don Owen, a MET board member from Orange County who in the early 1960s, as a young DWR engineer, had originated the idea of the Peripheral Canal, led the charge to change MWD's policy to support a "Through-Delta Facility." As he told others, "we have to stop chasing our tail over the Peripheral Canal." Owen felt that MET would gain more by dropping its quixotic quest for an isolated facility and that a peripheral canal eventually might emerge, but only if Northern California wanted one. MWD has stuck to this policy ever since.[72]

The ultimate judge of CALFED proposals would be the California electorate. With CALFED frozen in a "study-now, decide-later approach," critics were beginning to call it "Calfail." At this point, Governor Davis stepped in. Late in 1999 at his urging, the legislature slated Santa Claus–style environmental bond issues, Proposition 12 and Proposition 13, with something for everyone, to appear on the March 2000 ballot. Not to be confused with the 1978 property tax-reduction measure, the new Proposition 13 included $630 million for infrastructure programs, $468 million for watershed protection, $355 million for clean water and water recycling, $292 million for flood protection, $155 million for water conservation, and $70 million for safe drinking water. In 1996, Proposition 204 had been successfully sold to 63 percent of the voters as "The Safe, Clean, Reliable Water Supply Act." Public health considerations were a key factor in 2000 as well. Proposition 13 benefited from emotionally charged revelations that the process used to disinfect drinking water from the delta produced a byproduct—trihalomethanes—that may cause cancer and increase the risk of miscarriages.[73]

Yet soon after the two new bond issues passed, the underlying interest group conflicts began to resurface. By the summer of 2000, hard choices were increasingly difficult to postpone. Under pressure from both the governor and the secretary of the interior, CALFED moved behind closed doors to forge a Framework Agreement and a Record of Decision—*California's Water Future: A Framework for Action*. Essentially, "preferred program" status was bestowed on 1998's Alternative 2 for a modified or "enhanced" conveyance system that would require building a short, "through-Delta" canal (only 7 miles long) to carry fresher Sacramento River water into the Central Delta on its way to the Tracy pumps to the southwest. Although it supported this alternative, MWD was unsure whether the benefits justified the $400-million-plus cost. A new peripheral canal was kept off the drawing boards but was not ruled out as a future option if this more limited approach failed to produce a sufficient improvement in state water quality. CALFED released *California's Water Future*—an overview of the 7-year, $8.7-billion, Stage 1 of the 30-year CALFED program—at a June 2000 ceremony attended by the major water system stakeholders. Targets and timetables were spelled out in the 6,500-page EIR-EIS issued in July, and Secretary Babbitt met with Governor Davis in late August to sign an implementation plan.[74]

The veneer of consensus collapsed almost immediately. Up north, Assemblyman Mike Machado (D-Stockton) warned that "I know where the MWD is going to start looking, and I don't want them looking in my back yard." Down south, State Senator Steve Peace (D-San Diego) responded to a speech by MET's Tim Quinn about the "water-use efficiency ethic" with the riposte that it was "the first time I ever heard the words MET and ethics in the same sentence." The new state administration of Governor Davis also showed signs of indecision. On the one hand, it initially pleased environmentalists when State Resources secretary Mary Nichols announced support of Interior Department plans to help fisheries by releasing 800,000 AF of Central Valley Project water into the San Francisco Bay and Sacramento–San Joaquin Valley Delta. On the other hand, it seemed to shift position by claiming that the Interior Department should only act within the context of the CALFED process. Environmental Defense's Tom Graff spoke for environmentalists who felt betrayed by the Davis administration and by CALFED in August 1999 when the agency issued a revision suggesting that there might be circumstances where preserving water quality could require building of a peripheral canal after all.[75]

Yet according to *Los Angeles Times* reporter George Skelton, Governor Davis had always disliked MWD, which he described in a 1999 interview as "the most ineffective organization on the planet earth" that "should be [put out of] its misery." Further down the road—in 2003—the governor became even more piqued at MET for supposedly impeding the QSA and questioning his administration's proposal to redirect $250 million in Proposition 50 monies to lubricate the San Diego–Imperial Valley water deal. The governor responded by threatening to dump into the sea $10 million in water that MWD had purchased, rather than store it in an Oroville reservoir.[76]

The *Framework* and Record of Decision had precipitated a small flood of lawsuits in 2000. The Regional Council of Rural Counties was joined by the Central and South Delta water agencies in its suit against CALFED. The council chair Tom Bamert, who wanted to "get rid of" CALFED altogether, argued that the CALFED blueprint "over-promised water to Southern California" and threatened the groundwater supplies of "area of origin" counties, such as Placer, El Dorado, Sutter, and Yuba, all of which asserted a superior, prior claim to the water. The California Farm Bureau Federation joined the suit, charging that CALFED as proposed would put "a million acres of farmland in peril." An array of Northern California politicians attacked CALFED's governance commission as a Southern California power grab. Environmentalists were split. Even an Orange County water district sued. From its perspective, however, the plan had too little, rather than too much, water diversion, and it argued the plan was insufficient because a full-fledged peripheral canal was needed.[77]

In partisan terms, the year 2000 was the turn of Republicans, perhaps unhappy about CALFED's association with a Democratic State House and White House as well as its inaction on major water projects, to take their potshots at the agency. Congressmember John Doolittle (R-Rocklin) introduced legislation that, in return for $60 million in federal funding, would put CALFED under congressional oversight because "It's time to improve water supplies as well as water quality." Congressmember George Miller (D-Martinez), representing a Bay Area urban constituency and also a critic of CALFED from an environmental perspective, opposed the bill because it would reignite "the California water wars of the last century."[78]

CALFED's political ground in Washington remained insecure during the George W. Bush administration. In 2001, there was a semblance of bipartisanship when Senator Dianne Feinstein joined GOP Congressmember Ken Calvert in introducing legislation that would "preauthorize" up to $3 billion in CALFED projects, including controversial storage projects such as raising the Shasta Dam. The Davis administration and Metropolitan supported Feinstein's initiative, although it was opposed on environmental grounds by her colleague Senator Barbara Boxer. In the House, Congressmember George Miller introduced a bill, backed by 25 environmental groups, rejecting Feinstein's emphasis on storage in favor of recycling, desalination, and ecosystem restoration projects. Soon Feinstein discovered (as journalist Edward Epstein put it) that occupying the middle ground in water wars "can get you drowned." The seas failed to part for CALFED when it received no federal money for 2001. Then Senators Feinstein and Boxer jointly tried to get permanent, rather than annual, funding starting with the 2002 budget. They had to settle for $30 million for 2002 only. By 2003, the two California senators were again on the same side, as Feinstein changed positions and opposed Congressmember Calvert's continuing attempts to "untether" CALFED from the 2000 Record of Decision's environmental specifics as well as to "fast-track" major CALFED water storage projects.[79]

In addition to this legal and political barrage, CALFED, starting in 2000, suffered administrative and financial reversals in both Sacramento and Washington. CALFED's executive director resigned, hobbling for a time its lobbying ability. The California legislature rejected $135 million in CALFED funding that Governor Davis included in his 2000–2001 budget. The individual agencies comprising CALFED still had access to $700 million in bond funding under Propositions 204 and 13 as well as $28 million in other appropriations in the state budget. However, hopes that these resources would be supplemented by new federal money were dashed when the U.S. Senate, following the lead of the House, killed additional funding for CALFED. San Francisco environmentalist Gary Bobker said that "There's a lot of doubt over the sustainability of CalFed," and the new CALFED executive director Patrick Wright warned, "Next year, all bets are off unless we get a major infusion of federal money." The state and local agencies funded CALFED in 2000 with a combination of $739 million, but the full program would ultimately require at least $8.6 billion including $2.4 billion from Washington. The state and federal governments put the best face possible on the situation by jointly signing the "2000 CALFED Board Record of Decision" that mostly restated existing initiatives but was advertised as a new cooperative plan to meet California's water needs.[80]

During 2001, elements of the CALFED program were implemented on an incremental basis, but the fragmentation of its political support also continued. In Washington, Congressmember Calvert and Senator Feinstein each introduced CALFED reauthorization bills incorporating changes favored by farming interests. Next, Congressmember Miller offered his own, more environment-friendly version of CALFED reauthorization. The authors of these competing bills each claimed that their own legislative proposals embodied CALFED's true spirit and intent. At the same time, they criticized each other's bills for changing CALFED's provisions in fundamental ways that risked the program's collapse. "I think you're very close to destroying the CalFed process," Congressmember Miller warned of Senator Feinstein's proposal. As California legislators debated among themselves, the U.S. Congress in 2001, just as it had done in 2000, denied CALFED funding. No federal money was forthcoming, because California's representatives in Washington failed to agree on a reauthorization formula.[81]

CALFED's goal of a consensual plan for delta restoration remained an elusive one. CALFED had yet to secure state and federal monies needed to implement its expensive blueprint, but it had made real progress when nearly two thirds of Californians, in March 2000, voted for Proposition 12's and Proposition 13's nearly $4-billion bond authorization in environmental enhancements. This achievement was considerable, because it required overcoming the lingering shadow of the Peripheral Canal's 1982 defeat. In 1997, opponents of a new canal still outnumbered supporters 64 to 20 percent in Northern California and 45 to 36 percent in Southern California. CALFED supporters were able to persuade Californians by framing proposals in terms of water quality and safety at a time when the threat of contamination extended beyond Southern California to the Sacramento–San Joaquin Valley Delta and even San Francisco Bay and its estuaries. Public health concerns proved the most compelling arguments in the campaign to sell CALFED proposals to the public and its elected representatives.[82]

Even CALFED's sharpest critics admitted that the program's collapse might be far worse than the current policy battles. The spectacle of the delta farmers who had sued CALFED threatening to sue each other in 2000 offered a glimpse of a worse future. The Westlands Water District in Fresno County, which historically received all its water from the federal Central Valley Project, filed an application with the state to divert 520,000 annual AF from the San Joaquin River. This would leave no water in dry years and not much more in wet years for the 15,000 small farmers in 25 irrigation districts belonging to the Friant Water Users Authority on the east side of the San Joaquin Valley. Westlands claimed "area of origin" priority because it was located in the same western county as the Friant Dam supplying the eastern farmers for 50 years. Friant countered that the Westlands move was a selfish attempt to monopolize Central Valley Project flows that violated longstanding public and private understandings.[83]

Thus CALFED's biggest accomplishment to date has been its ability to foster dialogue among major water-policy stakeholders—farmers, environmentalists, and urban water agencies—that before 1994 not only disagreed but also rarely spoke to each other. And its Environmental Water Account appears to be a success. CALFED's survival is regarded by many as critical to the state's water resources "peace process." Much like proponents of democracy, CALFED advocates faced an imperfect process—except when compared to the alternatives. As long as CALFED continues to be the least bad alternative, it is unlikely to be scrapped.[84]

Proposition 50 to the Rescue

Except for Proposition 50, CALFED would be left "in a mode of triage."

CALFED spokesperson Marguerite Giddings, 2002[85]

The CALFED process was kept alive by the passage in November 2002 of the $3.4-billion Proposition 50—"The Water Security, Clean Drinking Water, Coastal and Beach Protection Act"—authorizing, among other priorities, $825 million for San Francisco–San Joaquin Delta restoration.

Absent federal money, Proposition 50 bailed out CALFED by underwriting the state's share of two years of program costs, including for the highly touted "environmental water account," which buys and stores surplus water for future salmon runs and environmental needs. Not put on the ballot by the legislature, where agricultural interests dominate the water committees, Proposition 50 was the product of a voter-initiative campaign masterminded by Joe Caves of the Nature Conservancy in cooperation with MWD. The initiative also opened the door to using public money for nongovernmental water projects undertaken by nonprofit and for-profit entities. The measure avoided the controversy surrounding water megaprojects by not authorizing money for dam and reservoir construction, and only allocating nominal sums for future study of such projects. Finally, it played on antiterrorist fears to fund additional security measures for California's existing reservoirs and dams.[86]

Proposition 50 passed easily despite the opposition of the California Chamber of Commerce, the California Farm Bureau, and the Regional Council of Rural Counties. Citing an analysis by the Legislative Analyst's Office that up to $1.5 billion of the bond issue could be used to buy land, opponents denounced the proposition as "a park and wetland protection bond" rather than a "water resources and coastal protection proposal." CALFED director Patrick Wright eased worries about heedless land acquisition by describing such purchases as among CALFED's lowest priorities for restoring habitat. Instead, according to Wright, CALFED would continue to forge partnerships with landowners rather than buy up their land and remove it from county tax rolls. The only major water agency in the state to initially support Proposition 50, MET strongly backed the inclusion of $100 million for desalination technology. "There is probably not going to be a state water project [completed] in my lifetime or in my grandchildren's [lifetime]," declared MWD vice president Tim Quinn, "so we're going to have to look to the ocean [and other local resources] as a new water supply."[87]

Under the new aegis of the CALFED Bay-Delta Authority (CFBDA), CALFED generated considerable controversy in 2003 when it hosted a special meeting of state and federal officials and private water contractors interested in the State Water Project (SWP) and Central Valley Project (CVP). Under the so-called Napa Proposal, the operations of the SWP and CVP would be integrated to increase pumping capacity. Wildlife refuges in the San Joaquin Valley would receive SWP rather than CVP water. As a result, federal CVP contractors would benefit by receiving as much as 100,000 annual AF more water. Environmentalists opposed to additional north-south water transfers feared that the ultimate beneficiary of increased pumping, however, might be MWD. This contentious issue, like many others, fell into the lap of new governor Arnold Schwarzenegger in Sacramento.[88]

In Washington, the logjam seemingly was broken in October 2004 when Congress (HR 2828) authorized $395 million for CALFED to continue work on four Northern California water-storage projects. The legislation also directed the federal government to study ways to restore the troubled Salton Sea. A bipartisan effort, the legislation secured the support of Senator Feinstein and Representatives Pombo, Calvert, and Napolitano in the House. Opposed by Bay Area environmentalists, the bill was supported by nearly all major California water agencies and organizations. It was a remarkable political accomplishment.[89]

The Challenge of Stewardship

The problem with water, though, is that the shortfalls don't show up until the very end. You can go on pumping unsustainably until the day you run out. Then all you have is the recharge flow, which comes from precipitation. This is not decades away, this is years away. We're already seeing huge shortages in China, where the Yellow River runs dry for part of each year.

Lester Brown, 1999[90]

Sadly, California history is replete with accounts of timber wars, budget wars, and water wars—all nasty conflicts conducted with unyielding passion and purpose. But too often they have been wars without winners. There is just too much at stake to risk losing again.

Governor Pete Wilson, speaking before a conference of water officials, 1992[91]

California's remarkable network of major water storage and conveyance facilities is often likened to "an empire." Stewardship of this empire in recent decades had been undergoing a succession crisis, with many pretenders to the throne—water agencies, urban consumers, water farmers and "real" farmers, environmental activists, and local and state politicians—but with no preeminent claimant to the imperial mantle. Leadership limitations were both symptom and cause of a fragmented policymaking environment in which all water policies were interconnected but few seemed to be in sync. Yet the policy linkages were obvious. CALFED could not succeed in reviving the delta without the support of Southern California water agencies and their consumers; yet CALFED also could not afford to alienate the Northern California constituencies that defeated the Peripheral Canal. The California 4.4 Plan could not achieve its goals without a successful delta restoration program to demonstrate to other western states and the federal government California's commitment to prudent water management. The challenge for water policy makers was to translate project and program interdependencies into positive reinforcement loops.[92]

Although deserving of some criticism, MWD has a regional mandate and mission that translate into a broader vision than is held by most other players in contemporary California water politics. Contrary to its critics, MWD never has been a mere "rubber stamp" for Los Angeles ambitions. In the 1990s, it became even more responsive to the perspectives of stakeholders far removed from its downtown L.A. headquarters. One reason for MWD's repeated clashes with San Diego was MWD's commitment to coordinated approaches to resource management such as the Integrated Water Resources Plan, demanding that all member agencies recognize a regional interest that transcends local self-interest. Proponents of "local water autonomy"—whether rural Inyo and Mono counties or metropolitan aspirants such as San Diego—cannot escape responsibility for the impact of their actions on all Californians.[93]

And Metropolitan has increasingly become an advocate of environmental restoration. In the early 1990s, the MET board added environmental values to its mission statement, stating that it would accomplish its reliability and water quality missions in "an environmentally and economically sound manner."[94] In 1994, to close the negotiations of the Bay-Delta Accord, Metropolitan provided $30 million of "seed money" to start the "Category III program"—the first effort to restore environmental habitat on a large scale in the Bay-Delta watershed. Since then,

MWD has partnered with local agricultural districts and other local entities to implement restoration projects to restore endangered fisheries. As a popular bumper sticker has it, "Think globally — act locally." MWD has a unique role and responsibility to forge the regional and statewide consensus needed for action in accordance with a coherent, disciplined vision of the state's water future if Californians are going to continue to "drink locally."

6 Turbulent Waters? Metropolitan Faces Water Markets

Farmers remain suspicious of the "Owens Valley syndrome." . . .
The theft of its water in the early 20th century has become the most
notorious water grab by a city anywhere. . . . The whole experience has
poisoned subsequent attempts to persuade farmers to trade their water
to thirsty cities.

The Economist, 2003[1]

We continue to struggle with a clear definition of what privatization
might mean. Is water going to be traded as a commodity? . . . What is
the role of public stewardship? I definitely see our industry becoming
more competitive. It's clear that water marketing and water transfers
are part of our future.

MWD general manager John "Woody" Wodraska, 1997[2]

California's big public wholesale water agencies [such as] Metropolitan
. . . have selected a cumbersome "command and control" regulatory
system instead of allowing a properly regulated water market to
emerge. . . . However, the wholesalers went beyond regulation: they
actually subverted the water market through a host of anti-competitive
pricing, market allocation and system access devices. . . . [This] means
that we will continue to have low reliability and higher costs than we
might have had if the market had not been strangled in its crib.

Western Water CEO Michael George, 2003[3]

No longer solely a water importer, MWD in recent decades
has been influenced—often reluctantly, according to critics—by a global
movement to use market mechanisms to meet burgeoning urban
water needs. Water and its market potential rank among the 10 cutting-
edge issues for the 21st century as identified by the economists of the

Copenhagen Consensus Project. Water markets involve the transfer, lease, or sale of water or water rights from one user to another. In California, water transfers began in the late 1970s with short-term (or spot-market) agreements among farmers in the same irrigation basin. Since the late 1980s, there have been a number of long-term (more than one year) agricultural-to-urban transfer agreements involving public water agencies. Private companies also have tried—albeit less successfully—to gain a foothold in the state by purchasing water or water rights and then selling them to willing buyers for a profit.[4]

A major advantage of market transactions is that water supplies can be shifted between users without the added expense of new dams or reservoirs. As a result, transfers have been blessed—but not always fully supported—by many environmentalists. Yet, as the Imperial Valley–San Diego deal attests, transfers also can have real environmental and economic costs, ranging from urban sprawl, to water cost shifting, and agricultural land fallowing. Negative externalities and mitigation burdens invite conflict over water transfers, going back to the Owens Valley. Regardless of what actually transpired there, the so-called "Owens Valley syndrome," replayed in the film *Chinatown*, has been a major disincentive for farmers to sell their water to thirsty cities.

From the mid-1980s onward, Metropolitan has been at the very center of agricultural-to-urban water market transactions and controversies in California.[5] Hailed as an innovative leader for the 1989 IID-MWD transfer agreement; for help in passing the Central Valley Project Improvement Act; for its Integrated Water Resources Plans featuring a host of Central Valley Project–State Water Project storage and transfer agreements; and, in 2004, for its 35-year Palo Verde Irrigation District crop rotation-transfer deal, MWD also has been castigated—perhaps unfairly so—for erecting stiff barriers, such as seemingly exorbitant wheeling rates, to market transactions involving its member agencies (such as San Diego) or private companies (such as Western Water). A central concern is whether Metropolitan has adequately embraced market forces, or has fought a stealth campaign to protect its privileges as a public monopolist.[6]

This chapter examines Metropolitan's on-and-off-and-on-again relationship with water transfers and markets. To be properly gauged, the market trend's impact needs to be placed—not just in regional and state perspective—but in national and even international contexts. In the

IID-SDCWA deal, MET's encounter with the giant French-owned conglomerate Vivendi (which purchased U.S. Filter, holder of the Bass brothers' Imperial Valley land interests) was but one of a growing number of market skirmishes between U.S. public water agencies and European multinational firms. MWD's market forays also are considered in terms of California water law development.

We then examine MET's early (pre-1990) forays into water transfer deals, involving the Imperial Valley and Kern County. For the post-1990 period, we analyze MWD's involvement in the State Water Bank, its Central Valley deal making, the ill-fated Cadiz conjunctive use-storage project in the Mojave Desert, and the recent Palo Verde agreement. Chapter 4 considered MET's controversial role in the landmark IID-SDCWA water transfer, and the ever-contentious wheeling charge issue. We conclude with a discussion of what role Metropolitan should play in the ongoing policy debate concerning water as a private commodity or public resource.

Water Markets and Privatization: Global and National Contexts

Water, like air, is a necessity of human life. It is also, according to *Fortune* magazine, "One of the world's great business opportunities. It promises to be to the 21st century what oil was to the 20th."

International Consortium of Investigative Journalists, 2002[7]

Gérard Payen, senior executive vice president of Suez, said that its U.S. subsidiary is still developing alliances with politicians and industry groups. The United States and China are the company's main expansion targets.

Erika Hobbs, 2003[8]

Multinationals and Global Markets

Founded in the Napoleonic era, Suez Lyonnaise des Eaux's ancestral company built and managed the Suez Canal until 1956. Preeminent among the triumvirate of the world's largest private water companies, Suez owed its 20th-century prosperity, not to the Nile's gift, but increasingly to "the blue gold" that flowed from its leverage of national and now international water markets. By the 1980s, 80 percent of France's water supply was controlled by corporate giants that excelled at increasing market share by tapping pipelines of political influence with the Gaullist power structure radiating outward to the provinces from the Elysée Palace. With home-market dominance secure, Suez and Vivendi set their sights on privatizing global water provision. By 2000 Suez owned or managed water services in 130 countries on five continents with some 115 million customers. Vivendi Environnement had 110 million customers in more than 100 countries. Completing the global "big three," Thames Water of the United Kingdom, owned by German conglomerate RWE AG, had 70 million customers. Significant but lesser players were Saur of France and United Utilities of England working in conjunction with the Bechtel Corporation. In terms of revenue, Vivendi's water-related earnings, for example, increased from $5 billion in 1990 to $12 billion in 2002.[9]

Both proponents and opponents of privatized water markets acknowledge that their heightened profile is a reflex of a global crisis. More than a billion people—a fifth of the world's population—currently lack access to clean water; by 2025, two thirds of a global population of 8 billion will live in countries facing moderate to severe water shortages. A major factor involves Malthusian pressures of growing numbers drawing on a finite resource, as exploding growth has made Latin America 77 percent urban and Africa 41 percent urban. Antiquated water delivery systems cannot keep pace with urban sprawl, and runoff from expanding cities produces pollution halos contaminating rural water sources. A complicating factor is skewed resource distribution, with the preponderance of fresh water found in only 10 countries, including the United States, Canada, Russia, and China. Increasing consumption is depleting local aquifers before they can be replenished, and 40 percent of people worldwide are already dependent on water transported from somewhere else. Southern California is of course a classic case, containing 60 percent of the state's population while storing only 3 percent of its surface water runoff.[10]

This is the crisis context in which multinational water firms have sold themselves as the cutting edge of a World Bank–promoted "efficiency revolution" to reduce costs, invest in new technology, modernize water delivery systems, and improve water quality. The appeal of market-based solutions is universal, but the record is decidedly mixed.

Although some studies indicate that the establishment of tradable water rights has benefited rural economies in Chile and Mexico, a Bolivian privatization experiment, implemented by Bechtel with the support of the World Bank, led to a tripling of prices, riots, and a return to public ownership. In Buenos Aires, public opinion regarding water privatization flipped from 59 percent favorable to 16 percent unfavorable in the late 1980s to essentially the reverse a decade later.[11]

A trans-Atlantic "French connection" linked the political economy of Parisian water, nicknamed "Chateau Chirac," to Argentina, which then became its own water market model to Third World countries, including the Philippines. Unfortunately, the conflicts of interest and kickbacks characteristic of French government-backed private water companies proved exportable to Latin America and Asia where they sluiced the hothouse corruption of Carlos Menem's Buenos Aires and the crony capitalism of post-Marcos Manila. In South Africa—where former President Nelson Mandela declared in 1994, "Privatization is the fundamental policy of our government. Call me a Thatcherite, if you will"—the French company Saur made major inroads. Townships began metering communal taps, causing the poorest townspeople to turn to cholera-ridden river water.[12]

Between 1983 and 1991, South Australia, followed by New South Wales and Victoria, legalized water markets. The economic gain derived by sheep farmers in the outback was offset by the ethical deficit in Adelaide, where a consortium controlled by Thames Water and Vivendi won a management contract in a bidding process clouded by charges of corruption. Promises from the water multinationals and the World Bank, that local operations would be "Australianized" and the country converted into a launching pad for entering the Asian region's water market, evaporated. Instead, Adelaide's waterworks, as a result of poor maintenance and monitoring under the new market regime, emitted for several months "the Big Pong," colloquial for a sulfurous stench.[13]

The United States: How Does Privatization "Play in Peoria"?

The situation in the United States, where public agencies meet the water needs of over 80 percent of the population, appears the inverse of the case in France. Yet U.S. public agencies are the big fish in a pond in which the small fish—private companies serving mostly rural communities—own 70 percent of all drinking water systems. The situation was ripe for European multinationals entering the market to consolidate smaller private firms as well as compete with larger public entities. Their selling points were improved management together with private capital to pay the huge national bill, estimated as high as $1 trillion, for water system improvements over the next three decades.[14]

To better position itself, Suez acquired United Water Resources Inc. in 2000, following Vivendi's purchase of U.S. Filter Corporation of Palm Desert, California, and RWE AG's purchase of American Water Works. Richard J. Heckmann, U.S. Filter's chairman, first approached Vivendi Chairman Jean-Marie Messier about possibly buying up Aqua Alliance, Vivendi's American arm. After Messier laughed at the idea of withdrawing from the American market, Heckmann decided that the partnership he needed would involve selling out to the European giant. Peter Spillet, head of Environment, Quality, and Sustainability for Thames Water, the London-based subsidiary of RWE AG, explained the multinationals' stateside sales strategy, which relied heavily on the recruitment of what were called "champions," or local influentials, to make their case: "With [American Water] we will inherit their existing political and lobbying skills. In Washington, we will employ useful lobbyists and so on."[15]

Historically, private water provision—far from being unknown—was the pre-20th-century norm in the United States. In the early Republic, the East Coast port cities all turned for sorely needed investment capital to private water companies, which constituted a tenth of all new incorporations during the 1790s. Incorporated in 1799, the inefficient, scandal-ridden Manhattan Company allied with water cart owners to block until 1834 the state legislature's creation of the New York Board of Water Commissioners that ultimately bought out the company (subsequently renamed Chase Manhattan) and built the Croton Aqueduct, later also tapping the Catskills and the Delaware River. Boston became a national model for municipal ownership, with the chartering of a Metropolitan Water District in 1895, yet it earlier took a long struggle before Boston's pioneering, public Cochituate Water Board was approved. Despite contaminated water and cholera epidemics long blamed on a private water monopoly, Baltimore did not municipalize until after mid-century. As late as 1850, 50 of the country's 83 water systems were still privately owned. Los Angeles had to await another half century, until 1902, for completion of the contentious buyout of the Los Angeles City Water Company and chartering of the municipal Board of Water Commissioners.[16]

The pattern of much-hyped expectations followed by disillusioned complaints about leaking pipes and price gouging that the private water giants have generated abroad has followed them to the United States. Peoria, Illinois—where politicians traditionally looked to measure the pulse of Middle America—had a long, uneventful history of private ownership until its water supplier was acquired by a subsidiary of American Water Works. "Our studies show the cost of water in Peoria is twice that of other similar-sized cities in the country," complained Terry Kolbuss of the Tri-County Regional Planning Commission. Peoria has moved to buy back and municipalize its water system.[17]

With major aquifers under stress, including the Ogallala in Texas and Potomac-Raritan-Magothy in New Jersey, the federal Environmental Protection Agency in 1996 called for improvements in water infrastructure and wastewater management. In 2001, Congress, over the objections of the Association of Metropolitan Water Agencies, required cities to consider private-public partnerships as a condition for federal money for improvement projects. The U.S. Conference of Mayors also joined with the National Association of Water Companies to lobby the Internal Revenue Service to stop penalizing cities that signed management contracts with private water companies of more than five years' duration. This opened the spigot for larger cities to negotiate such contracts, albeit with mixed results. It was a trophy contract for Suez when its subsidiary, United Water, signed a 20-year, $500-million agreement with Atlanta in 1999; but the relationship ruptured in 2003 when the New South capital griped about inferior service and broke its contract to resume public operation of its water utility. Replacing Mayor Bill Campbell, one of United Water's "champion" catches, the new mayor, Shirley Jackson, complained of poor maintenance and failure to collect outstanding water bills.[18]

The verdict is still out on Indianapolis, which in 2001 purchased the private water company that had served the city for over a century, and then signed a 20-year, $1.5-billion management contract with Vivendi's U.S. Filter. New Orleans' Sewerage and Water Board in 2002 had buyer's remorse even before signing and failed to approve a $1 billion management contract. A sewage spill at a U.S. Filter-operated plant and the guilty plea on bribery charges by executives of Aqua Alliance Inc., a wastewater treatment firm, poisoned the local atmosphere.[19]

California Water Rights and Markets

Water law evolved slowly in both California and the West, constructed piece by piece, like a quilt, rather than from whole cloth. Individual court cases and statutes were piled layer on layer, not welded together like links in a chain.

Donald J. Pisani, To Reclaim a Divided West *(1992)*[20]

If a creature from outer space dropped in on California and reviewed our water supply allocation, it would report back finding no sign of intelligent life here.

Carl Boronkay, former MWD general manager, 2005[21]

However the term is defined, California is no stranger to water markets. In 1850, the California legislature quickly adopted the English common law, including the "riparian rights" doctrine that protected against unreasonable upstream diversion of the natural flow of streams. A humid land carry over from the wet climes of "old" and "new" England, riparianism was already under attack in the early 19th century even in the East and Middle West by the "prior appropriation" doctrine privileging productive uses of water for industrial and irrigation purposes even if they interfered with downstream claims to unimpeded flow. Then in the West's gold fields, prior appropriation became the crusading mantra of miners' intent on exploiting rivers for placer, hard rock, and hydraulic operations without regard to disruption of natural flow, and in opposition to the stranglehold on water resources of monopolists with riparian claims based on their ownership of adjacent land.[22]

Yet the Forty-Niners were no fans of a water market that enabled speculators to buy up rights not for use but for sale. In 1855, the California Supreme Court defied them and upheld the market for water retailing. California and other Western states continued to muddy the definition of water rights as private property by failing to clarify the difference between the right to sell and lease water rights versus the sale and use of water.[23] Regarding water rights, California saw a halting evolution toward the distinctive "California doctrine" of "first in time, first in right" that was adopted by eight other West Coast and Great Plains states. In *Lux v. Haggin* (1886), the California Supreme Court reaffirmed riparianism as a general rule, but with a large loophole for prior appropriators who could establish that they, rather than riparian claimants, were the first to use the water. State courts tended to favor riparian claimants, but legislators were less sympathetic, and finally in 1928 a state constitutional amendment (Article X, Section 2) imposed a "reasonable and beneficial use" requirement on water rights.[24]

Antimonopolists carried over their antirailroad crusade to a campaign against price-gouging "water rings" allegedly exploiting farmers and city folk alike. Private water companies were turning the prior appropriation doctrine to their own advantage. California's first state water engineer, William Hammond Hall, disdained the doctrine for treating water resources "like a beast—to be shot down and dragged out by the first brute who came into sight of it." The preference for community control of water, enshrined since Mexican days at least south of the Tehachapi Mountains in places such as Los Angeles, received recognition in Article 14 of the California Constitution of 1879, which declared that "the use of water now appropriated, or that may hereafter be appropriated, for sale, rental or distribution, is hereby declared to be a public use, and subject to the regulation and control of the State." The Patrons of Husbandry, or Grange, even argued in the 1870s for complete public ownership of water resources and creation of a state-run distribution system. However, the new State Water Code placed the burden of public control on county commissions that were no match for increasingly powerful private water companies.[25]

Reformers searched for a new political vehicle more effective than prior appropriation to advance their agenda. One experiment with modest success was mutual water companies—privately owned, but collectively managed. A more important innovation was the Wright Act (1887) establishing irrigation districts, later joined by urban water districts, with the power to condemn land and water "in the public interest." Often working hand-in-glove with the federal Reclamation Service, founded in 1902 and later renamed the Bureau of Reclamation, they played an increasingly important, public role in water resource development. In the Imperial

Valley, for example, the Bureau of Reclamation challenged the control of water development by the private California Development Corporation, which was forced into receivership after the 1905 Colorado River flood. To avert bankruptcy, the corporation sold its assets to the public Imperial Irrigation District in 1911. IID general counsel and later congressmember Phil Swing negotiated the agreement with the Bureau of Reclamation for an All-American Canal that was incorporated into the Boulder Canyon Project Act of 1928. The close German-Mexican relationship during World War I had heightened desire for a canal north of the border that did not go through Mexico. Swing also was a moving force behind the creation of the Metropolitan Water District in the same year.[26]

In 1921, the California Progressive reform impulse to rationalize water policy culminated in an enactment directing the state engineer to develop a plan for the "maximum conservation, control, storage, distribution, and application of all the waters of the State." But the so-called "Marshall Plan," named after engineer-politician Robert Marshall, proposing to construct a state water project—including dams, aqueducts, and a tunnel through the Tehachapis—was 40 years ahead of its time and not enacted. Eventually, some 1,000 public water districts were formed in California. They were outnumbered by a spate of small, commercial water providers—most of which, however, were only marginally significant. The public boards were able to claim the right to market water, first as licensees under a permit system established in 1914 and then by applying to the State Water Resources Control Board, established in 1967. Under the prior appropriation doctrine, they could transfer and sell rights to water independent of land ownership, provided that their applications for a change in the purpose and place of use and point of diversion were approved as compatible with state water law.[27]

During the half-century romance of the building of the great public water works—from the Los Angeles Aqueduct to Hoover Dam, to the Colorado River Aqueduct, the Central Valley Project, and the State Water Project—local water markets continued to function, but as a rivulet flowing into the sea of the government-directed course of water resource development and allocation. Critics might view public water agencies as instruments of entrenched economic power, especially agribusiness and urban developers; but from another perspective the important point was the dependence of private interests on public formulation, operation, and validation of water policy. Ongoing local water markets allowed agricultural landowners to consolidate holdings and rationalize operations. Then in the 1940s and 1950s, an "exchange pool" system developed in the Central and West Coast basins of Los Angeles County. The price fluctuated, but was determined under court orders administered by the State Department of Water Resources acting as watermaster. The parties traded "surplus" allotments of groundwater, while still using the MWD as a peaking source for additional water purchases. The market was rudimentary, with no private bidders or water transfers outside circumscribed boundaries.[28]

The period after the 1982 voter defeat of the Peripheral Canal—a proposed conveyance facility to ship Northern California water around the fragile Bay-Delta ecosystem to Central Valley farms and Southern California consumers—was a step backward after Thermidor from the perspective of advocates of public water-resource development. However, it marked a renascence for water marketers who rode the new wave reallocating existing water supplies rather than tapping new ones. In an era when even a market for clean air existed in the form of pollution credits, water was deemed a quasi-public good. In theory, it was an indivisible benefit, free to all in its natural state; it also presented difficulties to those who wanted to exclude others from sharing its benefit. Yet in practice and law, ways were found to convert water into property by means of use, transfer, and storage. The result was an irresolvable tension between "public good" and "private property" conceptions of water.[29]

Market economists wanted to fully commodify water, with price solely determining its "highest and best" use. Yet whatever Milton Friedman's followers might think, water was too much "affected with a public purpose" and too fraught with third-party impacts, ever to be treated as purely private property. The prescriptive weight of centuries of law made land wholly alienable, but not water rights separate from it. The water market never entirely freed itself from the intrusive politics of the public trust and the regulatory impulse. Perhaps the first California law regulating groundwater, an 1874 act requiring that artesian wells be capped when not in use, declared water to be the property of the people, to be used for the "greatest possible good upon the greatest number." This public-regarding sentiment still remains an irreducible bedrock in California water law.[30]

An unlikely coalition of free-market ideologues and environmental activists struggled starting in the 1970s to move California more in the direction of privatized water allocation and administration. They were aided by both the promarket predilections of the times and the practical imperatives of managing an increasingly scarce and ecologically sensitive resource. During the 1976–1977 drought, there was an up-tick in water transactions, mostly short-term lease arrangements, primarily by private parties with clear title to water rights rather than public water districts. There also was a disappointing experiment with an emergency water bank to permit transfer of allocations from state and federal water projects. Most of these transfers occurred within the federal Central Valley Project. Reports by RAND (1978) and the California Governor's Commission to Review Water Rights Law (1978), following the lead of the National Water Commission (1970), also encouraged water marketing. The federal Emergency Drought Act of 1977 empowered the secretary of the Interior to authorize temporary transfers to reduce agricultural losses. The subsequent federal court decision in *Sporhase v. Nebraska* (1982) facilitated potential interstate water transfers by ruling that the interstate commerce clause barred the states from outlawing them.[31]

In the 1980s, as the Peripheral Canal proposal self-destructed under Governor Jerry Brown and failed to be resurrected under his successor, George Deukmejian, Sacramento gave its blessing to water marketing as a beneficial use of surplus water. In 1982, the state declared it established policy to "facilitate the voluntary transfer of water and water rights where consistent with the public welfare." State legislation authorized water agencies to transfer conserved or salvaged water; conserved water could be "sold, leased, exchanged or otherwise transferred." A 1986 wheeling bill (Assemblymember Richard Katz, D-L.A.) also mandated that at least 70 percent of unused capacity in water conveyance facilities, including aqueducts, be made available for water transfers.[32]

Testing the Waters: MWD Confronts Markets Before 1990

Mr. Abel told a story about the difference between heaven and hell. In hell, people have a long wooden fork attached to their arm, but they cannot bend their elbow and are starving to death because they are trying to feed themselves. In heaven, it is the same situation but they are feeding each other because they are cooperating. Mr. Abel looks at the water issue that way, and sees people trying to position themselves to the disadvantage of everyone else in California. We have to think about incentives and disincentives that encourage interregional collaboration. . . . Mr. Abel is looking to MWD to change and try to be a partner with the other regions and give us the capacity to deal with the challenges we face. There is a role for a water market, a regulated market, but a regulated market that does not mean one buyer. There has to be a "give and take" and not another [MWD] effort to colonialize the state.

David Abel, 2003[33]

IID/MWD Deal: Transfer or Sale?

As Southern California recovered from the severe drought of the mid-1970s, Imperial Valley was blessed—and cursed—with an abundance of rainfall. The rise in the Salton Sea threatened to swamp the agricultural empire of landowners John and Stephen Elmore, who responded by flooding state regulatory agencies and courts with complaints against the Imperial Irrigation District for wasteful practices under Section 275 of the California Water Code. In the legal and political hot seat, the California Department of Water Resources estimated that better drainage and conservation practices by Imperial Valley farmers could save 438,000 acre-feet (AF) of water a year—roughly the equivalent, as opponents of the Peripheral Canal were quick to point out, of what that ill-fated water project would have delivered annually to Southern California.[34]

The Ralph M. Parsons Company, hired by IID to do an environmental impact report, upped the state estimate of savings to over 500,000 AF. This analysis was the kernel of what became known as "the SWAP," the proposed transfer of at least 100,000 AF of conserved Imperial Valley water to MWD in return for conservation funding. A spinoff of Bechtel, Parsons had experience in dam building in Saudi Arabia and wastewater management in Phoenix. In the 1960s heyday of great water projects, when Congressmember Ed Roybal had floated the idea of a 1,700-mile pipeline under the Pacific Ocean from Alaska to Southern California, Parsons had proposed the grandiose North American Water and Power Alliance—diverting the waters of British Columbia to the American Southwest—that poet Wallace Stegner complained would be "a boondoggle visible from Mars." To stay afloat in the changing ideological currents of the Reagan administration, Parsons reformulated its vision into the privatization creed of "Build, Own, Operate." In the kernel of the IID/MWD SWAP, Parsons saw the oak of a full-grown water market like that also advocated by investment banker and government efficiency guru J. Peter Grace, who preached privatizing the Bonneville Dam.[35]

The Western Governors' Association joined the chorus, demanding that the Reclamation Bureau shift from "supplying capital for a few large projects to helping the West enhance the efficiency of use of the water that the Bureau already provides." In 1998, the bureau obliged by affirming the new, market-oriented approach, and declaring that water rights were commodities that could be bought and sold rather the inalienable property of the public and of taxpayers who had subsidized project development. Parsons' executives whispered into the ear of IID directors the dream of converting their water agency into the "new water market broker of the Southwest." Parsons advised the agency to seek, not just the cost of conservation, but a subsidy based on its estimate of environmental and other impacts. This translated into over $100/AF, which—if MWD refused the deal—might be paid by the San Diego County Water Authority, a top official of which had left to go work for Parsons.[36]

As early as 1984, at the recommendation of IID chief legal counsel John Carter, the IID board had adopted a resolution signaling its willingness to consider possible water conservation and transfer deals. Smarting from the Peripheral Canal defeat, MET signaled serious interest. After tortuous 1984–1988 negotiations, which MET general manager Carl Boronkay called an "off again, on again soap opera," an initial agreement was reached for MWD to pay $100/AF, or $10 million annually over 35 years, for the first 100,000 AF of water that IID conserved. Taking a page from *Alice in Wonderland*—where Humpty Dumpty states, "When I use a word, it means just what I choose it to mean"—the two agencies agreed to disagree over the nature of their transaction, which MWD defined as a limited conservation transfer but IID defined as a market sale. Although MET once had opposed the concept of markets as a Trojan horse used by conservationists whose ultimate purpose was to foil MWD's designs for expanding the State Water Project, MWD's Boronkay (1984–1993) would become the foremost champion of water marketing in California.[37]

Unfortunately for IID, its market strategy soon unraveled under embarrassing circumstances faintly reminiscent of the Mad Hatter's un-birthday party. The board's local opponents argued that Imperial Valley was being bought up cheap by an Owens Valley–style conspiracy of out-siders—including both Parsons and MWD. Parsons received its political comeuppance when the IID board first cut its fee and then canceled its contract. The board also circumvented MET's negotiators, making ques-tionable behind-the-scenes overtures to Metropolitan through board chair E. Thornton "Ibby" Ibbetson, whose Union Development Corpo-ration was active in Imperial Valley real estate. When MWD rejected as "outrageous" IID's "high-ball offer" of $250/AF, the IID board turned in desperation to San Diego.[38]

Imperial's hopes that San Diego would be interested in purchasing water were fueled after the implosion on legal and political grounds of the Galloway Plan calling for construction of a new dam on the upper Colorado River system to meet San Diego's growing thirst. Alas for IID, San Diego proved a tease—faulting MWD for tunnel vision and insufficient attention to conservation yet ultimately spurning an IID deal, ostensibly because of its obligation as a member agency to defer to MWD. Cynics speculated that the real reason was IID's inflated expectations that San Diego would pay as high as $250/AF for its water. As noted, San Diego later would be willing to pay such a price in exchange for political juice to secure low-cost access to MET's system.[39]

The IID board was under unrelenting legal and regulatory pres-sure—needing to raise water rates to pay for adverse court settlements—and was also buffeted by the statewide agricultural downturn that resulted in 15 percent of Imperial Valley land being removed from pro-duction by 1987, hitting hardest the valley's tenant farmers and farm workers. It now had to revisit MWD as a partner. New IID chief nego-tiator, water engineer Robert Edmonston, and MET assistant general manager Myron Holburt reached a proposed agreement in June 1988 that obligated MWD to pay capital construction costs and $23 million in indirect costs, including lost hydroelectric revenues and "mitigation of adverse impacts on agriculture from increased salinity in the water." The overall cost to MWD for conservation measures, mostly lining irrigation canals, appeared to be over $200 million. The State Water Code section governing water rights permits was changed to authorize the deal.

Implementation had to be delayed until December 1989 because of a lawsuit by the Coachella Valley Water District (CVWD), which claimed damages under its available Colorado River entitlement, specifically prior rights to water conserved through the IID-MWD agreement.[40]

New IID board member Don Cox successfully overturned the requirement that the Imperial Valley electorate approve the deal, but a lobbying campaign by "Imperial Valley Water Users for Fairness" was still a cause for concern. MWD mollified the grassroots by sweetening its deal with IID to the amount of $128/AF of water and also made a side agreement with the CVWD. In addition, MET tried to negotiate a dry-year exchange with the Palo Verde Irrigation District (PVID), a desert agency north and east of Imperial Valley where landowners included the San Diego Gas and Electric Company (SDG&E), owner of a stranded nuclear power plant site. The PVID deal initially failed primarily because of price disagreements in an atmosphere poisoned by local opponents who invoked the specter of the Owens Valley and editorialized, "MWD: Drop Dead."[41]

Supply-side economics notwithstanding, water transfers between rural and urban districts—lauded by privatization proponents—involved demand-side readjustments of existing resources rather than adding new water supplies. As Carl Boronkay later reflected, "politically, we knew that no new dams would be built. Reallocation would be the name of the game."[42] In the case of the SWAP, Metropolitan gained an entitlement to conserved IID water, but that water was still part of California's overall Colorado River allotment. In that sense, the deal was a transfer of rights from IID to MWD rather than the creation of new water in the way in which the Colorado River Aqueduct had tapped a new supply for Southern California. MET and other water agencies rationalized transfers (through sale, lease, or exchange) as a way of stretching existing supplies. They viewed this approach as inferior to building new water projects, but it was preferred to implementing some conservation programs that might not prove all that cost effective. MWD also could not complain about the $128/AF cost—only half of the $249/AF it was paying at the time for water from the State Water Project.[43]

Was the IID-MWD deal a market transaction? Yes, but of a highly regulated sort. No love match, the deal was far from a voluntary meeting of the minds between buyer and seller. Instead, it was more like a shotgun marriage into which both public parties were pressured by political and administrative imperatives. As a California appeals court opined in a 1991 ruling with respect to the Imperial Irrigation District, it had "occupied a position of great strength, discretion and vested interest in a geographical part of the country that is 'far western,' [but] recent trends in water use philosophy and the administration of water law have severely undermined the positions of districts such as IID."[44]

Kern County: MWD as Ultimate Buyer

MWD also confronted market challenges in the north. The struggle in the north pitted the Kern County Water Agency (KCWA) against its member agencies and farmers in the San Joaquin Valley of Central California. MET was independently involved as one of the biggest contractors of the State Water Project (SWP), which supplied both Central and Southern California. MET also was a potential buyer of water from interested sellers in Kern County, which was a large user of SWP water as well as an important customer of the federal Central Valley Project (CVP). During the 1970s, the Kern County agricultural economy underwent a tremendous speculative boom, particularly in cotton, which was a favorite tax shelter before the Tax Reform Act of 1986. The KCWA's two biggest members—the Wheeler Ridge–Maricopa and Berrenda Mesa water districts—lacked significant groundwater and were dependent almost entirely on purchases from the SWP. In the early 1980s, cotton prices collapsed at the same time that the SWP significantly raised rates to pay for higher energy costs to power its pumps. Following a flurry of bankruptcies in 1985–1986, several major corporate farmers decided to bail out.[45]

During the prior boom, Kern County landowners had shown little interest in water market proposals developed by Nancy Moore and Timothy Quinn (both then at the RAND Corporation, Dr. Quinn later at MWD), and agricultural economist Henry Vaux. By the mid-1980s, times had changed when Wheeler Ridge–Maricopa's two biggest corporate landowners decided to sell water rather than irrigate with it—Tenneco by leaving agriculture entirely; Tejon Ranch, a subsidiary of the *Los Angeles Times* parent company, by cutting back operations without generating too much bad publicity. At Berrenda Mesa, Ron Khachagian of the Blackwell Land Company was aggressively interested in bottom-line considerations, particularly the enticing (if illusory) prospect of selling his company's State Water Project entitlement for $800 to $1,000 per AF. (This was a capitalized price for permanent rights; the annualized cost was $80/AF.) Both Wheeler Ridge–Maricopa and Berrenda Mesa dutifully did the bidding of their agribusiness giants by entering the budding water market as sellers in search of buyers.[46]

The Kern County Water Agency was adamantly opposed to water transfers outside its boundaries. The fear was that these would erode its base and promote disinvestment in the Valley economy by reducing the supply and potentially raising the price of water to Kern County farmers who remained in the business of agriculture. The KCWA also had on its side the equity arguments that member agencies had assumed an obligation to other members not to jump ship in bad times and that Kern County taxpayers should be protected from adverse impacts because they had paid 15 percent of the cost of delivering water to farmers. Only in 1994, with the so-called Monterey Agreement to State Water Contracts, which stabilized supplies by authorizing permanent sales between SWP contractors, did KCWA's resistance to outside transfers dissipate.[47]

Years earlier, under Governor Jerry Brown, KCWA had reacted negatively to proposals to develop a state-controlled water bank. Shaken by the drought, it now established the Kern County Water Bank to encourage transfers between its member agencies. The KCWA also managed partly to satisfy Wheeler Ridge–Maricopa by arranging a water sale to an urban-based improvement district within Kern County.[48] Unappeased, by 1988 at the height of the drought, Berrenda Mesa had located three Orange County water agencies as potential buyers. In its continuing opposition to such sales, KCWA declared its disapproval both of transfers beyond district lines and of any revisions in State Water Project contracts, and by other State Water Project contractors claiming first right to any surplus water not used by Berrenda Mesa agribusiness. Berrenda Mesa, in contrast, had lawyers at the ready as well as friends in Sacramento including longtime MET critic L.A. assemblymember Richard Katz, who favored water markets (except for MWD sales of its surplus water at discounted rates to Kern County). Aware of the intricate weaving of legal and political issues involved, MWD chose to sit the conflict out.[49]

As hostilities in Kern County's civil war escalated, MET maintained what Robert Gottlieb, the Santa Monica maverick on the MWD board, called "a position of studied ambivalence." MWD adhered to its official supportive stance toward KCWA, whose manager Tom Clark, although fearful of MET as "an 800-pound gorilla," praised Carl Boronkay as "the major-domo in statewide water." Yet MWD executives listened politely when George Nickel of Tenneco dropped in at their Los Angeles headquarters to float the idea of some sort of water transfer. (About that same time, Kern County interests made unsuccessful approaches about water sales to the Parsons Company, then representing the Imperial Irrigation District, and to the San Diego County Water Authority). Fearful of being accused of "another Owens Valley land grab," MET spurned immediate offers for it to buy Kern County farms with water rights attached. More than a decade later, MET would buy up acreage in southern Riverside County as mitigation for the Diamond Valley Reservoir Project. Snatching the property out from under the developer's shovel for a generous price, MWD gave 8,300 acres to the Nature Conservancy as the Santa Rosa Plateau Ecological Reserve. This saved an ecologically sensitive area and made lasting friends of many environmentalists.[50]

Although the IID-MWD transfer enjoyed the strong support of the Environmental Defense Fund, Northern California environmentalists were not so enthusiastic about a transfer from the Central Valley to Southern California. In particular, there were many unanswered questions about potential impacts on drainage problems and water quality in the San Joaquin Valley that could result in additional legal complications. The State Department of Water Resources also declined to champion the deal. Faced with limited support and the prospect of huge litigation costs, Berrenda Mesa ultimately gave up. Yet, counseled by Tim Quinn, the economist Carl Boronkay had hired away from RAND, MET did not foreclose the possibility of other San Joaquin Valley deals. Perhaps more influential than water market logic, it was the regional argument for water transfers from Central Valley to Southern California that was the gift horse luring an otherwise skeptical Metropolitan.[51]

Poised between fear and desire, MWD seemed to have the luxury of some latitude about negotiating interregional water transfers. Despite the severe drought and the completion of the water-hungry Central Arizona Project, the SWP reservoirs serving MET were still full. California water executives in the 1980s also were more willing to risk lower reserves than would be deemed prudent a few years later. Even so, Tim Quinn was dispatched to explore the availability of prospective deals in the inevitable future when MWD faced dry-yield years. In Kern County, Quinn found a responsive partner in the Arvin-Edison Water Storage District (AEWSD).[52]

A KCWA member agency and major customer of the Central Valley project, the AEWSD was also drawing heavily on its groundwater, which, in addition, was increasingly expensive to pump. AEWSD's ingenious proposal was to pay to store MWD's unused State Water Project entitlement in Arvin-Edison's basin, where it would raise groundwater levels and reduce pumping costs. In dry years when MET needed the water, it would take it from AEWSD's Central Valley Project entitlement that would be carried to the SWP pipeline for delivery south by a short connector built and paid for by MWD. The deal was notable for its conjunctive use of surface and groundwater resources. It also involved a buy-back of federal project water rights that Arvin-Edison would surrender to the CVP. Thus, there would be no change in land title—and, technically, no legal transfer of water rights. MET also argued that, at least in ordinary years, Kern County water resources would not be depleted. Ultimately, MWD stored only SWP water; no CVP water was ever involved.[53]

Yet the proposed Arvin-Edison deal created a new conflict—between MWD and KCWA as well as Central Valley Project contractors. Kern County farmers were the regular buyers of the inexpensive surplus SWP water to which MET was entitled but did not use. KCWA wanted this good deal to continue. However, agricultural users of the federal water project were as hostile to MWD tapping the CVP in dry years for the benefit of Southern California urban users as Metropolitan was to Berrenda Mesa selling its entitlement to SWP water. Arvin-Edison liked the deal so much that it proposed starting immediately in 1989. Despite concerns over likely legal and political challenges, the MWD board agreed to go ahead. As the 1980s closed—and the drought further worsened—MWD's fears of stormy times ahead proved well-founded.[54]

The New Wild West: MWD and Water Markets Since 1990

As the 1980s drought continued, I could not avoid the concept of voluntary market transfers as the most sensible approach for most future water requirements. Now I realized the right political time had arrived.

Carl Boronkay, former MWD general manager, 2005[55]

Drought Crisis Politics: The State Water Bank and the CVPIA

In 1991, Governor Pete Wilson's administration and the state legislature launched new initiatives in response to the prolonged 1987–1992 drought that had reduced rainfall to 30 percent of normal and reservoir storage capacity to just above that level. In the fourth straight dry year, the State Water Project cut off agricultural contractors and limited urban purchasers to 30 percent of normal deliveries. There were demands for state involvement to supplement the increase in short-term spot sales between water agencies to meet shortages. The centerpiece of the governor's program was the Department of Water Resources' (DWR) emergency Drought Water Bank. State water contractors such as MWD and KCWA initially had developed the concept of the bank. Although DWR was initially skeptical about market mechanisms to deal with drought situations, once on board it was very effective in developing the bank.[56]

The state sought to meet the needs of water-short agencies by buying up to 1 million acre-feet (MAF) of water from willing sellers north of the delta for $125/AF. The water would then be resold in the south at $175/AF (with an additional $5/AF for administrative costs) to cover the carriage costs needed to maintain delta salinity levels. Initial results were disappointing as some water agencies discouraged sales and many water rights holders with surplus water held back either out of fear of compromising their future water rights or expectation of higher future prices. After the heavy rains in March 1991, demand lessened and selling resistance decreased. To demonstrate good faith for water it had negotiated for, the State Water Bank purchased 820,000 AF—half from growers who fallowed approximately 170,000 acres of land, one third from groundwater substitution, and the rest from stored water. Only about half the 820,000 AF were sold—the bulk to urban Southern California and San Francisco Bay area water agencies.[57]

According to a RAND study, the bank was a plus for urban buyers who received some $91 million in benefits. Although some agricultural regions that sold water and fallowed land may have lost money, farmers who bought water for increased production more than made up for the loss. Participating growers reduced operating costs by about 10 percent and increased farm investment in efficient irrigation. Crop sales dropped by 20 percent, but negative third-party impacts on employment and income in affected communities were minimal except in a few counties. In Yolo County, where 13 percent of the land was fallowed, local officials requested help with increased social welfare costs generated by increased unemployment.[58]

Environmentalists criticized the program's failure to protect rivers and the reduction of wildlife habitat due to fallowing. In response to such criticism, in late 1991 funding was approved for the purchase of 28,000 AF of water for the California Department of Fish and Game for in-stream flow releases and wildlife refuges in the San Joaquin Valley. In 1992, the bank was extended on an "as needed" basis, with water to be sold at $72/AF plus transportation costs. It should be emphasized that the bank—a government enterprise acting as a single buyer dictating prices—was hardly a free-market mechanism. In terms of Water Bank operations, the state assumed no liability for damage to third parties. After a California appeals court ruling in 1994 upholding the right of counties to exercise police powers over groundwater, 22 rural counties adopted ordinances regulating so-called "groundwater exports." San Joaquin County also incorporated restrictions on exports of water stored above ground. The major response by Democrats in Sacramento was a bill by Assemblymember Richard Katz repealing the veto by rural water agencies on for-profit, out-of-district sales to urban users of up to 2 million AF of SWP water. Ten percent of purchases would go to environmental protection. Decisively passing the Assembly with joint support by Los Angeles and San Francisco legislators, the bill represented a significant shift away from north-south antagonism to a new statewide, urban alliance. However, the Katz bill failed in the State Senate after gubernatorial lobbying against it.[59]

At the behest of leading CVP growers, the Wilson administration also lined up against MWD in Washington by opposing the Miller-Bradley bill or Central Valley Project Improvement Act (CVPIA) of 1992. Addressing environmental protection at the seeming expense of agriculture, the CVPIA also contained a market provision, allowing the Secretary of the Interior to sell water. This market opportunity caught the eye of MWD's Carl Boronkay. The CVPIA was only part of the multibillion-dollar Reclamation Projects Authorization and Adjustments Act, affecting 13 western states. However, Californians were at the center of the action. In addition to opposing the CVPIA, California Department of Resources secretary Douglas Wheeler urged Congress to surrender control of the Central Valley Project, which provided California with over 6 MAF of water per year, to California for state development of a more comprehensive water supply program.[60]

A decisive lobbying role in support of CVPIA was played by MWD's Boronkay, who persuaded the MWD board to "vigorously pursue . . . substantial increases in water transfers." Boronkay powerfully argued that, with Southern California producing more than half of the state's gross product with only 10 percent of its water, an increase of 1 acre-foot of water in perpetuity in importations to the region would, on average, produce 2,600 additional jobs and, in some industries, as many as 17,000 jobs. MWD hoped ultimately to acquire in incremental steps 10 percent of Central Valley Project water. Cosponsoring the CVPIA with Senator Bill Bradley (D-NJ), Congressmember George Miller, a liberal Democrat and environmentalist representing the San Francisco Bay area, wanted more federal money for delta conservation and an end to subsidized, long-term contracts for Central Valley agribusiness. Initially "very uncomfortable" with water marketing, he mused, "Look, what's worse? Having subsidized agriculture waste water, that's bad, but having field after field filled with ticky-tacky subdivisions is bad as well." Miller was ultimately convinced, however, that he "had to have the Met on his side," especially since the marketing paradigm was also strongly supported in Northern California by the Association of Bay Area Governments (ABAG) and the Bay Area Council.[61]

Passed in October 1992, the CVPIA was a compromise combining environmental mitigation and market incentives. On the one hand, it increased environmental restoration (at least 800,000 AF to be dedicated to in-stream flows and wetlands) and imposed some new restrictions, including shortened contract duration, on subsidized big farming. On the other hand, it marked an important shift from the conception of CVP water as a public resource that farmers used, but did not own, to a new conception of CVP water as a property right that recipients could buy and sell to other users. As Stephanie Pincetl observed, "The result was the privatization of a publicly developed, common property resource."[62]

Regarding MWD's enlightened, conservationist view of the CVPIA, it could be (and was) cynically noted that the act diverted to environmental purposes CVP water, to which MET had no entitlement, rather than SWP water, to which it was entitled. Carl Boronkay overexulted on the CVPIA's passage that "It's as if overnight a new reservoir was created." In reality, CVP sales to urban water districts were hedged with restrictions, including prior approval by the Interior Department, prohibition of surface water transfers that would be to the long-term detriment of groundwater supplies, the right of first refusal to buy by other CVP users, district approval of sales in excess of 20 percent of that district's supply, and environmental impact studies. The establishment a few years later of a computer-interactive Water Transfer Clearinghouse by the Westlands Water District in the west San Joaquin Valley partly eased the flow of water market transactions. Not satisfactorily resolved, however, was the question of where the ultimate authority to make sales should reside—with the water district or the farmer?[63]

By the end of the 1990s, though, not a drop of CVP water had been sold outside the project's service area, as the return of rainfall after 1992 slaked the interest of potential urban buyers. According to Tim Quinn, MET's point man on water marketing, the lack of CVP sales to MWD was also due to an economic impediment—a special surcharge for water transferred outside the CVP boundaries. After Boronkay's retirement in 1993, MET continued to pursue Central Valley purchases, although perhaps not with the same missionary zeal. Indeed, MWD has succeeded with water market transactions elsewhere in the Central Valley where competitive market pricing didn't bear the burden of the CVP surcharge. Since the CVPIA, MWD has continued to embrace both a pro-market and proenvironmental reform stance, which survives in board policy.[64]

Whatever the practical limitations, the CVPIA was a true political watershed for water transfers and marketing in California. In 1992, there was no gubernatorial veto when the legislature authorized river water to be transferred for environmental and in-stream beneficial uses. The next year, state legislation also authorized the transfer of surface and groundwater outside the State Water Project service area, although groundwater transfers had to be consistent with a management plan approved by the supplier. As noted, in 1994 SWP contractors and the DWR agreed to authorize permanent sales between SWP contractors. As Pincetl observed, "Clearly the balance of power [regarding water policy] in the state was shifting. But in whose interest?"[65]

Yet despite the apparent success of the drought water bank, in the early 1990s, with the sole exception of the Yuba County Water Agency (YCWA), Central Valley agricultural interests opposed voluntary water transfers (at least to urban Southern California). MWD's Boronkay initiated a number of water transfer initiatives—most notably a highly controversial legislative effort to allow individual water users to transfer water over the objections of their district, which actually held the water rights. In 1992, nearly 80 agricultural water agencies in the Sacramento Valley formed the Northern California Water Association for the sole purpose of going to war with MWD over the water marketing issue. Today, however, many of the same districts are eager to transfer water to MET. This change was led by a few large districts: the YCWA, Western Canal Water District, and Glenn Colusa Irrigation District. This northern California story is essentially one of public agency to public agency transfers, with most of the water made available by fallowing—but in a manner that strengthens farm businesses and the farm economy, and provides hundreds of thousands of acre-feet of options to buy water for Southern California. By 2005, the primary Central Valley complaint was that MWD had not sufficiently exercised its options and purchased their water.[66]

"Who's the Areias Brothers' Keeper?" MWD's Central Valley Deals

The eight-county Central Valley, running along Highway 99 north through the San Joaquin and Sacramento Valleys, produces about 25 percent of the nation's table food and is starting to suffer significant declines in crop yields from air pollution. When Carl Boronkay was still at MWD's helm, the agency entered the heart of this rich but environmentally and politically dicey realm of water transfers after an approach from John, Jess, and Rusty Areias, brothers owning a farm and dairy in Los Banos, in the heart of the Central Valley. Pressured by declining milk prices and dry year water reductions, the brothers Areias decided, in light of passage of the CVPIA (previously opposed by Assemblymember Rusty Areias who had called rural-to-urban water transfers "the equivalent of strip mining"), to keep the land but give up agriculture and sell the water rights.[67]

Secret negotiations culminated in 1993 with a proposed deal for MWD to buy 32,000 AF over 15 years for $175/AF from the Areias family, which paid the CVP $8/AF for water. Local opponents of the deal, demonstrating in the thousands, denounced the Areias brothers as "traitors" complicit in a "water grab" by "the region with the biggest checkbook" that was employing the same "divide-and-conquer campaign . . . used 90 years ago in the Owens Valley." According to one critic, "MWD had swaggered in with their cash and political power and told us it's either their way or the highway. They're going to suck this Valley dry so Los Angeles can grow more suburbs and swimming pools and golf courses all the way out to Palm Springs."[68]

The critics became even hotter than the desert palms when the Areias clan announced that, after all, they would continue dairy and farm operations, too, pumping groundwater for that purpose. Their neighbors complained that the local aquifer would be depleted by the export of high-quality drinking water that would probably end up feeding Southern California lawn sprinklers. The Areias brothers' supplier, the Central California Irrigation District (CCID), which had no objections to land fallowing to facilitate sales between Central Valley water users, made a specific complaint that its future would be imperiled by a deal with MET. Spurred by complaints, a Reclamation Bureau official associated himself with "the sense of unease" about water marketing and promised, "If it gets out of hand, we'll put on the brakes." Taken aback by the bureau's posture and concerned whether the brothers could legally transfer water, MWD made a good-faith payment, and (aided by the banks) consigned the proposal to a quiet death.[69]

Rather than give up, Carl Boronkay's successor, John "Woody" Wodraska, revisited MWD's forays made a decade earlier in the southern San Joaquin Valley. In 1994, MET reached a ground storage deal with the Semitropic Water Storage District, located about 25 miles northwest of Bakersfield. MWD provided SWP water during heavy rain years to replenish Semitropic's depleted underground aquifer, in return for the right to withdraw up to 170,000 AF of water during drought years.[70]

In 1997, a new agreement was negotiated with the Arvin-Edison Water Storage District. Unlike the abortive Areias deal, the negotiations were with a sister water district, not a private party, and were publicized rather than kept secret. In 1996, an agreement was concluded for MWD to purchase 350,000 AF over 25 years. The Friant Water Users Authority, an umbrella district with 25 members including Arvin-Edison, joined the Central Valley Water Coalition and the Natural Resources Defense Council in protesting the deal as a mortal threat to water districts and small farmers poor in groundwater reserves and as an environmental danger to the San Joaquin River. MET and Arvin-Edison entered broadened negotiations with the critics, who, in turn, promised Southern California "access to a new water supply"—but only if no land would be fallowed or rivers threatened and if local districts would receive permanent benefits and suffer "no adverse water supply or cost impacts." The new agreement, announced in 1997, upped the water to be purchased by MWD from 40,000 to 75,000 AF annually for 25 years, but only from flood runoff during wet years. In addition, MET would store a minimum of 250,000 AF of SWP water in the Arvin-Edison aquifer.[71]

This agreement satisfied everybody but the environmentalists concerned about the loss of flood runoff to the San Joaquin River. To circumnavigate this continuing obstacle, MWD and Arvin-Edison renegotiated yet again. Their ingenious new strategy involved using a middleman within the CVP service area. Recruited for this role, the Kern County Water Agency would receive and hold the CVP water sold by Arvin-Edison. But when Metropolitan wanted the water, KCWA would supply it, not with CVP water, but with SWP water from KCWA's own SWP entitlement. This way, technically, no CVP water would leave the Central Valley. Pleased that "we can now implement it without having to go to the state board," MET's Tim Quinn explained that "we structured something that looks like a duck, quacks like a duck, but is not a duck. . . . It's a bona fide exchange." Although the skies opened in the late 1990s, obviating immediate need, the successful deal provided a precedent for MWD's approach in 1999 to 500 potential public and private sellers statewide.[72]

In December 1998, the Bay area–based Western Water Company became the first private concern to sell Central Valley water southward using a public conveyance facility. The deal involved a one-time transfer of 1,000 AF from the Kings County Water District in the Central Valley to Orange County's Santa Margarita Water District. Contending that it should have made a $50,000 profit, Western Water blamed its $100,000 loss on higher-than-anticipated charges by MWD for wheeling the water. In 1999, Western Water teamed with the Natomas Central Mutual Water Company to sell 14,000 AF to Santa Margarita. In 2000, the State Water Resources Control Board cut back the allowable sale to one seventh that amount because it found that improved irrigation by Natomas rice farmers, reducing their consumption of Sacramento River water, did not create a conservation entitlement like that resulting from land fallowing. MET later effected its own deal to buy water from Sacramento Valley rice farmers. In 2002, Western Water concluded another small deal with the city of San Diego, which San Diego touted because the sales price was less than that charged by MWD.[73]

Parted Partners: MWD and Cadiz

We're working with the Metropolitan Water District on a program to provide storage of up to approximately 500,000 acre-feet of surplus Colorado River water. . . . Our program differs substantially from others that have been proposed in that it's both a banking and supply program, and in that it can be fully financed by the private sector.

Cadiz CEO Keith Brackpool, 1998[74]

Anytime someone tries to muck with the park [Mojave National Preserve], we get upset with them, and the Cadiz proposal would be a disaster for the preserve. We're tired of L.A. going out and stealing water. They stole it from Owens Valley and now they want to take it from the Mojave Desert.

Peter Burk, president of Citizens for Mojave National Park, 2002[75]

The 1990s ended much as the 1980s had began—with a groundswell for "market solutions" and "privatization" that even fed a passing enthusiasm to sell water on the Pacific Stock Exchange like any other commodity. MET was propelled into a defensive mode regarding privatization in response to a much-hyped global trend. On the world stage, the number of people receiving water under some sort of privatization arrangement was 51 million in 1990; this jumped to 300 million during the next dozen years.[76]

In the 1990s, MWD had to contend not only with the water crisis that threatened the regional economy but also with a political crisis that eroded its credibility and clout in state politics while undermining its preferred programmatic middle ground. Tarred with the brush of being a public water monopolist, MET risked guilt by association when it began negotiating a water-banking deal with the controversial Westlands Water District. Detested for ruthlessness worthy of private-sector robber barons, Westlands was a western San Joaquin Valley agency with 600 well-heeled members who responded in survival-of-the-fittest fashion to reductions in its water allotment under the CVPIA. The district filed a claim on the San Joaquin River that threatened the CALFED process and risked drying up the water of the Friant Water Users Authority on the east side of the Valley, made up of 15,000 small and middling farmers. "It is nothing short of a direct, Pearl Harbor-style attack intended to cripple agriculture," fumed a Friant official.[77]

Yet MWD's self-presentation as a public agency with an enlightened conscience did not impress militant apostles of a privatized water industry, either. Western Water Company CEO Michael George, for example, scorned MET as an archaic "command and control" bureaucracy that ought to be broken up by an antitrust lawsuit to free the water market from overbearing, self-interested regulators who buttress their power by means of "misleading analogies with energy deregulation." As MWD's then general manager "Woody" Wodraska put it, "The Met had an incentive to show it could do a public-private partnership."[78] Although many in the MET family supported long-term water markets as an appropriate way to encourage proper allocation of resources, they had a problem with the Western Water business plan that sought to use publicly paid infrastructure at marginal costs or at least substantially below amortized costs. This could result in larger water bills for smaller Metropolitan member agencies, particularly those not in a position to play an active role in the water market.[79]

Anxiously seeking to dilute toxic criticism with a show of ideological flexibility, MWD sought to consummate a blue-chip partnership with a sympathetic corporate soulmate. In the Cadiz Corporation it seemed to have found a veritable dreamboat for a public-private marriage. A water-marketing firm named after a desert hamlet near Barstow in San Bernardino County, Cadiz was known as an oasis for candidates trolling for campaign dollars. Its Sacramento political connections outshone its Dun & Bradstreet rating. Was this why a joint-storage project with Cadiz was fast tracked, given priority according to some critics even over the Hayfield project on MWD-owned land adjacent to its aqueduct? Cadiz was founded by English promoter Keith Brackpool. Transitioning from New York to the Golden State, he concluded that "California agriculture was in terminal decline." Then he made waves in California politics as a preeminent contributor to and fundraiser for the gubernatorial campaign of Gray Davis even as his Santa Monica–based firm speculated in banking water in the aquifer beneath the Mojave Desert. Given its high priority on increased water storage capacity, MET was initially able to rationalize a joint undertaking with Cadiz that would have involved storing up to 700,000 AF of surplus Colorado River water in Mojave Desert groundwater basins and to tap up to 1.5 MAF of native water from the aquifer.[80]

Cadiz had lost over $100 million since its incorporation in 1993 but hoped to make from $500 million to $1 billion off the deal over the next half century. Unfortunately, it had little immediate cash flow except for the income generated by its agriculture subsidiary, Sun World, which Brackpool hoped to sell to a Saudi prince. Cash-strapped and heavily indebted to ING Barings, Cadiz had little prospect of raising its half of the $150 million that would be required to build a short pipeline linking the desert storage facility to the Colorado River Aqueduct. MET was expected to help out by a prepayment of $54 million to Cadiz for water it would later store. Assuring skeptics after Gray Davis's 1998 electoral victory that "this is an administration that genuinely will promote water transfers," Brackpool used his Sacramento connections to have up to a $50-million subsidy for the proposed MWD-Cadiz deal written into the March 2000 state water bond initiative.[81]

The proposal was buffeted by political winds from all directions. Environmentalists, supported by U.S. senator Dianne Feinstein, darkly warned that it would degrade the Mojave aquifer and turn the desert towns into a dustbowl. Antiprivatization activists rejected it as corruption of a "public trust resource." Free-market proponents had no objections to its conceptual underpinnings but shared doubts about whether Cadiz had long-term financial viability and was a creditworthy partner. And political cynics surmised, in the words of Francesca Krauel, a San Diego MWD board member, that "the thinking [behind the deal] was that: You make a deal with Keith Brackpool, and you're on the good side of Gray Davis" who supposedly "had nothing but disdain" for MWD. James Edwards, an MWD board member representing the Foothill Municipal Water District, prognosticated, "If we had a new governor, I believe this thing would fall by the wayside and die a natural death." He proved a prophet.[82]

The MWD board voted down the deal by a close margin in October 2002, citing concerns about the environment, escalating project costs, and an uncertain water supply. And the next year California did indeed have a new governor, although by recall. The real deal breaker may not have been a weakened and soon-to-be-recalled governor or even the opposition of Senator Feinstein and leading environmentalists. For the professionals within the MET family, what mattered most was the lengthy drought and dwindling supply on the Colorado River, where water that was to be used for the storage component clearly was not going to be available. This fundamentally changed the economics and desirability of the project, because long-term supply reliability could no longer be assured.[83]

The abortive MWD-Cadiz deal was, among other things, a cautionary tale of how political influence peddling, real or perceived, can poison the prospects for public-private partnerships in water marketing. High transaction costs, especially wheeling charges, have combined with unresolved policy debates about the propriety of privatizing public-water resources to make California something of a mirage for firms—Cadiz, Western Water, Vidler Water, and Azurix (an Enron subsidiary)—in search of "blue gold."[84]

Fallow the Leader: MWD's Audacious Palo Verde Deal

By helping farmers better manage fluctuations in the crop market, this [deal] could well be one of the best-ever stimulants to Palo Verde's slow economy. At the same time, it will offer a valuable commodity for consumers throughout Metropolitan's service area.

> *PVID board chair Gary Bryce, 2002*[85]

Today's agreement is characterized by a business-like environment, free of the acrimony that was so commonplace in the history of water in California.

> *MWD board chair Phillip J. Pace, 2002*[86]

The MWD-Palo Verde Irrigation District Land Management, Crop Rotation, and Water Supply Program has a history (going back to 1986–1987) almost as tortuous as the Colorado River. Bordering southeastern Riverside County and northern Imperial County and approximately 200 miles east of Los Angeles, the Palo Verde Valley had an irresistible lure to rural-to-urban water marketers because the PVID has the highest priority among Southern California water agencies to Colorado River water, based on acreage in need of irrigation deriving from an 1877 appropriative claim on the Colorado River. After earlier negotiations fell apart over price disagreements, between 1992 and 1994 MET and PVID agreed to a short-term pilot program, enrolling some 22 percent of valley acreage, that compensated farmers at $135/AF for setting aside a portion of their land for two years, in return for the water that otherwise would have been used primarily to grow hay and cotton. MET received rights to 186,000 AF of additional Colorado River water as its payoff. A subsequent study of local impacts found that the farmers spent over 90 percent of the money paid for land fallowing on farm-related investments, purchases, and debt repayment, ostensibly strengthening the local agricultural economy.[87]

The pilot program was the precedent for a more ambitious deal negotiated in 2001, finalized in 2002, and implemented in 2004 despite protests over the years from some local interests concerned about a replay in their valley of the inequities (real and/or imagined) of San Diego's transfer deal with the Imperial Irrigation District. The new MWD-PVID program called for removal from cultivation of up to 29 percent of their land by signatory farmers who receive for each acre set aside a one-time payment of $3,170 plus $550 annually. The 35-year program would fallow as many as 26,500 acres of the valley during any one year, with the land taken out of production to be rotated in a five-year cycle. The annual savings of up to 110,000 AF of water in some years would be for immediate use or storage by MWD. Initiating the program at a cost of $94.3 million, MET would fund a local community foundation with $6 million to offset potential adverse third-party socioeconomic impacts on the local agricultural economy. Although proposals were made in Sacramento to mandate that the socioeconomic impacts of water deals be mitigated, the current rule under CEQA was that "evidence of social or economic impacts which do not contribute to, or are not caused by, physical impacts on the environment is not substantial evidence" of undue environmental impacts.[88]

The MWD-PVID deal made economic sense for several reasons. The vast majority of irrigated farmland in the valley is not designated Prime Farmland or Farmland of State Importance. The primary crops grown are not labor intensive, reducing the potential impact on farm worker employment. Local farm equipment dealers would likely suffer from a decline in machinery purchases, but this impact was not likely to be great on an already depressed agricultural region where not much equipment was being bought to grow new crops. The follow-up study to the 1992–1994 pilot program had shown a 1.3 percent total employment loss, no loss to non–farm-related businesses, with minimal losses to farm-related businesses counterbalanced by an overall positive outcome for the local economy of the infusion of MET money.[89]

At the crux of the deal were value-freighted, polarized assessments of the significance of land fallowing that transcended the realm of the merely economic. Proponents of farming as a way of life understandably recoiled at the prospect of taking land out of production. There were ways to save water from agricultural operations for rural-to-urban transfers that did not involve fallowing. For example, MWD's transfer deal with Arvin-Edison in the Central Valley involved the transfer solely of conserved flood runoff during wet years, and the original intent of SDCWA's deal with IID also was for savings solely from "efficiency measures" involving improved pumping, nonleaking gates, and on-farm and system conservation. The irony here was that environmentalists, who often had virtual veto power over such deals, considered fallowing a lesser evil than efficiency-generated flow or runoff reductions into the San Joaquin River or the Salton Sea.

After spilling much political blood on the environmental front, the San Diego County Water Authority in its IID negotiations finally switched to political damage control by admitting that it would be necessary to fallow some land in the Imperial Valley. The ultimate IID-SDCWA deal provided for fallowing 5 to 7 percent of the agricultural land under production during the first 15 years of the agreement, which also required adjusting the transfer schedule to lessen the impact. The deal's adverse economic impacts were mitigated by IID's purchase of the Bass brothers' landholdings, which had been transferred to U.S. Filter and later to the French conglomerate Vivendi. In contrast, MET was much more effective in floating its PVID deal. The *Western Farm Press* claimed this was a "high stakes five-card stud poker game" in which MWD would bet as much as necessary to win the pot. Money is political mother's milk on California's farms as well as in its cities. A $100-million infusion into the local economy made a true believer and water statesman out of PVID chair Gary Bryce, who saw prosperity just around the corner for local farmers and urban water consumers.[90]

In forging a "fallowship of the ring" in favor of the PVID deal, MWD was politically audacious in a manner suggesting that, even in the 21st century, the regional water giant had not entirely lost the legendary political skills that once had placed it on the level of skilled California practitioners such as former Assembly Speaker Jesse Unruh. In October, 2001, MET entered into an agreement with San Diego Gas and Electric Company (SDG&E) for MWD to purchase 16,344 acres of SDG&E land in the Palo Verde Valley for $42.5 million. This masterstroke made it a powerful Palo Verde landowner as well as a white knight to SDG&E officials and investors desperate to end their nuclear power plant exposure in the Valley. Then MET completed the political trumping of the San Diego water establishment by agreeing to sluice the initial phase of the IID/SDCWA transfer with water from its PVID deal. The deal's seeming moral was that economists and entrepreneurs could propose transfers, but they required savvy water bureaucrats as their political architects in order to come to fruition because of the inherently public nature of water in the United States.[91]

21st-Century Stakes

The introduction of marketable water rights signals the end of an era in California, even if that era was made up more of dreams than reality.

Stephanie Pincetl, Transforming California *(1999)*[92]

To paraphrase Winston Churchill about democracy, the market may be the worst kind of economic system—except for all the others. Yet not all markets are the same. The classic, laissez-faire marketplace was, at least in theory, a self-regulating affair in which the interaction of supply, demand, and fluctuating price determined the distribution of commodities. According to the institutional economic historian Karl Polanyi, markets through most of the past have not been free or self-regulating entities.

They have been administered or regulated—or subordinated to collective norms governing social status and reciprocal obligations often involving the redistribution of goods. In Polanyi's view, the transnational 19th-century "internal market" that subordinated Western society to economic values and transformed it in the process was quite different from the "external markets" pervasive throughout much of prior history. The latter involved trade and transfers, often over long distances, between self-regulating societies that did not subordinate their internal value systems to market imperatives.[93]

These observations may seem far afield in time and place from the emerging water markets in which MWD has become enmeshed as it searches for ways to supplement its water supplies. Yet they illuminate the very real tensions between the rival value emphases of those who want to create an internally self-regulating, commodified mechanism—a "free market in water"—and those who insist that market considerations should continue to be subordinated to a "trust resource" doctrine that defines water as public property to which private property holders are entitled to use rights but not ownership.[94]

Itself a public agency tasked with resource management for the common good of its members—and, by extension, of the regional economy and all Californians—MWD has had to straddle the tensions between these competing imperatives. Rather than plunge right into the free-market maelstrom, MWD has tested the waters of the new, increasingly globalized market economy in a resource that is as vital as the air we breathe. It has kept one foot, if not always firmly, on the traditional foundation of a regulated market that subordinated water transfers, however common and critically important, to essentially political determinations about priority uses and users. Implicitly, though with some important recent exceptions—such as the Cadiz deal—it has tried to make market price transactions "external" to the internal criteria determining how water is distributed, and redistributed, among its member agencies and the vital communities of interest that they serve.

Despite tentative beginnings, water transfers represent a key ingredient of Metropolitan's 21st-century water-reliability strategy. A major goal of MET's 1996 Integrated Resources Plan—a 20-year resource plan—was to develop additional supply reliability through the California Aqueduct by entering into flexible transfer and storage agreements with

Central Valley Project (CVP) and State Water Project (SWP) contractors. By 2003, Metropolitan had entered into eight major CVP-SWP transfer and storage programs—for 300,000 AF per year—available for meeting dry-year needs. Other spot-market transfer opportunities were identified to generate an additional 250,000 annual AF of buffer supply (reserves). In all, the promised 550,000 annual AF of CVP/SWP storage and transfer represented over 10 percent of Metropolitan's overall resource targets for the year 2025.[95]

The future of water provision in 21st-century Southern California will hinge to a considerable degree on whether and how well Metropolitan continues to navigate between the Scylla of authoritative, potentially authoritarian politics and the Charybdis of efficient, potentially soulless economics. In the future even more than the past, MWD's challenge will be to reconcile as best it can the ultimately incompatible definitions of itself as a state-sanctioned arbiter of an irreducible, indispensable public good or the servant of a commodified market in water. Most of all, and especially during the periodic waves of privatization enthusiasm that sweep American politics, this will require MET reminding the public—and itself—of its distinct advantages as a public agency, with public board decision making, long-term continuity of operations and borrowing, and run by board members and managers sworn to a public trust—albeit a trust that, according to some critics, is sometimes forgotten.

III   *At the Crossroads*

Water, water, everywhere,
And all the boards did shrink;
Water, water, everywhere,
Nor any drop to drink.

> *Samuel Taylor Coleridge, "The Rime of the Ancient Mariner," 1798*[1]

Adaptation is the covenant that all successful organisms sign with the dry country. . . . Water is safety, home, life, place. All around those precious watered places, forbidding and unlivable, is only space, what one must travel through between places of safety.

> *Wallace Stegner, "Living Dry," 1987*[2]

More prosaic than Wallace Stegner, Southern Californians take many things for granted, including 70-degree January temperatures, traffic congestion, and a reliable water supply. Unlike the warm winter weather (which they proudly showcase during the annual Rose Parade) and traffic delays (which they grudgingly tolerate), local residents rarely think about water. For water to have slipped so completely from public consciousness in a semiarid desert environment with limited local supplies is a testament to the reliability with which MET and its member agencies have supplied water.

In the early 21st century Metropolitan and its constituent members again find themselves as combatants, struggling to overcome a host of challenges to sustaining their estimable track record. This chapter examines key looming challenges, ranging from rapid growth to water supply, quality, and security concerns; the next chapter considers MWD's plans to meet them. We begin with population growth. How will millions more residents affect water demand in Southern California? Does rapid population growth elsewhere in the state and the Colorado River Basin threaten Metropolitan's imported supplies by creating greater competition for an increasingly scarce resource? Next, we turn to supply uncertainties created by climate patterns. To what extent was the 20th century an historical aberration—characterized by unusually wet years—and are there better guides for the future? We also consider the implications of global warming.

Metropolitan faces a number of environmental challenges. One involves the water needs of environmental projects, notably habitat restoration and preservation along with endangered species protection, which impinge on MWD's supplies. Another involves legislation mandating an assured water supply for new development and other stringent water requirements. Can MET provide such guarantees? We also examine water-quality concerns. How do contaminants such as perchlorate, MTBE, nitrates, and various volatile organic compounds affect Metropolitan's ability to provide safe water? Is MWD up to the task? Finally, we consider a more sinister meaning of "secure water supplies"—the daunting task of protecting Metropolitan's facilities and Southern California's water supplies from terrorist attack.

Population Growth: More Water Is Needed?

Los Angeles will remain the largest county in California, exceeding 11 million [people] in 2050. In numeric terms, Riverside County is expected to add more people than any other county with 2.8 million new residents. By 2050, Riverside is projected to overtake Orange County and become the third most populous county behind Los Angeles and San Diego.

California Department of Finance, 2004[3]

In a reversal from the 1940s—when MWD risked white elephant status because it had a costly long-term project built for future growth needs and was awash in water but not customers—Metropolitan's premier challenge in the coming decades will be to ensure that it doesn't find itself with more customers than water. Facing significant population growth in its service territory, will MET and its member agencies be able to provide sufficient water to meet heightened demand?

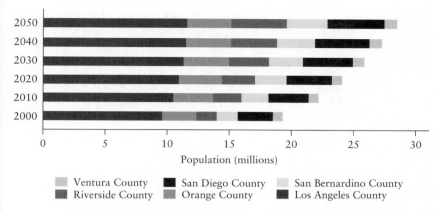

FIGURE **7.1**   **Southern California population projections, 2000–2050 (millions)**

SOURCE: State of California, Department of Finance, *Population Projections by Race/Ethnicity, Gender and Age for California and Its Counties 2000–2050.*

Backed by the promise of reliable water, Southern California has experienced a generations-long population boom. From fewer than 3 million residents when MWD was created in 1928, the combined population of Los Angeles, Orange, Ventura, Riverside, San Bernardino, and San Diego counties has increased more than sixfold, exceeding 20 million people in 2003. (MET now serves 85 percent of the six-county population.) In the 1990s, regional growth slowed from its historic pace but picked up again in 2000. The forecasted regional population growth, 2000–2050, depicted in Figure 7.1, will be quite robust, particularly in inland San Bernardino and Riverside counties. Current residents having children and a net influx of migrants, primarily from outside the United States, will combine to keep Southern California's population growing steadily well into the middle of the 21st century.

Between 2000 and 2020, the region is projected to grow by 24 percent, adding nearly 5 million new residents. This is equivalent to adding the population of Minnesota, which ranks 21st by state population. By 2050, Southern California is likely to have 28 million residents— a 45 percent increase over 2000, and equivalent to adding the population of Georgia, now the 9th most populous state. Forecasts extending out decades need to be treated with some caution, because minor changes in initial assumptions can lead to surprisingly divergent predictions. Indeed, different expectations for the level of migration to and from California and other states have produced statewide population estimates that differ by millions of people. Nonetheless, Metropolitan will have to prepare for millions of additional customers, since even the most divergent major forecasts for the state are consistently predicting a continued strong upward trend in the region's population growth.[4]

Forecasting Regional Water Needs

In the early 21st century, Southern California is poised to add millions of new residents, most of whom will live within Metropolitan's service area. How MWD will balance supply and demand under these circumstances is a major challenge. MET's annual deliveries vary considerably with changes in hydrology, retail demand, and other factors. The average annual delivery, 1990–2003, was just under 2.0 MAF. By 2003, in the middle of a lengthy drought, deliveries had risen to 2.4 MAF. If per capita deliveries of water remain constant as the population grows and nothing else changes, by 2010 MET will need to deliver 2.6 MAF under hydrological conditions similar to those in 2003. By 2050, MWD will need to deliver 3.3 MAF. To place the additional 946,000 AF required by 2050 (relative to 2003) in context, consider that State Water Project annual deliveries to MWD have averaged 1.5 MAF.[5]

How much Metropolitan will actually need to deliver each year is a function of retail demand and groundwater replenishment needs minus local supplies. MWD planners forecast water demand using a sophisticated in-house computer model, MWD-MAIN. This program calculates demand by sector, treating household, commercial and industrial, and agricultural users separately. MET incorporates population and economic forecasts from two regional planning agencies: the Southern California Association of Governments (SCAG) and the San Diego Association of Governments (SANDAG). (Their forecasts are broadly similar to those from the California Department of Finance—presented in Figure 7.1—although they suggest greater population growth within MWD's service area.)[6]

The MWD-MAIN model generates forecasts for wet-, average-, and dry-year hydrologies. The water demand forecasts for 2025 are

TABLE 7.1
Estimated MWD Water Demand, 2025 (millions of acre-feet per year)

	Multiple Dry Years*	Single Dry Year*	Average Year	Wet Year*
Retail Demand	5.07	4.99	4.94	5.05
Groundwater Replenishment	0.42	0.42	0.41	0.43
Demand Subtotal	5.49	5.41	5.35	5.48
Local Supplies	2.80	2.79	2.95	3.08
Demand on MWD	2.69	2.62	2.40	2.41

SOURCE: MWDSC, *Report on Metropolitan's Water Supplies* (Los Angeles: MWDSC, 2003), Appendix A, p. 8.

*Multiple-dry-year forecast based on a repeat of the hydrology observed 1990–1992; single-dry-year forecast is based on a repeat of 1977 hydrology; the wet-year forecast assumes a recurrence of 1985 hydrology.

presented in Table 7.1. MWD anticipates retail water demand will rise to between 4.9 and 5.1 MAF by 2025, with groundwater replenishment needs adding a further 400,000-plus AF per year to total demand. Local supplies will meet 51 to 56 percent of total demand, leaving MET to supply 2.4 to 2.7 MAF. Yet the small range of variation in MWD future demand may be unrealistic. In the last 15 years, Metropolitan has experienced a full 60 percent fluctuation in demand.

MWD's forecast of imported water supplies needed for its member agencies also appears lower than otherwise anticipated, because it incorporates higher reliance on local supplies. Yet the large local project numbers may be suspect. Local resources are a highly political issue within the MET family, with some member agencies wanting the glory and control of local supplies although not being in a position to come up with the needed money. In actuality, MET's needed deliveries through 2025 could be higher than forecast. As a result (as discussed in the next chapter), Metropolitan is creating a "buffer" supply to address such uncertainties without breaking the bank.

MWD's forecast also builds in allowances for continued conservation efforts. Metropolitan expects water savings from conservation to be offset by "the effect of increasing regional income, growing penetration rates of water-using appliances, and growth in hot and dry areas. As a result *per capita water demand is forecast to remain relatively constant* over the 25-year forecast horizon" (emphasis added). Thus MET expects millions of new customers and constant per-capita water use yet forecasts that its own deliveries will barely increase from 2.35 MAF in 2003 to between 2.40 and 2.69 MAF in 2025. As later argued, these figures may be on the low side. There is a real possibility of even more conservation savings than forecast. Together, moderate local resources growth and greater than expected conservation will provide some relief from boxed-in imported supplies, at least in the intermediate term.[7]

Thirsty Neighbors

MWD was created to import water, and for the foreseeable future securing water from far-flung sources will remain central to its mission. But Metropolitan is not the only party using the Colorado River and the State Water Project. Rapid urban population growth in the rest of California and in other Colorado River Basin states (plus Mexico) may soon lead these other areas to cast covetous eyes on MWD's imported water sources. And these fast-growing areas will be looking at the same sources as MET to augment core supplies—particularly agricultural water. California's population of nearly 35 million residents is expected to swell by 20 million more by 2050. Figure 7.2 shows that the state's population will likely exceed the 50-million mark by 2040.

The six counties of Southern California—already the state's largest population center and home to one in two Californians—are projected to account for 44 percent of the state's forecast growth. The most dramatic growth likely will be in the Central Valley, where in the foreseeable future millions of new residents will eclipse the still-growing San Francisco Bay area as the state's second most populous region. As Central and Northern California add people, Metropolitan may find itself in growing intrastate competition for Northern California agricultural water supplies.

Instead of being one of the few purchasers in a nascent State Water Project–Central Valley Project water market, Metropolitan could find itself in a more competitive environment for agricultural water. Rapid urbanization in the Central Valley may lead some local water agencies to curtail their marketing plans or raise their prices. They may prefer to see water banked for their own future needs, rather than sold off to the

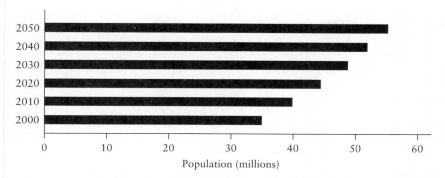

FIGURE **7.2**   California population projections, 2000–2050 (millions)

s o u r c e : State of California, Department of Finance, *Population Projections by Race/Ethnicity, Gender and Age for California and Its Counties 2000–2050.*

highest bidder. MWD's long-range plans through 2025 call for water market purchases to fill gaps in its water portfolio under dry hydrological conditions. Hence, the availability of spot markets is a big question facing MET. Further, the globalization of agriculture might free up water. Facing increased competition, Central Valley farmers might find water marketing attractive with appropriate social, economic, and environmental safeguards.[8]

Metropolitan also faces the prospect of increased interstate competition for water from growing Colorado River Basin states. California shares the Colorado River with six other states plus Mexico. These states grew by at least 20 percent, 1990–2000. Indeed, between 1990 and 2000 Nevada, Arizona, Colorado, and Utah had the highest population growth rates among all U.S. states. Table 7.2 displays population growth, 2000–2030, for the other Colorado River Basin states. Facing rapid growth, Arizona already has created a water bank. Later there could be pressure to revisit water allocations in the West, although such efforts would face the formidable "Law of the River" (compacts, statutes, contracts, and court opinions) that constitutes the foundation for existing Colorado River allocations.[9]

California has a basic claim to 4.4 MAF of Colorado River water, and Metropolitan has a fourth-priority base apportionment of 550,000 AF of the state's total allotment. Until recently, however, California has used more than its allotment, relying on its right to half of the

TABLE 7.2

Population Projections for Colorado River Basin States (excluding California),
2000–2030 (millions)

	2000	2010	2020	2030
Arizona	5.13	6.15	7.36	8.62
Colorado	4.30	5.14	6.13	7.16
Nevada	2.00	2.81	3.41	*
New Mexico	1.82	2.11	2.38	2.63
Utah	2.23	2.79	3.37	3.77
Wyoming	0.49	0.52	0.53	*
Total	15.98	19.51	23.20	*

SOURCE: State of Arizona, Arizona Department of Economic Security, Research Administration, Population Statistics Unit, *July 1, 1997 to July 1, 2050 Arizona County Population Projections* (February 1997); State of Colorado, Colorado Demography Office, *Draft Population Forecasts by Region, 2000–2030* (June 2003); State of Nevada, Nevada State Demographer's Office, *Population Projections for Nevada's Counties, 2004–2024* (n.d.); Bureau of Business and Economic Research (BBER), University of New Mexico, *Revised Population Projections for New Mexico and Counties, July 1, 2000 to July 1, 2030* (revised April 2004); State of Utah, Governor's Office of Planning and Budget, *Population Estimates and Projections by MCD 1940–2030* (n.d.); State of Wyoming, Department of A & I, Economic Analysis Division, *Population Estimates and Projections for Wyoming, Counties, Cities, and Towns: 2000 to 2020* (n.d.).

*Not available / not applicable.

"surplus" water. MWD was one of the largest users of "surplus" water. Under drought conditions, thoughts of surplus water vanish. It may take 15 or more years of average rainfall across the Colorado River Basin before the reservoirs along the river are sufficiently replenished so that the U.S. Department of the Interior can again declare surplus conditions. Although MET is not counting on a return to surplus conditions, by the time a surplus is declared there will be millions more residents in neighboring states anxious for a share. Figure 7.3 shows the historical supply and demand on the Colorado River, 1935–2003.[10]

Observe how demand has gradually crept up toward the dry-year average river runoff-inflow on the Colorado River. At current levels, demand would have exceeded river inflow in dry years—such as occurring in the decade between 1954 and 1964—where it previously did not. The growing population of other Colorado River Basin states is important for Metropolitan inasmuch as it places greater demands on future river runoff-inflow. So, too, is Mexico's increasing thirst for Colorado River water, guaranteed at 1.5 MAF per year under existing treaty rights. Thus MWD's contingency planning no longer relies on Colorado River surpluses.[11]

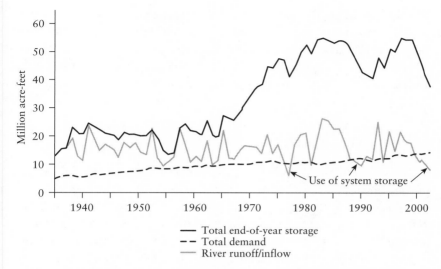

FIGURE **7.3**   Historical supply and demand on the Colorado River, 1935–2003

SOURCE: MWDSC, *Report on Metropolitan's Water Supplies* (Los Angeles: MWDSC, 2003), Appendix B, p. 11.

Hydrology and Water Supply

Events are mere "surface disturbances, crests of foam that the tides of history carry on their strong backs."

> *Fernand Braudel,* The Mediterranean and the Mediterranean World in the Age of Philip II *(1949)* [12]

Past performance is not necessarily indicative of future results.

> *Standard financial-industry disclaimer*

Historian Fernand Braudel insisted that history has three time scales: the fleeting "event time" of wars and revolutions; the longer *conjonctures*— the time span of economies and empires, of cyclical process that may last generations or even centuries; and the *longue durée*, the deeper geological time of the physical environment. Braudel considered the *longue durée* the most important time scale, underpinning and shaping faster-moving events. [13]

The notion of the *longue durée* is particularly relevant when considering long-term hydrology and its implications for future water availability. MET supply forecasts are based on almost 100 years of recorded observations. Compared to a human life span, a century is a long time indeed. On a geological scale, it is a mere instant. Here we consider Southern California's water prospects against the backdrop of the *longue durée*, using the severe 2000–2004 drought in the Colorado River Basin as a point of departure.

The Dry, Dry West

Droughts are difficult to define, because they can be alternatively expressed in terms of lower-than-usual precipitation, as low soil moisture or stream flows, or in relation to low groundwater or reservoir levels. The National Oceanic and Atmospheric Administration (NOAA) distinguishes between meteorological, climatological, atmospheric, agricultural, hydrologic, and water management droughts. Definitional difficulties aside, there is little doubt that the states of the Colorado River Basin other than California, along with several other western states (and northern Mexico), experienced a severe and prolonged drought in 2000–2004. This broke records on the Colorado River, including driest 5 years, driest single year, and lowest 3-year average stream flow since detailed record-keeping began almost 100 years ago. Measured at Lee's Ferry, the stream flow in two 3-year periods—2000–2002 and 2001–2003—are the first- and second-lowest recorded 3-year averages, displacing the previous low, 1953–1955.[14]

By spring 2005, despite a winter of wet storms, the two main reservoirs on the Colorado River remained quite low. Lake Mead (behind Hoover Dam in Nevada) was at roughly 60 percent of capacity, and close to its lowest level since the 1960s. Lake Powell (behind Glen Canyon Dam on the Arizona-Utah border) was less than 40 percent full. Other lake and reservoir levels across the West had precipitously dropped as well and had only begun to refill. Figure 7.4 shows the May 2005 reservoir levels across each of 11 Western states relative to average storage levels.[15]

The figure shows the percentage of usable storage remaining in each state's reservoirs. (Not all the water in a reservoir is usable; below certain levels it becomes impractical or impossible to drain additional water). Given usable water remaining, Colorado, Montana, Nevada, New Mexico, Oregon, Utah, and Wyoming were the hardest hit by the

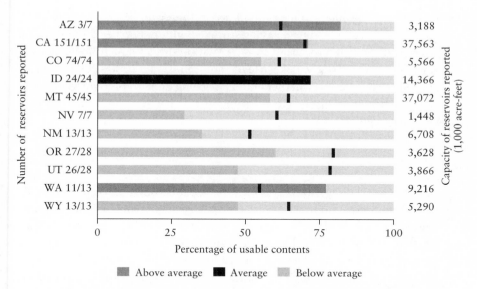

FIGURE **7.4**   **Water storage levels for western states, reservoir storage as of May 2005 (preliminary)**

SOURCE: USDA, Natural Resources Conservation Service, National Water and Climate Center, Portland, OR, http://www.wcc.nrcs.usda.gov.

lengthy drought. Statewide totals can mask considerable local variation, however. California was comparatively fortunate, although water agencies in Southern California were closely monitoring storage facilities on the Colorado River in Arizona, Nevada, and Utah.[16]

The drought had severe repercussions throughout the West. Power generation fell to 40 percent of capacity at Glen Canyon Dam. A further 85-foot drop in Lake Powell's level would force power generation to be curtailed entirely. At Lake Mead, the falling water level raised concern that Hoover Dam power generation might have to be curtailed. Even fossil-fuel power plants were threatened. Coal-fired plants such as the Navajo Generating Station in Arizona also draw water from the Colorado River. Agricultural production suffered, and recreational water use was affected. Environmental devastation included millions of dead or weakened trees, and sharply declining fish and animal populations.

In 2005, with one of the wettest years in recorded history, it appeared the drought might be over. Even so, it could take many years of normal rainfall to bring storage on the Colorado River back up to its

2000 level. Should average rainfall occur, there will be political pressures to release surpluses, thus delaying storage buildup. Further drought could turn Lake Powell into "dead storage" within three years, followed within another two years by Lake Mead. For some, the 2000–2004 drought raised concerns as to whether enough is being done to prepare for lengthy dry spells, particularly given rising water demand from the growing population in the West.

Another Dust Bowl?

Is the West in danger of becoming another Dust Bowl, adversely affecting MET's supplies and those of other western water agencies? Some climatic hints are contained in the recorded measurements of stream flow, precipitation, and other hydrological indicators, which in the West stretch back less than a century. During the 1930s and 1950s, there were severe droughts in the central United States, and the late 1980s and early 1990s were unusually dry on the West Coast. Yet these records cover a comparatively brief period of time, particularly in light of recent advances in understanding the complex interactions among ocean surface temperatures, climate patterns, and precipitation.[17]

First, scientists have developed a better understanding of the El Niño-Southern Oscillation (ENSO). The Southern Oscillation is the seesaw pattern of shifting sea-level atmospheric pressure between the Pacific and Indian oceans that causes the trade winds to either intensify or slacken. Strong trade winds pull cold water north, creating the cold La Niña phase of the ENSO; slack trade winds allow warm tropical water to spread south and east, producing the warm El Niño phase. ENSO phases last 6 to 18 months and have a strong influence on precipitation in the southwestern United States.[18]

Second, in the mid-1990s scientists discovered a long-term pattern of shifting surface water temperatures in the Pacific Ocean they dubbed the Pacific Decadal Oscillation (PDO). A full PDO cycle appears to take 50 years, meaning that "much of the North Pacific Ocean will be predominantly though not uniformly warm (or cool) for periods of about 15 to 25 years." More recent observations suggest that the PDO may also shift in shorter periods of just several years. Like ENSO, the PDO appears to have a strong influence on precipitation patterns in the

Southwestern United States. Third, scientists have recently discovered a similar long-term trend in surface ocean temperatures in the North Atlantic, called the Atlantic Multidecadal Oscillation (AMO). The AMO pattern appears to be one with warm and cool phases lasting 20 to 35 years each. The AMO also influences precipitation patterns in the southwestern United States, although the relationship is less well understood than with the ENSO and the PDO.[19]

Scientists speculate that rainfall patterns in the West are influenced by a complex interaction of the effects from these large patterns. Since these phenomena have lengthy (6-month to 35-year) oscillations that are not necessarily coincidental, the less than 100-year record of hydrological data in the West seems for some observers to be too brief a time scale in which to have encountered the full range of possible precipitation patterns. This highlights the significance of work being done by another group of scientists, who have pieced together a hydrological record stretching back centuries.

Paleoclimatologists use proxies—including tree rings; pollen in lakebeds, sand dunes, and ice core samples; and changes in lake levels and salinity—to reconstruct this historical record. Such records suggest that 20th-century droughts may not have been terribly unusual. Droughts on par with the 1950s-era drought appear to have occurred once or twice per hundred years in each of the past three centuries. Although the 1930s drought was probably the worst in the previous 300 years, an even more severe drought took place at the end of the 16th century. Indeed, most of the West seems to have been abnormally dry for 80 years beginning in the late 1500s. The 20th century, in contrast, seems to have been unusually wet, with the 20 years starting in the late 1970s marking the wettest period in the last 1,000 years.[20]

Although a megadrought about 700 years ago may have contributed to the demise of the Anasazi Indians, the Southwest's first known human settlers, most of today's Southern California residents have no memory of even the relatively recent 1930s-era Dustbowl experience. Lulled by nearly two decades of above-average precipitation that preceded the 2000–2004 drought, many western cities failed to acquire the water supplies needed to keep pace with their booming populations. Now they face the prospects of "water police" patrolling their streets to ticket scofflaws who fail to conserve. Given the vagaries of long-term climatic and hydrologic patterns, MET's planning does include provision for the next drought. Yet one of the major supply disasters facing MET may be not drought but earthquake. For example, liquefaction could occur in the Bay-Delta area following a major seismic event. This could force Southern California into water rationing for a number of years until natural flushing took place, or some sort of peripheral canal was finally built.[21]

MWD's Crystal Ball

Metropolitan forecasts its water supplies based on the last 77 years of observed hydrological conditions, 1921–1998. Metropolitan hydrologists run simulations in which probabilities are assigned to dry-year, multiple-dry-year, and wet-year scenarios. The dry-year scenario is based on a repeat of 1977 hydrology; the multiple-dry-year scenario is based on a repeat of the observed 1990–1992 hydrology; and the wet-year scenario is based on a recurrence of 1985 hydrology. Metropolitan "stress tests" its supplies using these scenarios by mapping past hydrology onto future years. Thus, in a model run that hypothesizes a repeat of 1977 dry-year hydrology in 2010, the next year's hydrology is based on 1978, 2012 hydrology is based on 1979, and so on. Using this type of modeling, MET predicts that it will be able to reliably meet its customers' demand for water through 2025. As we move forward in time, so does MWD's observed 77-year period move forward, thus incorporating current climate trends and melding them into the long-term trends. MWD's water supply forecasts, however, do not appear to allow for the type of perturbations that the complex interactions of the ENSO, PDO, and AMO suggest we might expect.[22]

Long-term hydrological patterns reconstructed from tree rings and other records suggest that the hydrology of the West is extremely variable and that any baseline data must be treated with caution. Yet MWD does not appear to be seriously considering the possible implications of wider hydrological fluctuations than observed since the 1920s. Metropolitan's primary water-supply documents do not include a discussion of the potential impact of a recurrence of conditions outside of the recorded hydrological history. However, MET did submit information highlighting the limitations of tree-ring analysis for a report on the potential consequences of climate variability for California. Metropolitan noted the potential bias in tree-ring data toward reporting dry conditions. Yet, the tree-ring data in question cover a *very* long record. Even if the data are biased toward dryness, the evidence of extended dry periods *relative to other extended periods covered by the same data* should give us pause when assessing future water reliability. At the very least, MWD may want to incorporate more severe drought scenarios in its modeling of future water supply reliability.[23]

However, the new sciences of historical hydrology and paleoclimatology provide cautionary guidance but not panaceas for water planners. Braudel's *longue durée* stretching over centuries is a valuable hermeneutic backdrop but of minimal use in predicting the day after tomorrow or even 20 years down the road. The most accurate predictive tools—for example, forecasts based on snowpack thickness and monsoon moisture—are useful for relatively short-term predictions. Essentially, MET is using a slowly-moving 20th-century baseline to model 21st-century climate trends. Although the 21st century may turn out to be very different, the last century's trend lines are the most plausible comparison from which MET modelers can extrapolate. Referring to economic policy making, John Maynard Keynes declared that "two generations is the practical alternative to eternity." For water resource planners, projections based on up to the last 100-year trends clearly remain the best practicable and primary predictive tool available.[24]

The Specter of Global Warming

Regional changes in climate, particularly increases in temperature, have already affected a diverse set of physical and biological systems in many parts of the world. Examples of observed changes include shrinkage of glaciers, thawing of permafrost, later freezing and earlier break-up of ice on rivers and lakes, lengthening of mid- to high-latitude growing seasons, poleward and altitudinal shifts of plant and animal ranges, [and] declines of some plant and animal populations.

> *Working Group II of the Intergovernmental Panel on Climate Change,* Climate Change 2001: Impacts, Adaptation, and Vulnerability *(2001)*[25]

It is vital that uncertainties not be used to delay or avoid taking certain kinds of action now. Water managers and policymakers must start considering climate change as a factor in all decisions about water investments and the operation of existing facilities and systems.

Peter Gleick, Water: The Potential Consequences of Climate Variability and Change for the Water Resources of the United States *(2000)*[26]

Global Warming?

Global warming and its impact on water supplies are steeped in uncertainty and controversy. Some skeptics doubt that global warming is real; others have acknowledged the trend but deny human culpability. The preponderance of scientific evidence points to a gradual warming trend that may herald widespread climate changes. The planet's average surface temperatures appear to be on course for a rise of between 2.5 to 10.4 degrees Fahrenheit, 1990 to 2100. The change in California will be most noticeable in winter, when the average temperature will increase more than it will in the summer. If it materializes, the warming will have far-reaching implications for Californians.[27]

From a water-systems management perspective, whether the human role is contributing is moot. What matters is whether and how a warming trend may affect water supplies. Scientists using computer models to simulate the effects of global warming have produced a wide range of possible impacts. They acknowledge uncertainties surrounding global warming predictions by characterizing the likelihood of particular changes occurring. For California's water system, they assign the highest level of confidence to changes in snowfall and snowmelt patterns, earlier peak runoff flows in the spring, and higher sea levels. Medium confidence is given to summer flow reductions, and lower confidence to area-specific changes such as rainfall in Southern California.[28]

In a warmer climate, the risk of mudslides caused by more frequent, intense storms will likely increase, as will coastal erosion hastened by rising seas. Reduced stream flows and less stored water could imperil the generation of hydroelectric power. Entire ecosystems could be affected, and animal species may see their ranges shift—if there is time and space available for them to adjust. California farmers will be particularly vulnerable to climate change. The state's most valuable crops tend to be perennials such as nuts, grapes, and tree fruits, which take years to mature to the point where they are commercially productive. Such crops cannot be quickly substituted or moved elsewhere in response to changing conditions. And all Californians could be affected if warming lessens the supply of available water, thereby heightening existing competition among agricultural, urban, and environmental uses.[29]

What's at Risk

The greatest threat to Southern California's water supply related to global warming is the potential shift in snowfall and snowmelt patterns. As the climate warms, the snowline—the elevation below which precipitation falls as rain and above which it falls as snow—will rise. Many areas that currently accumulate snow during the winter will see a shift to a mix of snow and rain, or just rain, greatly reducing the statewide snowpack. The Sierra Nevada range, for example, may receive just 30 to 70 percent as much snow as it does today. The snow that does fall will likely melt sooner, which, combined with the change from snow to rainfall in many areas, will mean an earlier peak in the seasonal runoff. (Snowfall is largely unaffected at higher, colder elevations.) These changing snowfall patterns threaten Southern California's water supply by making it more difficult to capture and store water.[30]

The dams that store much of California's water are also used for flood control. During peak winter rainfall months, the dams are deliberately kept below capacity—by releasing water if necessary—so they have room to capture any sudden surge of water during major storms. Once the threat of flooding has receded, the dams are refilled by the spring snowmelt. California's mountain snowpack, therefore, acts as a massive natural reservoir, with the Sierra Nevada range storing in typical winters more (frozen) water than the combined capacity of the state's three largest reservoirs. Water accumulates in the mountains each winter as snow before being gradually released during spring and summer melts. This convenient arrangement spreads the runoff from winter precipitation over many months, lessening winter floods, and allowing dams to serve their dual function of flood control and water storage. If global warming shifts enough winter precipitation from snow to rain, it could disrupt the transition from flood control to storage.[31]

More rain in the winter could exacerbate floods by increasing the volume of runoff. Floods may also be more frequent in addition to being more intense, although climate models cannot yet reliably predict the type of heavy, localized rainfall patterns that give rise to them. With less snow in the mountains, there may not be enough runoff to fill the reservoirs after the peak winter flood hazard has passed. One obvious response would be to refill the reservoirs earlier in the year before the flood threat has passed. Such a move may prove risky, however, particularly in the context of increased winter runoff. Indeed, with climate-change researchers warning that a warmer climate may usher in an era of more frequent and intense storms, there will be a powerful incentive to retain as much flood prevention capacity as possible.[32]

Another possible response would be to add storage capacity. Large-scale dam projects, however, are costly and controversial because of their adverse environmental impacts, making them an unlikely option. Alternatively, raising the height of dams—where practicable—could increase the capacity of existing reservoirs with fewer adverse impacts. Using existing underground storage by recharging natural aquifers also may be a viable alternative to building new dams. Nonetheless, water would still have to be conveyed to recharging sites (and out of flood zones) rapidly enough and on a large-enough scale to replace surface storage without impeding flood prevention activities.[33]

Smaller snowpack also could also imperil Southern California's water imports because of the need to accommodate species affected by reduced summer river flows. MWD and other State Water Project contractors already have had their water deliveries curtailed when water has been needed for protected species. Less snowmelt means lower water levels in the rivers of Northern California, which could increase seasonal salinity. With lower summer river flows, more stored water may have to be released to prevent high salinity levels and to control water temperatures. Thus climate change may increase demands to use water that previously would have been available for Southern California to protect wildlife habitat.[34]

Similarly, increasing hydraulic pressure both from increased storm runoff, earlier and more intense snowmelts, and seawater intrusion will threaten the physical integrity of the fragile Bay-Delta ecosystem. Higher flows of fresh water into the San Joaquin–Sacramento River Delta may be required to offset rising salinity levels created by lower summer runoff and intruding salt water forced further inland by rising seas. The water level in the delta rose 4 inches in the previous 150 years, and hastened melting of the polar ice caps and worldwide glaciers is expected to push the sea level up another 8 to 12 inches in the coming decades. If the seas rise sufficiently, saltwater intrusion could upset the delta ecosystem's delicate balance, exacerbating the impact of freshwater diversions. Extreme intrusion would affect the SWP Delta Pumping Plant, imperiling Metropolitan's deliveries of drinking water. Thus, some argue that California may need to expand export pumping capacity away from the delta or to secure the ability to move water by constructing an isolated facility through or around the delta.[35]

Climate change also may increase urban demand for water, particularly if it leads to more prolonged (and warmer) heat waves. Changes in urban demand will hinge on water uses, particularly the extent of irrigation. In general, urban and industrial demand for water is not expected to change dramatically in response to warming; water conservation policies will likely have a greater (offsetting) impact. Agricultural demand, in contrast, is considerably more sensitive to climate change and could increase or even decrease, depending on local conditions and the crops involved. The uncertain impact on agricultural demand could create problems for MET in the long run if it disrupts water transfers. Farmers may discover they need more water or may simply desire larger reserves as a hedge against uncertain and changing water needs. In such a scenario, agricultural water districts may find it prudent to limit rural-to-urban water transfers, and decline to recommit to existing transfer agreements that come up for renewal. Alternatively, to reflect growing agricultural risk the price asked per transferred acre-foot well may increase.[36]

Although at least over the next 20 years, changes due to global warming are likely to be "very small relative to other pressures," Metropolitan will need to begin incorporating possible climate-induced changes in its supply forecasts, at the very least acknowledging an extra degree of uncertainty added to Southern California's water supply. Going forward, more severe weather may alter our conception of "normal" and notions such as "one-hundred-year and five-hundred-year floods may completely lose their meaning and usefulness as planning tools."[37] Prudently, the American Water Works Association in 1997 already was urging water agencies to prepare their systems for climate change. Those who link the imperfect science of climate change to the management of uncertain water resources do so at their peril—but so, too, do those who do not.[38]

Environmental Challenges

Nature provides a free lunch, but only if we control our appetites.
William Ruckelshaus, 1990[39]

Even laws that respond to new public values can add to pressures on fixed supplies. Laws promoting efficient water use, environmental protections, and maintenance of stream flows are intended to add balance to the system, but they too are water demand that can stress the system.
David H. Getches, 2003[40]

Environmental factors also impinge on Metropolitan's future water supplies. Ranked by their potential impacts on MET, key factors include the need to provide water for environmental mitigation; environmentalist opposition to building additional water facilities and power plants; and legislative efforts to use water supply to rein in California's future growth. In this section I consider their implications for MWD's supplies and reliability.

Environmental Restoration

A relatively recent claimant for water resources involves environmental protection and restoration. To correct various forms of presumed environmental harm, the legislature and courts increasingly restrict urban and agricultural water diversions. The harm may have been caused by water diversions themselves (as in the case of loss of habitat); some other human action (as in low stream flow caused by diversions or dams); a natural phenomenon (such as saltwater intrusion); or some combination of these (such as increased salinity caused by the combined impact of agricultural runoff, reduced stream flow, and saltwater intrusion). Good examples are the court decisions regarding the Mono Basin and Owens River Valley—

which significantly curtailed water diversions to Los Angeles in order to mitigate supposed environmental damage, reduce dust storms, and restore portions of dry Owens Lake.[41]

Thus, Metropolitan may lose some of its previously secure supplies to environmental purposes. The State Department of Water Resources (DWR) has had to change operations of the State Water Project (SWP), as has the U.S. Bureau of Reclamation's Central Valley Project (CVP), to comply with biological findings on endangered species issued by state and federal fisheries agencies. For example, findings regarding the delta smelt and Chinook salmon indicated the requirement for various changes, most notably lowered pumping when the fish are spawning, and closing of cross-channel gates. Such changes in SWP and CVP operations combined with dry-year hydrological conditions in 1993 to create shortages in the California water system. State water-contract deliveries were cut 50 percent for many Central Valley users.[42]

Similar efforts to improve or protect the environment—including "the CVPIA [Central Valley Project Improvement Act] compliance, Delta accord agreements, reductions from upstream diverters, Shasta Dam operations, Trinity River, and others"—have reduced annual extractions of water from the delta area by 1 to 3 MAF. Reduced water extractions around the state, particularly during dry years, may be necessary to protect endangered species, improve water quality, and restore habitat. Although beneficial to the environment, such water reductions complicate Metropolitan's efforts to secure reliable water supplies. Environmental restoration represents a major issue—and bone of contention—in the CALFED deliberations.[43]

The health and restoration of the Salton Sea also has had potential implications for water deliveries to Southern California. The sea was a dry lakebed until accidentally diverted Colorado River water in the early 20th century filled the depression during nearly two years of unimpeded flow. Today, the Salton Sea is a federally designated agricultural sump sustained solely by runoff from agricultural irrigation and seepage from canals. This unlikely setting has become an important, environmentally sensitive habitat, although mostly by default. With the loss of 95 percent of the state's wetlands and at least 80 percent of the state's riparian habitat, the Salton Sea has become an important resource for migrating birds. The sea provides a surprising variety of habitats, including shallow open water, islands, freshwater and brackish marsh, mudflats, mesquite bosque (thickets), and agricultural fields.[44]

These habitats form an important stopover for millions of migratory birds on the Pacific flyway; support various bird species endemic to the Lower Colorado River Basin; and serve as the winter home for a variety of species, including endangered or threatened species such as the mountain plover, white snowy plover, and the burrowing owl. The disappearance of viable habitat elsewhere has increased the importance of the Salton Sea by concentrating the populations of many bird species there. At the same time, increasing salinity threatens the entire Salton Sea and its ecosystem. The sea lacks an outlet, so that the salt concentrations are greater than seawater and are slowly rising further. Without intervention, the fish in the sea will eventually die off, threatening the rest of the species in the ecosystem that depend on them for food.[45]

The Imperial Valley–San Diego water transfer plan appeared to aggravate the problem. The planned linings of the All-American and Coachella canals—with savings going to the SDCWA—would reduce flows into the Salton Sea by eliminating seepage from existing earthen facilities. Environmentalists became deeply concerned, fearing loss of habitat protection and potential species loss. In the absence of a comprehensive, funded plan to protect the sea, environmental lawsuits challenging the Imperial Valley–San Diego water transfer (and possibly requiring additional Colorado River water for the Salton Sea) were filed and consolidated. The revised transfer agreement does include a corrective mechanism—land fallowing that would free up more Colorado River water to replenish the sea.[46]

Saving the Salton Sea is a fiendishly complex, expensive, contentious, and uncertain enterprise. There is no clear baseline for restoration or rehabilitation; local geology precludes certain solutions; divergent interest groups lack a shared vision of what preservation should accomplish; and there are comparatively few funds—roughly $300 million provided as part of the Quantification Settlement Agreement (QSA, discussed earlier)—available for a restoration project that could cost upward of $2 billion. Other basin states have taken a hard-line position against using Colorado River water for sea restoration. Given such difficulties, the final QSA bifurcated Salton Sea environmental restoration from the water transfer so that the latter could proceed. The state now has responsibility for restoration, the water transfer beneficiaries are contributing toward that effort, but the actual movement of water is no longer dependent on the success or failure of efforts to restore the sea. The QSA mitigation provisions regarding the Salton Sea now provide for a 15-year window of opportunity to find more comprehensive, long-term solutions.[47]

Water, Power, and Air Pollution

Moving water around California is an energy-intensive endeavor. The State Water Project is the largest consumer of electrical power in the state. During California's 2000–2001 energy crisis, the pumps lifting water out of the Central Valley over the mountains to the South Coast plain were occasionally shut down during periods of peak electrical demand because of their large energy consumption. In normal years, the DWR's eight hydroelectric power plants and a coal-fired plant produce enough power to cover two thirds of their power requirements, but the remainder is purchased. DWR would need additional power if it were to deliver its full allotment of water. Similarly, "Colorado River water supplies require about 2,000 kWh/AF (kilowatt-hours per acre-foot) for conveyance to the Los Angeles basin." Most of the power is supplied by hydroelectric projects on the Colorado River—notably the Hoover and Parker Dam power plants—but the rest is purchased. Severe drought conditions throughout the Southwest during 2000–2004 forced federal officials to cut hydroelectric power deliveries to state utilities. "Clearly, we are in a multiyear drought that has impacted our hydroelectric power generation," said a spokesperson for the Western Area Power Administration, a U.S. Department of Energy agency that markets and delivers power in 15 states.[48]

Power availability and costs become greater concerns for Metropolitan and its member agencies because of plans for greater reliance on SWP-CVP water transfers. Moving more water requires extra power, which may not be available. California already has difficulty siting, permitting, and building power plants, in part because of environmental concerns about air quality. Additional power may also be required as MWD's local-project subsidies encourage member-agency desalination facilities. Desalination is an expensive process—largely driven by power costs, which also include uphill pumping charges to a gravity-flow reservoir-and-pipeline distribution system.[49]

Growth Management

A different challenge to Metropolitan and its member agencies is posed by legislative efforts to use water supply to limit future development. In part, these laws reflect the efforts of environmentalists and slow-growth advocates to use water as a means to curtail sprawling new development. Thus, in 2001, California passed new laws—SB 221 (Kuehl) and SB 610 (Costa)—which "require new development to meet certain criteria and provide 'substantial evidence' of available water supplies in the event of drought."[50]

SB 221 prevents local governments from approving projects of more than 200 residential units unless there is verification that a sufficient water supply is available. SB 610 encourages long-term water planning by requiring cities and counties to identify public water systems that may supply water to new projects, and to assess whether projected water supplies will meet the expected water needs of the projects. Not addressed by these laws, higher density in existing housing stock in older cities such as Los Angeles also is a key factor in rising water demand. Complying with the new laws, MET has issued its 20-year water supply forecast, claiming sufficient water to meet future development needs.[51]

Water Quality

The quality of California's surface waters and groundwater is deteriorating inexorably. Toxic wastes, residues from irrigated agriculture, and shortsighted watershed management practices all threaten to reduce water quality even further. . . . By permitting the degradation of water quality to continue, Californians contribute to a worsening of the future water-supply situation as surely as if they destroyed existing water-supply facilities.

Henry Vaux, "Global Climate Change and California's Water Resources," 1991[52]

For decades, Metropolitan has provided safe, reliable drinking water. Yet water quality is fast becoming one of the most significant issues affecting both supply and cost. Contaminants and pollutants in MWD's and member agencies' major water sources—including the Colorado River, the

San Francisco Bay–San Joaquin Delta, and local Southern California groundwater—loom as major challenges. High, toxic levels of pollution pose health risks. Contaminated water has to be cleaned up before it can be safely distributed for drinking, and severe contamination may render a water source unusable. With growing public concerns about water quality and safety, Metropolitan is energetically addressing water contamination and pollutant issues (discussed in chapter 8). MET water already meets federal and state water-quality standards. Here, I briefly survey general sources of water pollution, describe pollutants of critical concern, and consider the implications for Metropolitan's supplies, costs, and customers.

A River Runs Through?

California's groundwater has been contaminated to varying degrees by a multitude of sources. Notable nonagricultural sources of water contamination and pollution include leaks and spills from commercial and industrial operations, industrial wastewater discharge, urban stormwater runoff, landfills, mining operations, leaky and overflowing sewers, faulty septic tank systems, and natural causes. Agricultural sources include fertilizers, pesticides, animal waste, and naturally occurring contaminants flushed into the water system by crop irrigation. Some of California's water pollution is part of an historic legacy of industrial and commercial development that took place when the effects of water pollution were poorly understood, of little apparent concern, and were rarely examined and mitigated. Indeed, "for decades it was widely believed that all contaminants, including chemicals, were removed by percolation through soil and sediment"—an attitude that in hindsight seems quaintly naïve. Thus, it was common for fuels, solvents, and other liquid wastes to be dumped into pits, regardless of the potential for contamination of groundwater.[53]

Efforts to reduce water pollution have been driven by an improved scientific understanding of how pollutants interact with the environment and the potential effects on humans and wildlife. This has been translated into stricter antipollution measures (notably the Clean Water Act), enforcement lawsuits brought by environmental groups, and a broader awareness of water pollution issues among the general public. However, even with improved awareness and better efforts to control water pollution, contamination from legacy and recurrent sources remains a major challenge. Mining operations are the poster child of legacy water pollution. Mercury was used in gold mining, and during the state's gold rush, two California mines—New Almaden and New Idna—accounted for 90 percent of all mercury produced in North America. Today, mercury (and other unpleasant contaminants) leaches from closed mining operations. The mercury is converted by bacteria into methyl mercury, which then moves into the food chain and eventually to people who consume fish and wildlife. Although it is not currently impacting MWD's water supplies, mercury rising still bears close scrutiny.[54]

Landfills represent both an historic and ongoing problem. Materials leaching from former and current garbage dumps have contaminated groundwater. Older landfills are of greater concern because prior to the early 1980s, they were constructed without consideration for groundwater contamination. Changes to the regulations governing the operation of landfills (and the disposal of household toxic materials) have reduced water contamination from landfills, but even some sites explicitly designed to contain contaminated groundwater have failed. Similarly, water contamination from agricultural operations is an ongoing concern. Although the use of the nastiest chemicals has been phased out, fertilizers and pesticides continue to pose challenges. Urban land uses such as golf courses and lawns also contribute to the contamination created by excessive fertilizer and pesticide use. Even without the addition of chemicals, runoff from agricultural areas may still be contaminated by animal wastes and naturally occurring contaminants, such as arsenic, boron, chromium, mercury, and selenium, which can be leached out of the soil when crops are irrigated.

Urban stormwater runoff is another ongoing contamination problem that generally remains unmitigated. In California, stormwater runoff regulations have been put in place, but enforcement is intermittent. Southern California is covered with impermeable surfaces such as roads, homes, and buildings, which greatly reduces the amount of water that seeps into the ground after heavy rains, increasing the volume of runoff. Stormwater runoff flushes pollutants, including motor oil, zinc (from catalytic converters and tire dust), asbestos (from vehicle brakes), cadmium, lead, bacteria and feces from backed-up sewers, and trash into storm drains that discharge into rivers and the ocean.[55]

The Wrong Kinds of Additives

Perchlorate, typically combined with ammonium, potassium, or sodium, is the primary ingredient in solid rocket fuel. Also used in matches, flares, military ordnance, explosives, air bags, and fireworks, perchlorate has become a widespread water contaminant in California chiefly because of its use as a propellant for civilian (space) and military rockets and missiles. Much of the contamination is related to improper disposal by the military and defense contractors of chemicals containing perchlorate. Perchlorate is considered a health hazard because it disrupts the thyroid (which helps regulate metabolism and contributes to normal mental function) by interfering with the intake of iodine. The problem is more severe in expectant mothers, because thyroid damage can harm the fetus, leading to delayed development and decreased learning capacity; and in children, because thyroid damage can interfere with proper development, particularly of the nervous system.[56]

There is no consensus on safe levels of perchlorate. Draft reports by the National Academy of Sciences and the United States Environmental Protection Agency suggest perchlorates may pose a risk, particularly to fetuses and infants, at levels higher than one part per billion (PPB). The Office of Environmental Health Hazard Assessment set a public health goal for perchlorate in drinking water of 6 PPB, and the California Department of Health Services recommends discontinuing the use of water sources with perchlorate levels exceeding 40 PPB. However, the Defense Department claims that perchlorate is safe at concentrations of up to 200 PPB.[57]

Additional contaminants include methyl tertiary butyl ether (MTBE)—now banned in California—which was a gasoline additive that helped reduce ozone levels by making fuel burn cleaner. This potential carcinogen has been showing up in groundwater throughout California, primarily from leaking underground gasoline storage tanks. MTBE does not degrade on its own; and, over time it tends to migrate, which can spread the contamination to rivers and aquifers. Further, some volatile organic compounds (VOCs) used in fuel ingredients and cleaning solvents tend to linger in groundwater. The category of VOC includes numerous contaminants. One VOC is trichloroethylene (TCE)—used mainly as a solvent for cleaning grease from metal parts. Long-term exposure to small amounts of TCE (that is, in drinking water) may harm the liver, kidneys, and immune system. There is heavy contamination in the San Gabriel and San Fernando valleys, a legacy of improper disposal by defense contractors. Another familiar VOC is perchloroethylene (PERC), a popular solvent commonly used in dry cleaning. PERC is a probable carcinogen.[58]

Other man-made contaminants found in California water sources include 1,2,3-trichloropropane (1,2,3-TCP), *n*-nitrosodimethylamine (NDMA), and hexavalent chromium (chromium 6). 1,2,3-TCP, a possible carcinogen, was used as a paint and varnish remover, a degreaser, a cleaning solvent, an input in industrial chemical processes, and in pesticides. NDMA, which has been used in the production of liquid rocket fuel, is also a by-product of drinking water treatment and a probable carcinogen. Chromium 6, a carcinogen, is used in chrome plating, dyes and pigments, leather tanning, and wood preserving and is a by-product of chemical manufacturing and the combustion of fossil fuels. Naturally occurring contaminants found in some California water sources include arsenic, boron, manganese, mercury, and selenium. Human activity may add to the naturally occurring levels of these contaminants.[59]

A Hidden Thief

Local groundwater supplies about one third of Southern California's water needs, and Metropolitan is counting on local sources to meet much of the increase in regional demand over the next 20 years. In California, groundwater sources are already overextended. During normal years, almost 2 MAF more water is extracted than is recharged naturally or artificially, with the overdraft being larger still during dry years. Nonetheless, the overdraft has been shrinking because of recharge efforts. In Southern California, MWD expects to provide additional water for recharge, particularly during wet years, to support higher local extractions of groundwater. MET forecasts that total local supply in dry years will rise from 1.97 MAF in 2003 to 2.45 MAF in 2025, an increase of almost 500,000 AF.[60]

What happens, however, if the water is physically present but unsuitable for drinking? Contamination can potentially undermine the future reliability of local groundwater sources. For example, perchlorate has been showing up in wells in the counties of Los Angeles, San

Bernardino, and Riverside, and could become a serious problem. The standard treatment for volatile organic compounds does not remove perchlorate, and the California Department of Toxic Substances Control is still in the process of developing best practices for statewide management of the chemical. In the San Gabriel Valley, high concentrations of perchlorate (along with the volatile organic compounds PCE and TCE) have forced the closure of 50 wells that formerly produced about 127,000 AF per year. These pollutants are migrating and may eventually threaten groundwater in the central basin of Los Angeles County. Perchlorate contamination has also closed 20 wells, which used to produce almost 62,000 AF annually for three cities in the Inland Empire.[61]

MTBE, another pollutant that could render additional local supplies unusable, has been found in groundwater throughout California. MTBE contamination traced to gas stations already prevents the city of Santa Monica from using local water supplies totaling almost 7,000 AF per year. Nitrate contamination, which has been responsible for the closure of more wells than any other contaminant in Southern California, is a perennial nuisance. Common sources of nitrates are fertilizers from rural and urban users, animal manure, and waste ponds. Leaking septic tanks and sewers are another problem, one that the 2004 court decision compelling Los Angeles to upgrade its inadequate and leak-prone sewer system throws into stark relief.[62]

Local groundwater is not the only component of Metropolitan's supplies at risk of contamination. Although there is only a minuscule chance of MWD's imported water being rendered unusable, these sources are not entirely risk free. Perchlorate has been detected in low concentrations (5 to 9 PPB) in the Colorado River, most likely from a solid rocket fuel manufacturer in Nevada. There is also a 10-million-ton radioactive waste pile sitting on the banks of the river in Moab, Utah, at the site of a former uranium mill. In April 2005, the U.S. Department of Energy announced a long-awaited plan to move and bury the waste about 30 miles from the river. And the growing population throughout the river basin increases the risk of accidental sewage spills and contamination from nitrates, which can leach into the river from leaking septic tanks.[63]

Water from Northern California may contain higher contaminant loads if rapid urbanization in the Central Valley contributes more pollutants being swept into stormwater runoff. The Sacramento River, which flows into the Bay-Delta, already contains significant amounts of copper, mercury, and pesticides. And Metropolitan may face another challenge as it switches from chlorination to ozonation for treating SWP water. The water from the delta has elevated levels of bromide because of saltwater intrusion, and the bromides can react with the ozone to produce bromates.[64]

Metropolitan's supplies do not have to be contaminated directly to cause problems for Southern California's water future, because pollution effectively reduces the overall supply. Thus, perchlorate is present in high concentrations at sites in Northern California, notably in Santa Clara and Sacramento counties. In Rancho Cordova, east of Sacramento, drinking water was contaminated when the cleanup of volatile organic chemicals backfired. Contaminated shallow groundwater was successfully treated to remove VOC and injected into the local aquifer before people realized that the water also contained high concentrations of perchlorate. The contamination has disabled 12 wells that collectively produced almost 13,000 AF per year.

Pesticides represent a similar problem in the San Joaquin Valley. Dibromochloropropane, a soil fumigant banned in 1977, has been found at worrisome levels in groundwater at locations throughout the valley. And in Fresno, nitrate contamination from fertilizers and leaking septic tanks forced the closure in 2002 of seven wells with an annual capacity of 8,000 AF. If water districts around the state heretofore willing to market water to MET find some of their own supplies contaminated, they may decide such transfers are no longer a viable option. Yet as serious as water contamination problems appear to be, they are not unsolvable (see chapter 8).[65]

Protecting MWD from "Evil-Doers"

Water supply facilities offer a particularly vulnerable point of attack to the foreign agent, due to the strategic position they occupy in keeping the wheels of industry turning and in preserving the health and morale of the American populace.

FBI Director J. Edgar Hoover, 1941[66]

For decades, MWD has been able to secure Southern California's water supply by ensuring that it has had adequate supplies to meet demand. As if this original task were not challenge enough, today MET must also guard against a possible terrorist attack. Water can be wielded as a weapon of war in two ways: by harnessing its potential destructive power and by denying an opponent its use. Metropolitan's water system is vulnerable on both counts. Here we consider what such an attack might look like, the likelihood it might occur, and MWD's vulnerability.[67]

First, Metropolitan's surface reservoirs and storage facilities throughout California and the southwestern United States that hold Colorado River and California Aqueduct water make tempting targets for terrorists seeking to wreak havoc. Destroying dams and dikes and diverting rivers has a long history in international warfare. If terrorists were able to destroy a major dam or reservoir, it could cause substantial loss of life and major property damage.[68] Metropolitan might be temporarily crippled, particularly during dry years when it relies on stored water to make up for reduced imports. Although the Diamond Valley Lake reservoir is a key component of MET's flexible in-basin storage strategy and can provide up to 400,000 AF in a dry-year scenario, it may be a possible attack site.[69]

Second, terrorists could attempt to deny the Southern California region water by interrupting the flow through MWD's aqueducts or by making the water undrinkable. Such tactics have been tried elsewhere in the past, and although nations appear to have forsaken poisoning water supplies as a permissible military tactic, terrorists may yet attempt it. Here, too, Metropolitan is vulnerable simply because its sprawling infrastructure is so vast. There are simply too many miles of aqueduct and too many storage facilities to protect all of them all of the time. Yet an attack aimed at disrupting an aqueduct or a pumping station would be problematic, and the damage could be repaired. Metropolitan's diverse portfolio of water resources, storage facilities, and strategically placed repair supplies (in the event of natural as well as human-made disaster) may be sufficient to avoid service interruptions.[70]

For an attack to be truly devastating, it would have to render surface or groundwater storage facilities unusable for an extended period of time, perhaps through some form of poisoning or other contamination. (Even sham attacks—such as with food dyes—could have the intended effect of scaring people into not using municipal water supplies.) In response to the terrorist threat, MET has stepped up its program of testing water supplies for contamination. Frequent testing should reduce the risk. The long-term loss of major water storage capabilities is less horrifying than loss of life, yet could still seriously hamper MWD's efforts to provide a reliable supply of water to Southern California. However, effective poisoning of large volumes of water is quite difficult.[71]

Nonetheless, Al Qaeda appears determined to attack Americans at home. Terrorists may consider the nation's critical infrastructure, including reservoirs, as prime targets. In May 2003, Al Qaeda threatened doing so, to poison America's water supply. In summer 2004, a federal bulletin warned that prior to the 9/11 attacks Al Qaeda had considered infiltrating water treatment facilities to poison urban water supplies. Terrorists appear quite willing to use such tactics, having demonstrated in the words of an FBI spokesperson that "they have no inhibitions and they have no rules."[72]

Securing Metropolitan's far-flung facilities, encompassing hundreds of miles of aqueducts, multiple surface reservoirs, pumping stations, and distribution infrastructure against a determined and ruthless enemy may ultimately prove all but impossible. At the very least, it will require redirecting to security considerable resources and energy that might be productively applied elsewhere. Small comfort can be gleaned from the sheer number of possible terrorist targets in the United States and from the continued efforts of local, state, and federal law enforcement agencies to try to deter such attacks.

As the 21st century begins, how is Metropolitan responding to this daunting array of old and new challenges? Chapter 8 considers the courses of action being charted by MWD and its member agencies, and the global lessons to be learned.

The issues of water—water development, water quality, the pattern of urban, industrial, and agricultural development—are preeminently social issues. They address value systems. They influence the quality of life. The debates over the future direction of water policy are really debates about the future direction of social change.

Robert Gottlieb, A Life of Its Own *(1988)*[1]

At the most basic level, two paths lie before us. One, a "hard path," relies almost exclusively on centralized infrastructure to capture, treat, and deliver water in order to expand the available supply. The other, the "soft path," aims to improve the efficient and wise use of water through investments in decentralized facilities, efficient technologies and policies, smart application of economics, and community management and planning.

Peter H. Gleick, "A Soft Path" (2003)[2]

The paths of "water development" and "water management," or the so-called hard and soft paths, are not mutually exclusive. Metropolitan has and will continue to pursue both. At times, the two overlap.

Ron Gastelum, former CEO, Metropolitan Water District of Southern California, 2005[3]

Without crystal ball or divining rod, MWD is ambitiously planning to meet the challenges of 21st-century supply reliability, affordability, water quality, sustainability, and security for Southern California. Metropolitan is pledged to meet these goals in the context of a projected regional population increase from nearly 20 million residents in 2000 to almost 30 million in 2050. There are also growing supply-side constraints. For example, the Colorado River Basin state precipitation shortfalls of 2000–2004 may well preview 21st-century climatic austerities.

The other half of a daunting supply-side equation is political. An unfinished monument to California's vast infrastructure dreams, the State Water Project was decisively set back in the civil war between Northern and Southern California by the 1982 voter defeat of the Peripheral Canal and of subsequent anticlimactic campaigns for scaled-down delta improvements. Even if CALFED's investment in shoring up the Bay-Delta succeeds, the likelihood is small that the State Water Project will ever be completed along the lines of its ambitious blueprint.[4]

Hence, two seemingly irresistible tidal forces—imported supply constraints relative to still-rapid regional growth, and what the "water buffaloes" claim is a deficit of political will at state and federal levels to augment supplies—have converged to chart MET's growing involvement in regional water-resources management.[5] Moving beyond its traditional mission of simply importing water, Metropolitan now uses financial inducements to encourage (albeit indirectly) member agency water-resource strategies. In concert with these changes in planning and philosophy, MWD also has reformed its financing, rate, project construction, and governance structures.

Analyzed here, the Integrated Resources Plan (IRP) process is Metropolitan's state-of-the-art compass for navigating shrinking imported supplies, growth in demand, and member agency desires for self-determination in water resources development. The IRP represents long-term supply and demand management utilizing computer modeling, data collection, and analysis to map out "constrained optimization of multiple objectives," including affordability, system reliability, water quality, diversification of water sources, regional adaptability, inclusive decision making, public outreach, social equity concerns, and environmental sustainability. The IRP's objective is to further these diverse goals with a least-cost planning methodology, while also advancing technical solutions and "best practices" in storage, groundwater recovery, conjunctive use, watershed and habitat conservation, flood control, storm drain management, recycling, and desalination.[6]

This chapter essays MET's efforts to forecast and mold the region's turbulent water-resources future. It evaluates MWD's (and its lead member agencies') progress and prospects in plotting a course toward a reliable, affordable, sustainable, and safe water future for Southern California, and considers Metropolitan's lessons for global water management.

MWD and California's Thirst for Planning

All benefits that are dispersible
Should be, perhaps, non-reimbursable.
But people should be made to pay
For benefits that come their way—
Unless we want to subsidize
The good, the needy, or the wise.
(It would be well to be quite sure
Just who *are* the deserving poor,
Or else the state-supported ditch
May serve the undeserving Rich.)

> Kenneth Boulding, *"The Feather River Anthology or 'Holy Water'"* [7]

MWD is both a product and agent of California's 150-year experiment in water resources planning. Its creation was a culminating achievement of the Progressive era, when California moved beyond single-purpose water development for mining or agriculture by individual corporate interests and irrigation districts to municipally organized, multipurpose projects such as the Los Angeles Owens Valley and San Francisco Hetch-Hetchy aqueducts that combined urban water provision with hydroelectric power generation. In Sacramento, state government rationalized the trend toward superlocal, technocratically planned water-resource development by means of the Municipal Water Act of 1911; Municipal Utility District Act of 1921; the Metropolitan Water District Act of 1928; the State Water Plan of 1931 (template for the federally funded Central Valley Project); the County Water Authority Act of 1944; the State Water Resources Control Board and Department of Water Resources (chartered, respectively, in 1945 and 1956); and the California Water Plan of 1957 that was the blueprint for the State Water Project. [8]

From the 1960s through the 1980s, MET's ambitions as regional water provider were affected by the California water establishment's hubristic roller-coaster experience. This up-and-down ride led from the 1960s narrow ratification of the State Water Project to the 1980s ballot-box rout of the Peripheral Canal. Nor were the Peripheral Canal's sinking political fortunes lost on state legislators and the governor, who in

1983 approved the Urban Water Management Planning Act that laid down conservation and efficient utilization (not augmentation) of existing supplies as the new governing parameters for water resource planning.

Strengthened by subsequent legislation (SB 901 in 1995, SB 610 and SB 221 in 2001), the Urban Water Management Planning Act imposes a mandatory obligation on local water agencies directly or indirectly supplying water to 3,000 customers or in amounts of 3,000 AF or more to submit a plan. MET is complying with this requirement, as well as providing a service to its member agencies. With a 20-year time horizon and a 5-year update requirement, the UWMP is the closest equivalent among water agencies to city or county general plans, although with a specific focus on water supply and demand projections. Metropolitan goes far beyond the minimum requirements by incorporating detailed population estimates into a sophisticated forecasting program called MWD-MAIN that breaks down data to predict retail urban water demand among different types of land uses throughout the region. (Urban demand in California is approximately 55 percent residential, 25 percent commercial and industrial, and 10 percent public with the remaining 10 percent "unaccounted for.")[9]

Metropolitan also has adapted to a rising environmentalist tide that led to the enactment of the California Environmental Quality Act (CEQA), the federal National Environmental Protection Act (NEPA), and subsequent state and federal legislation. Interpreted broadly by the California Supreme Court under the "public trust doctrine," CEQA's expanded environmental impact review requirements ended the era when water agencies could plan and implement new supply projects using narrow cost-benefit analyses. MET was better prepared than most to pass environmental muster. In contrast to the federal Army Corps of Engineers and Bureau of Reclamation projects, MWD's projects are justified with a needs analysis and assessment of available alternatives. Because member agencies, not the state or federal government, are expected to pay the costs, the ultimate test is whether the members agreed with the needs assessment and are willing to pay. Significantly, Metropolitan built the mammoth Diamond Valley Lake reservoir project in an era of strict environmental review and post–Proposition 13 fiscal constraints because it was willing to comply with the rules and to shoulder full project costs (including mitigation).[10]

In recent years, other major state legislation, including Senator Sheila Kuehl's SB 221 (passed in 2001), has strengthened "show-me-the-water" linkage requirements between approval of large subdivisions and assessment/verification of adequate water supplies for such projects. MWD supported SB 221 largely because it promoted greater transparency in water supply planning and more accountability for accurate demand forecasts at the retail level. Although (as Justice Holmes long ago cautioned) logic is not the life of the law, common sense has reinforced legislation in moving water agencies and land use planners toward more information sharing and closer collaboration. Litigation has also provided a push in the same direction as courts have ruled that counties cannot approve developments on the basis of "paper water," purportedly to be delivered by unbuilt SWP facilities. Nor can water agencies rely in estimating water supply on dubious declarations in unadopted provisions of county general plans.[11]

While developing and sharing its Regional Urban Water Management Plan with land-use planning agencies to use in assessing water availability for new development projects, Metropolitan has innovated beyond the state mandate. In particular, it embarked on the Integrated Resources Planning process. This marked a new departure in water resource planning in which cost-benefit determination of the most economical way to augment supply was supplemented if not supplanted by "least-cost planning" also weighing alternative ways of managing demand. In addition, MET proceeded in parallel with "reliability planning" that modeled how to meet demand at various supply levels.[12]

A Glass Half Full? MWD's Integrated Resources Plans: From 1996 to 2003

With lessons learned . . . , Metropolitan recognized the importance of working collaboratively with our member public agencies to diversify our supply mix, with special emphasis on increasing local supplies.

MWD board chair Phillip J. Pace, 2004[13]

Touted as Metropolitan's answer to California's failure to finish the State Water Project, its *1996 Integrated Resource Plan* was the locus classicus of a new planning philosophy traceable back to the 1980s. The new approach crystallized in the MWD board's 1992 *Goals and Objectives*, adopted in the last year of a six-year drought that had stimulated significant soul-searching about MET's methodologies and, to a lesser extent, its mission. A somewhat uneasy marriage between time-tested and innovative techniques, the IRP was adopted as a reasonable, midstream course to follow. The IRP used both supply augmentation strategies and "least cost" and "reliability planning" approaches to plan for an adequate, affordable water supply within politically acceptable boundaries.

As MWD declared, "the major objective for the IRP was developing a comprehensive water resources plan that ensures (1) reliability; (2) affordability; (3) water quality; (4) diversity of supply; and (5) adaptability for the region, while recognizing the environmental, institutional and political constraints to resource development."[14] Notable among the new principles enunciated were commitments "to integrating environmental values and awareness into Metropolitan's decision-making" and "to an open and participatory process that involved major stakeholders," including a wide spectrum of "participants representing environmental, business, agricultural, community and water interests."[15]

In the wake of the 1987–1992 drought, Metropolitan was faced with growing demand, increased competition for existing supplies, and intensifying political infighting within "the MET family." The existential question confronting both MWD and its member agencies was whether the regional parent agency could any longer be relied on to provide the margin of safety—indeed, the guarantee of protection against drought—promised in the Laguna Declaration of 1952. In 1993, MET initiated a two-stage, 3-year process of introspection and information gathering followed by development of a new supply strategy—the Preferred Resource Mix—linking resource diversification to a greater emphasis on local supply to restore member agencies' confidence in the drought safety margin.[16]

The emphasis on "process" was both analytical (involving updating and enhancing the MWD-MAIN demand model, and developing an IRP supply projection simulation model) and political in the form of "an open, participatory process." The latter featured numerous, carefully planned staff and interagency workgroups, together with public forums and three "Regional Assemblies" involving for the first time senior

Metropolitan management in formal outreach efforts designed to galvanize broad support for a 25-year comprehensive water-resource strategy and regional planning framework integrating the goals of "reliability, affordability, water quality, (source) diversity, flexibility, and environmental and institutional constraints."[17]

The "Preferred Resource Mix" established regional targets for resource development in the areas of improved conservation, increased local supplies, greater surface and underground storage, State Water Project and Colorado River imports, and Central Valley transfers. The 1996 Report's unprecedented embrace of conservation as a core water-resource development strategy set the stage for MET's sustained campaign "pushing the envelope of water conservation technology with a portfolio of innovative conservation programs" and high-profile involvement in the California Urban Water Conservation Council's best-management-practices campaign. In terms of conservation, small incremental reforms—such as requiring that the retrofitting or replacement of water-guzzling toilets, shower heads, and washing machines, and sprinkler systems, and doing water audits for homes, hotels, and commercial establishments—can make a big cumulative difference. The water required to flush a toilet has been reduced by 75 percent, and further savings of 40 percent in overall commercial and industrial uses of water are possible.[18]

Because of such measures—together with the Damocles threat of water rationing—MWD's service area used about the same amount of water in 1998 as it did in 1983 despite a 30 percent increase in population. In the 1990s, water use in Southern California actually dropped by 16 percent at the same time as the population was increasing by that same percentage. Between 1996 and 2003, MET increased its estimate of "dry year" savings from conservation by almost 200,000 annual AF. In 2003, the Pacific Institute estimated that increased savings of at least 30 percent (over 1 MAF per year) can be made in current California residential water use through more efficient use of existing indoor and outdoor technologies; similar savings are practicable in the commercial and industrial sectors. Such gains are possible if not probable.[19]

MWD's Local Resources Program, involving over a $100-million investment in recycling and groundwater partnerships with member agencies, achieved results that made possible Metropolitan's politically vital

"100 percent assurance that retail-level demands can be satisfied under all foreseeable hydrologic conditions."[20] By 2001, MWD had committed an average of $110/AF to develop new recycling and groundwater production, instituted its new innovative conservation-credits program, and started moving toward its current production goal of 150,000 annual AF for seawater desalination to take advantage of the declining cost of technology. Having completed a new strategic plan, rate restructuring, and IRP review, Metropolitan also responded to the passage of state legislation (SB 221 and SB 610) that tightened the linkage between land use and water-supply availability planning and required "urban water suppliers to prepare and adopt comprehensive management plans on a timely basis."[21]

In November 2001, MET's board launched a work plan with the purposes of providing "a report card" on implementation of the 1996 IRP, updating forecasts and targets, and extending the time horizon from 2020 to 2025. Publicly presented in a series of outreach meetings during the first half of 2004, and then approved by the MWD board, the *Integrated Resources Plan 2003 Update* offered an upbeat assessment of progress under the 1996 plan and of future prospects—including 100 percent reliability—despite important caveats and qualifications involving supply factors, including the imposition of new federal drinking-water regulations. Particularly significant, the update projected 500,000 AF in annual demand savings through the combination of conservation and local supply-development initiatives. The update increased its estimate of available water to be stored in Diamond Valley Lake that would be connected, at least indirectly, to the Inland Feeder pipeline beginning by 2007 or shortly thereafter. New state monies could help fund IRP projects. Proposition 13, approved in 2000, furnished MWD $45 million in funding for groundwater conjunctive-use projects. MET also could indirectly gain from Proposition 50 grants for water-savings projects by its member agencies.[22]

A very substantial increase—250,000 AF per year—was estimated from MWD's eight major storage and transfer programs with CVP and SWP contractors, including Semitropic, Arvin-Edison, Kern Delta, San Bernardino, and Coachella Valley, with North Kern and Mojave projects in the pilot stage. Although Metropolitan had assumed historic lows for SWP dry-year supplies at 450,000 annual AF, a successful CALFED program could add an additional 200,000 AF. MET also has proven that it can augment its dry-year SWP supplies through storage and transfer agreements outside of CALFED. In addition, it projected greater recycling savings and increased its target for desalination to 150,000 AF per year. MET also proposed to take advantage of improved demand-supply forecasts, and to cushion against the possibility of future adverse "water quality risk" and "implementation risk" consequences, by creating an annual 500,000-AF Planning Supply Buffer, constituting 10 percent of projected annual retail demand in 2025, to be drawn equally from local supplies and imported supply sources. With climatic and other conditions being so variable that hard planning beyond 10 to 15 years out was sheer speculation, MWD chose the buffer approach to handle uncertainty in a cost-effective manner.[23]

MWD board chair Phil Pace and CEO Ron Gastelum framed the 2003 update as a successful watershed in the ongoing process of regional water resource adaptation that began with the 1987–1992 drought. According to Gastelum, "Metropolitan's supply reliability over the next five to seven years is a result of the successful implementation of the 1996 plan and investment decisions by Metropolitan's Board."[24] Critics instead saw the 2003 IRP update as a glass half empty. From an environmentalist perspective, the upward revision of the 1996 estimate of how much water MET reasonably could expect to import from the Colorado River in 2020–2025 displayed the misleading cosmetic profile of "rosy scenario." The 2003 update increased by 50,000 AF per year to 1.25 MAF the estimate of what Metropolitan could expect to import in the distant future from the Colorado River, notwithstanding that, as MWD itself admitted, "in the short-term programs are not yet in place to provide the full target, even with the adoption of the QSA." MWD countered that its projections were actually conservative, reflecting support for the QSA, cooperative management of limited river supplies with other Colorado Basin states and California contractors, the PVID program, support for the river's multispecies protection program, and California's firm stance on shortage rights vis-à-vis Arizona.[25]

Despite an abundant winter 2004–2005 rainfall, the Bureau of Reclamation warned that it might be forced to curtail deliveries as early as 2007, denying California for the first time its basic 4.4-MAF allotment. And skeptics viewed MET's decision to "forbear," that is, to take a voluntary immediate reduction of 700,000 AF in Colorado River deliveries, as merely an attempt to put the best possible face on looming disaster. MWD officials countered that the decision reflected a "best assessment" of the unavailability of surplus water under the Interim Surplus Guidelines and of Metropolitan's obligation to provide 1 MAF (up to 500,000 AF in a given year) to Arizona in a shortage, should MWD begin taking surplus water after the QSA. Taking stock of its other supplies, MET officials decided that it wasn't worth the risk of undertaking a new obligation to Arizona to gain a possible short-term surplus. It should be noted that following adoption of the QSA, Metropolitan's Colorado River supplies grew from 684,000 AF in 2003 to 761,000 AF in 2004, and are expected to be at least 750,000 AF in 2005.[26]

As argued previously, new paleoclimatological science injected further uncertainties into conventional hydrological predictions. Metropolitan's guarded optimism regarding increased future Colorado River Aqueduct imports hinged, partly, on gains from its current conservation, storage, and transfer projects, such as the IID-MWD Conservation Program, the Coachella and All-American Canal Lining projects, the IID-SDCWA Transfer Program, the PVID Land Management Program, and the Hayfield Storage Program. But it also depended on the successful fruition of other projects—such as the Lower Coachella Storage Program, the Chuckwalla Storage Program, the Central Arizona Water Bank Program—that to date are only under development.[27]

Metropolitan's frequent nemesis—the San Diego County Water Authority—also discerned sleight-of-hand involving water rates and preferential rights. SDCWA found particularly objectionable MWD's presentation, prior to finalization of the 2003 Update's selection of future water-supply projects, of its *2003 Long Range Finance Plan* projecting rate increases for 2004–2013 of between $76 and $100 per acre-foot, depending on water sales. Putting a negative spin on these cost estimates, the *San Diego Union-Tribune* editorialized that local rate payers could expect "average rate increases of 3.8 percent to 4.6 percent per year between 2004 and 2013, with possible increases of 4 percent to 7.5 percent in the next three years—not counting a possible $1.8-billion increase in the MWD's capital improvement program." Voting to defer approval of MET's new finance plan until the IRP update was adopted, SDCWA assumed a position akin to that of a thirsty horse whose rider wanted to be led to the watering hole first—before being asked to pay more to drink. From MET's perspective, the rider had to commit to the journey first for the horse ever to get to the watering hole.[28]

Cutting-Edge Issues: Drought Management and Water Quality

The unprecedented drought on the Colorado River and the unpredictable nature of State Water Project supplies warrant a more thorough analysis of likely and worst case supply scenarios.
SDCWA chairperson Bernie Rhinerson, 2004[29]

Metropolitan's Planning Supply Buffer was a proactive response to two major negatives—"water quality risk" and "implementation risk"—threatening Southern California's water-resources future. The first was technically complicated, but otherwise easy to understand in lay terms as "unsafe water." The second involved the possibility not only of unexpected rainfall shortfalls—unrelenting drought—but unanticipated project failures as well. Defending the 2003 IRP update, MWD CEO Gastelum admitted the wild card of natural disaster by declaring, "This plan assumes droughts, earthquakes, unexpected events." The apocalyptic eventuality that was all too possible would be a continuation of the lengthy western states drought that, according to some estimates, was the worst to hit the Colorado River Basin in 500 years. Yet the heavy 2004–2005 winter rains replenished MET's near-term storage as well as local groundwater resources. MWD's bottom line has always been as an ultimate "drought insurance policy" for member agencies afraid to gamble on the adequacy of local supplies in the event of a severe dry siege.[30]

Despite MET's assurances to its member agencies of 100 percent overall reliability through 2025, its IRP supply projection model identified a worst-case, dry-year or "peak need" scenario—most likely to occur in 2008–2009, according to the model—producing a deficit of 900,000 AF. This was far in excess of the 500,000 AF buffer and would require the acquisition of additional supplies to meet demand. The probability of the worst-case scenario happening was deemed at only 8 percent. Not content with this level of protection, Metropolitan bought its own insurance by empowering its Water Surplus and Drought Management Team to pursue drought mitigation projects. These included dry-year spot purchases of 125,000 AF from the Central Valley for 2005, and a new deal for MWD to bank 30,000 AF annually of Southern Nevada's Colorado River entitlement in the next several years, to be returned during a future time period at Southern Nevada's call. MWD also showed interstate statesmanship by voluntarily surrendering some potential purchases to reduce the draw on depleted Lake Mead. "We don't worry about drought until it's dry. We don't worry about floods until it rains," observed Sid Wilson, general manager of the Central Arizona Project, with which MWD also had a water-banking arrangement that might bail out Southern California with additional interstate water absent the much-needed proverbial rainy day.[31]

Created by new science in league with federal and state regulatory bureaucracies, more stringent water-quality standards constituted a multipronged assault that could conceivably puncture holes in the levee of MET's positive reliability prognostications. After high levels of total organic carbons were detected in the East Branch of the California Aqueduct, the EPA's Microbial Disinfectants Bi-Products Rule forced Metropolitan to accelerate the complex, expensive process of converting from chlorine (which generates trihalomethanes as by-product) to ozonation as a primary method of purification at all five of its treatment plants. (Two of MWD's treatment plants only purify State Water Project supplies; they were required to upgrade to ozone prior to July 2005.) The other three plants had relied on blending State Water Project supplies with Colorado River water that had lower carbon and bromide levels than SWP water. But even these plants would require ozonation to comply with the new treatment standards, albeit on a slower time path. MET also supported CALFED's delta improvement program to reduce by 20–30 percent bromide and salt concentrations in its SWP and CVP imports.[32]

Colorado River supplies also raised serious water-quality concerns. In addition to high salinity (the target desirable goal is 500 mg/L), Metropolitan had to consider a more stringent public health goal recommended by the California Office of Environmental Health Assessment to counter the danger of drinking water from the Colorado River being contaminated by perchlorate, a chemical used to manufacture rocket fuel and fireworks that seeped into the river from a Kerr-McGee plant near Lake Mead in Nevada. Further, there was the specter of the 10-million-ton pile of radioactive waste near Moab, Utah, that could leak 15,000 gallons of toxic chemicals and minerals (including uranium tailings) daily into the Colorado River if the pile were not removed or otherwise sealed. Its now-planned removal could cost the federal government a cleanup bill of as much as $540 million. And, an energy company contributes contamination in the form of Chromium 6 from a site across the river from Topock, Arizona.[33]

Potential harmful levels of carbons, bromides, perchlorate, radon, chromium, gasoline additives, pesticides, sewage contaminants, and salt are only a few of over 160 organic and inorganic compounds (90 requiring mandatory monitoring) for which MWD each year conducts 300,000 water-quality tests to detect their presence and levels. Effective January 2004, MET imposed a new surcharge of $10/AF or 2 percent for treated water, the first rate increase in seven years. Part of the cost of water quality compliance went to fund nearly $11 million in new security measures adopted by MWD in partnership with federal and state governments in the wake of the 9/11 attacks.[34]

The mantra of Metropolitan's Water Quality Initiative is "protecting water at the source, so you can trust it at the tap." The imposition of increasingly more stringent water-quality standards is likely to enhance water source protection. Beginning to have an impact, AB 901 (passed in 2001) is a state mandate requiring MET and other agencies to include in their Urban Water Management Plans information "relating to the quality of existing sources of water . . . and the manner in which water quality affects water management strategies and supply reliability." The federal Clean Water Act is also being interpreted to define urban storm drains and culverts—and even gutters and ditches—as "navigable waters of the United States" subject to water quality regulation. Although MET's supplies are not affected by urban storm drain and culvert runoff in Southern California, they can be negatively affected by agricultural and urban runoff upstream of the Colorado River intake facilities at Parker Dam and the State Water Project's pumping plants. For MWD, more regulation of such upstream dischargers would be beneficial.[35]

As bad as water contamination problems potentially are, they are not unsolvable. Cutting-edge technologies are becoming available to provide both detection and even cure. The Shimadzu TOC-4110 is an online total organic carbon and TN analyzer. Other firms market an ion chromatography–mass spectrometry method for detecting perchlorate in drinking and surface water. Endocrine-disrupting chemicals can also now be easily detected in environmental samples. The portable Orion AQUAfast AQ4000 multiwavelength colorimeter rapidly signals the presence of cyanide in the water by turning it blue. Argonide Corporation is developing a radically new portable water-filtration system that attracts, captures, and destroys electronegative bacteria and small viruses. The filter can also trap viruses from aerosols and may be adapted to detecting SARS, bird flu, influenza, and other nonwaterborne respiratory diseases. The water community is equipping itself with new technologies in response to water quality concerns.[36]

Bottom Up: MWD Member Agency Strategies

You know that there are two schools of thought on what regional water agencies do, particularly agencies like ours that are growing. One is that we rely on MWD for anything and everything needed in terms of reliability and adequate supply to meet not only the current customers' needs, but also . . . for new development. The other school of thought is that an agency like ours goes out and puts its own transactions together, ensuring that there is a sufficient supply in the event that MWD misses the mark.

John Schatz, general manager, Santa Margarita Water District, 2004[37]

Metropolitan's 26 member agencies have become an increasingly important front line managing Southern California's water resources. Regionwide policy may be made at MWD's headquarters, but implementation largely occurs in the trenches or *zanjas* (irrigation ditches) where local agencies pursue their own policies at the same time as they interact with Metropolitan. According to MET's projections, local resource development projects will increase production by 21 percent over 20 years, meeting up to 56 percent of total retail demand by 2025.[38]

Traditionally misidentified as "the shadow government" that runs Metropolitan, the Los Angeles Department of Water and Power now purchases roughly 15 percent of MWD's overall supplies. Yet despite the lack of fundamental policy disagreements with Metropolitan, LADWP continues to have—as it has historically—its own distinctive priorities.

Recently, six consecutive years of low snowpack in the Eastern Sierra, together with environmental commitments reducing imports from the Owens Valley by as much as a third, have tilted Los Angeles's water acquisition toward MWD. The older L.A. source mix involved 50 percent dependence on Owens Valley supplies, and 30 percent reliance on MWD deliveries. The new balance involves over 50 percent reliance on more expensive MET supplies and only 30 percent dependence on the Owens Valley. This costs the city 20 percent or more for water than previously.[39]

The cost differential between municipal supplies and Metropolitan deliveries was one of several reasons for the defeat in 2003 of San Fernando Valley and Hollywood secession initiatives that could have resulted in those new cities paying more for water. Aided by a Los Angeles city population growing more slowly than previously predicted, the LADWP appears as a conservation success story that has managed to cut annual demand by 15 percent. Despite cordial MWD-LADWP relations, Los Angeles is eyeing building a new direct north-south connection with the State Water Project linking the Los Angeles and California Aqueducts where the two systems intersect in the Antelope Valley. L.A. could buy Central Valley water and wheel it through an integrated system. Requiring DWR approval, the deal would replace up to 40,000 annual AF of water from the Owens Valley that is no longer available to L.A. because of dust remediation efforts.[40]

Still a prime MWD beneficiary but more often than not MWD's leading *bête noir*, the San Diego County Water Authority continues to pursue water independence. SDCWA director Mike Madigan believes that the region needs to wean itself from imported water and instead create a more sustainable local water supply through a combination of seawater desalination ("a no-brainer for San Diego"), conservation, and recycling.[41] The County Water Authority's 2020 Plan envisages 21 percent of its total supply from the long-term contract to purchase conserved Imperial Irrigation District water, to be wheeled to San Diego through Metropolitan's aqueduct system; a 9 percent supply from the transfer of conserved water from the All-American and Coachella Canal lining projects; 6 to 15 percent from desalination; and 24 to 35 percent from MWD, down from 85 percent in 2003. In 2004, the County Water Authority Board approved 21 local development projects, including plans to raise the San Vincente Dam to increase storage capacity and to build a new treatment plant near San Marcos, with an estimated price tag of $2 billion, to be paid for by bond issues financed by unspecified future water rates.[42]

The County Water Authority remains MET's largest customer—purchasing over a quarter of its supplies—and also leads all member agencies with 20 MWD-funded (and critics say subsidized) local resource-development projects. SDCWA's thirst for independence has not diminished its taste for entitlement as the biggest drinker at Metropolitan's bar. A telling example is the proposed Carlsbad-area seawater desalination plant in partnership with a private firm, Poseidon Resources, and the city of Carlsbad but with a hefty MWD subsidy of $250/AF. Yet when Metropolitan CEO Gastelum expressed skepticism about the appropriateness of MET funding such an expensive SDCWA-linked project at least so long as the SDCWA reserved its so-called "rights" to try and change the QSA deal to get cheaper subsidized wheeling charges from MET for IID-SDCWA transfer water, San Diego water officials reacted indignantly. The County Water Authority's general manager fumed as if Metropolitan were somehow obligated to bankroll the project.[43]

Whether due to inhospitable geography (hilly terrain and a lack of aquifers), or inhospitable politics (in 1999 the San Diego City Council sank an effort to turn sewage into drinking water), or the two in combination, San Diego recycles only about one third of the water per capita as the statewide average, despite pouring more than $450 million from federal and other grants into water reclamation since 1994. In San Diego County, the Otay Water District is developing a $34-million facility to provide recycled wastewater to parks and other open spaces. Yet the South Bay Sewage Reclamation Plant—having only recently made its first sale of water—functions at only 10 percent of capacity, while almost all of the city's treated sewage is still flushed into the sea.[44]

Orange County water politics historically have revolved around disputes over groundwater (North County versus South County), and schemes to get secure water at below MET's regular rates. South County has no groundwater, and North County won't share. Orange County's huge northern aquifer, stretching from Anaheim to Irvine, until recently provided 75 percent of the drinking water for northern and central county residents. Yet with drought-induced supply reductions from local river flows, the overtapped, under-replenished aquifer sank as much as 30 feet below sea level in some places. This was also due to calculated local de-cisions not to buy MET replenishment water when available.

Orange County member agencies such as the Municipal Water District of Orange County (MWDOC) have largely avoided high-profile conflicts with MWD while pursuing local conservation and development initiatives ranging from low-volume toilets and shower heads, to swim-ming pool covers, to water education campaigns. MWDOC supplies ap-proximately 2 million people with potable water. The population is ex-pected to increase to almost 3 million within the next 20 years. MWDOC has supported the Orange County Water District's joint development with the Orange County Sanitation District of a cost-effective solution to provide a supplemental source of high-quality water. The two agencies sponsored a water purification project, known as the Groundwater Re-plenishment System (GWRS), to purify for reuse additional highly treated wastewater. The $487-million GWRS recharges groundwater with highly treated wastewater, providing supplies during droughts and replenishing the saltwater intrusion barrier. The GWRS will be capable of supplying approximately 22 percent of the water needed to recharge the groundwa-ter basin by the year 2020.[45]

When MWD secured $45 million of voter-approved state funding for groundwater conjunctive use in its service area, it approached MW-DOC and others to expand local storage. MWDOC and the Orange County Water District then agreed to store for their own use 63,000 AF of MWD supplies in the local water basin in exchange for MWD funding additional well capacity and facilities to protect Orange County's groundwater supply. And in southeastern Orange County, the fast-growing Santa Margarita Water District (a MWDOC member agency) contracted with the Cucamonga Valley Water District to store water to be made available in the event of an MWD supply shortage.[46]

MWD Family Squabbles: Governance and Rate Structure Reforms

Watersheds come in families; nested levels of intimacy. . . . The big river is your nation, a little out of hand. The lake is your cousin. The creek is your sister. The pond is her child. And, for better or worse, in sickness and in health, you're married to your sink.

Michael Parfit, "Water" (1993)[47]

> Metropolitan General Manager Ron Gastelum proposed a new policy
> that would ban the [San Diego County] Water Authority from accepting
> a critical subsidy to build the desalination plant—unless the Water
> Authority promises not to challenge Metropolitan's rate system in court
> or the state Legislature. . . . This irked Water Authority General
> Manager Maureen Stapleton. "This is not a charity where Met receives
> revenue separate and apart from its member agencies and then out of
> the goodness of its heart hands us some," Stapleton said.
>
> *Gig Conaughton,* North County Times *reporter, 2004*[48]

With the protracted controversy over the Imperial Valley–San Diego
transfer finally being resolved, two contentious issues still generated interagency conflict within Metropolitan: governance reform and rate restructuring. At stake were answers to three interrelated questions: Who
benefits? Who pays? Who governs?

San Diego found in Metropolitan governance reform an attractive
battle cry. Here it could rally allies who did not necessarily share the
SDCWA's bottom-line objective to have its water purchases from IID
wheeled through the Colorado River Aqueduct at bargain rates (with possible system-wide cost shifting to other member agencies). In 1931,
Metropolitan's membership was limited to 13 cities in two counties. The
governance system featured as least one representative from each member
agency (the U.S. Senate approach), plus additional voting entitlement
based on assessed valuation, a proxy for early tax-based infrastructure
investments. By 1998—when Sacramento rained down proposals to re-
structure MWD governance—its then 51-member board presided over a
diverse six-county confederation of 27 members (including 13 cities, 13
municipal water districts, and 1 county water authority), ranging in size
from tiny San Marino to giant Los Angeles. Over the years there have been
calls for making the MWD board more accountable, such as by direct election of members or by using population as the basis of representation.[49]

Los Angeles's decades-long decline in numbers and influence in
MWD's policymaking circles has reduced the City of Angels from the
proverbial 800-pound gorilla to a much more diminutive ape. Yet critics
continued to find it intolerable that—based on its large assessed valuation
and historic investment in the Colorado River Aqueduct—Los Angeles
still had more representatives on the MWD board (7 out of 51) and a

greater preferential rights claim in the event of drought (22 percent) than any other member agency including San Diego, the long-time purchaser of the largest share of MET water.[50]

In 1992, MWD had successfully opposed Assemblymember Richard Polanco's AB 3522 that would have replaced the Metropolitan board with 15 directors elected for two-year terms. In 1998, three bills, including Tom Hayden's SB 1875 and Ruben Ayala's SB 1885, proposed a fundamental revamping. Understandably, MWD is highly resistant to tinkering with the Metropolitan Act. The MWD board countered by hiring academic John Carver, former attorney general John Van De Kamp, and PricewaterhouseCoopers to advise it on self-reform. Despite concerns that reduction in the board size might slow progress toward ethnic diversity, the end result of these external and internal initiatives was a reform package, adopted during the 1999–2000 state legislative session. It reduced MWD board membership from 51 to 37, but without changing relative member-agency voting strength, or disenfranchising any of the smaller city members as was sought by some. The new, smaller board assumed power in 2001.[51]

Arguably, board size and selection procedure were less important than rate restructuring. From MWD's perspective, the problem—as chief financial officer Brian Thomas put it—was that "Over 80 percent of our costs are fixed, yet 80 percent of our revenues are dependent on sales. . . . There is no commensurate responsibility (or obligation) for anyone to buy Metropolitan water." MWD loyalists feared changes that would further entice member agencies—for whom "the game is to avoid buying Metropolitan water"—to "roll off the system" by relying on local supplies or buying water from third parties. From the perspective of critics such as San Diego, the problem was rate "bundling" that prevented member agencies from picking, choosing, and paying separately for the "buffet or cafeteria" of Metropolitan services—supply, treatment, consulting, and so on—they preferred.[52]

This dispute also raised fundamental questions about the nature and extent of MWD's mission. Critics such as San Diego asked whether Metropolitan should solely be a supply conduit—and, if so, whether the exclusive supply conduit—for regional water importation. Or, as others contended, should MWD be a planner, facilitator, and manager of a full range of functions and services, including water-issue advocacy, interagency dialogue, technical research, and project development? The broader MWD's functions were, the greater its need for a large financial reserve that was anathema to those wanting to shrink the agency's size and mission as well as its budget.[53]

Metropolitan fended off attempts in successive legislative sessions to shift some of its rate-making powers to the Public Utilities Commission or State Water Resources Control Board, ostensibly to increase the opportunities for a water market. Ultimately, MWD's member agency managers internally negotiated a new contractual rate system providing an acceptable compromise for loyalists desirous of a fixed revenue source and critics intent on unbundling rates by ending MWD's inclusive "postage stamp" rate. Adopted by the MWD board in 2001 and to be gradually implemented starting in 2003, a new "unbundled" two-tier water rate system was created. The rate structure included a readiness-to-serve charge that would help finance facilities to meet emergency and drought needs. Rate unbundling provided a much more transparent picture of various service costs. The components of the new rate system included a system access charge, a power rate, a water stewardship rate (funding MET's incentive payments for conservation, recycling, and seawater desalination), and two basic supply rates.[54]

The lower Tier 1 Supply Rate allowed member agencies to long-term contract for baseline volumes in exchange for higher quantities of supplies. Of MET's 26 member agencies, 24 elected to do so. The Tier 2 Rate reflected the higher cost of acquiring additional reliable, long-term imported water supplies, particularly needed by growing member agencies. Other wrinkles included a capacity charge to recover the cost of peaking on the distribution system, a treatment rate for all treated water deliveries, an ongoing Water Surplus and Drought Management Plan to equitably allocate water in times of crisis, and the option to contract with third parties for additional supplies. Metropolitan itself purchased water from Palo Verde farmers under a contract with the PVID. The initial rate structure announced and implemented in 2003 was modified, effective 2005. Some unbundled rates went up, and others down—with an overall increase of $25/AF, or only 4.4 percent, primarily to pay for rising water treatment and power transmission costs.[55]

San Diego initially sought to delay adoption of the new rate structure until drought emergency reductions were removed. SDCWA general manager Maureen Stapleton insisted that it would prove meaningless if preferential rights were ever implemented. Yet in 2004 the California Supreme Court denied San Diego's appeal of an appellate court ruling supporting MWD's authority, subject to the State Water Code and the legislature, to set preferential rights. San Diego abandoned its early threat to appeal all the way to the U.S. Supreme Court, thus ending challenges to the new rate system.[56]

There followed Metropolitan's board election in October 2004 of a new chair, Wesley Bannister, a former Huntington Beach mayor and representative of the Municipal Water District of Orange County, by a narrow 51 percent board majority—including a unanimous phalanx of Orange County and San Diego votes, but with little or no support from Los Angeles–area directors. "We've got to put our house back together," declared Bannister, and he joked about making MWD a "kinder, gentler, more lovable, sweeter agency." He also observed that "San Diego really wants independence from MWD, and I understand that we should really be supportive of agencies being more independent. We have to change our philosophy." Bannister echoed similar inaugural conciliatory statements as former board chairs Phil Pace and Jack Foley, both of whom eventually grew distrustful of San Diego.[57]

Bannister appointed a San Diegan as a board vice chair, and pushed for MWD to consider building desalination plants of benefit to agencies such as the SDCWA and MWDOC. Yet the new chair disappointed San Diego when he unsuccessfully opposed board passage of a measure penalizing member agencies such as San Diego that sued MWD by withholding MWD subsidies for local projects such as desalination. It remained to be seen whether Bannister's calculated appeasement of San Diego in Metropolitan's civil war would prove successful. In April 2005, the appointment of veteran Dennis Underwood as MET's new chief executive officer allayed some fears, as the new CEO pledged to diversify water supplies, focusing on reclamation and desalination.[58]

What remained to be seen was the strength of the new leadership's commitment to MWD's regional mission. In the late 1990s, MET's board unanimously had reaffirmed the agency's strong regional mission. MWD was to remain the major voice of the region's water interests statewide and nationally; provide imported water to meet baseline needs; manage the region's importation, distribution, treatment, and storage systems; serve as drought allocator during times of shortage; and encourage local recycling, reclamation, and conservation programs.

MWD in the Global Balance

If we link accountability and innovation, we can begin to change the discourse about water in Southern California. . . . The commodity value of water . . . , which has for so long shaped the discourse and set the policy framework, is essentially what is at question in this debate. In its place can emerge a conception of the *community* value of water, and with it, a new public agency central to community life and fulfilling the community's objectives.

> *Robert Gottlieb and Margaret FitzSimmons,* Thirst for Growth *(1991)*[59]

Are we going to permit water to become a commodity like oil, to be over pumped, under priced, and used wastefully, leading to water wars, international conflict and competition, and environmental destruction?

> *Peter H. Gleick, "A Soft Path" (2003)*[60]

What is the overall report card on Metropolitan—a regional resource agency—in a world that increasingly "thinks globally but acts locally"? Although not perfect, MWD has done a remarkable job to date. MWD's original mission to provide reliable and inexpensive supplies of high-quality water to meet present and future needs so far has been fulfilled. Contrary to conventional wisdom about MET's traditional leadership as archaic "water buffaloes," this is a contemporary Southern California institution that is a quite up-to-date water provider, especially when judged by current world standards. Its overall performance might be considered in the context of a world where the United Nation's "Millennium Goals and Targets" (2000) include as desperately needed objectives reducing by half the huge masses of people without safe drinking water while increasing to more than half those who earn at least one dollar a day.[61]

It should be noted that current global trends in regionalizing water planning and management rely far more heavily than Metropolitan does on mixed public-private resource development. The United Kingdom regionalized water services under the 1973 Water Act, creating 10 multipurpose regional water authorities. The process was completed under the 1989 Water Act, which copied the privatization of the gas and telecommunications public authorities. Each regional water authority corresponded to a hydrological division or catchment area—to be headed by "public" companies that, given 25-year leases, shared the field with 25 private water companies. The 10 investor-owned public utilities were virtual monopolies in their respective services areas in which they did not compete with each other directly, though they were competitively priced in the capital markets. They were also extensively regulated in terms of rates and service by the Office of Water Services in conjunction with Customer Service Committees.[62]

Sometimes called the "Anglo-Saxon model" of quasi-monopolistic water companies, owned by private investors but highly regulated by independent government bodies, this is actually a hybrid market-sensitive model. In fact, the United Kingdom's divergence from the pure market model has become more, not less, pronounced in recent years. An attempt to inject more competition into the system in 1991 produced a backlash by unhappy rate payers. A 1996 study by Save the Children showed that low-income consumers were dangerously reducing consumption to save on water bills. The result was heightened governmental regulation.[63]

France's three powerful corporate water purveyors are unusual compared to other countries because of their long history of private ownership. However, water in France remains publicly owned, as does most water infrastructure. Typically, it is privately managed, with water giants Vivendi, Suez, and Saur sharing the national stage with 36,000 municipal providers and with the central government that provides regional regulation at the level of six river basins under the Decentralisation Laws of 1982 and 1983. In the Far East, Japan as early as 1950 regionalized into a system of basin development agencies that operate somewhat akin to the United States' vaunted New Deal–era Tennessee Valley Authority (TVA), which publicly provides water and power. (The TVA was modeled after the LADWP and MWD.) In China (as throughout India) ground and surface water both are public property where the national Ministry of Water Resources also functions through the instrumentality of seven regional river basin commissions. The problem in the People's Republic is not public ownership per se, but poor management.[64]

Regarding regionalization trends elsewhere, all across Europe the planning, construction, management, and financing of water systems are devolving from the central level to regional and local levels. In Australia, the Murray–Darling Basin Ministerial Council now coordinates land, water, and environmental planning for the basin states of Queensland, New South Wales, Victoria, and South Australia. And Mexico's economic crisis of the 1980s stimulated a radical decentralization of the water provision sector with much of state control shifted to local and regional nongovernmental water-user organizations. Although the mix between private and public, for-profit and nonprofit, water provision and management differs considerably between countries, the regionalizing trend cuts across national divisions as water agencies are organized not only around geographical "watersheds" but around water "problem-sheds" at an intermediate regional level. This avoids both overcentralization and excessive fragmentation, fosters cooperation and coordination, and promotes infrastructure investment by encouraging economies of scale. The regional water agency model has been praised for efficient management, effective coordination, valuable interagency planning, sharing of expertise, and pooling of financial resources.[65]

In the United States, Southern California's Metropolitan Water District and Northern California's East Bay Municipal Utility District find parallels in Florida's Water Resources Act (enacted in 1972), which organized the state into six (later five) regional districts, set up according to hydrologic basin boundaries, and with the authority to plan and manage surface water and also to tax. The cities of St. Petersburg and Tampa and the counties of Hillsborough, Pinellas, and Pasco followed (in 1974) with interlocal agreements encouraging regional supply development by issuance of revenue bonds. The federal-state Delaware River Commission does the same for five states. Where and when regionalization succeeds, the reasons are "70 percent politics, 20 percent engineering, and 10 percent luck."[66]

Metropolitan combines the regional functions of water supplier and allocator with water planning, development and management authority, interagency coordinator, local project subsidizer, public educator, and political lobbyist and cheerleader. The question that critics who wish to reduce or eliminate all or some of these functions must answer is: what would take MET's place? In particular, would reducing Metropolitan to a mere water conveyor sluicing water market sales and purchases really meet the need for an agency dedicated to vindicating water resources as the pulse of regional values beyond the cash nexus? The underlying philo-sophical question—as once posed by poet and novelist Wallace Stegner—is "to determine what is the greatest good, and whether the several goods are compatible or whether one will destroy the others."[67]

Paradoxically, water privatizers who criticize Metropolitan for inefficient "business principles" fail to recognize that MWD was created to operationalize a "public utility model" of how to conduct business in the public interest. This resonates with reformers around the world try-ing to overcome histories of corporately corrupt water-resource develop-ment. Unlike private water companies that they replaced, Metropolitan and its member agencies must conduct their affairs by preparing annual business plans and budgets, clearly defining their methods and objectives, and opening themselves to financial and public accountability. Although MET and its members may on occasion honor these principles in the breach, the problem may lie in occasional poor implementation rather than in fundamental defects in institutional arrangement or mission.[68]

Metropolitan enjoys distinct institutional advantages as a water-resource management agency. In the complicated, technical water busi-ness in California, MWD's special-district status makes it easier to carry out its mission compared to state and local water agencies—such as the California Department of Water Resources and even Los Angeles's De-partment of Water and Power—that are part of general-purpose govern-ments directly exposed to potentially sharp budgetary and electoral swings. MET enjoys independent revenue sources and thus escapes the periodic budgetary crises afflicting California's general-purpose govern-ments. By largely eliminating the property tax as a source of revenue, MET is not as susceptible as other local governments in California to post–Proposition 13 state fiscal raids. Further, Metropolitan's reliance on revenue-bond financing for capital projects brings needed market disci-pline in the form of adequate equity-debt ratios and debt service coverage. The market also encourages water rates to rise to reflect cost recovery, and thus sends valuable signals to customers about the need to conserve. Finally, MWD's large appointed board may provide needed continuity in carrying out its long-term mission, unlike small, elected boards where single elections can produce sharp personnel and policy swings.[69]

Rather than dismantle a viable regional water-resource agency, the challenge arguably is to encourage greater cooperation among member

agencies to achieve MWD's priorities and extend its linkages by emphasizing water quality as much as water affordability; by focusing more
on the demand management side of the demand-supply equation; by
furthering the conjunctive development of surface and groundwater
resources; by heightened coordination of water policy with land use
planning; and by embracing equitable concerns and environmental
sustainability.[70]

Of course, critics have a point that Metropolitan—in the most
venerable of California's traditions—has characteristically favored
"growth" over other values. Regarding "blue gold," Golden Staters have
heretofore believed that "build a city—and the water will come." Or
rather, that MWD—the growth religion's once-regional demigod—could
be relied on to provide the water. MWD officials do not deny that there
is a difference between growth narrowly conceived as an economic met-
ric and sustainable development that incorporates environmental quality
goals and also the equitable protection of weaker localities and future
generations against spoliation of their right to water. Yet MET has been
reluctant to embrace the distinction, on the grounds that it cannot transform itself into the high priest of "no growth." MWD's Carl Boronkay argues that "Metropolitan is responsible for ensuring adequate and reliable
supply of water to meet increasing demand within the service area. . . .
Metropolitan does not initiate or implement 'no growth' policies. By
adopting plans or policies intended to limit water supplies to levels that
would not meet the projected demands, . . . Metropolitan would be
engaging in de facto regional growth control that is beyond its legal
capacity."[71]

Although it is true that MWD is a limited powers agency whose
statutory mandate does not extend to land use planning, the line between
real estate development and water resource allocation—to the extent it
ever existed—is being redefined and sometimes muddied into oblivion by
every legislative session in Sacramento. It is no longer easy, if it ever was,
for Metropolitan to navigate between meeting its responsibilities to
member agencies and its obligation to decide matters in the broader
public interest.[72]

Water historian William Kahrl observes that the "history of
California in the twentieth century . . . [is] the story of a state inventing
itself with water."[73] This epic tale is particularly true for modern

Southern California, and is not yet over. In the future, the region is likely to place greater emphasis on what Peter H. Gleick calls "the soft path" to a supposedly more sustainable water-resources future. Yet even a more environmentally friendly approach has costs. As former MWD CEO Gastelum cautions, "The soft path . . . is highly dependent upon subsidies since it is generally more costly than existing supplies, and won't really accelerate unless there are shortages or a real conservation enforcement policy at the state and federal levels. Water policy decisions in California have always been drawn by economics and parochial self-interest to a greater extent than considered public policy."[74]

Notwithstanding *Chinatown*'s *noir* inscrutabilities, MWD has successfully mixed economics, member agency self-interest, and public policy to conjure into existence a mighty yet fragile regional archipelago on the Pacific Rim. Metropolitan's challenge is to find the right formulas to nourish this improbable desert civilization well into the 21st and future centuries.

Notes

Chapter 1

1. Metropolitan Water District of Southern California (MWDSC), *Water from the Colorado River* (Los Angeles: MWDSC, 1931), p. 5.

2. Quoted in Vandana Shiva, *Water Wars: Privatization, Pollution, and Profit* (Cambridge, MA: South End Press, 2002), p. ix.

3. The Los Angeles metropolitan area includes Los Angeles, Orange, Ventura, Riverside, and San Bernardino counties. The San Diego metropolitan area consists of San Diego County.

4. Regarding L.A.'s early role in regional water development and the formation of MWD, see Joel Schwarz, *A Water Odyssey: The Story of the Metropolitan Water District of Southern California* (Los Angeles: MWDSC, 1991), pp. 14–44. Regarding Pasadena's key role, see Timothy F. Brick, "Partners: Pasadena's Role in the Formation of the Metropolitan Water District of Southern California," unpublished manuscript, November 22, 1997, 8 pp.

5. Interview with Paul Engstrand, former general counsel, San Diego County Water Authority, 2005.

6. Quoted in Kevin Starr, *Endangered Dreams: The Great Depression in California* (New York: Oxford University Press, 1996), p. 307, describing the building of the Colorado River Aqueduct.

7. Terry McDermott, "Knee-Deep Disputes for 'Water Buffaloes,'" *Los Angeles Times*, November 1, 1998.

8. *Harry Griffen Manuscript*, chapter 6.2.doc, n.p. This is an unpublished late 20th-century manuscript by Harry Griffen (d. 7/12/03) concerning the history of

water development in San Diego and Southern California. It is provided courtesy of the Helix Water District Archives, La Mesa, California. I wish to thank Kate Breece, Helix Water District Senior Public Affairs Representative, and Pam Griffen, Harry's daughter, for their assistance in securing access to this invaluable manuscript. San Diegan Harry Griffen, known as "Mr. Water," was a force in the Southern California water industry for half a century. Griffen served on the Helix Water District board of directors from 1951 to 1978; the San Diego County Water Authority board of directors from 1956 to 1995; and the Metropolitan Water District board of directors from 1963 to 1995.

9. In accord with the provisions of the Boulder Canyon Project Act of 1928.

10. Brick, "Partners"; Scott Harris, "Metropolitan Water District: A Giant in Southern California's Success," *Los Angeles Times*, April 1, 1990, p. A34.

11. "MWD's Wodraska: A Coherent Strategy for State's Urban Interests," *Metro Investment Report* II: 2 (July 1994), pp. 1, 13; Brick, "Partners"; Frederick M. Muir, "Challenge to MWD's Old Ways," *Los Angeles Times*, August 11, 1991, pp. A1, A24, A25.

12. In 1928 voters in 11 cities—Anaheim, Beverly Hills, Burbank, Colton, Glendale, Los Angeles, Pasadena, San Bernardino, San Marino, Santa Ana, and Santa Monica—approved joining MWD. Voters in Glendora and Orange vetoed the measure. In 1931, 4 other cities—Compton, Fullerton, Long Beach, and Torrance—agreed to be annexed to MWD, while Colton and San Bernardino withdrew. The resulting 13 municipalities are considered MWD's founding members. See Schwarz, *A Water Odyssey*, p. 43; McDermott, "Knee-Deep Disputes for 'Water Buffaloes.'"

13. Under the Metropolitan Water District Act, each member agency has at least one board representative, plus an additional board member for each full 5 percent of assessed property valuation in MWD's service territory. Voting also is based on assessed valuation. Each member agency casts one vote for each $10 million or major fractional part of $10 million of assessed property valuation.

14. Member-agency supplemental water needs have varied greatly over time. For example, the city of Los Angeles historically got up to 75 percent of its total water supply from the Owens Valley, 15 percent from local groundwater, and only 10–20 percent from MWD. For 2000–2004, with Owens Valley reductions because of restoring the level of Mono Lake and lowering dust levels at Owens Lake, coupled with below-average years of snow pack in the eastern Sierra, Los Angeles has averaged over 50 percent of its supply delivered from Metropolitan. MWD likely will remain L.A.'s single largest source of water for years to come.

15. McDermott, "Knee-Deep Disputes for 'Water Buffaloes.'"

16. The San Diego County Water Authority (SDCWA) is a 23-member agency. The city of San Diego is the largest member. With the weighted (financial

contribution) vote, the city controls over 40 percent of the total vote of SDCWA's board of directors.

17. For example, see Dennis E. O'Connor, *The Governance of the Metropolitan Water District of Southern California: An Overview of the Issues* (Sacramento: California Research Bureau, August 1998), 60 pp.; and Dennis E. O'Connor, *Governance of the Metropolitan Water District of Southern California: Options for Change* (Sacramento: California Research Bureau, December 1998), 45 pp.

18. Quoted in Frederick M. Muir, "MWD's Thirst for New Customers Continues," *Los Angeles Times*, March 31, 1991, p. A32.

19. MWDSC, *2004/05 Proposed Budget* (Los Angeles: MWDSC, 2004), p. 3.

20. Major Los Angeles water studies include Remi Nadeau, *The Water Seekers* (Santa Barbara, CA: Crest Publishers, 1997 [originally published in 1950]); Vincent Ostrom, *Water and Politics: A Study of Water Policies and Administration in the Development of Los Angeles* (Los Angeles: Haynes Foundation, 1953); Abraham Hoffman, *Vision or Villainy: Origins of the Owens Valley-Los Angeles Water Controversy* (College Station, TX: Texas A&M University Press, 1981); William Kahrl, *Water and Power: The Conflict over Los Angeles' Water Supply in the Owens Valley* (Berkeley: University of California Press, 1982); and Catherine Mulholland, *William Mulholland and the Rise of Los Angeles* (Berkeley: University of California Press, 2000). More general studies of water and western development include Erwin Cooper, *Aqueduct Empire: A Guide to Water in California, Its Turbulent History and Its Management Today* (Glendale, CA: Arthur H. Clark, 1968); Norris Hundley Jr., *Water and the West: Colorado River Compact, and the Politics of Water in the American West* (Berkeley: University of California Press, 1975); Donald Worster, *Rivers of Empire: Water, Aridity, and the Growth of the American West* (New York: Oxford University Press, 1985); Marc Reisner, *Cadillac Desert: The American West and Its Disappearing Water* (New York: Viking, 1986); John Walton, *Western Times and Water Wars: State, Culture, and Rebellion in California* (Berkeley: University of California Press, 1992); Philip L. Fradkin, *A River No More: The Colorado River and the West* (Berkeley: University of California Press, 1996); David Carle, *Water and the California Dream: Choices for the New Millennium* (Westport, CT: Praeger, 2000); Ted Simon, *A River Stops Here: Saving Round Valley, A Pivotal Chapter in California's Water Wars* (Berkeley: University of California Press, 2001); Norris Hundley Jr., *The Great Thirst: Californians and Water—A History*, rev. ed. (Berkeley: University of California Press, 2001); and Donald J. Pisani, *Water and American Government: The Reclamation Bureau, National Water Policy, and the West, 1902–1935* (Berkeley: University of California Press, 2002). For an historiographic overview, see Norris Hundley, "Water and the West in Historical Imagination," *Western Historical*

Quarterly 27:1 (Spring 1996), pp. 4–31. Regarding MWD, see Schwarz, *A Water Odyssey*; Kazuto Oshio, "Urban Water Diplomacy: A Policy History of the Metropolitan Water Supply in the Twentieth Century Southern California," doctoral dissertation, UC Santa Barbara, 1992; Robert Gottlieb, *A Life of Its Own: The Politics and Power of Water* (New York: Harcourt Brace Jovanovich, 1988); Robert Gottlieb and Margaret FitzSimmons, *Thirst for Growth: Water Agencies as Hidden Government in California* (Tucson: University of Arizona Press, 1991). Also see Norris Hundley Jr., *The Great Thirst*, chapter 7, "Water Policy at a Crossroads," pp. 365–542; and William Fulton, *The Reluctant Metropolis: The Politics of Urban Growth in Los Angeles* (Baltimore: Johns Hopkins University Press, 2001), chapter 4, "Redefining *Chinatown*," pp. 101–124.

21. For biographies of MWD board chairs and general managers, 1929–1990, see Schwarz, *A Water Odyssey*, pp. 189–201.

22. See John C. Bollens, *Special District Governments in the United States* (Berkeley: University of California Press, 1961); Donald Axelrod, *Shadow Government: The Hidden World of Public Authorities—and How They Control over $1 Trillion of Your Money* (New York: Wiley, 1992); Nancy Burns, *The Formation of American Local Governments: Private Values in Public Institutions* (New York: Oxford University Press, 1994); Kathryn A. Foster, *The Political Economy of Special Purpose Government* (Washington, DC: Georgetown University Press, 1997); Vincent Ostrom, Charles M. Tiebout, and Robert Warren, "The Organization of Government in Metropolitan Areas: A Theoretical Inquiry," *American Political Science Review*, 55:4 (December 1961), pp. 833–34; William A. Niskanen, *Bureaucracy and Representative Government* (Chicago: Aldine-Atherton, 1971); James Q. Wilson, *Bureaucracy: What Government Agencies Do and Why They Do It* (New York: Basic Books, 1991); Megan Mullin, "Specialization and Responsiveness in Local Policy Making: The Case of Water Districts," unpublished manuscript, University of California at Berkeley, September 2004, 44 pp.

23. Over the years, MWD has had both powerful board chairs and general managers, with influence appearing to shift from chairs to managers. See McDermott, "Knee-Deep Disputes for 'Water Buffaloes.'" Close observers claim that MET appears most effective when strong chair-manager alliances are forged. Such was the case in the 1980s with board chairs E. Thornton "Ibby" Ibbetson, Lois Krieger, and Les Balmer and general manager Carl Boronkay; from 1999 to 2004, there was a similar close working relationship between MWD Chair Phil Pace and CEO Ron Gastelum. Regarding strategies elected officials use to control bureaucracies, see Mathew D. McCubbins and Thomas Schwartz, "Congressional Oversight Overlooked: Police Patrols versus Fire Alarms," *American Political Science Review*, 28:1 (February 1984), pp. 165–79; Mathew D. McCubbins, Roger G. Noll, and Barry R. Weingast, "Administrative Procedures

as an Instrument of Political Control," *Journal of Law, Economics, and Organization*, 3 (1987), pp. 243–77; Mathew D. McCubbins, "Abdication or Delegation? Congress, the Bureaucracy, and the Delegation Dilemma," unpublished manuscript, University of California at San Diego, n.d., 25 pp.

24. Mullin, "Specialization and Responsiveness in Local Policy Making"; Darwin C. Hall, "Public Choice and Water Rate Design," in Aniel Dinar, ed., *The Political Economy of Water Pricing Reforms* (New York: Oxford University Press for the World Bank, 2000), pp. 189–212. I wish to thank my colleague Sam Kernell for suggesting this line of inquiry regarding accountability and principal-agent relations.

25. United Nations, Environment and Sustainable Development Division (ESDD), *Guidelines on Water and Sustainable Development, Principles and Policy Options* (Bangkok: ESDD, 1997), pp. 1, 54; Neil S. Grigg, *Water Resources Management: Principles, Regulations and Cases* (New York: McGraw-Hill, 1996), p. 444; Peter Rogers, *America's Water: Federal Roles and Responsibilities* (Cambridge, MA: MIT Press, 1993), p. 15.

26. MWDSC, *2004/05 Proposed Budget*, Table 23, "Population," p. 88.

27. Ralph Vartabedian, "Drought Has West in Chokehold," *Los Angeles Times*, December 22, 2003, pp. A1, A24; Michael Gardner, "Drought Creates a River of Doubt," *San Diego Union-Tribune*, April 25, 2004, pp. A3, A23; Miguel Bustillo, "State Gets Warning on Global Warming," *Los Angeles Times*, April 17, 2004, pp. B1, B10; Dan Cayan, "Climate Change: A Challenge Looming for California," *San Diego Union-Tribune*, August 15, 2004, pp. G1, G6; Julie Cart, "Threats to Colorado River Cited," *Los Angeles Times*, April 14, 2004, p. B6.

28. W. H. Auden, "First Things First," in W. H. Auden, *Collected Poems*, ed. Edward Mendelson (New York: Vintage International, 1991), pp. 583–84.

29. Quoted in Chris McGreal, "Deadly Thirst," *The Guardian*, January 13, 2004, www.guardian.co.uk/.

30. Jim Motavalli, "Down the Drain: The Coming World Water Crisis," *In These Times*, April 17, 2000, p. 18.

31. Testimony as to how the public's appetite has been whetted is the sheer number of recent water books. These include Roger D. Masters, *Fortune Is a River: Leonardo Da Vinci and Niccolo Machiavelli's Magnificent Dream to Change the Course of Florentine History* (New York: Plume, 1999); Diane Raines Ward, *Water Wars: Drought, Flood, Folly, and the Politics of Thirst* (New York: Riverhead Books, 2002); Sandra Postel and Linda Starke, eds., *Last Oasis: Facing Water Scarcity* (New York: W.W. Norton, 1997); John M. Donahue and Barbara Rose Johnson, eds., *Water, Culture, and Power: Local Struggles in a Global Context* (Washington, DC: Island Press, 1997); Paul Simon, *Tapped Out: The Coming World Crisis in Water and What We Can Do about It* (New York: Welcome Rain

Press, 1998); Peter H. Gleick, *World's Water 2000–2001* (Washington, DC: Island Press, 2000); Marq de Villiers, *Water: The Fate of Our Most Precious Resource* (New York: Houghton Mifflin, 2001); Jeffrey Rothfeder, *Every Drop for Sale: Our Desperate Battle over Water in a World About to Run Out* (Los Angeles: J.P. Tarcher Press, 2001); Robert Jerome Glennon, *Water Follies: Groundwater Pumping and the Fate of America's Fresh Waters* (Washington, DC: Island Press, 2002); Vandana Shiva, *Water Wars*; Sandra Postel and Brian Richter, *Rivers for Life: Managing Water for People and Nature* (Washington, DC: Island Press, 2003); Bernadette McDonald and Douglas Jehl, eds., *Whose Water Is It? The Unquenchable Thirst of a Hungry World* (Washington, DC: National Geographic Society, 2003); Maude Barlow and Tony Clarke, *Blue Gold: The Fight to Stop the Corporate Theft of the World's Water* (New York: W.W. Norton, 2003).

32. Igor A. Shiklomanov, "World Fresh Water Resources," in Peter H. Gleick, ed., *Water in Crisis: A Guide to the World's Fresh Water Resources* (New York: Oxford University Press, 1993), p. 13; Peter H. Gleick, "Water in the Twenty-First Century," in *Water in Crisis*, pp. 105–06.

33. Fradkin, *A River No More*; Steven J. Shupe et al., "Western Water Rights: The Era of Reallocation," *National Resources Journal*, 29 (1989), p. 413; Malin Falkenmark and Gunnar Lindh, "Water and Economic Development," in *Water in Crisis*, p. 87; Michael Gardner, "Drought Creates a River of Doubt," p. A3.

34. Douglas Jehl, "A New Frontier in Water Wars Emerges in the East," *New York Times*, March 3, 2003, p. A1; Stephen A. Thompson, *Water Use, Management, and Planning in the United States* (San Diego: Academic Press, 1999); Christopher Conte, "Dry Spell," [Congressional Quarterly] *Governing Magazine*, March 2003, p. 20; Charles W. Petit, "The Great Drying," *U.S. News and World Report*, May 20, 2002, p. 12.

35. Andrew A. Dzurik, *Water Resources Planning* (London: Rowman and Littlefield, 1990), pp. 41–42; "Ebro Eddies," *The Economist*, January 8, 2004, www.economist.com; Marlise Simons, "Spain's Sunny Coasts Look for Water from North," *New York Times*, June 13, 2004, p. A8.

36. "Spain Plans to Divert Ebro River Basin Water," UPI, September 6, 2000; "Protesters Clog Streets of Madrid to Denounce Water Project," *AP Wire*, March 11, 2001; David Guillet, "Water Property Rights and Resistance to Demand Management in Northeastern Spain," in Bryan Randolph Bruns and Ruth S. Meinzen-Dick, eds. *Negotiating Water Rights* (London: International Food Policy Research Institute, 2000), pp. 222–44; "Whose Water, Exactly?" *The Economist*, August 23, 2001, www.economist.com.

37. Harald D. Fredriksen, *Water Resources Institutions* (Washington, DC: World Bank, 1992), pp. 31, 33; Dugold Black, "Sustainable Water Resources Management in Australia," in United Nations, Economic and Social Commission

for Asia and the Pacific, *Sustainable Development of Water Resources in Asia and the Pacific: An Overview* (New York: United Nations, 1997), pp. 8–12; "Drying Out," *The Economist*, July 10, 2000, www.economist.com.

38. De Villiers, *Water*, pp. 146–165; Marc Reisner, *Cadillac Desert: The American West and Its Disappearing Water* (New York: Viking, 1986); Peter H. Gleick, "Water and Energy," in *Water in Crisis*, pp. 68–69; Dzurik, *Water Resources Planning*, pp. 146–47; Joe Nick Patoski, "Boone Pickens Wants to Sell You His Water," *Texas Monthly*, August 2001, p. 120.

39. "High and Dry," *The Economist*, March 28, 2002, www.economist.com; "Bangkok Gets that Sinking Feeling," *The Economist*, April 27, 2000, www.economist.com; "Problems of the Big Thirst," *The Economist*, April 27, 2000, www.economist.com; Sandra Postel, "Water and Agriculture," in *Water in Crisis*, pp. 57–58; R. Vidyasagar Rao, "Water and Sustainable Development: Indian Scenario," in United Nations, Economic and Social Commission for Asia and the Pacific, *Sustainable Development of Water Resources in Asia and the Pacific: An Overview*, pp. 47–59.

40. Gleick, "Water in the 21st Century," pp. 105–13; Barlow and Clarke, *Blue Gold*, pp. 51–78.

41. Stephen C. McCaffrey, "Water, Politics, and International Law," in *Water in Crisis*, pp. 92–104; Barlow and Clarke, *Blue Gold*, pp. 79–182.

42. Peter H. Gleick, "An Introduction to Global Fresh Water Issues," in *Water in Crisis*, pp. 3–12.

43. John Bulloch and Adel Darwish, *Water Wars: Coming in the Middle East* (London: Gollancz, 1993); Diane R. Ward, *Water Wars*.

44. Peter H. Gleick, "Water Policies and Politics," in *Water in Crisis*, pp. 438–49, Tables I-6, I-7; Babacar N'Diaye, "Water and African Development," in Asit K. Biswas, Mohammed Jellali, and Glenn E. Stout, eds., *Water for Sustainable Development in the Twenty-First Century* (Delhi: Oxford University Press, 1993), pp. 18–23.

45. Asit K. Biswas, ed., *International Waters of the Middle East: Euphrates-Tigris to Nile* (New York: Oxford University Press, 1994); Saul Arlosoroff, "The Water Sector in the Middle-East: Potential Conflict Resolutions," in Manas Chatterji, Saul Arlosoroff, and Gauri Guha, eds., *Conflict Management of Water Resources* (London: Ashgate, 2002), pp. 47–68.

46. McCaffrey, "Water, Politics, and International Law," p. 94; P. P. Howell and J. A. Allan, eds., *The Nile, Sharing a Scarce Resource: A Historical and Technical Review of Water Management and of Economic and Legal Issues* (Cambridge: Cambridge University Press, 1994); Kristin Wiebe, "The Nile River: Potential for Conflict and Cooperation in the Face of Water Degradation," *Natural Resources Journal*, 41:3 (Summer 2001), pp. 731–54.

47. M. Kassas and Samir I. Ghabbour, eds., *The Nile and Its Environment* (New York: Pergamon Press, 1980); Wiebe, "The Nile River"; Bonaya Adhi Godana, *Africa's Shared Water Resources: Legal and Institutional Aspects of the Nile, Niger, and Senegal River Systems* (London: F. Pinter, 1985).

48. W. S. Ellis, "The Aral: A Soviet Sea Lies Dying," *National Geographic*, 177:2 (1990), pp. 73–92; Eric W. Sievers, "Water, Conflict, and Regional Security in Central Asia," *New York University Environmental Law Journal*, 10 (2002), pp. 356–402; Genady N. Golubev, "State and Perspectives of Aral Sea Problem," in *Water for Sustainable Development in the Twenty-First Century*, pp. 245–54; "Liquid Dominoes," *The Economist*, March 4, 2004, www.economist.com; "Hanging Separately," *The Economist*, July 24, 2004, www.economist.com; "Saving the Last Drop," *The Economist*, June 29, 2000, www.economist.com; "Tajikistan's Water Politics," *The Economist*, July 2, 1998, www.economist.com.

49. Norris Hundley Jr., *Dividing the Waters: A Century of Controversy Between the United States and Mexico* (Berkeley: University of California Press, 1966), pp. 153–80; Myron B. Holburt, "International Problems," in Dean F. Peterson and A. Barry Crawford, eds., *Values and Choices in the Development of the Colorado River Basin* (Tucson: University of Arizona Press, 1978), pp. 220–37; Stephen Mumme, "Innovation and Reform in Transboundary Resource Management: A Critical Look at the International Boundary and Water Commission, United States and Mexico," *Natural Resources Journal*, 33 (1993), p. 93; Rudy E. Verner, "Short Term Solutions, Interim Surplus Guidelines, and the Future of the Colorado River Delta," *Colorado Journal of International Environmental Law and Policy*, 14 (Spring 2003), p. 241; David H. Getches, "Water Management in the United States and the Fate of the Colorado River Delta in Mexico," *U.S.-Mexico Law Journal*, 11 (Spring 2003), p. 107; Damien M. Schiff, "Rollin', Rollin', Rollin' on the River: A Story of Drought, Treaty Interpretation, and Other Rio Grande Problems," *Indiana International and Comparative Law Review*, 14 (2003), p. 117; "A Water Debt Boils Over," *The Economist*, June 20, 2002, www.economist.com; Will Weissert, "Mexico Ready to Pay Off a Massive Water Debt," *San Diego Union-Tribune*, March 27, 2005, p. A17.

Chapter 2

1. American Film Institute, "On Refining Story: A Conversation with Robert Towne," 2002, www.fathom.com/feature/122390/; Liahna K. Babener, "Chinatown, City of Blight," in David Fine, ed., *Los Angeles in Fiction: A Collection of Essays* (Albuquerque: University of New Mexico Press, 2000), p. 276.

2. Robert Towne, *"Chinatown" and "The Last Detail": Two Screenplays by Robert Towne* (New York: Grove Press, 1997), p. 12.

3. In the words of Hannah Arendt, "whatever brotherhood human beings may be capable of has grown out of fratricide, whatever political organization men may have achieved has its origin in crime." See Arendt, *On Revolution* (New York: Viking Press, 1963), pp. 10–11. Also see Norman M. Klein, *The History of Forgetting: Los Angeles and the Erasure of Memory* (London: Verso, 1997), p. 61; Charles Champlin, "'Chinatown' Tour de Force," *Los Angeles Times*, June 21, 1974, p. D1; Samuel A. Kimball, "Laius a Tergo, the Symbolic Order, the Production of the Future: *Chinatown*'s Primal Scene," *Literature and Psychology*, 48 (2002), pp. 1–31; Vernon Shetley, "Incest and Capital in Chinatown," *MLN*, 114:5 (December 1999), pp. 1092–1109.

4. Towne, "*Chinatown,*" pp. 3–146.

5. Klein, *History of Forgetting*, pp. 60, 247–48; Babener, "Chinatown, City of Blight," p. 275; Towne, "*Chinatown,*" pp. 3–146.

6. James Mayfield, "'Injustice of It All': Polanski's Revision of the Private Eye Genre in Chinatown," in Jerome H. Delamater and Ruth Prigozy, eds., *The Detective in American Fiction, Film, and Television* (Westport, CT: Greenwood Press, 1998), pp. 93–102; Karen Lynch, "Orientation via Orientalism: Chinatown in Detective Narratives," *Popular Culture Review*, 11:1 (February 2000), pp. 13–29; David Fine, *Imagining Los Angeles: A City in Fiction* (Albuquerque: University of New Mexico Press, 2000), pp. 148, 228; Towne, "*Chinatown,*" p. 80.

7. Jim Shepard, "Jolting Noir with a Shot of Nihilism: It Was 25 Years Ago That 'Chinatown,' to Renovate the Genre, Gave It a New Ferocity," *New York Times*, February 7, 1999, p. L24; Mike Wilmington, "Roman Polanski's 'Chinatown,'" *Velvet Light Trap*, 13 (Fall 1974), p. 15; Mayfield, "'Injustice of It All,'" p. 99; Garrett Stewart, "*The Long Goodbye* from *Chinatown*," *Film Quarterly*, 28: 2 (Winter 1974–1975), p. 31.

8. Chris Citron and Greg Hobbs, "Colorado's Life Written in Water," *Denver Post*, June 30, 2002, www.coloradocenterforthebook.org/ROW_Denver_Post_article.htm; William Galperin, "'Bad for the Glass': Representation and Filmic Deconstruction in *Chinatown* and *Chan Is Missing*," *MLN*, 102:5 (December 1987), p. 1156.

9. John Cawelti, "Chinatown and Generic Transformation in Recent American Films," in Gerald Mast and Marshall Cohen, eds., *Film Theory and Criticism: Introductory Readings*, 4th ed. (New York: Oxford University Press, 1992), pp. 498–511; Babener, "Chinatown, City of Blight," p. 273; Vernon Shetley, "Incest and Capital in Chinatown," *MLN*, 114:5 (1999), pp. 1092–1109; Towne, "*Chinatown,*" pp. 122–24; Klein, *History of Forgetting*, p. 89.

10. Towne, "*Chinatown,*" pp. 139–40.

11. Catherine Mulholland, *William Mulholland and the Rise of Los Angeles* (Berkeley: University of California Press, 2000), p. 4.

12. Klein, *History of Forgetting*, pp. 80, 89.

13. Kevin Starr, "It's Chinatown," *New Republic*, 173 (July 26, 1975), p. 31; Gerald Forshey, "Exploring Uncharted Depths of Depravity," *Christian Century*, September 18, 1974, pp. 860–61; Towne, "*Chinatown*," pp. 16–18, 79–82, 138–44; Robert Gottlieb and Irene Wolt, *Thinking Big: The Story of the Los Angeles Times, Its Publishers, and Their Influence on Southern California* (New York: Putnam, 1977), pp. 1–120; Marshall Berges, *The Life and Times of Los Angeles: A Newspaper, a Family, and a City* (New York: Atheneum, 1984), pp. 25–27.

14. Mulholland, *William Mulholland*, pp. 81, 186, 206–07, 211–15, 227; Frederic Cople Jaher, *The Urban Establishment: Upper Strata in Boston, New York, Charleston, Chicago, and Los Angeles* (Urbana: University of Illinois Press, 1982), p. 639; William L. Kahrl, *Water and Power: The Conflict over Los Angeles' Water Supply in the Owens Valley* (Berkeley: University of California Press, 1982), pp. 133, 181–83; Marc Reisner, *Cadillac Desert: The American West and Its Disappearing Water* (New York: Penguin Books, 1993), pp. 74–75.

15. Towne, "*Chinatown*," pp. 11, 65, 71.

16. Vincent Ostrom, *Water and Politics: A Study of Water Policies and Administration in the Development of Los Angeles* (Los Angeles: Haynes Foundation, 1953), pp. 40–48, 90–97; Mulholland, *William Mulholland*, pp. 75–87; Abraham Hoffman, *Vision or Villainy: Origins of the Owens Valley-Los Angeles Water Controversy* (College Station: Texas A&M University Press, 1981), pp. 25–46.

17. Steven P. Erie, "How the Urban West Was Won: The Local State and Economic Growth in Los Angeles, 1880–1932," *Urban Affairs Quarterly*, 27:4 (June 1992), pp. 538–47; Donald J. Pisani, *To Reclaim a Divided West: Water, Law, and Public Policy, 1848–1902* (Albuquerque: University of New Mexico Press, 1992), p. 40; Ostrom, *Water and Politics*, pp. 31–37; Peter L. Reich, "Mission Revival Jurisprudence: State Courts and Hispanic Water Law Since 1850," *Washington Law Review*, 69 (October 1994), pp. 869–90; Carey McWilliams, *Southern California Country: An Island on the Land* (Santa Barbara, CA: Peregrine Smith, 1973 [1946]), p. 188; Mulholland, *William Mulholland*, pp. 83–86, 103–04. Credit should be given to Remi Nadeau and W. W. Robinson for noting McWilliams's error concerning water dumping. See Remi Nadeau, *The Water Seekers* (Garden City, NY: Doubleday, 1950).

18. Hoffman, *Vision or Villainy*, pp. 126–28, 154; Norris Hundley Jr., *The Great Thirst: Californians and Water: A History*, rev. ed. (Berkeley: University of California Press, 2001), pp. 155–62; Mulholland, *William Mulholland*, p. 211; Kahrl, *Water and Power*, pp. 96–99, 138.

19. Mulholland, *William Mulholland*, pp. 29, 44–45, 113–14, 192, 240, 245–46; Hoffman, *Vision or Villainy*, pp. 19–24, 103, 275; Nadeau, *The Water*

Seekers, p. 17; Kahrl, *Water and Power*, pp. 12–17, 47–50; Jaher, *Urban Establishment*, pp. 624–25, 639. Modern theorists of bureaucracy see public entrepreneurs such as Mulholland driven by desires for influence/power and for their near- and long-term reputation. Yet there is little in the historical record suggesting that such factors seriously influenced William Mulholland.

20. Hundley, *The Great Thirst*, p. 155; Mulholland, *William Mulholland*, p. 133.

21. Kahrl, *Water and Power*, pp. 48–49, 54; Hoffman, *Vision or Villainy*, p. 65.

22. Mulholland, *William Mulholland*, pp. 169, 211, 243–44; Reisner, *Cadillac Desert*, pp. 88, 90–91; Ostrom, *Water and Politics*, p. 151; John Walton, *Western Times and Water Wars: State, Culture, and Rebellion in California* (Berkeley: University of California Press, 1991), p. 167.

23. Towne, "*Chinatown*," pp. 11, 139; J. David Rogers, "A Man, a Dam, and a Disaster: Mulholland and the St. Francis Dam," in Doyce B. Nunis Jr., ed., *The St. Francis Dam Disaster Revisited* (Los Angeles: Historical Society of Southern California, 1995), pp. 20–28; Reisner, *Cadillac Desert*, p. 100; Mulholland, *William Mulholland*, pp. 330, 382.

24. Hundley, *The Great Thirst*, p. 160; Hoffman, *Vision or Villainy*, pp. 245–46; Kahrl, *Water and Power*, p. 311.

25. Kahrl, *Water and Power*, p. 98 (quote).

26. Margaret Leslie Davis, *Rivers in the Desert: William Mulholland and the Inventing of Los Angeles* (New York: HarperCollins, 1993), p. 128; Matthew W. Roth, "Mulholland Highway and the Engineering Culture of Los Angeles in the 1920s," in Tom Sitton and William Deverell, eds., *Metropolis in the Making: Los Angeles in the 1920s* (Berkeley: University of California Press, 2001), p. 59; Erie, "How the Urban West Was Won," pp. 538–47.

27. Reisner, *Cadillac Desert*, pp. 64–65, 68, 70; Hoffman, *Vision or Villainy*, pp. 67–85, 273–74; Kahrl, *Water and Power*, 49, 58–63; Mulholland, *William Mulholland*, pp. 113–14, 127–28.

28. Ostrom, *Water and Politics*, p. 80; Hundley, *The Great Thirst*, pp. 153–54, 167–70; Reisner, *Cadillac Desert*, pp. 64–65, 88–89; Mulholland, *William Mulholland*, pp. 83–86, 100–104, 319–32; Martin Schiesl, "Politicians in Disguise: The Changing Role of Public Administrators in Los Angeles, 1900–1920," in Michael H. Ebner and Eugene M. Tobin, eds., *The Age of Reform: New Perspectives on the Progressive Era* (Port Washington, NY: Kennikat Press, 1977), pp. 108–16; H. Eric Shockman, "Los Angeles: Toward the 21st Century," in Norman M. Klein and Martin J. Schiesl, eds., *20th Century Los Angeles: Power, Promotion, and Social Conflict* (Claremont, CA: Regina Books, 1990), p. 230; Joel Schwarz, *A Water Odyssey: The Story of the Metropolitan Water District of*

Southern California (Los Angeles: MWDSC, 1991), p. 15; Hoffman, *Vision or Villainy*, p. 242. Cf. Kahrl, *Water and Power*, pp. 83–84.

29. See Gary D. Libecap, "*Chinatown*: Transaction Costs in Water Rights Exchanges—The Owens Valley Transfer to Los Angeles," unpublished manuscript, November 2004, 46 pp., at p. 30.

30. Reisner, *Cadillac Desert*, pp. 90–97; John Walton, *Western Times and Water Wars*, pp. 167, 194–95; Gary Brechin, *Imperial San Francisco: Urban Power, Earthly Riches* (Berkeley: University of California Press, 1999), pp. 53, 73.

31. Mulholland, *William Mulholland*, pp. 59–60, 227; Hundley, *The Great Thirst*, pp. 167–71.

32. Robert M. Fogelson, *The Fragmented Metropolis: Los Angeles, 1850–1930* (Berkeley: University of California Press, 1967), p. 98; Erie, "How the Urban West Was Won," Table 5, p. 542; Ostrom, *Water and Politics*, pp. 63, 71; Kahrl, *Water and Power*, pp. 341–42. Also see Boyle Workman, *The City That Grew* (Los Angeles: Southland Publishing, 1935), pp. 386–87.

33. Hundley, *The Great Thirst*, pp. 174, 177, 187–202; Walton Bean, *Boss Ruef's San Francisco* (Berkeley: University of California Press, 1967), pp. 140–44; Brechin, *Imperial San Francisco*, pp. 100–101, 113–14; Sarah S. Elkind, *Bay Cities and Water Politics: The Battle for Resources in Boston and Oakland* (Lawrence: University of Kansas Press, 1998), pp. 6–7, 27; Kevin Starr, *Endangered Dreams: The Great Depression in California* (New York: Oxford University Press, 1996), pp. 276–77, 281, 286; Mike Davis, *City of Quartz: Excavating the Future in Los Angeles* (London: Verso, 1990), p. 113.

34. Morrow Mayo, *Los Angeles* (New York: Knopf, 1933), pp. 245–46.

35. Alex Pappademas, "Burn, Hollywood, Burn," http://articles.student.com/musicreview/celebrityskin, 1998.

36. Kevin Roderick, *The San Fernando Valley: America's Suburb* (Los Angeles: Los Angeles Times Books, 2001), p. 65.

37. Rebecca Fish Ewan, *A Land Between: Owens Valley, California* (Baltimore: Johns Hopkins University Press, 2000), pp. 131–33; Fine, *Imagining Los Angeles*, pp. 37–38; Hoffman, *Vision or Villainy*, pp. 102–3, 142–45, 234–43; Kahrl, *Water and Power*, pp. 155–57, 319–20, 323–25, 327–29; Ostrom, *Water and Politics*, p. 58.

38. Mulholland, *William Mulholland*, p. 279; Ostrom, *Water and Politics*, pp. 81–83; Jules Tygiel, *The Great Los Angeles Swindle: Oil, Stocks, and Scandal During the Roaring Twenties* (New York: Oxford University Press, 1994), pp. 12, 80. See chapter 109, *Statutes and Amendments to the Codes of California, 1925*, making cities that tapped a watershed liable for damages.

39. Hoffman, *Vision or Villainy*, pp. xiii, 235–42, 266–68, 275–76; Walton, *Western Times and Water Wars*, pp. 227–28; Kahrl, *Water and Power*, pp. 318,

405, 417. Although *Chinatown* has a scene filmed at LADWP's Stone Canyon Reservoir complex (where Mulwray's body is pulled up the channel), it is uncertain whether any of the movie actually was filmed in the Owens Valley.

40. Hoffman, *Vision or Villainy*, pp. xiii, 266–68; Kahrl, *Water and Power*, pp. 318, 405, 417; Walton, *Western Times and Water Wars*, p. 255.

41. Klein, *History of Forgetting*, p. 80; Robert Gottlieb, *A Life of Its Own: The Politics of Power and Water* (New York: Harcourt Brace Jovanovich, 1988), p. 275; Kahrl, *Water and Power*, p. 400.

42. Despite newspaper accounts of "ecoterrorism," this incident appears to have been a prank by youngsters and apparently was not politically motivated.

43. Walton, *Western Times and Water Wars*, pp. 231–32, 292.

44. Hundley, *The Great Thirst*, p. 423.

45. Robert A. Jones, "Death of 'Chinatown,'" *Los Angeles Times*, February 12, 1997, p. A2; Harold Brackman and Steven P. Erie, "California's Water Wars Enter a New Century," in Ali Modarres and Jerry Lubenow, eds., *California Policy Issues Annual: California's Future in the Balance* (Los Angeles: The Edmund G. "Pat" Brown Institute of Public Affairs, California State University, Los Angeles, and the Institute of Governmental Studies, University of California, Berkeley, 2002), pp. 180–83.

46. Quoted in Kahrl, *Water and Power*, p. 302.

47. Tom Kirk, "Don't Blame the IID for Failed Water Transfer Deal," *San Diego Union-Tribune*, December 21, 2002, p. B11.

48. Jerome W. Milliman, "The History, Organization, and Economic Problems of the Metropolitan Water District of Southern California," doctoral thesis, University of California, Los Angeles, 1956, pp. 97–100, 133–35; Mulholland, *William Mulholland*, pp. 277, 296; Kahrl, *Water and Power*, pp. 296, 302; Ostrom, *Water and Politics*, pp. 174–81; Walton, *Western Times and Water Wars*, pp. 201–2, 227; chapter 720, *California Statutes of 1931* (Senate Bill 141-Crittenden), enacted the County of Origin Law.

49. Fine, *Imagining Los Angeles*, pp. 37–38; Hoffman, *Vision or Villainy*, pp. 102–3, 142–45, 215–28, 234–43; Kahrl, *Water and Power*, pp. 155–57, 319–20, 323–29; Mulholland, *William Mulholland*, p. 203; Ostrom, *Water and Politics*, p. 58.

50. Kahrl, *Water and Power*, p. 321; Hoffman, *Vision or Villainy*, pp. 210–12, 224–27.

51. *Sacramento Union*, April 3, 1927, quoted in Kahrl, *Water and Power*, p. 316.

52. Kazuto Oshio, "Urban Water Diplomacy: A Policy History of the Metropolitan Water Supply in the Twentieth Century Southern California," doctoral thesis, University of California at Santa Barbara, 1992, pp. 78, 143, 150–54, 215.

53. Oshio, "Urban Water Diplomacy," p. 309; Committee on Western Water Management, Water Science and Technology Board, Commission on Engineering and Technical Systems, *Water Transfers in the West: Efficiency, Equity, and the Environment* (Washington, DC: National Academy Press, 1992), p. 224.

54. Interview with former MWD General Manager Carl Boronkay, 2005; Paul Jacobs, "Surplus Water Is Available, But Goes Unclaimed, Report Says," *Los Angeles Times*, May 22, 1985, p. A3.

55. Hundley, *The Great Thirst*, p. 507; William Fulton, *The Reluctant Metropolis: The Politics of Urban Growth in Los Angeles* (Baltimore: Johns Hopkins University Press, 2001), p. 119; Robert Gottlieb and Margaret FitzSimmons, *Thirst for Growth: Water Agencies as Hidden Government in California* (Tucson: University of Arizona Press, 1991), p.187; Virginia Ellis, "Urban Water Bill Okd by Assembly," *Los Angeles Times*, July 3, 1991, p. A3; David H. Getches, "Essays from Ashabad to Welton-Mohawk to Los Angeles: The Drought in Water Policy," *University of Colorado Law Review*, 64 (Spring 1993), p. 535.

56. "Water Persuasion," editorial, *San Diego Union-Tribune*, May 26, 2002; "Parting of Waters," editorial, *San Diego Union-Tribune*, December 11, 2002; Tony Perry, "Proposal to Sell Valley Water Stirs Anger," *Los Angeles Times*, October 25, 1995, p. A1; Rick Orlov, "Southland Divided by Water Fight," *Los Angeles Daily News*, June 2, 1997.

57. "Buy Low, Sell High: Imperial Valley Finds Fortune in Its Water," editorial, *San Diego Union-Tribune*, February 12, 2004, p. B10; "MWD Hypocrisy," editorial, *San Diego Union-Tribune*, October 18, 2001; Beverly Kelley, "If San Diego Gets a Free Water Ride, We'll Pay," *Ventura County Star*, June 18, 2001, p. B7; Tom Kirk, letter to the editor, *San Diego Union-Tribune*, December 21, 2002; Tony Perry, "Water Talks Send Ripple of Fear North," *Los Angeles Times*, August 24, 2003, p. B1; "Water Sharing," editorial, *San Diego Union-Tribune*, March 29, 2004.

58. Fulton, *The Reluctant Metropolis*, p. 101.

59. Christopher Parkes, "From Dust to Dust," *Financial Times* (London), November 8, 1997, p. 1.

60. Gottlieb, *A Life of Its Own*, pp. 6–9, 113–51.

61. Gottlieb, *A Life of Its Own*, pp. 126–27.

62. Gottlieb and FitzSimmons, *Thirst for Growth*, p. 8; Schwarz, *Water Odyssey*, p. 189; Erwin Cooper, *Aqueduct Empire* (Glendale, CA: Arthur H. Clark, 1968), pp. 97–98; Gottlieb, *A Life of Its Own*, p. 8 (quote).

63. Gottlieb and FitzSimmons, *Thirst for Growth*, p. 8.

64. Nelson S. Van Valen, "Power Politics: The Struggle for Municipal Ownership of Electric Utilities in Los Angeles, 1905–1937," doctoral thesis, Claremont Graduate School, 1963; Oshio, "Urban Water Diplomacy," pp. 63,

98; William Fulton, *The Reluctant Metropolis*, p. 106; Mulholland, *William Mulholland*, p. 302.

65. Oshio, "Urban Water Diplomacy," p. 67; *Los Angeles Times*, April 23, 1925.

66. *Los Angeles Times*, April 28, 1927; Oshio, "Urban Water Diplomacy," pp. 66–67, 71; Tom Sitton, *John Randolph Haynes: California Progressive* (Stanford, CA: Stanford University Press, 1992), p. 221.

67. Gottlieb and FitzSimmons, *Thirst for Growth*, pp. 22–24, 122–25; Oshio, "Urban Water Diplomacy," p. 87; James Jamieson et al., *Some Political and Economic Aspects of Managing California Water Districts* (Los Angeles: Institute of Government and Public Affairs, University of California, Los Angeles, 1974), pp. 112–13.

68. Nadeau, *Water Seekers*, pp. 220–21; Kahrl, *Water and Power*, pp. 339–40; Oshio, "Urban Water Diplomacy," p. 81; Milliman, "The History, Organization, and Economic Problems of the Metropolitan Water District of Southern California," pp. 21–23.

69. Gottlieb and FitzSimmons, *Thirst for Growth*, p. 8; Fulton, *The Reluctant Metropolis*, pp. 106–7; Milliman, "The History, Organization, and Economic Problems of the Metropolitan Water District of Southern California," pp. 407–8, 460, 510–12, 515; Oshio, "Urban Water Diplomacy," p. 179; Donald Worster, *Water, Aridity, and the Growth of the American West* (New York: Oxford University Press, 1985), p. 7; Kevin Starr, *Material Dreams: Southern California Through the 1920s* (New York: Oxford University Press, 1990).

70. Oshio, "Urban Water Diplomacy," pp. 114, 257–58, 266–68; Gottlieb and FitzSimmons, *Thirst for Growth*, pp. 144, 214; Milliman, "The History, Organization, and Economic Problems of the Metropolitan Water District of Southern California," pp. 177, 183, 228–31; John R. Logan and Harvey L. Molotch, *Urban Fortunes: The Political Economy of Place* (Berkeley: University of California Press, 1987), p. 225.

71. Oshio, "Urban Water Diplomacy," p. 77, 126–27, 148, 150–54; Gottlieb and FitzSimmons, *Thirst for Growth*, pp. 12–13, 35, 194, 215.

72. Boronkay interview; Gottlieb, *A Life of Its Own*, pp. 28–31; Mark Arax and Rick Wartzman, *The King of California: J. G. Boswell and the Making of a Secret American Empire* (New York: Public Affairs, 2003), pp. 351–56; Brackman and Erie, "California's Water Wars Enter a New Century," p. 161; Oshio, "Urban Water Diplomacy," pp. 194, 307.

73. Arendt, *On Revolution*, p. 201. Cf. Ronald J. Schmidt, *This Is the City: Making Model Citizens in Los Angeles* (Minneapolis: University of Minnesota Press, 2005), pp. xiii, 20–24, 111. Also see Lance deHaven-Smith and John R. Wodraska, "Consensus-Building for Integrated Resources Planning," *Public*

Administration Review, 56:4 (1996), pp. 367–71; and Annmarie H. Walsh, *The Public's Business: The Politics and Practices of Government Corporations* (Cambridge, MA: MIT Press, 1978), pp. 207, 333, for a contrary view of public corporations as inherently unaccountable and conflict-of-interest prone.

Chapter 3

An earlier version of this chapter appeared in Jennifer Wolch, Manuel Pastor Jr., and Peter Dreier, eds., *Up Against the Sprawl: Public Policy and the Making of Southern California* (Minneapolis: University of Minnesota Press, 2004), pp. 45–70.

1. Quoted in Joseph Jensen, "Developing California's Natural Resources" (Oral History Program, Department of Special Collections, UCLA Library, University of California at Los Angeles, 1970), p. 131.

2. William Fulton, *The Reluctant Metropolis: The Politics of Urban Growth in Los Angeles* (Baltimore: Johns Hopkins University Press, 1997, 2001), p. 105.

3. Norris Hundley Jr., *The Great Thirst: Californians and Water—A History*, rev. ed. (Berkeley: University of California Press, 2001), pp. 217, 219.

4. I wish to thank Jim Doig for suggesting this line of inquiry.

5. Jensen, "Developing California's Natural Resources," p. 129.

6. Fulton, *The Reluctant Metropolis*, pp. 106–7.

7. Population projections for Los Angeles, Orange, Riverside, San Diego, San Bernardino, Imperial, and Ventura Counties are from the state of California, Department of Finance, *Interim County Population Projections* (Sacramento, CA: Department of Finance, 2001).

8. See Center for Continuing Study of the California Economy, "Land Use and the California Economy: Principles for Prosperity and Quality of Life," 1998, available at www.calfutures.org. Regarding processes of suburbanization, see Kenneth Jackson, *Crabgrass Frontier: The Suburbanization of the United States* (New York: Oxford University Press, 1985); Robert Fishman, *Bourgeois Utopias: The Rise and Fall of Suburbia* (New York: Basic Books, 1987); and Joel Garreau, *Edge City: Life on the New Frontier* (New York: Doubleday, 1991). Regarding the impact of state and local policies on suburban development, see Jon Teaford, *City and Suburb: The Political Fragmentation of Metropolitan America* (Baltimore: Johns Hopkins University Press, 1976); Michael N. Danielson, *The Politics of Exclusion* (New York: Columbia University Press, 1976); and Mark Gottdiener, *Planned Sprawl: Private and Public Interests in Suburbia* (Beverly Hills, CA: Sage Publications, 1977). Regarding state and local policies encouraging Southern California suburbanization and sprawl, see Gary J. Miller, *Cities by Contract: The Politics of Municipal Incorporation* (Cambridge, MA: MIT Press,

1981); Fulton, *The Reluctant Metropolis*; and Jennifer Wolch et al., eds., *Up Against the Sprawl*.

9. See, for example, Peter Wiley and Robert Gottlieb, *Empires in the Sun: The Rise of the New American West* (New York: Putnam, 1982); Donald Worster, *Rivers of Empire: Water, Aridity, and the Growth of the American West* (New York: Pantheon, 1985); Marc Reisner, *Cadillac Desert: The American West and Its Disappearing Water* (New York: Viking, 1986); and Norris Hundley Jr., *The Great Thirst*. And see Robert Gottlieb, *A Life of Its Own: The Politics and Power of Water* (New York: Harcourt Brace Jovanovich, 1988), p. 126.

10. As Joseph Jensen, the long-serving MWD board chair (1949–1974) observed, "In fact, the failure of Los Angeles to take all the MWD water it was entitled to has been a benefit to outside agencies which have taken much more than the proportionate share they are entitled to—Orange and San Diego Counties are entitled to 10% each of MWD's water but get 25% each of actual deliveries. . . . This is a good thing both ways, for the counties and for the District, because the water is being used." Jensen, "Developing California's Natural Resources," p. 114.

11. William Mulholland's belief in bountiful water resources in the Owens Valley was confirmed by reports of the United States Geological Survey. See, for example, Willis T. Lee, *Geology and Water Resources of Owens Valley, California*, Water Supply and Irrigation Paper No. 181, United States Geological Survey (Washington, DC: U.S. Government Printing Office, 1906), 25 pp.

12. Interview with Robert V. Phillips, former general manager and chief engineer, L.A. Department of Water and Power, 1995. Also see Hundley, *The Great Thirst*, pp. 216–17. For the early history of the Colorado River Aqueduct, see Metropolitan Water District of Southern California (MWDSC), *History and First Annual Report* (Los Angeles: MWDSC, 1939). For another view of the policy dynamics behind frenetic suburban incorporation in postwar Los Angeles County, see Miller, *Cities by Contract*.

13. The Laguna Declaration states, "The Metropolitan Water District of Southern California is prepared, with its existing governmental powers and its present and projected distribution facilities, to provide its service area with adequate supplies of water to meet expanding and increasing needs in the years ahead. The District now is providing its service area with a supplemental water supply from the Colorado River. When and as additional water resources are required to meet increasing needs for domestic, industrial and municipal water, The Metropolitan Water District of Southern California will be prepared to deliver such supplies." Statement of Policy Approved by the Board of Directors of the Metropolitan Water District of Southern California, December 16, 1952, item 44 of supporting documents in MWDSC, *Source Materials on Metropolitan Water*

District Act Section 135—Preferential Rights (Los Angeles: MWDSC, 1996). Also see Joel Schwarz, *A Water Odyssey: The Story of the Metropolitan Water District of Southern California* (Los Angeles: MWDSC, 1991), pp. 103–18.

14. Jensen, "Developing California's Natural Resources," p. 137.

15. MWD's early fiscal problems involved power costs as well as water. MWD faced large power expenses with limited revenue. In 1946, MWD entered into a contract with LADWP and Southern California Edison to buy unused MWD power. Still, MWD paid millions of dollars for power it did not use and could not sell. See Joe Jenson, "Developing California's Natural Resources," pp. 106–7.

16. MWDSC, *Thirty-Fourth Annual Report, 1972* (Los Angeles: MWDSC, 1972), p. 147; MWDSC, *2004/05 Proposed Budget* (Los Angeles: MWDSC, 2004), Table, "2004/05 Water Rates and Charges," p. 12.

17. Although Los Angeles's share of Colorado River Aqueduct bond financing (in 2003 dollars) was 42 percent, San Diego taxpayers and ratepayers only contributed an 8 percent share. Source: MWDSC, Budget and Financial Planning Group, Water Information System (WINS).

18. In 1961 the MWD Act was amended to provide that its water rates "so far as practicable" shall cover operating expenses, repairs and maintenance, and principal and interest on bonded debt. See California Legislature, *Statutes of California, 1961 Regular Session* (Sacramento: State Printing Office, 1961), chapter 862, pp. 2268–69.

19. As former MWD board chair Joe Jensen observed, "Some San Diego MWD directors have tried to keep the price of water down—the [more] MWD taxes they make L.A. County pay, the less they [San Diegans] pay for water." Jensen, "Developing California's Natural Resources," p. 149. Yet former MWD general manager Julian Hinds criticized demands by L.A. MWD directors that SWP capital costs "be loaded onto satellite cities as a day-to-day water charge— if so, L.A. would get a free ride until using [MWD] water. . . . Satellite cities can't afford to carry L.A.'s share of the capital burden." See Julian Hinds, "Western Dam Engineer," pp. 127–28, UCLA Oral History Program, 1971. Also see Steven P. Erie and Pascale Joassart-Marcelli, "Unraveling Southern California's Water/Growth Nexus: Metropolitan Water District Policies and Subsidies for Suburban Development, 1928–1996," *California Western Law Review*, 36:2 (Spring 2000), pp. 267–90, at p. 273.

20. See MWDSC Board of Directors, Resolution 5821 (1960).

21. In 1960, the San Diego County Water Authority's MWD directors opposed raising MWD water rates to include payments of principal and interest on bonded debt. Later, Metropolitan's board of directors considered setting a higher price for State Water Project supplies (to include capital costs) relative to Colorado River water. According to an unofficial history of Metropolitan Water

District Act provisions: "SDCWA and other heavy water users resisted the concept of any such difference [in water price based on] source amendment to the Act [to Section 133, derived from the original Act's Section 5(10) and Section 6(8) (Stats. 1961, Ch. 862)]. A majority of the board, though, approved . . . a legislative draft containing this concept. However, the [Los Angeles] City's Department of Water and Power then entered into a Memorandum of Understanding with SDCWA (in order to dissuade the Authority from lobbying for defeat of the bill). The Memorandum contained these points: . . . [t]he legislation is permissive only." George Flewelling, "Derivation and History of Various Metropolitan Water District Act Provisions," unpublished manuscript, MWDSC, n.d., p. 93. Finally, starting in 1979 with the settlement of a lawsuit brought by the city of Los Angeles regarding MWD water and tax rate–setting policies, MWD began to fully implement a water charge-based system of capital financing. See Flewelling, "Derivation and History", pp. 92–107. See also MWDSC Resolution 5821 (1960); MWDSC Board of Directors, Resolution 7446 (1972); MWDSC Board of Directors, Minutes, November 13, 1979, p. 9.

22. See MWDSC Board of Directors, Resolutions 8464–65 (1995).

23. See MWDSC, *Thirty-Fourth Annual Report, 1972* (Los Angeles: MWDSC, 1972), p.146. The merger of MWD member agencies Coastal MWD and MWD of Orange County (MWDOC) in January 2001 reduced the number of MWD members to its present total of 26.

24. Phillips interview.

25. Interview with Paul Engstrand, former SDCWA general counsel, 2005.

26. See *Harry Griffen Manuscript* (n.d.), chapter 6-3.doc, n.p.

27. See Mark P. Berkman and Jesse David, "Water Subsidies in Southern California: Do They Exist and Have They Contributed to Urban Sprawl? A Comment on an Article by Steven P. Erie and Pascale Joassart-Marcelli Titled 'Unraveling Southern California's Water/Growth Nexus: Metropolitan Water District Policies and Subsidies for Suburban Development, 1928–1996,'" *California Western Law Review*, 37:1 (Fall, 2000), pp. 121–46.

28. For a critique of the Berkman and David approach to calculating Los Angeles subsidies for San Diego water provision, see Steven P. Erie, "Mulholland's Gifts: Further Reflections upon Southern California Water Subsidies and Growth," *California Western Law Review*, 37:1 (Fall 2000), pp. 147–60.

29. Alternative definitions of subsidy—based on stand-alone costs and incremental costs—lead to the same conclusion: that a subsidy relationship existed between original MWD members, particularly the city of Los Angeles, and later joiners such as San Diego County. See Erie, "Mulholland's Gifts," pp. 149–51.

30. See, for example, "Water Sharing: San Diego Pays More But L.A. Has Control," editorial, *San Diego Union-Tribune*, March 29, 2004.

31. There also are sizable unit-cost disparities between particular member agencies in a given county. For instance, much of Orange County's low unit cost is generated by one agency, the Municipal Water District of Orange County (MW-DOC). The county's three smallest agencies, Anaheim, Santa Ana, and Fullerton, were MWD founders, joining between 1928 and 1931. MWDOC, the county's largest agency, which draws 70 percent of its Metropolitan water deliveries, only joined MWD in 1951. Riverside County's member agencies with low unit costs are Eastern and Western MWD, having joined Metropolitan in 1951 and 1954, respectively.

32. Surprisingly, in the 1929–1970 period member agencies in Ventura (Calleguas MWD) and San Bernardino (Chino Basin MWD) counties paid a high $525 and $783 per acre-foot, respectively. Given that Ventura and San Bernardino unit costs, 1929–2003, closely approximate the overall member-agency average, these pre-1970 figures are anomalous. Calleguas only joined MWD in 1960 to receive State Water Project deliveries and, through 1970, had paid annexation charges but had received little MWD water. Chino Basin, which had joined in 1951, chose to draw little MWD water in the pre-1970 period relative to its payment of annexation fees.

33. Gottlieb, *A Life of Its Own*, p. 126.

34. Former L.A. Mayor Fletcher Bowron interview with Don J. Kinsey, July 2, 1965, in Bowron (Fletcher) Collection, Box 65, "Water and Power," Huntington Library, San Marino, California. Bowron also interviewed James H. Howard regarding his role in drafting the MWD Act. Howard observed that "I wrote the MWD Act in the first instance. It was modified during the course of negotiating very considerably. I had the benefit of W.B.'s [Mathews] advice all the time; we worked very closely together on it." According to Howard, "the primary difficulty was the form of government. The smaller communities were fearful that the dominant population of the City of L.A. would turn the control of any district that might be incorporated [over] to the City." Thus, "we worked out the very odd system of government that now controls the operation of the District—the idea that members should vote assessed valuation, but no one city should have more than 50% of the vote, and no city less than one vote." Fletcher Bowron interview with James H. Howard, August 27, 1965, in Bowron (Fletcher) Collection, Box 65, "Water and Power," Huntington Library.

35. As for MET's disputed paternity, some claim that the idea originated with the L.A. Chamber of Commerce. See Robert Gottlieb and Margaret FitzSimmons, *Thirst for Growth: Water Agencies as Hidden Government in California* (Tucson: University of Arizona Press, 1991), p. 8. Former MWD board chair Joseph Jensen, a mining engineer appointed to the chamber's Water and Power Committee in 1927, and to the MWD board in 1940, argues that "in 1925, under the

chairmanship of Lucius K. Chase, the L.A. chamber appointed a committee of 15 to develop and formulate a plan for bringing water from the Colorado River. This report of the committee of 15 formed the basis of the organization of the MWD of Southern California." Jensen, "Developing California's Natural Resources," p. 96. In his oral history, Jensen also discusses the formative roles of Los Angeles and Pasadena: "Since it was observed that the organization should not appear to be dominated by Los Angeles, the City of Pasadena was used as the vehicle for the organization of the District and took a prominent part in its creation," p. 96. Yet there was an equally—if not more important—public side to MET's creation, involving the city of Los Angeles, the LADWP, and other founding members such as Pasadena. See Schwarz, *A Water Odyssey*, pp. 14–44; Hundley, *The Great Thirst*, pp. 216–17; and Timothy F. Brick, "Partners: Pasadena's Role in the Formation of the Metropolitan Water District of Southern California," unpublished manuscript, November 22, 1997, 13 pp. Regarding how L.A. debt-ceiling limits and annexation issues influenced Mulholland's support for MWD, see Gerald W. Jones, "Water for Los Angeles," p. 110, UCLA Oral History Program, 1987. Jones was a former LADWP engineer in charge of the water-operating division. Also see Kahrl, *Water and Power*, pp. 265–68.

36. According to Joe Jensen, "both Mulholland—a man of great vision—and E. F. Scattergood [LADWP chief electrical engineer] looked to the Colorado River—the one, as a source of water, and the other, as a source of power." Jensen, "Developing California's Natural Resources," p. 96. Some scholars have depicted MWD and the Colorado River Aqueduct, not as a source of extra water supply, but as a front for enlarging LADWP's so-called "public power machine." See Jerome W. Milliman, "The History, Organization, and Economic Problems of the Metropolitan Water District of Southern California," doctoral thesis, University of California at Los Angeles, 1956, pp. 67–76, 510–15. Northcutt "Mike" Ely, a noted water attorney and former executive assistant to U.S. Secretary of Interior Ray Lyman Wilbur involved in the Boulder Canyon Project Act power negotiations, 1930–1931, observed that private utilities such as Southern California Edison, serving the hinterland outside L.A. city limits, had serious misgivings concerning Metropolitan. Edison feared that MWD "would turn into Metropolitan Water and Power District," using its Hoover Dam power not only for water pumping but also for distribution to Southern California residents and businesses, thereby becoming a competitive threat. Interview with Northcutt "Mike" Ely, 1995.

37. MWDSC, *Significance of Colorado River Aqueduct Water Supply to Southern California* (Los Angeles: MWDSC, 1936), 8 pp., at p. 2, reprinted from *Western City* (June 1936); Central Citizens Colorado River Committee, brochure, "Why We Need the Colorado River Aqueduct" (1931), MWDSC Engineering Library, Los Angeles.

38. Steven P. Erie, "How the Urban West Was Won: The Local State and Economic Growth in Los Angeles, 1880–1932," *Urban Affairs Quarterly*, 27:4 (June 1992), pp. 519–54.

39. Gottlieb, *A Life of Its Own*, p. 126.

40. Interview with former MWD General Manager Carl Boronkay, 2005.

41. On June 28, 1924, the city of Los Angeles filed with the state authorities for a flow of 1,500 cubic feet per second—equivalent to 1.1 million acre-feet annually—from the Colorado River. Los Angeles's original filing, which was transferred to Metropolitan, represents 90 percent of MWD's Colorado River priority rights. MWD's other Colorado River entitlement consists of the city of San Diego's 112,000 annual acre-feet. San Diego granted its filing to MWD on annexation in 1946. See MWDSC, *History and First Annual Report*, p. 36; and Schwarz, *A Water Odyssey*, pp. 84–86.

42. See Metropolitan Water District Act, Section 5 1/2, chapter 323, California Statutes 1931. Preferential rights now appear in Section 135 of the Metropolitan Water District Act, chapter 209, California Statutes 1969, as amended. See MWDSC, *Source Materials on Metropolitan Water District Act Section 135* (1996); Los Angeles Department of Water and Power, "Projected Preferential Rights," unpublished table, 2001.

43. Jensen, "Developing California's Natural Resources," pp. 129–30.

44. In the period 1928–1999, there were 27 agencies; this analysis is based on 27 agencies. In 2001 two Orange County MET member agencies merged.

45. *Harry Griffen Manuscript* (n.d.), chapter 6-1.doc.

46. See David Rusk, *Cities Without Suburbs*, 2nd ed. (Washington, DC: Woodrow Wilson Center Press, 1995); and Manuel Pastor Jr., Peter Dreier, J. Eugene Grigsby III, and Marta Lopez-Garza, *Regions That Work: How Cities and Suburbs Can Grow Together* (Minneapolis: University of Minnesota Press, 2000).

47. For FY 2004/05, Metropolitan has proposed a capital investment plan of $400 million, with nearly $100 million coming from property taxes and annexation fees. See MWDSC, *2004/05 Proposed Budget* (Los Angeles: MWDSC, 2004), Table 7, p. 20, and Table 12, p. 30.

48. "We seem, as it were, to have conquered and peopled half the world in a fit of absence of mind." Sir John Robert Seeley, "The Expansion of Empire," 1883 Lecture, in Robert Andrews, ed., *The Columbia Dictionary of Quotations* (New York: Columbia University Press, 1993), p. 273.

49. Regarding the British Empire, see Niall Ferguson, "British Imperialism Revised: The Costs and Benefits of 'Angloglobalization,'" Development Research Institute Working Paper Series, No. 2 (April 2003), http://www.nyu.edu/fas/institute/dri/DRIWP02.pdf; Ferguson, "The British Empire and Globalization: A

Forum," in *Historically Speaking: The Bulletin of the Historical Society*, 4:4 (April 2003), http://www.bu.edu/historic/hs/april03.html.

50. See Ralph Waldo Emerson, "The Problem," in Humphrey Milford, ed., *Poems of Ralph Waldo Emerson* (London: Oxford University Press, 1921), p. 8.

Chapter 4

1. Quoted in Robert Gottlieb and Margaret Fitzsimmons, *Thirst for Growth: Water Agencies as Hidden Government in California* (Tucson: University of Arizona Press, 1991), p. 34.

2. Spoken at the San Diego County Water Authority (SDCWA) board of directors meeting, February 12, 1998.

3. Anonymous San Diego County water official, in private correspondence with author, 2005.

4. See Albert O. Hirschman, *Exit, Voice, and Loyalty: Responses to Decline in Firms, Organizations, and States* (Cambridge, MA: Harvard University Press, 1970).

5. Michael Gardner, "S.D. Thirsts for Independence," *San Diego Union-Tribune*, August 9, 1999, pp. A1, A10; and Amy Wallace, "Water Dependence Bodes a Dry San Diego Future," *Los Angeles Times*, February 24, 1991, p. A1.

6. Dan Walker, *Thirst for Independence: The San Diego Water Story* (San Diego: Sunbelt Publications, 2004), p. 65.

7. *Harry Griffen Manuscript* (n.d.), chapter 5-2g.doc, n.p., provided courtesy of the Helix Water District Archives, La Mesa, California.

8. For a distillation of San Diego revisionist history, see Walker, *Thirst for Independence*, passim.

9. Metropolitan Water District of Southern California (MWDSC), *Twenty-Third Annual Report 1961* (Los Angeles: MWDSC, 1961), Table 1, p. xvii, and Table 20, p. 50.

10. SDCWA general manager Maureen Stapleton claimed that "Preferential rights [were] invoked in 1991 by a simple phone call. Los Angeles called Met and said deliver this much water. Met said, in order to deliver that water, I must take away from others. And Met did it." SDCWA, "Partial Transcript of 12/7/00 Meeting of the Water Policy Committee of the San Diego County Water Authority Board of Directors," p. 7. However, Jerry Gewe, chief operating officer of Los Angeles Department of Water and Power's Water System states that "I am unaware of any such action [invoking preferential rights] and would find such action totally inconsistent with the opinion of the Los Angeles City Attorney's Office that preferential rights were unenforceable in a drought based upon an overriding

position of the [State] Water Code." Interview with Jerry Gewe, 2005; and interview with former MWDSC general manager Carl Boronkay, 2005.

11. *Harry Griffen Manuscript*, chapter 5-1g2.doc, and chapter 5-2g.doc; Steve
La Rue, "Pipeline Brought Water, Prosperity," *San Diego Union-Tribune*, November 23, 1997, pp. B1, B2; SDCWA, *First Annual Report for the Period June 9, 1944
to June 30, 1946* (San Diego: SDCWA, 1946), passim. For an excellent account of
events leading up to the creation of the San Diego County Water Authority and its
annexation to MWD, see Theodore Andrew Strathman, " 'Dream of a Big City':
Water Politics and San Diego County Growth, 1910–1947," doctoral thesis, University of California at San Diego, 2005. For early San Diego water history as told
by one of its water leaders, see Col. Ed Fletcher, *Memoirs of Ed Fletcher* (San Diego:
Privately printed, 1952). For a general history of San Diego water development, see
San Diego County Water Authority, *To Quench a Thirst: A Brief History of Water
in the San Diego Region* (San Diego: SDCWA, 2003), 76 pp.

12. *Harry Griffen Manuscript*, chapter 5-2g.doc; SDCWA, *Second Annual
Report for Period July 1, 1946 to June 30, 1948* (San Diego: SDCWA, 1948),
pp. 28–29; interview with Lin Burzell, former SDCWA general manager, 2005;
Kazuto Oshio, "Urban Water Diplomacy: A Policy History of the Metropolitan
Water Supply in Twentieth Century Southern California," doctoral thesis,
University of California at Santa Barbara, 1992, p. 128. The initial 50/50 MWD/
SDCWA split financing for San Diego pipeline 1 has been followed for subsequent
pipelines 2 through 5 serving San Diego.

13. MWDSC, *Annual Reports*, various years; MWDSC, *Annual Report 1998*
(Los Angeles: MWDSC, 1998), "Historical Roll of Directors," pp. xxi–xxix;
Kazuto Oshio, " 'Who Pays and Who Benefits?' Metropolitan Water Politics in
Twentieth-Century Southern California," *The Japanese Journal of American
Studies*, 8 (1997), pp. 65, 81–82.

14. Oshio, "Urban Water Diplomacy," pp. 5, 75; Norris Hundley Jr., *The
Great Thirst: Californians and Water, A History*, rev. ed. (Berkeley: University of
California Press, 2001), pp. 219, 290.

15. MWDSC, *Annual Reports*, various years; MWDSC, "Historical Roll
of Directors"; Robert E. Melbourne, "San Diego County's Water Crusader,
Fred A. Heilbron," *Journal of San Diego History*, 32:4 (Fall 1986) at www
.sandiegohistory.org/journal/86fall/heilbron.htm; and Kyle Emily Ciani," "A
Passion for Water: Hans H. Doe and the California Water Industry," *Journal of
San Diego History*, 39: 4 (Fall 1993) at www.sandiegohistory.org/journal/93fall/
water.htm.

16. John F. Hennigar, personal letter to author, 2004. Hennigar was a member of the SDCWA board of directors, 1976–1989, and served as an MWD director, 1986–1989; interview with Lin Burzell, 2005.

17. "William H. Jennings: Water Lawyer," Oral History Program, University of California at Los Angeles, 1967, p. 97.

18. "Riordan Names New MWD Board Members," *Metro Investment Report*, I:5 (October 1993), p. 4; "Carolyn Green: MWD Board Leadership Changes 'A Wash,'" *Metro Investment Report*, 1:8 (January 1994), pp. 1, 8, 9; MWDSC, "Historical Roll of Directors."

19. Critics countered that San Diego actually received a disproportionate share of Metropolitan's capital improvement benefits. For example, they claimed that although the SDCWA paid for 25 percent of the $2-billion plus Domenigoni Reservoir (now Diamond Valley Lake), it received fully half of the benefits. See West Basin Municipal Water District, Memorandum, "Analysis of San Diego's Relative Financial Contribution and Water Supply Benefits with the Metropolitan Water District," October 2, 1995, 6 pp.

20. Interview with Greg Quist, member, SDCWA board of directors, and director, Rincon del Diablo Municipal Water District, 2005.

21. Quoted in Tony Perry, "San Diego, MWD Water War Heats Up," *Los Angeles Times*, April 29, 1996, p. A1. In contrast, former SDCWA general counsel Paul Engstrand observes, "Ironically, in 1990 the Authority received 674,993 acre-feet from MWD. The water 'brought with us' was only 112,000 acre-feet of low fifth priority which would not be available at all when California is limited to its basic right of 4.4 million acre-feet per year. Instead of 'servitude,' San Diego has received fair and even generous treatment by MWD." Interview with Paul Engstrand, 2005.

22. See "Erosion of Authority: How L.A. Controls San Diego's Water Decisions," editorial, *San Diego Union-Tribune*, January 17, 1996; "The Met's Dry Well," editorial, *San Diego Union-Tribune*, March 24, 1996; "Water: A Clearer View," editorial, *San Diego Union-Tribune*, August 30, 1996; "Power Plays with Water: The MWD Has Become a Rogue Agency," editorial, *San Diego Union-Tribune*, November 10, 1996, p. G6; "Mismanagement Flood: State Needs to Rein in Rogue Water District," editorial, *San Diego Union-Tribune*, September 8, 1997; "In L.A.'s Shadow: San Diego's Water Supply Not Guaranteed," editorial, *San Diego Union-Tribune*, January 25, 2001; and information provided by anonymous San Diego water officials.

23. Interview with Annette Hubbell, general manager, Rincon del Diablo Municipal Water District, 2005.

24. "Water: A Clearer View."

25. "Quest for Water Unites the Region," *Ventura County Star*, December 27, 1998.

26. See Paul Engstrand, "The Controversy About Preferential Rights and Water Pricing." n.d., 4 pp.; Engstrand, "San Diego's Wake-up Call," n.d., 3 pp.

27. Interview with Mike Madigan, SDCWA director and former MWD director, 2005.

28. SDCWA officials warned of a 50 percent cutback if L.A. claimed its full preferential rights entitlement. See Chris Moran, "Water Authority Seeks a New Deal," *San Diego Union-Tribune*, January 23, 2001.

29. SDCWA, "Landmark Water Conservation and Transfer Agreement Ratified," press release, April 29, 1998; Steve La Rue, "'Historic' Imperial Water Deal Approved," *San Diego Union-Tribune*, April 30, 1998.

30. Mike Davis, "Imperial Pirates: Texas Duo Is Staging a Historic Water Heist," *L.A. Weekly*, February 2–8, 1996, pp. 11–12; Chris Moran, "Water Wars," *North County Times*, March 3, 1996, pp. A1, A6; James Sterngold, "A Blow for Water Independence," *New York Times*, August 6, 1996, p. A11; Charles McCoy and G. Pascal Zachary, "A Bass Play in Water May Presage Big Shift in Its Distribution," *Wall Street Journal*, July 11, 1997, pp. A1, A6; Marc Lifsher, "Why Shipping Water to San Diego Has Been Harder Than It Looked," *Wall Street Journal*, July 1, 1998; Tony Perry, "Proposal to Sell Imperial Valley Water Stirs Anger," *Los Angeles Times*, October 2, 1995, p. A1; Robert A. Jones, "Trolling for Bass," *Los Angeles Times*, March 13, 1996, p. B2.

31. Rudy Yniquez, "Bass-San Diego Fallowing Scheme Revealed in Documents," *Imperial Valley Press*, June 30, 1998, pp. A1, A6; Charles McCoy, "Lee, Ed Bass to Sell Their Water Rights to U.S. Filter Corporation," *Wall Street Journal*, August 4, 1997, p. A1; Steve La Rue, "$274 Million Imperial Valley Water Deal May Help County," *San Diego Union-Tribune*, August 5, 1997, pp. C1, C4; "Our Opinion: Some Neighborly Advice," editorial, *Imperial Valley Press*, September 23, 1997; Stephanie S. Pincetl, *Transforming California: A Political History of Land Use and Development* (Baltimore: Johns Hopkins University Press, 1999), p. 264; William Fulton, *The Reluctant Metropolis: The Politics of Urban Growth in Los Angeles* (Baltimore: Johns Hopkins University Press, 2001), pp. 123–24; Hundley, *The Great Thirst*, pp. 478–79; Steven P. Erie, "A San Diego/Imperial Valley Water Deal: Who Stands to Gain? Who to Lose?" *Metro Investment Report*, 10:1 (June 1997), pp. 19–20; Phil Diehl, "Water Authority Deal Questioned," *North County Times*, February 14, 1998; Imperial Grand Jury, *Final Report, 1995–1996* (June 27, 1996), pp. 18–29; "One-Stop Shopping for Water: U.S. Filter's Richard Heckmann," *Metro Investment Report*, 5:9 (February 1998), pp. 1, 14–15, 21.

32. Jonathan Heller, "Water Debate Boils Down to Price Issue," *North County Times*, March 15, 1998; Gary Broomell, Dale Mason, and Greg Quist, "Deal with Imperial Is Just Not Worth It," *North County Times*, April 4, 1998; San Diego County Grand Jury, *Final Report, 1996–1997* (June 27, 1997), p. 87; Hundley, *The Great Thirst*, pp. 480–81.

33. La Rue, "'Historic' Imperial Water Deal Approved." The Imperial Irrigation District bowed to local pressure by inserting contract language that there would be no "fallowing" of land to meet water sales targets; but it did not offer a precise definition of the term.

34. In terms of negotiating parameters with IID, SDCWA pledged that "the price must be comparable to other market transfers but in no case at a price to the Authority, including conveyance and salinity control costs, which is greater than MWD's untreated rate plus applicable charges." See Maureen Stapleton, SDCWA general manager, "Memo to [SDCWA] Board of Directors," July 20, 1996, p. 6.

35. Quist interview; Steven P. Erie, "A San Diego 'Chinatown' with Los Angeles as Victim," *Los Angeles Times*, August 25, 1996, pp. M1, M6; Erie, "San Diego Must Share in Blame for Water Debacle," *San Diego Union-Tribune*, February 6, 2003, p. B11.

36. Quist interview.

37. Communications with anonymous San Diego water officials, 2004.

38. Engstrand interview.

39. Heller, "Water Debate Boils Down to Price Issue"; Broomell, Mason, and Quist, "Deal with Imperial Is Just Not Worth It"; San Diego County Grand Jury, *Final Report, 1996–1997*, p. 87; George Rooney, "Discount Offered in Water Deal," *Riverside Press-Enterprise*, December 10, 1997; Rudy Yniguez, "MWD Funds Would Quench Its Own Thirst," *Imperial Valley Press*, May 22, 1998; Hundley, *The Great Thirst*, pp. 482–83.

40. MWDSC, "Wheeling: Gearing for the Future of Water Marketing," February 1997, p. 2; Tony Perry, "Southland's Water Future May Hinge on Bitter Dispute," *Los Angeles Times*, August 3, 1997; Chris Moran, "County Backs Down on Pipe," *North County Times*, November 14, 1997; Hundley, *The Great Thirst*, p. 484; "MWD's GM Woody Wodraska: 'Wheeling' & Dealing Water," *Metro Investment Report*, 4:12 (May 1997), pp. 13–14; Rooney, "Discount Offered in Water Deal," *Riverside Press-Enterprise*, December 10, 1997.

41. Robert V. Phillips and Steven P. Erie, "San Diego Takes Aim at L.A.'s Hegemony," *Los Angeles Times*, March 3, 1996, pp. M1, M6; Yniguez, "MWD Funds Would Quench Its Own Thirst"; Fulton, *Reluctant Metropolis*, p. 123; Hundley, *The Great Thirst*, pp. 485, 487.

42. Tony Perry, "Judge Rejects MWD Stand on Aqueduct Fees," *Los Angeles Times*, January 14, 1998; Perry, "Tensions Rise over Bill to Alter Water Delivery Policy," *Los Angeles Times*, May 6, 2001, p. B8; Steve La Rue, "Judge Tosses Out MWD Rate Plan for Transporting Water," *San Diego Union-Tribune*, January 14, 1998; Tony Perry, "Appeals Court Ruling a Victory for MWD," *San Diego Union-Tribune*, May 31, 2000, pp. A3, A16; Michael Gardner, "Court Won't

Take MWD Water Fees Case," *San Diego Union-Tribune*, September 15, 2000, p. A4; Hundley, *The Great Thirst*, pp. 488–89.

43. Steve La Rue, "Answer Offered for S.D. Water Imports," *San Diego Union-Tribune*, January 6, 1998; George Rooney, "Framework Proposed for Settling Water Dispute," *Riverside Press-Enterprise*, January 6, 1998; Paula Story, "State Water Department Makes Recommendation to End Water War," *Hemet News*, January 7, 1998.

44. See Koenig and Dorsey, *Research Report on the Bass Brothers*, n.d.; Steve La Rue, "Water District Shuts Off PR Effort," *San Diego Union-Tribune*, September 3, 1997, pp. A1, A4; Steve La Rue, "County Water Leaders Are United in Anger at Publicity Campaign," *San Diego Union-Tribune*, September 12, 1997, p. B3; "Dynamite the Dam," editorial, *San Diego Union-Tribune*, December 9, 1997; Bill Boyarsky, "MWD's Dirt-Digging Scheme Is All Wet," *Los Angeles Times*, January 15, 1998; Dan Walters, "A Showdown in the Water War," *San Diego Union-Tribune*, January 29, 1998; Walters, "Water Kremlin Facing Revolt," *Sacramento Bee*, May 22, 1998; Jonathan Heller, "Water Officials Decry Probe," *North County Times*, January 7, 1998; Rudy Yniguez, "2.24 Million Spent on Legal, Consulting Fees, IID Says," *Imperial Valley Press*, May 14, 1998.

45. Thor K. Biberman, "Metropolitan Water Dist. Offers to Pay $1 Billion for Water Importation," *San Diego Daily Transcript*, May 21, 1998; Tony Perry, "Possible Solution Seen in Southland Water War," *Los Angeles Times*, June 23, 1998; "Fund the Water Deal, Imperial Transfer Would Benefit Whole State," editorial, *San Diego Union-Tribune*, June 28, 1998; Hundley, *The Great Thirst*, pp. 491–92.

46. Michael Gardner, "Water Issue Is Back on Ballot in Prop. 13," *San Diego Union-Tribune*, February 21, 2000; Hundley, *The Great Thirst*, pp. 491–92, 497.

47. "California Water Policy Demystified: An MIR Interview with State Senator Jim Costa," *Metro Investment Report*, 8:3 (August 2000), p. 5; Tony Perry, "Tensions Rise over Bill to Alter Water Delivery Policy," *Los Angeles Times*, May 6, 2001, p. B8.

48. Ron Gastelum, "A Public Monopolist Considers Private Alliances to Meet Regional Water Needs," *Metro Investment Report*, VIII:8 (January 2001), p. 14; Tony Perry, "Tensions Rise over Bill to Alter Water Delivery Policy," *Los Angeles Times*, May 6, 2001, p. B8; Andy McCue, "Water Transfer Plan Stirs Waves," *Riverside Press-Enterprise*, October 5, 1997, p. A1; Ed Manning, "Finding 'New Water' for a Thirsty State: SB 506 Suggests Water Marketing May Be Answer," *Metro Investment Report*, 6:11 (April 1999), p. 4; "Wheeling—and Dealing," editorial, *San Diego Union-Tribune*, April 27, 2000, p. B10; Jim Gogek, "A Deal to Secure Water for Southern California Falls Through, But Is Not Dead," *San Diego Union-Tribune*, January 12, 2003; Robert Fellmeth, "Plunging into

Darkness: Energy Deregulation Collides with Scarcity," *Loyola University of Chicago Law Journal,* 33 (Summer 2002), p. 845; Joe Mozingo, "MWD Eyes Possible Effects of Competition," *Los Angeles Times,* August 22, 2000, p. B2.

49. Perry, "Tensions Rise over Bill to Alter Water Delivery Policy"; "Sen. Kuehl Links Development to Water: Is a Workable Water Market Needed?" *Metro Investment Report,* 8:12 (June 2001), p. 12; Beverly Kelley, "If San Diego Gets a Free Water Ride, We'll Pay," *Ventura County Star,* June 18, 2001, p. B7; Steve La Rue, "Quick OK Urged for Water from Imperial Valley," *San Diego Union-Tribune,* August 11, 2001; Hundley, *The Great Thirst,* p. 495.

50. Alec Rosenberg, "IID Board Votes to Give Public More Time to Review Pact," *Imperial Valley Press,* February 25, 1998; "Buy Low, Sell High; Imperial Valley Finds Fortune in Its Water," editorial, *San Diego Union-Tribune,* February 12, 2004, p. B10; Rosenberg, "Study: Transfer Benefits County," *Imperial Valley Press,* February 13, 1998.

51. Steven P. Erie, "A Good Deal?" *San Diego Daily Transcript,* September 11, 1996; Steven P. Erie and Pascale Joassart-Marcelli, "New Battle Fronts in the L.A. vs. San Diego Water War," *Los Angeles Times,* January 30, 2000; Thair Peterson, "State Will Mediate Southland Water Fight," *Long Beach Press-Telegram,* October 15, 1998; "Quest for Water Unites the Region," editorial, *Ventura County Star,* December 27, 1998; Robert Gottlieb, *A Life of Its Own: The Politics and Power of Water* (New York: Harcourt Brace Jovanovich, 1988), pp. 129–33; Gottlieb and FitzSimmons, *Thirst for Growth,* pp. 34–36, 115. Boronkay's musing was in response to San Diego's determination to pursue the ill-fated Galloway Plan after being warned that it was legally flawed and politically doomed. Boronkay interview.

52. Erie, "A Good Deal?"; Chris Moran, "County Eyes Aqueduct via Mexico," *North County Times,* August 15, 1997; Peterson, "State Will Mediate Southland Water Fight."

53. Quist interview; Erie, "San Diego Must Share in Blame for Water Debacle"; Jim Gogek, "Water War," *San Diego Union-Tribune,* January 12, 2003, pp. G1, G5; Lloyd Allen, "Plenty of Blame, But There Is Not Plenty of Water," *San Diego Union-Tribune,* January 15, 2003, p. B7. Allen was the president of the IID board of directors.

54. "A Dying Sea," editorial, *San Diego Union-Tribune,* February 2, 2003, p. G2.

55. Chris Moran, "County Backs Down on Pipe," *North County Times,* November 14, 1997; Bill Ainsworth, "MWD Members Considered Plan to Punish S.D.," *San Diego Union-Tribune,* March 28, 1998.

56. Tony Perry, "Imperial Valley Told to Cut Its Water Use," *Los Angeles Times,* December 19, 1997; Guy Kelley, "U.S. Puts California on 'Water Diet,'"

San Francisco Examiner, December 29, 1997; Coachella Valley Water District, "Imperial Irrigation District and San Diego County Water Authority Propose Illegal Water Transfer," July 1, 1996; Alec Rosenberg, "MWD: Quantify Before Approving Water Transfer," *Imperial Valley Press*, February 20, 1998; Rosenberg, "Draft State Water Plan Praises IID for Use Efficiency," *Imperial Valley Press*, March 25, 1998.

57. "William H. Jennings: Water Lawyer," Oral History Program, University of California at Los Angeles, 1967, p. 96.

58. "Water Sharing: San Diego Pays More But L.A. Has Control."

59. "Water Authority Board Seeks Legal Clarification of Water It Can Depend Upon from MWD," SDCWA Press Release, January 25, 2001, 3 pp.; Tony Perry, "San Diego to Fight Old L.A. Water Claim," *Los Angeles Times*, January 26, 2001, pp. A3, A20; Steve La Rue, "S.D. Agency Takes Water Rights Fight into Court," *San Diego Union-Tribune*, February 12, 2001, pp. B1, B3; Steven P. Erie, "What Does San Diego Really Want from the MWD?" *Los Angeles Times*, February 25, 2001; MWDSC, "MWD Act—Sec. 135 Preferential Rights to Purchase Water—6/30/2001." Also see MWDSC, *Source Materials on Metropolitan Water District Act Section 135—Preferential Rights* (Los Angeles: MWDSC, January 11, 1996). As early as 1961, the city of Los Angeles and the SDCWA agreed that preferential rights calculations should be modified in the state legislature to include all member-agency contributions, regardless of source, to capital costs. See MWDSC, *Source Materials*, Supporting Document 38, "Memorandum of Understanding between Department of Water and Power of the City of Los Angeles and San Diego County Water Authority, dated April 18, 1961."

60. Madigan interview.

61. Following the severe 1976–1977 California drought, the MWD board in 1981 adopted an interruptible water-pricing program whereby member agencies were able to purchase water at discounts for agricultural, reservoir, and groundwater-replenishment purposes. They agreed to have such supplies interrupted during a future time of shortage, thus reserving water for full-price noninterruptible municipal and industrial purposes. In November 1990, the MWD board adopted a modified plan called the "Incremental Interruptible and Conservation Plan" (IICP). Under the IICP, noninterruptible water also would be cut back, but by a smaller percentage than interruptible water. The plan also provided that adjustments would be made for loss of local supplies. Through much of the drought year 1991, MWD was implementing Stage V of the IICP, which provided for a 20 percent reduction for noninterruptible water and a 50 percent reduction for interruptible water. Interview with Duane L. Georgeson, former MWDSC assistant general manager, 2005. And see Michael B. Young, assistant chief of

operations, MWDSC, memo to member agency managers, "Draft Paper on Events Leading Up to and Chronology of the 1990–92 Drought Years and Supply Reliability Improvements Achieved as a Result of the Drought," August 25, 1998, 12 pp. Also see Gregory M. Quist, "A Regional Water Perspective on *Preferential Rights*," January 17, 2001, 3 pp.

62. Madigan interview.

63. See Paul D. Engstrand, SDCWA general counsel, letter to Duane L. Georgeson, assistant general manager for water, Los Angeles Department of Water and Power (LADWP), January 25, 1985; and Duane L. Georgeson, letter to Paul D. Engstrand, January 30, 1985. Also see Engstrand, Memo to San Diego County Water Authority, Water Policy and Administrative Policy Committees, Re MWD's Section 135 [Preferential Rights], January 10, 1985; and L.A. MWD director Mark Lainer, letter to E. Thornton Ibbetson, MWDSC board chair, August 10, 1984. Regarding Los Angeles's willingness to modify MWD's preferential rights calculations to give credit for future water payments that apply to capital costs, see letter from Los Angeles mayor Tom Bradley et al., to E. Thornton Ibbetson, MWDSC board chair, February 17, 1984. Also see, LADWP, "Chronological History of Preferential Rights Computation," 2001, 4 pp. "However, if the preferential rights formula is modified to include capital contributions from water sales, then the original member agencies should also be credited with the time value of the money that they have paid in taxes." In LADWP, "SDCWA's Preferential Rights Lawsuit Briefing Paper," 2001, 3 pp., at p. 3; and Quist interview.

64. This chart represents a best guess based on current events; the actual rate of change in preferential rights could differ depending on hydrology and other conditions. Thus, in the early 1990s, it was projected that well before 2010, the L.A. and San Diego lines would cross. However, the changing Owens Valley situation and L.A.'s growing purchase of MWD deliveries altered that projection. From San Diego's standpoint, when the lines cross around 2015 L.A. still will have more than enough water to meet its needs and San Diego will still be short in terms of meeting its needs.

65. Madigan interview.

66. See California State, First Appellate Court, *San Diego County Water Authority v. Metropolitan Water District of Southern California*, A098526, March 25, 2004, 26 pp.; Jose Luis Jimenez, "Water Authority Loses in Court— Justices Decline to Alter Drought Allocations," *San Diego Union-Tribune*, March 26, 2004, pp. B1, B10; "Ruling Secures Water Access," *San Diego Daily Transcript*, March 26, 2004.

67. Quist interview.

68. County Water Authority officials claimed they wanted the Inland Feeder pipeline to go around the mountains, rather than through them. Critics countered that San Diego's MWD delegates voted against the Inland Feeder to absolve the SDCWA of any project financial responsibility should the County Water Authority decide to sue. Later, San Diego MWD delegates chose to abstain on Inland Feeder project votes.

69. Hubbell interview.

70. Kim Peterson, "Water Authority Awash in Turmoil," *San Diego Daily Transcript*, December 13, 1996, pp. 1A, 14A.

71. Mark Watton, "Let's Focus on the Real Water Issues," *San Diego Union-Tribune*, February 18, 1997, p. B9.

72. Economic Study Group (ESG), "The Case for Withdrawal," n.d.

73. Peterson, "Water Authority Awash in Turmoil"; "Water Bully: San Diego Pulls Power Play," editorial, *North County Times*, December 14, 1996.

74. Quist interview; Steve La Rue, "County Water Dispute Eases as City's Clout Is Cut," *San Diego Union-Tribune*, July 11, 1997, p. B2.

75. Tony Perry, "San Diego Aims to Cut Reliance on L.A. Water," *Los Angeles Times*, June 25, 2004, pp. B1, B8.

76. "Transcription of Comments by Senator Peace at the Council of Water Utilities Meeting, November 16, 1999"; Watton, "Let's Focus on the Real Water Issues," p. B9.

77. ESG, *Draft Report: Analysis of San Diego County Water Authority's Rates, Charges, and Fees With Respect to Cost of Service Equity Among Member Agencies* (Bookman-Edmonston Engineering Inc. [San Diego], May 1999); Bruce Lieberman, "Water Rates Are Soaking N. County, Study Says," *San Diego Union-Tribune*, May 18, 1999, pp. B1, B5; Jonathan Heller, "Water Agencies Seek Rate Relief," *North County Times*, May 18, 1999, pp. A1, A4; Bruce Lieberman, "North County Water Officials Push Reduced Rates for Their Customers," *San Diego Union-Tribune*, May 21, 1999, pp. B1, B6; Bradley J. Fikes, "Water Fee Plan May Splinter County Agency," *North County Times*, May 28, 1999, pp. A1, A4; Bradley J. Fikes, "Agency Member Urges Secession from Water Authority, *North County Times*, May 21, 1999; Economic Study Group, "Why AB 1385?" March 2003, 3 pp.

78. Quist interview; ESG, "A Change in Governance at the San Diego County Water Authority," n.d., 2 pp.

79. Quist interview.

80. Ibid.

81. MWDSC, "MWD Board Preserves Integrity of Rate Structure by Moving to Maintain Incentives for Water Management," press release, December 14, 2004, 2 pp.

82. Jason Felch, "MWD Taps Ex-Mayor to Lead Board; Bannister is elected with support of O.C. and San Diego Directors," *Los Angeles Times*, October 13, 2004, p. B3; Jose Luis Jimenez, "S.D. Gains Ally at L.A. Water Agency," *San Diego Union-Tribune*, March 14, 2005, pp. B1, B3.

Chapter 5

1. The quotation is attributed. See "Directory of Mark Twain's Maxims, Quotations, and Various Opinions," http://www.twainquotes.com/WaterWhiskey .html.

2. Quoted in Diane Raines Ward, *Water Wars: Drought, Flood, Folly, and the Politics of Thirst* (New York: Riverhead Books, 2002), p. 60.

3. Norris Hundley Jr., *The Great Thirst: Californians and Water, A History*, rev. ed. (Berkeley: University of California Press, 2001), p. 441; Carl Boronkay and Warren Abbott, "Water Conflicts in the Western United States," *Studies in Conflict & Terrorism*, 20 (1997), pp. 136–66, especially 147–60; Michael Gardner, "Water Funds Diverted to Help Pay Energy Bills," *San Diego Union-Tribune*, February 3, 2001, p. A1. Senator Dianne Feinstein, for example, compared the California water picture—with population growth but little done for three decades in terms of new water development—to the electricity shortages. See Mike Taugher, "Congressman Introduces Third Competing Water Plan for California," *Contra Costa Times*, June 29, 2001. Environmentalists criticize current estimates of future water needs for failing to factor in further efficiencies in usage resulting from additional conservation. See "Farm Bureau Sues Cal-Fed to Protect Farmland and Water," *Business Wire*, September 28, 2000.

4. Clean Water Fund, "We All Live Downstream," http://www.denver.feb .gov/cfc/earthsharefamo.htm.

5. Water Education Foundation (WEF), *Layperson's Guide to the Colorado River* (Sacramento, CA: Water Education Foundation, 1995), pp. 9, 11, 13–16; James S. Lochhead, "Synopsis of Major Documents and Events Relating to the Colorado River," *University of Denver Water Law Review*, 3 (Spring 2000), pp. 339–56; Kara Gillon, "Watershed Down? The Ups and Downs of Watershed Management in the Southwest," *University of Denver Water Law Review*, 5 (Spring 2002), pp. 395–403.

6. California Department of Water Resources, *California Water Plan*, Bulletin 160–98 (Sacramento: California Department of Water Resources, January 1998), Table 9–17.

7. Hundley, *The Great Thirst*, pp. 307, 340–42, 347–60; 406–7; William Kahrl, *Water and Power: The Conflict over Los Angeles' Water Supply in the Owens Valley* (Berkeley: University of California Press, 1982), pp. 429–36; Frances

Spivey-Weber, "The Mono Lake Committee Taught L.A.'s DWP That by Doing Good, L.A. Would do Well!" *Metro Investment Report*, VII:4 (September 1999), pp. 5, 14, 15; interview with Timothy Quinn, vice president, MWDSC, 2005.

8. James S. Lochhead, "An Upper Basin Perspective on California's Claims to Water from the Colorado River, Part II: The Development, Implementation, and Collapse of California's Plan to Live within Its Basic Apportionment," *University of Denver Water Law Review*, 6 (Spring 2003), p. 325; "U.S. EPA Approves Historic Owens Lake Dust Control Plan," press release, *E-Wire*, August 18, 1999; "LADWP's Water Guru, Gerald Gewe Opines on Owens Valley, Water Marketing & Desal," *Metro Investment Report*, XI: 5 (January 2004), pp. 4, 18, 19.

9. Hundley, *The Great Thirst*, pp. 307, 362–64; Robert Gottlieb, *A Life of Its Own: The Politics of Water and Power* (New York: Harcourt Brace Jovanovich, 1988), pp. 14–33.

10. William Fulton, *The Reluctant Metropolis: The Politics of Urban Growth in Los Angeles* (Baltimore: Johns Hopkins University Press, 2001), pp. 106–13, 123; Ron Gastelum, "Reorganizing Its Troops: Will MWD Adjust in Time?" *Metro Investment Report*, VII:2 (July 1999), pp. 1, 14; Jennifer Warren, "MWD Chief's Style Stirs the Waters at Changing Agency Management," *Los Angeles Times*, August 12, 1991, p. A1; Frederick M. Muir, "Challenge to MWD's Old Ways," *Los Angeles Times*, August 11, 1991, p. A1; James Rainey and Virginia Ellis, "MWD Chairman Gage Resigns from Board at Riordan's Request," *Los Angeles Times*, September 22, 1993, p. A3; "New MWD Chairman Phillip Pace's Millennium 'State of the Met Address,'" *Metro Investment Report*, VI:8 (January 1999), p. 8; "Governing the Ungovernable? Met Water Selects a New GM," *Metro Investment Report*, VI:12 (May 1999), pp. 1, 16. Board turnover is a two-edged sword regarding reform. In 1993 newly elected Los Angeles mayor Richard Riordan purged MWD chairman Michael J. Gage, a reformer, and other sympathetic Bradley appointees from the MWD board.

11. Fulton, *The Reluctant Metropolis*, pp. 119–20; Hundley, *The Great Thirst*, pp. 468, 502.

12. Hundley, *The Great Thirst*, pp. 469 (Boronkay quote), 476, 514–15.

13. Interview with Carl Boronkay, former MWDSC general manager and general counsel, 2005.

14. Frederick M. Muir, "MWD May Seek Aid in Lobbying Water Agency," *Los Angeles Times*, June 26, 1990, p. A3; Phillip J. Pace, "A Water-Use Ethic: Striving to Ensure Southern California's Water Supply," *San Diego Union-Tribune*, March 19, 1999.

15. Hundley, *The Great Thirst*, pp. 442–44, 459; "Utah Radioactive Waste," *Associated Press*, July 3, 1999, http://www.efc-inc.com/News/july99.html #730991.

16. Hundley, *The Great Thirst*, pp. 404–95.

17. Southern California Association of Governments, "Population Growth in the SCAG Region, 1950–2025," http://www.scag.ca.gov/livable/download/pdf/ GV1950_2025.pdf; Hundley, *The Great Thirst*, pp. 559–60.

18. Thomas E. Sheridan, "The Big Canal: The Political Ecology of the Central Arizona Project," in John M. Donahue and Barbara Rose Johnson, eds., *Water, Culture, and Power: Local Struggles in a Global Context* (Washington, DC: Island Press, 1997), pp. 153–86; Michelle Rushio, "Arizona Cities Buy Farms Just for Water," *San Diego Union-Tribune*, May 7, 1998.

19. California Resources Agency, "DWR to Hold Hearings in Southern California on Water Supply Outlook," press release, February 13, 1998; California Resources Agency, "California Water Plan Forecasts Water Shortage; Water Management Options Would Offer Relief," press release, January 30, 1998.

20. Robert V. Phillips and Steven P. Erie, "San Diego Takes Aim at L.A.'s Hegemony," *Los Angeles Times*, March 3, 1996; Steve La Rue, "Agency Will Sue on Rights to Water," *San Diego Union-Tribune*, January 26, 2001, p. B1.

21. San Diego County Water Authority (SDCWA), "Quantification Settlement Agreement," October 2003, http://www.sdcwa.org/manage/mwd-QSA.phtml# overview. See also Senate Agriculture and Water Resources Committee, "Bill No. SB 654," Hearing, September 10, 2003, http://info.sen.ca.gov/pub/bill/sen/ sb_0651-0700/sb_654_cfa_20030910_120952_sen_comm.html.

22. Hundley, *The Great Thirst*, pp. 487, 490, 497; Elliot Diringer, "Water Chief Revives Talk of Peripheral Canal," *San Francisco Chronicle*, March 21, 1992, p. A1.

23. California Department of Water Resources, *California Water Plan: Update 2003*, California Department of Water Resources, http://www.waterplan .water.ca.gov/b160/pdf/Water%20Plan.pdf; Hundley, *The Great Thirst*, pp. 470–501.

24. Lochhead, "An Upper Basin Perspective," pp. 341–50; Fulton, *The Reluctant Metropolis*, pp. 328–30.

25. Seth Hettena, "Governor's Aide Threatens to Cut Metropolitan Out of Water Talks," *Associated Press*, August 22, 2003.

26. Susan Greene, "California Scolded for River Water Use," *Las Vegas Review Journal*, August 13, 1997.

27. Bernadette Tansey, "State's Water System Plan Assailed," *San Francisco Chronicle*, June 25, 1998, p. A14; Hundley, *The Great Thirst*, p. 487.

28. Fulton, *The Reluctant Metropolis*, pp. 101–2, 115–17; Hundley, *The Great Thirst*, pp. 375–78; Alex Barnum, "California Water Plan Shown Off," *San Francisco Chronicle*, December 19, 1998, p. A1; MWDSC, "Integrated Resources Plan," http://mwdh2o.org/mwdh2o/pages/yourwater/irp/integrated01.html.

29. California Department of Water Resources, *California Water Plan*, Bulletin 160–98, Chap. 9; U.S. Department of the Interior Office of the Secretary, press release, "California's Colorado River Water Talks Successful," August 4, 1999; California Department of Water Resources, *California Water Plan: Update 2003*, http://www.waterplan.water.ca.gov/b160/pdf/Water%20Plan.pdf.

30. Robert B. Gunnison, "Babbitt Delivers Water Warning," *San Francisco Chronicle*, March 18, 1999, p. A20; Lochhead, "An Upper Basin Perspective," pp. 370–71, 384–88; Ken Ellingwood and Tony Perry, "Delta a Snag in Babbitt's Plan for Colorado River," *Los Angeles Times*, December 26, 2000, p. A3; Rudy E. Verner, "Short Term Solutions, Interim Surplus Guidelines, and the Future of the Colorado River Delta," *Colorado Journal of International Environmental Law*, 14 (Spring 2003), pp. 241–49.

31. Quoted in Tony Perry, "Imperial Valley Told to Cut Its Water Use," *Los Angeles Times*, December 19, 1997, p. A3.

32. Perry, "Imperial Valley Told to Cut Its Water Use"; MWDSC, "Key Terms for a Quantification Agreement," http://www.mwd.dst.ca.us/mwdh2o/pages/yourwater/supply/colorado/colorado03.html; Coachella Valley Water District, Resolution No. 2003–227, "A Resolution of the Board of Directors of the Coachella Valley Water District Approving . . . the Implementation of the Quantification Settlement Agreement," September 24, 2003, http://www.cvwd.org/Public_Docs/RESOLUTION_APPROVING_IMPLEMENTATION_OF_QSA.pdf.

33. Gig Conaughton, "San Diego Water Officials Discuss Impending Shortage," *North County Times*, November 28, 2001; "From Dust to Dust, *Financial Times* (London), November 8, 1997, p. 1; Sue McClurg, "The California Plan and the Salton Sea," *Western Water*, November–December 2001, pp. 4–13.

34. Lochhead, "An Upper Basin Perspective," pp. 390–91; Steve La Rue, "Quick OK Urged for Water from Imperial Valley," *San Diego Union-Tribune*, August 11, 2001.

35. Ken Calvert, "Restoring Confidence in Water Policy," *San Diego Union-Tribune*, July 1, 2003, p. B7; "Salton Sea Restoration, Desal Plant Studied," *Western Water*, 47:1 (January 2003); Conaughton, "San Diego Water Officials Discuss Impending Shortage" *North County Times*; James F. Turner, "A Water Problem We Can't Solve Alone," *San Diego Union-Tribune*, December 14, 2001, p. B9; Michael Cohen, "Salton Sea Must Be Addressed in Water Deal," *San Diego Union-Tribune*, February 20, 2003, p. B11; Congressman Duncan Hunter, "Colorado River Quantification Facilitation Settlement Agreement," H. R. 2764, 107th Congress 1st Session, August 2, 2001, http://www.theorator.com/bills107/hr2764.html; Lochhead, "An Upper Basin Perspective," pp. 390–91 (Raley quote).

36. David Herrmann, "Salton Sea Warning Issued," *Los Angeles Times*, January 13, 2004, p. B1; Jonathan Shikes, "Salton Sea Solutions," *Riverside Press-Enterprise*, March 2, 2003, p. A1; Claire Vitucci, "Bono Favored to Take the 45th District," *Riverside Press-Enterprise*, February 26, 2004, p. B3.

37. Robert M. Hertzberg, "Solving California's Water Problem," *San Diego Union-Tribune*, May 15, 2002, p. B11; Lochhead, "An Upper Basin Perspective," p. 394; Coachella Valley Water District, "CVWD Board Formally Recognizes State Legislature's Concern About QSA," http://www.cvwd.org/pressrel/QSAlegislature.pdf.

38. "Colorado River—Imperial Negotiations Navigated by Ex-Speaker Hertzberg," *Metro Investment Report*, X: 2 (September 2002), pp. 1, 8, 18; Lochhead, "An Upper Basin Perspective," pp. 380–81, 390–96, 405–6.

39. Hundley, *The Great Thirst*, p. 498; Lochhead, "An Upper Basin Perspective," pp. 394–95; MWDSC, press release, "Agreement Reached on Landmark Colorado River Water Accords," October 16, 2002, http://www.mwd.dst.ca.us/mwdh2o/pdf/QSA-accord.pdf.

40. Lochhead, "An Upper Basin Perspective," pp. 395–96, 407; Daniel B. Wood, "In Water Transfers, Farmers vs. Sprawl," *Christian Science Monitor*, December 11, 2002; Coachella Valley Water District, press release, "Another $150 Million in Loan Guarantees from Sacramento Also Is Sought by IID," http://www .cvwd.org/pressrel/ruling.pdf.

41. Lochhead, "An Upper Basin Perspective," pp. 396–97 (Raley quote); and F. Scott Fitzgerald, *The Great Gatsby* (New York: Scribner's, 1953 [1925]), p. 182.

42. Lochhead, "An Upper Basin Perspective," pp. 392–93, 400–402; William Booth and Kimberly Edds, "California Supply of Surplus Water Shut Off," *Washington Post*, January 6, 2003, p. A3; Jose Luis Jimenez, "Interior Secretary Says River Talks Are Local Matter," *San Diego Union-Tribune*, February 21, 2003, p. B1.

43. Lochhead, "An Upper Basin Perspective," pp. 401–2.

44. "Answers Sought for California Water Woes," *Western Water*, 47:1 (January 2003), http://www.awwa.org/Communications/mainstream/2003/jan/Lead01_California%20water.cfm; Lochhead, "An Upper Basin Perspective," pp. 318, 401–8.

45. Lloyd Allen, "MWD's Public Policy vs. Its Private Policy," *San Diego Union-Tribune*, June 17, 2003, p. B7; Hundley, *The Great Thirst*, p. 465; "MWD's Ron Gastelum Argues Glass Half Full: Threats of Water Crisis 'Playing to People's Fears,'" *Metro Investment Report*, X:1 (August 2002), pp. 4, 12–13, 17.

46. MWDSC, letter to the Honorable Gray Davis, June 24, 2003, http://www .mwd.dst.ca.us/mwdh2o/pdf/news/Governor%20Davis.pdf.

47. Lochhead, "An Upper Basin Perspective," pp. 405–6.

48. Steven P. Erie and Pascale Joassart-Marcelli, "New Battle Fronts in the L.A. vs. San Diego Water War," *Los Angeles Times*, January 30, 2000; Seth Hettena, "Governor's Aide Threatens to Cut Metropolitan Out of Water Talks," *Associated Press*, August 22, 2003; Gig Conaughton, "Water Transfer in Trouble Again," *San Diego Union-Tribune*, May 28, 2003; Carl Ingram, "Two Water Bill Backers May Change Votes," *Los Angeles Times*, July 7, 1987, p. A17.

49. Seth Hettena, "Three Water Agencies Seek to Cut MWD Out of Colorado River Talks," *Associated Press*, August 22, 2003; Tony Perry, "Tensions Rise over Bill to Alter Water Delivery Policy," *Los Angeles Times*, May 6, 2001, p. B8; Michael Gardner, "Reserves of Water Seller Are Targeted," *San Diego Union-Tribune*, May 22, 2001, p. A3; Tony Perry, "Water Talks Send Ripple of Fear North," *Los Angeles Times*, August 24, 2003, p. B1. Earlier, in 2001, the legislature had considered bills forcing MWD to make refunds, but ultimately adopted a less stringent requirement that it cut back on its financial reserves. There also was continuing talk of legislation to invoke antitrust legislation against MET as "a water monopolist."

50. Michael Gardner, "Water Skirmishes Resurface," *San Diego Union-Tribune*, September 11, 2003; "Senate Bill 317," http://www.saltonsea.water.ca .gov/docs/sb317.pdf.

51. Gardner, "Water Skirmishes Resurface"; MWDSC, "Agreement Reached on Landmark Colorado River Water Accords," press release, October 16, 2002, http://www.mwd.dst.ca.us/mwdh2o/pdf/QSA-accord.pdf.

52. Gardner, "Water Skirmishes Resurface."

53. Gig Conaughton, "Water Deal Is Official After Years of Talks," *North County Times*, October 3, 2003.

54. Conaughton, "Water Deal Is Official After Years of Talks."

55. U.S. Department of the Interior Office of the Secretary, press release, "California's Colorado River Water Talks Successful," August 4, 1999. California Department of Water Resources, *California Water Plan: Update 2003*, http:// www.waterplan.water.ca.gov/b160/pdf/Water%20Plan.pdf; California Department of Water Resources, *California Water Plan*, Bulletin 160–98 (Sacramento: California Department of Water Resources, January 1998).

56. Hundley, *The Great Thirst*, p. 416.

57. Gottlieb, *A Life of Its Own*, pp. 14–33; Michael Hiltzik, "State, Local Spats Set Water Wars on the Boil," *Los Angeles Times*, June 16, 2003, p. D1.

58. Hundley, *The Great Thirst*, pp. 318, 320, 330; Mark Arax and Rick Wartzman, *The King of California: J. G. Boswell and the Making of a Secret American Empire* (New York: Public Affairs, 2003), pp. 351–56.

59. Interview with Tim Quinn; MWDSC, "CALFED: Reinvesting in California's Future" (Los Angeles: MWDSC, 1998); "Delta Debate," *Western Water*, March–April, 1998, p. 7.

60. Daniel K. Macon, "What California Agriculture Would Like from CALFED," *Sacramento Bee*, March 6, 1998; Tom Philip, "Cities, Farmers, Enviros Try to Cut a Water Deal," *Sacramento Bee*, April 14, 1998; David Friedman, "The Divining Rod of Water Politics," *Los Angeles Times*, April 19, 1998; Mark Grossi, "Study Finds Valley Water Among Worst," *Fresno Bee*, May 1, 1998.

61. CALFED, "Programmatic EIS/EIR Executive Summary" (Sacramento: CALFED Bay-Delta Program, March 1998), pp. 4–5; "CALFED: A Framework for Action on Water and a Work in Progress," *Metro Investment Report*, 8:1 (June 2000), pp. 4, 10–11.

62. Alex Barnum, "Water Warriors Prepare for New Battle in Delta," *San Francisco Chronicle*, March 16, 1998; Tony Perry, "Bond Measures Win," *Los Angeles Times*, March 9, 2000, p. 19; Elliott Diringer, "S.F. Fighting Bay-Delta Water Pact It Signed in '94," *San Francisco Chronicle*, July 23, 1996, p. A11.

63. John Howard, "Wilson, Babbitt to Confer on Plans for Restoring Delta," *Riverside Press-Enterprise*, May 8, 1998; Frank Clifford, "Draft of Delta Plan Coming by Year's End," *Los Angeles Times*, May 12, 1998.

64. CALFED, "Programmatic EIS/EIR Executive Summary," pp. 15, 22–24.

65. Mark Grossi, "Peripheral Canal Idea Resurrected," *Fresno Bee*, April 22, 1998; Hundley, *The Great Thirst*, p. 412.

66. Christopher Heredia, "Delta Plan Presented, Attacked," *San Francisco Chronicle*, March 17, 1998; "The Delta's Destiny," editorial, *Sacramento Bee*, March 22, 1998; Tony Perry, "Water Canal Plan, Debate Resurface," *Los Angeles Times*, March 17, 1998; Vic Pollard, "Water Plan Unveiled, Attacked," *Bakersfield Californian*, March 17, 1998; Chief Executive Officers of Major California Employers and Members of California Business Roundtable, California Council for Economic and Environmental Balance, and Bay Area Council, "Letter to The Honorable William Jefferson Clinton and The Honorable Pete Wilson," April 15, 1998; Steve La Rue, "Business Leaders Weigh in on Water," *San Diego Union-Tribune*, May 5, 1998; "Delta Debate," p. 13; Mark Arax, "Water Deal Splits San Joaquin Valley," *Los Angeles Times*, July 29, 1997; California Farm Water Coalition, "A Closer Look at CALFED's Farmland Conversion Proposals: Farmers Must Weigh In on California Water Decisions," *Farm Water Report*, May–June 1998.

67. MWDSC, "Refinement of Policy Principles Relating to the CALFED Bay-Delta Program and Preliminary Comments on CALFED's Draft PEIR/S," Memo from General Manager to Board of Directors, May 11, 1998, p. 3; "MWD's

Wodraska: A Coherent Strategy for State's Urban Interests," *Metro Investment Report*, 2:2 (July 1994), p. 14; George Rooney, "Inland Officials Favor Canal Plan," *Riverside Press-Enterprise*, April 27, 1998; Chris Frahm, Chair, SDCWA, "Letter to Jack V. Foley, Chairman of the Board of the Metropolitan Water District of Southern California," May 12, 1998; "Wrench in the Works," editorial, *San Diego Union-Tribune*, May 3, 1998.

68. Bay Area Council, "Sunne Wright McPeak," http://www.bayareacouncil.org/orgprofl/sdr/SunneMcPeak.pdf.

69. Hundley, *The Great Thirst*, p. 414.

70. Nancy Vogel, "Wilson Promises Canal Decision," *Riverside Press-Enterprise*, May 7, 1998; George Skelton, "To Little Fanfare, Lundgren Wades into Water Wars," *Los Angeles Times*, November 24, 1997; Tony Perry, "Politicians Wade into Water Issue," *Los Angeles Times*, May 3, 1998.

71. "Delta Debate," *Western Water*, p. 15; Hundley, *The Great Thirst*, p. 417; "MWD's Woody Wodraska: Water Politics and Policy Distilled," *Metro Investment Report*, 4:4 (September 1996), pp. 1, 14–16.

72. Interview with Tim Quinn.

73. California, Office of the Governor, press release, "Governor Davis Signs Historic Water Bond Legislation for March 2000 Ballot," October 7, 1999; California Department of Water Resources, "Safe Drinking Water, Clean Water, Watershed Protection, and Flood Protection Act," http://wwwdwr.water.ca.gov/dir-Water_Bond_2000/Major_Features.html; Denis Cuff, "Cancer Fear May Sweeten Peripheral Canal Appeal," *Contra Costa Times*, March 16, 1998; Hundley, *The Great Thirst*, pp. 391–92, 418–19. "CALFED Today: A Roundtable Discussion," *Western Water*, September–October 2002, p. 10.

74. Hundley, *The Great Thirst*, pp. 419–20; Sue McClurg, "Introduction," *Western Water*, July–August 2000, http://water-ed.org/julyaug00.asp#introduction; Tim Stroshane, "To Decimate Delta Farming," *Environmental News*, Winter 2000–2001, http://www.becnet.org/ENews/0001WiDeltaFarming.html; Stuart Leavenworth, "Rural Coalition Sues State over Water Plan," *Sacramento Bee*, September 28, 2000.

75. Alex Barnum, "California Water Plan Shown Off," *San Francisco Chronicle*, August 4, 1999, p. A15.

76. Michael Hiltzik, "State, Local Spats Set Water Wars on the Boil," *Los Angeles Times*, June 16, 2003, p. D1.

77. Stroshane, "To Decimate Delta Farming," *Environmental News*, Winter 2000–2001, http://www.becnet.org/ENews/0001WiDeltaFarming.html; Leavenworth, "Rural Coalition Sues State over Water Plan," *Sacramento Bee*, September 28, 2000; "Suits Filed Against Cal-Fed Water Plan," *San Francisco Chronicle*, September 30, 2000.

78. Otto Kreisher, "GOP Bill Would Give Congress Power over CalFed Water Pact"; Barnum, "California Water Plan Shown Off," *San Francisco Chronicle*, September 21, 2000, p. A4.

79. Eric Brazil, "Feinstein Fast-Tracks Water Storage Plans," *San Francisco Chronicle*, May 25, 2001, p. A4; Eric Brazil, "Challenge to Water Bills in Congress," *San Francisco Chronicle*, June 30, 2001, p. A2; Edward Epstein, "Feinstein's Water Plan Rained on by Critics," *San Francisco Chronicle*, July 20, 2001, p. A3; Glen Martin, "Congress OKs Funding for 2002 CalFed Program," *San Francisco Chronicle*, November 2, 2001; Epstein, "Dueling Water Bills Split Congress," *San Francisco Chronicle*, July 28, 2003, p. A2.

80. Sue McClurg, "Delta Deal?" *Western Water*, July–August 2000; Bart Jansen, "Senate Panel, Following House, Kills Funding for CalFed Water Plan," *Tahoe Commercial Appeal*, July 22, 2000; Michael Gardner, "Water Officials Plan Strategy to Salvage Program," *San Francisco Chronicle*, December 13, 2000, p. A3.

81. Mike Taugher, "Congressman Introduces Third Competing Water Plan for California," *Contra Costa Times*, June 29, 2001; Calvert, "Restoring Confidence in Water Policy," p. B7; Jansen, "Senate Panel, Following House, Kills Funding for CalFed Water Plan."

82. Mark Grossi, "Peripheral Canal Idea Resurrected," *Fresno Bee*, April 22, 1998; Denis Cuff, "Cancer Fear May Sweeten Peripheral Canal Appeal," *Contra Costa Times*, March 16, 1998.

83. "A Giant Sucking Sound near the Banks of the San Joaquin," editorial, *Sacramento Bee*, August 29, 2000; "Water Wars," *Western Water*, July–August 2000; Hundley, *The Great Thirst*, pp. 504–5, 531–32.

84. "Gut Check for Cal-Fed: Lawsuits and Politics Challenge Delta Water Plan," editorial, *Sacramento Bee*, October 17, 2000; McClurg, "Introduction," *Western Water*, July–August 2000, http://water-ed.org/julyaug00.asp#introduction.

85. Douglas Fischer, "Prop. 50 Atypical," *Oakland Tribune*, October 18, 2002; Colleen Valles, "Environmental Measure Is a Landmark in Funding," *Associated Press*, March 7, 2002.

86. Fischer, "Prop. 50 Atypical"; John Krist, "A Big State Water Bond for November," *Ventura County Star*, June 8, 2002, p. B10.

87. Chris Rizo, "Water District Throws Support Behind Prop. 50," *San Gabriel Valley Tribune*, September 30, 2002; Michael Gardner, "Powerful Foes Line Up Against November Water Bond," *Copley News Service*, January 15, 2002; interview with Tim Quinn.

88. "CALFED Governance," *Western Water*, September–October 2002, p. 11; "Calfed Reauthorized," *Aqueduct Magazine*, 1:3 (December 2001), http://www.mwd.dst.ca.us/aqueduct/calfedissue/calfed3.htm; Nancy Vogel,

"State Wants Firms to Get Share of Water Funds," *Los Angeles Times*, March 12, 2004, p. B1; "The CALFED Plan: Making It Happen," *Western Water*, January–February 2004, pp. 7–8.

89. Richard Simon and Bettina Boxall, "Delta Water Projects Bill OKd," *Los Angeles Times*, October 7, 2004, pp. B1, B10; interview with Tim Quinn.

90. Quoted in Bill McKibben, "Taking the Text of the Planet," *Audubon*, November–December 1999, http://magazine.audubon.org/population.html.

91. Elliot Diringer, "Water Foes Praise Wilson for Stepping In, But His Apparent Strategy Quickly Draws Some Flak," *San Francisco Chronicle*, April 7, 1992, p. A1.

92. Fulton, *The Reluctant Metropolis*, pp. 102–4, 124; S. Joshua Newcom, "The Colorado River: Coming to Consensus," *Western Water*, March–April 2002, pp. 4–13, 17; "A Worthy Water Trade: Southern California, San Joaquin Explore Partnership," *Sacramento Bee*, July 29, 2000; Hundley, *The Great Thirst*, pp. 485–86; Lance deHaven-Smith and John R. Wodraska "Consensus-Building for Integrated Resources Planning," *Public Administration Review*, 56:4 (1996), pp. 367–71; "A Public Monopoly Considers Private Alliances to Meet Regional Water Needs," *Metro Investment Report*, 8:8 (January 2001), pp. 1, 14.

93. Hundley, *The Great Thirst*, p. 561; MWDSC, "Metropolitan Board Sets New Water Plan Pricing Rates," press release, March 12, 2002, http://www.mwd.dst.ca.us/mwdh2o/pages/news/press_releases/2002-03/WaterPricing.htm; Thair Peterson, "Strategic Plan," *Aqueduct Magazine*, March 2001, http://www.mwd.dst.ca.us/aqueduct/march2001/strategic.htm.

94. Champions of the new environmentally oriented mission statement included MET directors Tim Brick of Pasadena, and Christine Reed, a Republican environmentalist and Santa Monica city councilwoman.

Chapter 6

1. *The Economist*, July 19, 2003, p. 15.

2. "The Future of Water in So. California: MWD's Woody Wodraska," *Metro Investment Report*, 5:5 (October 1997), p. 14.

3. "Western Water's Michael George on the Viability of Water Markets Post the Colorado-IID Deal," *Metro Investment Report*, 9:4 (December 2003), p. 10.

4. Bjorn Lomborg, "Problems, Problems," *Wall Street Journal*, May 5, 2004, p. A14; Water Education Foundation (WEF), *Layperson's Guide to Water Marketing* (Sacramento: WEF, 2000), pp. 2–3. For an analysis of the development of the Golden State's water market, see Ellen Hanak, *California's Water Market, by*

the Numbers (San Francisco: Public Policy Institute of California, October 2002), 28 pp.

5. A key factor in successful transactions involves establishing an acceptable price to be paid. This can range from a low charge equal to the value of the water for agricultural production plus a premium needed to induce the transaction to a high price equal to the cost of the next best alternative. Interview with Paul Engstrand, 2005.

6. See Metropolitan Water District of Southern California (MWDSC), *Integrated Water Resources Plan: 2003 Update* (Los Angeles: MWDSC, May 2004), pp. 49–52.

7. CBC News, "Water for Profit: How Multinationals Are Taking Control of a Public Resource," February 3–9, 2003, http://www.cbc.ca/news/features/water/.

8. Erika Hobbs, "Low Rates, Needed Repairs Lure 'Big Water' to Uncle Sam's Plumbing," Center for Public Integrity, February 12, 2003, http://www.publicintegrity.org/water/report.aspx?sID=ch&rID=54&aID=54.

9. Andre Guillerme, "The Genesis of Water Supply and Sewerage Systems in France, 1800–1850," in Joel A. Tarr and Gabriel Dupuy, eds., *Technology and the Rise of the Networked City* (Philadelphia: Temple University Press, 1988), pp. 99–115; Marq de Villiers, *Water: The Fate of Our Most Precious Resource* (New York: Houghton Mifflin, 2001), p. 252; Maude Barlow and Tony Clarke, *Blue Gold: The Fight to Stop the Corporate Theft of the World's Water* (New York: New Press, 2002), pp. 101–53; "Creating a Gusher in Power and Energy," *Business Week*, June 17, 2002, http://www.keepmedia.com/pubs/Business Week/2002/06/17/22710-53; Vandana Shiva, *Water Wars: Privatization, Pollution, and Profit* (Cambridge, MA: South End Press, 2002), pp. 91–92, 97–98; International Consortium of Investigative Journalists, "Cholera and the Age of the Water Barons," *ENN News*, February 4, 2002, http://www.enn.com/news/2003-02-03/s_2479.asp.

10. Shiva, *Water Wars*, pp. 1–18; Villiers, *Water*, pp. 3–26; Bonnie Colby Saliba and David B. Bush, *Water Markets in Theory and Practice* (Boulder, CO: Westview Press, 1987), p. 107; Stephanie S. Pincetl, *Transforming California: A Political History of Land Use and Development* (Baltimore: Johns Hopkins University Press, 1999), pp. 48–49.

11. Renato Gazmuri Schleyer, "Chile's Market-Oriented Water Policy: Institutional Aspects and Achievements," in Guy Le Moigne et al., eds., *Water Policy and Water Markets* (Washington, DC: World Bank, 1994), pp. 65–78; Connie Watson, "How the Privatization of Water Caused Riots in Cochabamba, Bolivia," CBC Radio, February 4, 2003, http://www.cbc.ca/news/features/water/bolivia.html; Meena Palaniappan, Peter H. Gleick, Catherine Hunt, and Veena

Srinivasan, "Water Privatization Principles and Practices," in Peter H. Gleick et al., *The World's Water, 2004–2005* (Washington, DC: Island Press, 2004), p. 47.

12. International Consortium of Investigative Journalists, "The Aguas Tango: Cashing In on Buenos Aires' Water Privatization," *ENN News*, http://www.enn .com/news/2003-02-07/s_2544.asp; Roel Landingin, "Loaves, Fishes and Dirty Dishes: Manila's Privatized Water Can't Handle the Pressure," Center for Public Integrity, http://www.publicintegrity.org/water/report.aspx?aid=51&sid=100; Jacques Pauw, "Metered to Death: How a Water Experiment Caused Riots and a Cholera Epidemic," Center for Public Integrity, http://www.icij.org/water/ report.aspx?sID=ch&rID=49&aID=49.

13. Robert R. Hearne and K. William Easter, "The Economic and Financial Gains from Water Markets," *Agricultural Economics*, 15:3 (1997), pp. 187–99; Gary L. Sturgess and Michael Wright, *Water Rights in New South Wales: The Evolution of a Property Rights System* (Sydney: The Center for Independent Studies, 1993), p. 23–24; Shiva, *Water Wars*, pp. 99–101; William Birnbauer, "The Big Pong Down Under," Center for Public Integrity, http://www.publicintegrity .org/water/report.aspx?aid=59&sid=100.

14. Marianne Lavelle, "The Coming Water Crisis," *U.S. News and World Report*, August 12, 2002, http://www.keepmedia.com/ShowItemDetails.do?itemID =1928&extID=10032&oliID=213; Hobbs, "Low Rates, Needed Repairs Lure 'Big Water' to Uncle Sam's Plumbing."

15. Claudia H. Deutsch, "Vivendi of France Acquiring U.S. Filter," *New York Times*, March 23, 1999, p. C10; International Consortium of Investigative Journalists, "Cholera and the Age of the Water Barons," *ENN News*, February 4, 2002, http://www.enn.com/news/2003-02-03/s_2479.asp. In late 2004, Vivendi sold U.S. Filter to Germany's industrial conglomerate Siemens AG. Allegedly stymied by Vivendi in working abroad, U.S. Filter hoped to capture the growing worldwide market for industrial water and wastewater treatment.

16. Nelson M. Blake, *Water for Cities: A History of the Urban Water Supply Problem in the United States* (Syracuse, NY: Syracuse University Press, 1956), pp. 276–82; Charles H. Weidner, *Water for a City: A History of New York City's Problem from the Beginning to the Delaware River System* (New Brunswick, NJ: Rutgers University Press, 1974); Fern L. Nelson, *Great Waters: A History of Boston's Water Supply* (Hanover, NH: University Press of New England, 1983), pp. 1–14, 23, 24; Sarah S. Elkind, *Bay Cities and Water Politics: The Battle for Resources in Boston and Oakland* (Lawrence: University of Kansas Press, 1998), pp. 17–27; Vincent Ostrom, *Water and Politics: A Study of Water Policies and Administration in the Development of Los Angeles* (Los Angeles: Haynes Foundation, 1953), pp. 40–48, 90–97.

17. Alex Tysbine, "Water Privatization: A Broken Promise," *Public Citizen,* October 2001, pp. 12–13, http://www.citizen.org/documents/ACF146.pdf; Joyce Morrison, "Germany Owns My Water," February 4, 2003, http://www .propertyrightsresearch.org/germany_owns_my_water.htm.

18. National Association of Water Companies, "Government Relations," http://www.nawc.org/gov.html; Tysbine, "Water Privatization: A Broken Promise"; Hobbs, "Low Rates, Needed Repairs Lure 'Big Water' to Uncle Sam's Plumbing"; "Atlanta Signs United Water,' http://www.waterindustry.org/UWR-atlanta1.htm.

19. Geoffrey Segal, "Indianapolis Selects U.S. Filter to Operate Water Utility," in Reason Foundation, *Annual Privatization Report, 2003,* http://www.rppi .org/apr2003/indianapolisselects.html; "The Big Greedy," *Public Citizen,* http://www.citizen.org/documents/Big_Greedy_(PDF).PDF; Hobbs, "Low Rates, Needed Repairs Lure 'Big Water' to Uncle Sam's Plumbing."

20. Donald J. Pisani, *To Reclaim a Divided West: Water, Law, and Public Policy, 1848–1902* (Albuquerque: University of New Mexico Press, 1992), pp. 11–12.

21. Interview with Carl Boronkay, 2005.

22. Morton J. Horwitz, *The Transformation of American Law, 1780–1860* (Cambridge, MA: Harvard University Press, 1977), p. 31; Norris Hundley Jr., *The Great Thirst,* rev. ed. (Berkeley: University of California Press, 2001), pp. 76, 85–93; Theodore Steinberg, *Nature Incorporated: Industrialization and the Waters of New England* (Cambridge, MA: Harvard University Press, 1991); Robert Kelley, *Battling the Inland Sea: American Political Culture, Public Policy, and the Sacramento Valley, 1850–1986* (Berkeley: University of California Press, 1989), pp. 75–78.

23. Pisani, *To Reclaim a Divided West,* pp. 16, 28, 100–101; Joseph L. Sax, Robert H. Abrams, and Barton H. Thompson Jr., *Legal Control of Water Resources,* 2nd ed. (St. Paul, MN: West Publications, 1991), p. 190; Charles H. Shinn, *Land Laws of the Mining Camps* (Baltimore: Johns Hopkins University Press, 1984), p. 235.

24. Douglas R. Littlefield, "Water Rights During the California Gold Rush: Conflicts over Economic Points of View," *Western Historical Quarterly,* 14 (October 1983), pp. 415–34; State of California, *Governor's Commission to Review California Water Rights Law* (Sacramento: State of California, 1978), p. 9; Donald J. Pisani, *From Family Farm to Agribusiness: The Irrigation Crusade in California and the West, 1850–1931* (Berkeley: University of California Press, 1984), pp. 30–53; Hundley, *The Great Thirst,* pp. 85–99, 245; Wells A. Hutchins, *The California Law of Water Rights* (Sacramento: California State Printing Division, 1956), pp. 67–178; S. T. Harding, *Water in California* (Palo

Alto, CA: N-P Publications, 1960), pp. 42–43; "Whose Water Is It Anyway? State Supreme Court Clarifies Priorities," *Metro Investment Report,* 8:4 (September 2000), p. 14.

25. Pisani, *To Reclaim a Divided West,* pp. 41–43, 52–53, 99–100, 154–90; Pisani, *From Family Farm to Agribusiness,* pp. 129–282; Daniel Tyler, *The Mythical Pueblo Rights Water Doctrine: Water Administration in Hispanic New Mexico* (El Paso: Texas Western Press, 1991).

26. Pisani, *From Family Farm to Agribusiness,* pp. 378–80; Donald Worster, *Rivers of Empire: Water, Aridity, and the Growth of the American West* (New York: Oxford University Press, 1985), p. 193; Otis B. Tout, *The First Thirty Years 1901–1931: Being an Account of the Principal Events in the History of Imperial Valley, Southern California,* U.S.A. (San Diego: Otis B. Tout, 1931), pp. 98–114; Beverly B. Moeller, *Phil Swing and Boulder Dam* (Berkeley: University of California Press, 1971), p. 104.

27. Harding, *Water in California,* pp. 45, 84–85, 189; Hundley, *The Great Thirst,* pp. 103–6, 243–44, 246; Saliba and Bush, *Water Markets in Theory and Practice,* pp. 66, 109–10; Nancy Y. Moore, Morlie H. Graubard, and Robert Shishko, *Efficient Water Use in California: Groundwater Use and Management* (Santa Monica, CA: RAND Corporation, 1978).

28. Robert Gottlieb, *A Life of Its Own: The Politics and Power of Water* (New York: Harcourt Brace Jovanovich, 1988), pp. 262–63; Saliba and Bush, *Water Markets in Theory and Practice,* pp. 113–14; J. C. Bliss and Samuel Imperati, "The Legal Aspects of Appropriative Water Rights Transfers in California," *University of California Davis Law Review,* 11 (1977–1978), p. 441; Elinor Ostrom, "Public Entrepreneurship: A Case Study in Groundwater Basin Management," doctoral thesis, University of California at Los Angeles, 1965.

29. R. A. Young, "Why Are There So Few Transactions Between Water Users?" *American Journal of Agricultural Economics,* 19 (1983), pp. 143–51; Saliba and Bush, *Water Markets in Theory and Practice,* pp. 187–97.

30. Pisani, *To Reclaim a Divided West,* pp. 100–101; Harry N. Scheiber, "The Road to *Munn*: Eminent Domain and the Concept of Public Purpose in the State Courts," *Perspectives in American History,* 5 (1971), pp. 327–42; Joseph W. Dellapenna, "The Importance of Getting Names Right: The Myth of Markets for Water," *William and Mary Environmental Law and Policy Review,* 25 (Winter 2000), pp. 317–35; Charles J. Meyers and Richard A. Posner, "Market Transfers of Water Rights: Toward an Improved Market in Water Resources," *National Water Commission Legal Study,* 4 (1971), pp. 2–7; Richard A. Posner, *Economic Analysis of Law,* 5th ed. (New York: Aspin Law and Business, 1998), sections 1.1–1.2; Helen Ingram, *Measuring the Community Value of Water: The Water and Public Welfare Project* (Tucson: University of Arizona Press, 1989), pp. 1–42.

31. Peter Passell, "Soaking Lawns, Not Taxpayers," *New York Times*, February 5, 1992, p. D2; Gottlieb, *Life of Its Own*, pp. 99, 213–14; Saliba and Bush, *Water Markets in Theory and Practice*, pp. 50, 77, 112–13; Richard W. Wahl and Robert K. Davis, "Satisfying Southern California's Thirst for Water: Alternatives," in Kenneth D. Frederick, ed., *Scarce Water and Institutional Change* (Washington, DC: Resources for the Future Inc., 1986), pp. 102–33; Charles E. Phelps, Nancy Y. Moore, and Morlie H. Graubard, *Efficient Water Use in California: Water Rights, Water Districts, and Water Transfers* (Santa Monica, CA: RAND Corporation, 1978); Angelides Sortirus and Eugene Bardach, *Water Banking: How to Stop Wasting Agricultural Water* (San Francisco: Institute of Contemporary Studies, 1978); WEF, *Layperson's Guide to Water Marketing*, p. 5; *Sporhase v. Nebraska* 458 U.S. 941 (1982).

32. California Water Code, Sections 109, 380–87, 1010–011; California State Assembly, AB 3491 (1982), AB 1029 (1985), AB 1746 (1986); Saliba and Bush, *Water Markets in Theory and Practice*, pp. 112–13; Gottlieb, *Life of Its Own*, p. 265.

33. David Abel, Remarks Before the Southern California Water Committee, "Regional Self-Reliance: A Vision of California's Water Future," Forum 3, p. 2, http://www.socalwater.org/download/Forum3summary.pdf.

34. Gottlieb, *Life of Its Own*, p. 98; Robert Gottlieb and Margaret Fitz-Simmons, *Thirst for Growth: Water Agencies as Hidden Government in California* (Tucson: University of Arizona Press, 1991), pp. 79–82; Robert N. Stavins, *Trading Conservation Investments for Water* (Berkeley: Environmental Defense Fund, 1983); Paul Jacobs, "Surplus Water Is Available, But Goes Unclaimed, Report Says," *Los Angeles Times*, May 22, 1985, p. A3; California Water Resources Control Board (CWRCB), "Waste and Unreasonable Use of Water by Imperial Irrigation Dist.," Order No. WR 88-20, at 44 (Sacramento: CWRCB, 1988); Tom Graff, "Environmentalist Graff Reflects on Reform Efforts: A Past, Present & Future of California Water," *Metro Investment Report*, 9:2 (August 2001), pp. 5, 14–15.

35. Gottlieb and FitzSimmons, *Thirst for Growth*, pp. 82–83; Imperial Irrigation District and Metropolitan Water District of Southern California, "Agreement for the Implementation of a Water Conservation Program and Use of Conserved Water," Los Angeles, MWDSC, December 1989; Marc Reisner, *Cadillac Desert: The American West and Its Disappearing Water* (New York: Penguin Books, 1993), p. 489; Gottlieb, *Life of Its Own*, pp. 101, 258–61, 263.

36. Gottlieb and FitzSimmons, *Thirst for Growth*, pp. 82–83, 188; Gottlieb, *Life of Its Own*, pp. 265, 271.

37. "Keeping the Peace: A Conversation with the IID's John Carter," *Valley Grower*, November–December 1999, p. 8; Gottlieb, *Life of Its Own*, p. 99;

Gottlieb and FitzSimmons, *Thirst for Growth*, pp. 83–87, 178, 245 note 61; Cheryl Clark, "Water Sale Bypassing MWD Said Feasible," *San Diego Union-Tribune*, August 9, 1985.

38. Gottlieb, *Life of Its Own*, p. 100; Bill Boyarsky, "MWD Rejects 'Outrageous' Imperial Offer to Sell Water," *Los Angeles Times*, November 10, 1987, p. A1.

39. Boronkay interview; Hundley, *The Great Thirst*, p. 333; Gottlieb and FitzSimmons, *Thirst for Growth*, pp. 37–39, 81–85.

40. Hundley, *The Great Thirst*, pp. 476–78; Gottlieb and FitzSimmons, *Thirst for Growth*, pp. 85–88; WEF, *Layperson's Guide to California Water* (Sacramento: WEF, 2003), p. 21; Committee on Western Water Management, Water Science and Technology Board, *Water Transfers in the West: Efficiency, Equity, and the Environment* (Washington, DC: National Academy Press, 1992), p. 243.

41. Myron Holburt, Richard W. Atwater, and Timothy H. Quinn, "Water Marketing in Southern California," *Journal of the American Water Works Association*, 80 (March 1988), pp. 36–45; Timothy H. Quinn, "Shifting Water to Urban Uses: Activities of the Metropolitan Water District of Southern California," in L. MacDonnell, ed., *Moving the West's Water to New Uses: Winners and Losers* (Boulder, CO: Natural Resources Law Center, 1990), pp. 23–24; Committee on Western Water Management, *Water Transfers in the West*, p. 245; Gary D. Weatherford, Mary Wallace, Lee H. Storey, *Leasing Indian Water: Choices in the Colorado River Basin* (Washington, DC: Conservation Foundation, 1988), pp. 1–54.

42. Boronkay interview.

43. Gottlieb, *Life of Its Own*, pp. 271, 279; Gottlieb and FitzSimmons, *Thirst for Growth*, pp. 184, 187–88, 217; Steven J. Shupe, Gary D. Weatherford, and Elizabeth Checchio, "Western Water Rights: The Era of Reallocation," *Natural Resources Journal*, 29:2 (Spring 1989), pp. 413–34; Committee on Western Water Management, *Water Transfers in the West*, pp. 234–48. As later noted, MWD's deal with the Palo Verde Irrigation District was resurrected and implemented. See Jerry Hirsch and Marc Lifsher, "Landmark Water Pact Is Expected," *Los Angeles Times,* May 11, 2004.

44. Barton H. Thompson Jr., "Institutional Perspectives on Water Policy and Markets," *California Law Review*, 81 (May 1993), pp. 729–30; Committee on Western Water Management, *Water Transfers in the West*, p. 237.

45. Gottlieb and FitzSimmons, *Thirst for Growth*, pp. 17–18, 89–90, 180; *Imperial Irrigation District v. State Water Resources Control Board*, 275 Cal. Rptr. 250, 267 California Court of Appeals, 4th District (1991); Brian E. Gray, "Water Agencies and Water Transfers in California: A Case Study of the Kern County Water Agency," in *Moving the West's Water to New Uses*, pp. 11–41.

Notes for Chapter 6 315

46. Henry J. Vaux Jr. and Richard E. Howitt, "Managing Water Scarcity: An Evaluation of Interregional Transfers," *Water Resources Research*, 20 (1984), pp. 785–92; State of California, Assembly Office of Research, *Water Trading: Free Market Benefits* (Sacramento: State Printing Office, 1985).

47. Committee on Western Water Management, *Water Transfers in the West*, pp. 223–24, 226–27.

48. Gottlieb and FitzSimmons, *Thirst for Growth*, pp. 180, 201–2; Saliba and Bush, *Water Markets in Theory and Practice*, p. 116; Russell Kletzing, "Imported Groundwater Banking: The Kern Water Bank—A Case Study," *Pacific Law Journal*, 19 (1988), p. 1225.

49. Boronkay interview; Gottlieb and FitzSimmons, *Thirst for Growth*, pp. 180–81; Carl Ingram, "Two Water Bill Backers May Change Votes," *Los Angeles Times*, July 7, 1987, p. A17; Virginia Ellis, "Urban Water Bill OKd by Assembly," *Los Angeles Times*, July 3, 1991, p. A3; Dale Kasler and Stuart Leavensworth, "The Water's Hot," *Sacramento Bee*, July 14, 2002.

50. Jennifer Warren, "MWD Chief's Style Stirs the Waters at Changing Agency Management," *Los Angeles Times*, August 12, 1991, p. A1; Gottlieb and FitzSimmons, *Thirst for Growth*, pp. 183, 270; "Trading Land for Water," editorial, *Riverside Press-Enterprise*, October 22, 2001; "Water Officials Purchase Land to Provide Water to Coastal," *Associated Press*, October 17, 2001.

51. Committee on Western Water Management, *Water Transfers in the West*, pp. 214, 224, 228–30, 246.

52. Virginia Ellis, "State Criticized for Worsening Water Crisis," *Los Angeles Times*, May 5, 1991, p. A1; Gottlieb and FitzSimmons, *Thirst for Growth*, pp. 184–85.

53. Interview with Tim Quinn; Committee on Western Water Management, *Water Transfers in the West*, pp. 244–46; Gottlieb and FitzSimmons, *Thirst for Growth*, p. 185; Brian E. Gray, "A Primer on California Water Transfer Law," *Arizona Law Review*, 31 (1989), p. 745; EIP Associates, *Arvin-Edison Water Storage District/Metropolitan Water District of Southern California Water Storage and Exchange Program* (January 1992).

54. Gottlieb and FitzSimmons, *Thirst for Growth*, pp. 185–88, 207–8; Richard W. Wahl, *Markets for Federal Water: Subsidies, Property Rights, and the Bureau of Reclamation* (Washington, DC: Resources for the Future, 1989), pp. 135–40.

55. Boronkay interview.

56. Quinn interview; WEF, *Layperson's Guide to the State Water Project* (Sacramento: WEF, 2003), p. 9; WEF, *Layperson's Guide to California Water*, p. 21.

57. Quinn interview; WEF, *Layperson's Guide to Water Marketing*, p. 17; Hundley, *The Great Thirst*, pp. 467, 501.

58. WEF, *Layperson's Guide to Water Marketing*, p. 17; Lloyd S. Dixon, Nancy Y. Moore, and Susan W. Schechter, *California's 1991 Drought Water Bank: Economic Impacts in the Selling Regions* (Santa Monica, CA: RAND Corporation, 1991); Brian E. Gray, "The Market and the Community: Lessons from California's Drought Water Bank," *Hastings West-Northwest Journal of Environmental Law and Policy*, 17 (1994), p. 1; Richard E. Howitt, "Empirical Analysis of Water Market Institutions: The 1991 California Water Market," *Resource and Energy Economics*, 16 (1993), p. 357; Ray Coppock et al., "California Water Transfers: The System and the 1991 Drought Water Bank," in Harold O. Carter, Henry J. Vaux Jr., and Ann F. Scheuring, eds., *Sharing Scarcity: Gainers and Losers in Water Marketing* (Davis: Agricultural Issues Center, University of California, Davis, 1994), p. 21; Ellen H. C. Dyckman, "Counties Wresting Control: Local Responses to California's Statewide Water Market," *University of Denver Water Law Review*, 6 (Spring 2003), p. 494; Harold O. Carter and Henry J. Vaux Jr., "Third-Party Effects: The Research Challenge," in Carter et al., eds., *Sharing Scarcity*, pp. 55, 97.

59. WEF, *Layperson's Guide to Water Marketing*, p. 17; Dellapenna, "The Importance of Getting Names Right," pp. 323, 362–65; Dyckman, "Counties Wresting Control," pp. 490–95; "The Agreement of Ancient Wranglers," editorial, *Los Angeles Times*, July 29, 1991, p. B4; "No Time for Politics as Usual," editorial, *Los Angeles Times*, August 19, 1991, p. B4; Carl Ingram, "Senate Panel Kills Bill to Ease Sales of Water Supplies," *Los Angeles Times*, August 21, 1991, p. A3; Hundley, *The Great Thirst*, pp. 502, 666; William Fulton, *The Reluctant Metropolis: The Politics of Urban Growth in Los Angeles* (Baltimore: Johns Hopkins University Press, 2001), pp. 119–20.

60. Interview with Tim Quinn; Carl Boronkay and Warren J. Abbott, "Water Conflicts in the Western United States," *Studies in Conflict & Terrorism*, 20 (1997), pp. 137–66, esp. pp. 143–47; Pincetl, *Transforming California*, pp. 259–62; Hundley, *The Great Thirst*, p. 502; Fulton, *The Reluctant Metropolis*, p. 120.

61. Fulton, *The Reluctant Metropolis*, pp. 119–20; WEF, *Layperson's Guide to Water Marketing*, p. 12; Jim Carlton, "Is Water Too Cheap?" *Wall Street Journal*, March 17, 2004, p. B1; Pincetl, *Transforming California*, p. 261; Bay Area Economic Forum, *Using Water Better: A Market-Based Approach to California's Water Crisis* (San Francisco: Bay Area Economic Forum, October 1991), p. 1.

62. Joseph L. Sax et al., *Legal Control of Water Resources*, 3rd ed. (St. Paul, MN: West Publications, 2000), pp. 675–76; Harrison C. Dunning, "Confronting the Environmental Legacy of Irrigated Agriculture in the West: The Case of the Central Valley Project," *Environmental Law*, 23 (1993), p. 943; Ernest A. Conant, "The Central Valley Project Improvement Act Proposed Reforms," *San*

Joaquin Agricultural Law Review, 6 (1996), pp. 27–30; Pincetl, *Transforming California*, pp. 260–61; David Zilberman, Neal MacDougall, Farhed Shah, "Changes in Water Allocation Mechanisms for California Agriculture," *Contemporary Economic Policy*, 12:1 (January 1994), pp. 122–34; Marca Weinberg "Federal Water Policy Reform: Implications for Irrigated Farms in California," *Contemporary Economic Policy*, 15:2 (April 1997), pp. 63–74; Boronkay and Abbott, "Water Conflicts in the Western United States," pp. 143–47.

63. WEF, *Layperson's Guide to Water Marketing*, p. 12; WEF, *Layperson's Guide to the Central Valley Project* (Sacramento: WEF, 2002), pp. 14–15; Graff, "Environmentalist Graff Reflects on Reform Efforts," p. 15.

64. Boronkay interview; Quinn interview.

65. WEF, *Layperson's Guide to the State Water Project*, pp. 9, 17; WEF, *Layperson's Guide to Water Marketing*, p. 9; Pincetl, *Transforming California*, p. 261; "Court Reports," *University of Denver Water Law Review*, 4 (Fall 2000), p. 154; Hundley, *The Great Thirst*, p. 512.

66. Quinn interview.

67. Pincetl, *Transforming California*, p. 263; Hundley, *The Great Thirst*, pp. 506–7; Ellis, "Urban Water Bill OKd by Assembly," *Los Angeles Times*, July 3, 1991, p. A3; Elliot Diringer, "San Jose Assemblyman to Profit from Law He Fought," *San Francisco Chronicle*, September 23, 1993, p. A22.

68. Hundley, *The Great Thirst*, p. 507.

69. Boronkay interview; Quinn interview; Ernest A. Conant, "The Central Valley Project Improvement Act Proposed Reforms," *San Joaquin Agricultural Law Review*, 6 (1996), pp. 35–40; Mark Grossi, "Areias Farms' Water Deal for L.A. on Tap," *Fresno Bee*, June 30, 1994, p. A1.

70. Dyckman, "Counties Wresting Control," p. 515; Hundley, *The Great Thirst*, pp. 500, 508, 665; Andy McCue "Groundwater Reservoirs Take the Dust Out of Drought," *Riverside Press-Enterprise*, May 5, 1997, p. A7.

71. Mark Grossi, "Valley Farmers Weighing Revised L.A. Water Deal," *Fresno Bee*, October 25, 1997, p. A12.

72. WEF, *Layperson's Guide to Water Marketing*, p. 12; Hundley, *The Great Thirst*, p. 508.

73. WEF, *Layperson's Guide to Water Marketing*, pp. 12–13; Noel Brinkerhoff "Water Marketing: Let's Make a Deal," *California Journal*, August 1, 1999, http://www.wwtr.com/; Nancy Vogel, "State Looks Hard at Who Can Sell Conserved Water," *Modesto Bee*, May 28, 2000, p. G2; Kasler and Leavensworth, "The Water's Hot"; "Water Transfer Deal to Save City $160,000," *San Diego Union-Tribune*, February 7, 2002, p. B4.

74. "Water for Sale in California: Cadiz CEO Keith Brackpool," *Metro Investment Report*, 5:8 (January 1998), p. 14.

75. Quoted in Vince Lovato, "A Look Back at the Cadiz Water Proposal," *San Bernardino Sun*, October 9, 2002, p. 1.

76. Brinkerhoff, "Water Marketing: Let's Make a Deal"; Palaniappan et al., "Water Privatization Principles and Practices," in Peter H. Gleick et al., *The World's Water, 2004–2005*, p. 46.

77. Hundley, *The Great Thirst*, pp. 501, 504–5; Glen Martin, "California's Water Pact Threatened," *San Francisco Chronicle*, April 14, 2002, p. A1.

78. Michael George, "Water for Southern California: Critical Policy Decisions Must Be Made," *Metro Investment Report*, 5:10 (March 1998), p. 4; "Western Water's New CEO, Michael George, Evaluates Opportunities," *Metro Investment Report*, 5:12 (May 1998), pp. 1, 12–15; "Western Water's Michael George on the Viability of Water Markets Post the Colorado-IID Deal," *Metro Investment Report*, pp. 9–11.

79. Interview with Jerry Gewe, former LADWP Assistant General Manager/Chief Operating Officer, Water System, 2005.

80. Michael A. Hiltzik, "Critics Raising Concerns About Cadiz Water Project," *Los Angeles Times*, May 19, 2002, p. C1; Ron Gastelum, "Reorganizing Its Troops: Will MWD Adjust in Time?" *Metro Investment Report*, 7:2 (July 1999), p. 14; "Agency Rejects Plan to Store Water Under Mojave Desert," *Associated Press*, October 2, 2002.

81. Hiltzik, "Critics Raising Concerns About Cadiz Water Project," p. C1; Brinkerhoff "Water Marketing: Let's Make a Deal."

82. Glen Martin, "Water Controversy Percolates in Desert," *San Francisco Chronicle*, April 9, 2001, p. A1.

83. Andrew Silva, "Desert Water Plan Dies: MWD Rejects Cadiz Storage Project," *San Bernardino Sun*, October 9, 2002; "MWD's Ron Gastelum Argues Glass Half Full: Threats of Water Crisis 'Playing to People's Fears,'" *Metro Investment Report*, 10:1 (August 2002), p. 13; Gewe interview.

84. WEF, *Layperson's Guide to Western Water*, pp. 21–22; Michael A. Hiltzik, "Water as Business Taps into Fears," *Los Angeles Times*, September 20, 2002, p. C1.

85. "Water Transfer," *City News Service* (Los Angeles), October 22, 2002, p. 1.

86. San Diego Metropolitan Daily Business Report, October 23, 2002, http://metro.sandiegometro.com/dbr/index.php?dbrID=190.

87. Interview with Tim Quinn; Karen E. Johnson and Jeff Loux, *Water and Land Use: Planning Wisely for California's Future* (Point Arena, CA: Solano Press Books, 1994), pp. 124–25; Palo Verde Irrigation District (PVID), *Draft Environmental Impact Report for the Proposed Palo Verde Irrigation District Land Management, Crop Rotation and Water Supply Program*, State Clearinghouse No.

2001101149 (Blythe, CA: PVID, May 2002), pp. ES-1, 6–2; James S. Lochhead, "An Upper Basin Perspective on California's Claims to Water from the Colorado River. Part II: The Development, Implementation and Collapse of California's Plan to Live Within Its Basic Apportionment," *University of Denver Law Review*, 6 (Spring 2003), pp. 338–39.

88. Holburt, Atwater, and Quinn, "Water Marketing in Southern California," 36–45; Quinn, "Shifting Water to Urban Uses," pp. 86–87; Gottlieb and Fitz-Simmons, *Thirst for Growth*, pp. 186–87; "Landmark Ag-to-Urban Water Transfer Further Diversifies and Buttresses Southland's Water Supplies for Coming Decades," MWDSC press release, May 11, 2004; MWDSC, *Metropolitan Water District of Southern California Palo Verde Land Management, Crop Rotation and Watersupply Program at a Glance*, n.d., http://www.mwdh2o.com/mwdh2o/pdf/at%20a%20glance/Palo_Verde.pdf; PVID, *Draft Environmental Impact Report*, n.d., p. ES-16; California Public Resources Code, sec. 21082.2(c).

89. PVID, *Draft Environmental Impact Report*, pp. ES-2, ES-6, Table 1-1.

90. "Water Transfer," p. 1; "Upstart Imperial Valley Wins This Round in the Water War," editorial, *Western Farm Press*, January 4, 2003, p. 1; David J. Hayes, "Accommodation Turns to Conflict: Lessons from the Colorado," in Bernadette McDonald and Douglas Jehl, eds., *Whose Water Is It? The Unquenchable Thirst of a Water-Hungry World* (Washington, DC: National Geographic, 2003), p. 147.

91. "Water Transfer," p. 1; "Metropolitan Water District of Southern California Enters into Two Agreements Furthering California's Colorado River '4.4 Plan,'" *Western Water News*, December 2001, http://www.argentco.com/htm/f20011201.916442.htm.

92. Pincetl, *Transforming California*, p. 263.

93. Karl Polanyi, *The Great Transformation: The Political and Economic Origins of Our Time* (Boston: Beacon Press, 1957 [1944]), pp. 47–53; Polanyi, "Ports of Trade in Early Societies," in George Dalton, ed., *Primitive, Archaic, and Modern Economies: Essays of Karl Polanyi* (New York: Doubleday, 1968), pp. 38–60; J. Ron Stanfield, *The Economic Thought of Karl Polanyi* (New York: St. Martin's Press, 1986), pp. 65–92.

94. Saliba and Bush, *Water Markets in Theory and Practice*, pp. 187–261; Dellapenna, "The Importance of Getting Names Right," pp. 317–35; Victor Brajer, Al Church, Ronald Cummings, and Phillip Farah, "The Strengths and Weakness of Water Markets as They Affect Water Scarcity and Sovereignty Interests in the West," *Natural Resources Journal*, 29:2 (Spring 1989), pp. 489–509; David H. Getches, "Essays from Ashabad to Wellton-Mohawk to Los Angeles: The Drought in Water Policy," *University of Colorado Law Review*, 64 (Spring 1993), pp. 335–40, 547–51; Terry L. Snyder and Pamela Snyder, *Water Markets: Priming the Invisible Pump* (Washington, DC: Cato Institute, 1997); Lawrence K. MacDonnell,

From Reclamation to Sustainability: Water, Agriculture, and the Environment in the American West (Niwot: University of Colorado Press, 1999).

95. MWDSC, *Integrated Water Resources Plan: 2003 Update*, pp. 10, 49–52.

Chapter 7

1. Samuel Taylor Coleridge, "The Rime of the Ancient Mariner," in M. H. Abrams et al., eds., *Norton Anthology of English Literature*, 5th ed., vol. 2 (New York: W. W. Norton, 1986), pp. 335–52.

2. Wallace Stegner, in Page Stegner, ed., *Marking the Sparrow's Fall: Wallace Stegner's American West* (New York: Henry Holt, 1998), pp. 213, 226–27.

3. State of California, Department of Finance, "New Projections Show 20 Million More Californians by 2050," May 2004, http://www.dof.ca.gov/HTML/DEMOGRAP/DRU_Publications/Projections/P1_Press_Release_5-04.pdf.

4. State population and rankings from U.S. Census Bureau, *Statistical Abstract of the United States*, "Table NST-EST2003-01—Annual Estimates of the Population for the United States and States, and for Puerto Rico: April 1, 2000 to July 1, 2003," December 18, 2003, http://eire.census.gov/popest/data/states/tables/NST-EST2003-01.php; Hans P. Johnson, "How Many Californians? A Review of Population Projections for the State," *California Counts: Population Trends and Profiles*, 1:1 (October 1999), pp. 1–12.

5. Metropolitan Water District of Southern California (MWDSC), *Integrated Water Resources Plan: 2003 Update* (Los Angeles: MWDSC, 2004), p. 95; MWDSC, *Report on Metropolitan's Water Supplies* (Los Angeles: MWDSC, 2003), Appendix C, p. 1.

6. MWD has supplemented SCAG and SANDAG population forecasts with long-range population forecasts to 2050 from the Center for the Continuing Study of the California Economy (CCSCE). See MWDSC, *Integrated Water Resources Plan: 2003 Update*, p. 68. SCAG's Los Angeles County population forecast is higher than the Department of Finance (DOF) estimate because the DOF forecast extrapolates from growth over the previous decade, whereas SCAG discounts the decade-long trend in favor of emphasizing higher growth since 2000. The SCAG approach is sensible given that the economic recession and restructuring of the early 1990s depressed net migration, and a repeat is unlikely. Details of the SCAG population forecasts are available at http://scagrtp.migcom.com/docmanager/1000000042/tac.agenda.081203.pdf; and see SANDAG, *2030 Regional Growth Forecast* (June 2004), http://www.sandag.org/uploads/publicationid/publicationid_1077_3212.pdf.

7. From MWDSC, *Report on Metropolitan's Water Supplies*, Appendix A, p. 3; Sandra Postel, *Last Oasis: Facing Water Scarcity* (New York: W. W. Norton,

1992), pp. 141–42; Peter H. Gleick, "A Soft Path: Conservation, Efficiency, and Easing Conflicts over Water," in Bernadette McDonald and Douglas Jehl, eds., *Whose Water Is It? The Unquenchable Thirst of a Water-Hungry World* (Washington, DC: National Geographic, 2003), pp. 189–91.

8. See MWDSC, *Integrated Water Resources Plan: 2003 Update*.

9. Marc J. Perry and Paul J. Mackun, *Census 2000 Brief: Population Change and Distribution, 1990 to 2000* (Washington, DC: U.S. Census Bureau, April 2001); Christopher Conte, "Dry Spell," (Congressional Quarterly) *Governing Magazine*, March 2003, p. 20.

10. Replenishment estimate based on remarks by Dennis Underwood, MWD vice president, Colorado River Resources, at the Water Education Foundation (WEF) Water Law and Policy Briefing, San Diego, July 2004.

11. Mexico has been receiving more Colorado River water than its entitlement under the governing 1944 treaty. See Chris Kraul, "U.S. and Mexico Water Dispute Settled, Rice says," *San Diego Union-Tribune*, March 11, 2005, p. A7.

12. Fernand Braudel, *The Mediterranean and the Mediterranean World in the Age of Philip II*, Siân Reynolds, trans. (New York: Harper and Row, 1972–1973), p. 21.

13. Braudel, "History and the Social Sciences: The Longue Duree," in Peter Burke, ed., and Keith Folca, trans., *Economy and Society in Early Modern Europe* (London: Routledge and Kegan Paul, 1972), pp. 11–42.

14. California Department of Water Resources, http://watersupplyconditions.water.ca.gov/background.htm. See National Oceanic and Atmospheric Administration (NOAA) drought definitions at http://www.erh.noaa.gov/lwx/drought/droughtdef.htm. Also see United States Geological Survey (USGS), *Climatic Fluctuations, Drought, and Flow in the Colorado River Basin*, USGS Fact Sheet 2004–3062 version 2 (August 2004); remarks of Jeff Kightlinger, MWDSC general counsel, at Los Angeles Water and Power Associates Board of Directors meeting, September 2004.

15. Michael Gardner, "Drought's Grip Has West by Throat," *San Diego Union-Tribune*, August 16, 2004; "Six-Year Drought Reigns Across Much of West," *U.S. Water News Online*, April 2004; Associated Press, "West Drought Could Be Worst in 500 Years," *MSNBC.com*, July 9, 2004; Associated Press, "Western Storms Help Raise Lake Mead Water Level," *USA Today*, February 18, 2005. See also *U.S. Drought Monitor* at www.drought.unl.edu/dm/monitor.html.

16. Colorado Water Resources Research Institute, "Severe Sustained Drought: Managing the Colorado River System in Times of Water Shortage," http://cwrri.colostate.edu/pubs/newsletter/specinterest/drought.htm.

17. See NOAA Paleoclimatology Program, *North American Drought: A Paleo Perspective,* November 12, 2003, http://www.ncdc.noaa.gov/paleo/drought/drght_home.html.

18. USGS, *Climatic Fluctuations.*

19. USGS, *Climatic Fluctuations;* "Pacific Dictates Droughts and Drenchings," January 28, 2004, http://www.gsfc.nasa.gov/topstory/2004/0116west coast.html.

20. NOAA Paleoclimatology Program, *North American Drought;* Flam, "Dry, Dry West"; California Department of Water Resources, http://watersupplyconditions.waterca.gov/background.htm; California Regional Assessment Group for the U.S. Global Change Research Program (CRA Group), *Preparing for a Changing Climate: The Potential Consequences of Climate Variability and Change for California,* http://www.ncgia.ucsb.edu/pubs/CA _Report.pdf, June 2002, p. 4-148.

21. Gregory J. Hobbs Jr., "Symposium: The Role of Climate on Shaping Western Water Institutions," *University of Denver Water Law Review,* 7 (Fall 2003), p. 6; Alex Markels, "Water Fights," *U.S. News and World Report,* May 19, 2003, p. 58; interview with Jerry Gewe, former assistant general manager/chief operating officer, Los Angeles Department of Water and Power Water System, 2005.

22. See MWDSC, *Integrated Water Resources Plan, 2003 Update;* MWDSC, *Report on Metropolitan's Water Supplies.*

23. See MWDSC, *Integrated Water Resources Plan, 2003 Update;* MWDSC, *Report on Metropolitan's Water Supplies;* CRA Group, *Preparing for a Changing Climate,* p. 4-1–50.

24. Michael Kiparsky and Peter H. Gleick, "Climate Change and California Water Resources," in Peter H. Gleick et al., *The World's Water, 2004–2005* (Oakland, CA: The Pacific Institute, 2004), pp. 162, 178; C. Booth Wallentine and Dave Matthews, "Can Climate Predictions Be of Practical Use in Western Water Management?" in William M. Lewis Jr., ed., *Water and Climate in the Western United States* (Boulder: University of Colorado Press, 2003), pp. 165–67.

25. Working Group II of the Intergovernmental Panel on Climate Change (Working Group II), *Climate Change 2001: Impacts, Adaptation, and Vulnerability* (Geneva: IPCC Secretariat/World Meteorological Organization, 2001), p. 3.

26. Peter H. Gleick et al., *Water: The Potential Consequences of Climate Variability and Change for the Water Resources of the United States: The Report of the Water Sector Assessment Team of the National Assessment of the Potential Consequences of Climate Variability and Change,* U.S. Global Change Research Program, Pacific Institute for Studies in Development, Environment, and Security, 2000, p. 2; see http://www.gcrio.org/NationalAssessment/water/.

27. Working Group II, *Climate Change 2001*, p. 3.

28. Gleick et al., *Water*, p. 125; Maurice Roos, quoted in CRA Group, *Preparing for a Changing Climate*, pp. 4-1–51; Working Group II, *Climate Change 2001*, pp. 16, 197; National Academy of Sciences, *Reconciling Observations of Global Temperature Change* (2000); and California Climate Choices, www.climatechoices.org/ (a project of the Union of Concerned Scientists). Skeptics include the Frontiers of Freedom, at www.ff.org/, and the George C. Marshall Institute, at www.marshall.org.

29. K. Hayhoe et al., "Emissions Pathways, Climate Change and Impacts on California," *The Proceedings of the National Academy of Sciences*, 101:34 (August 24, 2004), pp. 12422–27; Union of Concerned Scientists, www.ucsusa.org.

30. Christopher Field in *Proceedings of the National Academy of Sciences*, quoted in Maggie Fox, "Global Warming Menaces California Wine Industry," *Reuters*, August 17, 2004; Working Group II, *Climate Change 2001*, pp. 200, 203; CRA Group, *Preparing for a Changing Climate*, pp. 4-1–34 to 4-1–35, 4-1–41, 4-1–59, 4-1–64.

31. CRA Group, *Preparing for a Changing Climate*, p. 4-1–64; and Maurice Roos, State Hydrologist, California Department of Water Resources, quoted in CRA Group, *Preparing for a Changing Climate*, pp. 4-1–70 to 4-1–73.

32. Working Group II, *Climate Change 2001*, p. 205. On modeling climate change impacts on water resources in California, see D. Cayan, M. Dettinger, R. Hanson, T. Brown, A. Westerling, and N. Knowles, http://meteora.ucsd.edu/~meyer/acpi_progress_jun01.html#wholeresp. On incentives to keep flood prevention space open, see Maurice Roos, in CRA Group, *Preparing for a Changing Climate*, p. 4-1–74. See also "Projected Changes in Average Annual Runoff" in CRA Group, *Preparing for a Changing Climate*, pp. 4-1–53, 4-1–56.

33. Dennis Brownridge and Steve Hinchman, "The Grand Canyon Is Just Another Turbine," in Char Miller, ed., *Water in the West: A High Country News Reader* (Corvallis: Oregon State University Press, 2000), pp. 93–99; Neil S. Grigg, *Water Resources Management* (New York: McGraw-Hill, 1996), pp. 381–88; Marcus Moench, "Groundwater: The Challenge of Monitoring and Management," in Gleick et al., *The World's Water, 2004–2005*, pp. 79–100.

34. Kiparsky and Gleick, "Climate Change and California Water Resources," pp. 160–61.

35. Jim Mayer, *Layperson's Guide to Groundwater* (Sacramento: Water Education Foundation, 2003), p. 13; California Department of Water Resources, *Bulletin 160-98, The California Water Plan Update*, November 1998, p. ES 3-7; Working Group II, *Climate Change 2001*, p. 199; CRA Group, *Preparing for a Changing Climate*, pp. 4-1–34, 4-1–35, 4-1–87, 4-1–88.

36. Working Group II, *Climate Change 2001*, pp. 193, 211–212.; David J. Hayes, "Accommodation Turns to Conflict: Lessons from the Colorado," in McDonald and Jehl, eds., *Whose Water Is It?* pp. 139–62; Postel, *Last Oasis*, pp. 93–94.

37. CRA Group, *Preparing for a Changing Climate*, p. 4-1–77.

38. Working Group II, *Climate Change 2001*, pp. 197, 207, 218; American Water Works Association, "Climate Change and Water Resources: Committee Report of the AWWA Public Advisory Forum," *Journal of the American Water Works Association*, 89:11 (November 1997), pp. 107–10.

39. William Ruckelshaus, quoted in *Business Week*, June 18, 1990.

40. David H. Getches, "Constraints of Law and Policy on the Management of Western Water," in William M. Lewis Jr., ed., *Water and Climate in the Western United States* (Boulder: University of Colorado Press, 2003), p. 214.

41. *National Audubon Society v. Superior Court of Alpine County*, 33 Cal. 3d 419, 189 Cal. Rprtr. 346 (1983), cert. denied, 464 U.S. 977 (1983), cited in CRA Group, *Preparing for a Changing Climate*, p. 4-1–5, note 21.

42. WEF 2004 Water Law and Policy Briefing, "Panel 2: *Tulare Lake v. United States*: An Analysis of the Endangered Species Act Takings Compensation Case."

43. California Department of Water Resources, *California Water Plan Update, Bulletin 160-93*, vol. 1 (Sacramento: California Department of Water Resources, 1994), p. 57; Harrison C. Dunning, "Confronting the Environmental Legacy of Irrigated Agriculture in the West: The Case of the Central Valley Project," *Environmental Law*, 23 (1993), p. 943; Ernest A. Conant, "The Central Valley Project Improvement Act Proposed Reforms," *San Joaquin Agricultural Law Review*, 6 (1996), pp. 27–30; David Zilberman, Neal MacDougall, Farhed Shah, "Changes in Water Allocation Mechanisms for California Agriculture," *Contemporary Economic Policy*, 12:1 (January 1994), pp. 122–34; Marca Weinberg, "Federal Water Policy Reform: Implications for Irrigated Farms in California," *Contemporary Economic Policy*, 15:2 (April 1997), pp. 63–74.

44. Remarks by Dan Cooper, "Overview—Birds of the Salton Sea," presented at the WEF Salton Sea Conference, Sacramento, California, January 2004.

45. Ibid.

46. WEF 2004 Salton Sea Conference, "Status of Salton Sea Fish and Wildlife Resources"; Margaret Kriz, "Water Wars," *California Journal*, 47:3 (March 1, 2003), p. 40; Dean E. Murphy, "Agreement in West Will Send Farms' Water to Urban Areas," *New York Times*, October 17, 2003, p. A1; "Demand to Fallow Farmland Latest in Salton Sea Saga," editorial, *Western Farm Press*, June 15, 2002.

47. WEF 2004 Salton Sea Conference, "What Do We Mean When We Say

Restoration?"; Laura McCoy, "Desert Water Wars Looming Vote Could Determine the Future of the Salton Sea," *Sacramento Bee*, December 7, 2002, p. A1; Mark van de Kamp, "Historic Water Pacts Fill Attorney's Resume," *Santa Barbara News-Press*, November 9, 2003, p. 1; Megan Hennessy, "Colorado River Water Rights: Property Rights in Transition," *University of Chicago Law Review,* 71 (Fall 2004), pp. 1673–74.

48. CRA Group, *Preparing for a Changing Climate*, pp. 4-1–22, 4-1–26 to 4-1–29; Paul Rosta, "Long Dry Spell Taxes Utilities in the West," *Water Management*, 253:3 (July 19, 2004), p. 10.

49. California Department of Water Resources, press release, "Department of Water Resources Signs Long-Term Power Contracts for Peak Power," August 17, 2001; "Water Rates Not Affected as Metropolitan Board Appropriates $133 Million for Increased Power Costs," *Business Wire*, June 12, 2001; MWDSC, "Metropolitan Power Agreement with California ISO to Help Ease Electrical Crisis This Summer," press release, May 9, 2001.

50. MWDSC, *Report on Metropolitan's Water Supplies*, p. 1.

51. Waterman, "Addressing California's Uncertain Water Future by Coordinating Long-Term Land Use and Water Planning: Is a Water Element in the General Plan the Next Step?" *Ecology Law Quarterly*, 31 (2004), pp. 129–33; Karen E. Johnson and Jeff Loux, *Water and Land Use: Planning Wisely for California's Future* (Point Arena, CA: Solano Press Books, 1994), pp. 237–48.

52. Henry Vaux, "Global Climate Change and California's Water Resources," in Joseph B. Knox, ed., *Global Climate Change and California: Potential Impacts and Responses* (Berkeley: University of California Press, 1991), p. 95.

53. Noel Brinkerhoff, "Who's Minding the Aquifer?" *California Journal*, 32:7 (July 1, 2001), p. 16; Mayer, *Layperson's Guide to Groundwater*, p. 14.

54. Linda Nash, "Water Quality and Health," in Peter H. Gleick, ed., *Water in Crisis: A Guide to the World's Fresh Water Resources* (New York: Oxford University Press, 1993), pp. 25–39; Steve Hinchman, "EPA to Denver: Wake Up and Smell the Coffee" in Miller, ed., *Water in the West*, pp. 203–5; Khalil Abu-Saba, "Mercury Rising: Dealing with History's Toxic Legacy," presentation at the WEF 2004 Water Law and Policy Briefing.

55. Elizabeth McCarthy, *Layperson's Guide to San Francisco Bay* (Sacramento: Water Education Foundation, 1997), p. 13; Jim Mayer, *Layperson's Guide to Water Pollution* (Sacramento: Water Education Foundation, 1996), p. 11; CRA Group, *Preparing for a Changing Climate*, p. 4-1–75.

56. See http://www.epa.gov/safewater/ccl/perchlorate/perchlorate.html; http://thyroid.about.com/cs/perchloratedanger/a/perchlorate.htm; http://www.dhs.ca.gov/ps/ddwem/chemicals/perchl/perchlindex.htm; http://www.basinwater.com/ss/contaminant.htm. See http://www.epa.gov/safewater/ccl/perchlorate/

perchlorate.html; http://thyroid.about.com/cs/perchloratedanger/a/perchlorate
.htm; http://www.dhs.ca.gov/ps/ddwem/chemicals/perchl/perchlindex.htm; and
Mayer, *Layperson's Guide to Groundwater*, p. 15.

57. See http://www.oehha.ca.gov/water/phg/perchphg31204.html; http://
www.dhs.ca.gov/ps/ddwem/chemicals/perchl/perchlorateMCL.htm; and Mayer,
Layperson's Guide to Groundwater, p. 15.

58. See http://www.dhs.ca.gov/ps/ddwem/chemicals/MTBE/mtbeindex.htm;
http://www.atsdr.cdc.gov/tfacts19.html; http://www.atsdr.cdc.gov/tfacts18.html;
and Mayer, *Layperson's Guide to Groundwater*, p. 15.

59. See http://www.dhs.ca.gov/ps/ddwem/chemicals/arsenic/newmcl.htm;
http://www.dhs.ca.gov/ps/ddwem/chemicals/NDMA.NDMAindex.htm; http://
www.dhs.ca.gov/ps/ddwem/chemicals/123tcp/actionlevel.htm; http://www.dhs
.ca.gov/ps/ddwem/chemicals/Chromium6/Cr+6index.htm; http://www.atsdr.cdc
.gov/tfacts7.html

60. "Table A2-1: Total Local Supply for Consumptive Uses—Dry Year," and
"Table A2-10: Total Local Supply (Consumptive and Non-consumptive—Dry
Year," in MWDSC, *Integrated Water Resources Plan: 2003 Update*, pp. 73, 82;
Mayer, *Layperson's Guide to Groundwater*, p. 11.

61. Environment California Research and Policy Center (ECRPC), "Down
the Drain: Six Case Studies of Groundwater Contamination That Are Wasting
California's Water," January 2003, http://www.environmentcalifornia.org/
envirocalif.asp?id2=8874 and http://www.dhs.ca.gov/ps/ddwem/chemicals/
perchl/perchlindex.htm, http://www.dhs.ca.gov/ps/ddwem/chemicals/perchl/
monitoringupdate.htm and http://www.gci.ch/Communication/DigitalForum/
digiforum/ARTICLES/article2002/californiahigh.html.

62. Gary Pitzer, *Layperson's Guide to Drinking Water* (Sacramento: Water
Education Foundation, 2002), p. 18; Environment California Research and Policy Center (ECRPC), "Down the Drain"; Mayer, *Layperson's Guide to Groundwater*, pp. 14, 16.

63. See, for example, the American Rivers' list of the most endangered rivers
of 2004, http://www.disasternews.net/news/news.php?articleid=2209. Also see
David Hasemyer, "Huge Toxic Pile by River to Be Moved," *San Diego Union-
Tribune*, April 7, 2005, pp. A1, A12.

64. McCarthy, *Layperson's Guide to San Francisco Bay*, p. 9; Pitzer, *Layperson's Guide to Drinking Water*, p. 15. MWD still plans to use chlorine for
distribution-line disinfection.

65. Mayer, *Layperson's Guide to Groundwater*, p. 14; see http://www.dhs
.ca.gov/ps/ddwem/chemicals/perchl/earlyfindings.htm; ECRPC, "Down the
Drain"; "Water Testing and Treatment Reflect the Times," *R&D Magazine*, 46:5
(May 2004), p. 52.

66. J. Edgar Hoover, "Water Supply Facilities and National Defense," *Journal of the American Water Works Association*, 33:11 (1941), p. 1861, quoted in Claudia Copeland and Betsy Cody, *Terrorism and Security Issues Facing the Water Infrastructure Sector* (Washington, DC: Congressional Research Service, 2005), p. CRS-1.

67. "US Responds to Potential Threats to Water Supply," *Water & Waste Water International*, 17:4 (August 2002), p. 5.

68. In World War II, both sides bombed dams, and the Wehrmacht even attacked British troops crossing the Liri River by destroying the Isoletta Dam in 1944. The Wehrmacht also repeatedly blocked rivers to slow the Allied advance across western Europe, notably flooding the Ay River in France (1944) and, during the Battle of the Bulge, the Ill River Valley (1944–45). More recently, the United States bombed dikes in North Vietnam (1972); Iran diverted water to flood Iraqi positions during the Iran-Iraq war (1980–1988); and Cuban and Angolan forces attacked the Calueque Dam in Angola (1988). See Peter H. Gleick, "Environment and Security: Water Conflict Chronology Version 2002," in Peter Gleick et al., *The World's Water: The Biennial Report on Freshwater Resources, 2002–2003* (Oakland, CA: The Pacific Institute, 2002) pp. 196–206.

69. See MWDSC, *Integrated Water Resources Plan, 2003 Update*, pp. 44–45; MWDSC, *Report on Metropolitan's Water Supplies*, Appendix D, pp. 6–12.

70. For evidence of combatants destroying water facilities or introducing poison into local water supplies during wartime, see Peter H. Gleick, "Environment and Security," pp. 196–206.

71. MWDSC, "Commitment to Water Quality: Tighter Security and Persistent Monitoring," in *Annual Water Quality Report for 2003* (Los Angeles: MWDSC, 2003), http://mwdh20.com/mwdh2o/pages/yourwater/2003%5Freport/protect%5F02.html.

72. "Report: Terrorists Considered Poisoning Water Supplies," *U.S. Water News Online*, August 2004, http://www.uswaternews.com/archives/arcquality/4repoterr8.html; Shaun Waterman, "Al Qaeda Warns of Threat to Water Supply," *Washington Times*, May 29, 2003, http://washingtontimes.com/national/20030528-102548-4938r.htm; "FBI: Al Qaeda Might Use Poison," *CBS/AP*, September 5, 2003, http://www.cbsnews.com/stories/2003/09/05/national/main 571778.shtml.

Chapter 8

1. Robert Gottlieb, *A Life of Its Own: The Politics of Water and Power* (San Diego: Harcourt Brace Jovanovich, 1988), p. 247.

2. Peter H. Gleick, "A Soft Path: Conservation, Efficiency, and Easing Conflicts over Water," in Bernadette McDonald and Douglas Jehl, eds., *Whose*

Water Is It? The Unquenchable Thirst of a Water-Hungry World (Washington, DC: National Geographic, 2003), p. 190.

3. Interview with Ron Gastelum, former chief executive officer, Metropolitan Water District of Southern California (MWDSC), 2005.

4. Lloyd S. Dixon, Nancy Y. Moore, Ellen M. Pint, "Drought Management Policies and Economic Effects in Urban Areas of California, 1987–1992" (Santa Monica, CA: RAND Corporation, 1993), Doc. No. MR-251-CUWA/RC; Pacific Northwest National Laboratory, "Model Casts Cloud over Mountain Snowfall," http://www.pnl.gov/main/highlights/global.html; John D. Landis and Michael Reilly, "How We Will Grow: Baseline Predictions of California's Population Through 2100," http://www.energy.ca.gov/reports/2003-10-31_500-03-058CF_A03.PDF, p. 9.

5. Norris Hundley Jr., *The Great Thirst: Californians and Water—A History,* rev. ed. (Berkeley: University of California Press, 2001), pp. 316, 329; John N. Barbour, "Water Politics in California: The Peripheral Canal Bill," doctoral thesis, University of California at Santa Barbara, 1982; Stephanie S. Pincetl, *Transforming California: A Political History of Land Use and Development* (Baltimore, MD: John Hopkins University Press, 1999), pp. 206–12; Steven J. Shupe et al., "Western Water Rights: The Era of Reallocation," *National Resources Journal,* 29 (1989), p. 413.

6. Interview with Ron Gastelum; Michael F. Domenica, ed., *Integrated Water Resources Planning for the 21st Century: Proceedings of the 22nd Annual Conference,* Cambridge, Massachusetts, May 7–11, sponsored by the Water Resources Planning and Management Division, American Society of Civil Engineers (New York: American Society of Civil Engineers, 1995); MWDSC, *Southern California's Integrated Water Resources Plan,* vols. 1–2 (Los Angeles: MWDSC, 1996); Ryan Waterman, "Addressing California's Uncertain Water Future by Coordinating Long-Term Land Use and Water Planning: Is a Water Element in the General Plan the Next Step?" *Ecology Law Quarterly,* 31 (2004), pp. 160–63; Karen E. Johnson and Jeff Loux, *Water and Land Use: Planning Wisely for California's Future* (Point Arena, CA: Solano Press Books, 1994), pp. 129–44.

7. Kenneth Boulding, "The Feather River Anthology or 'Holy Water'" (unpublished), quoted in Gurmukh S. Gill, Edward C. Gray, and David Seckler, "The California Water Plan and Its Critics: A Brief Overview," in David Seckler, ed., *California Water: A Study in Resource Management* (Berkeley: University of California Press, 1971), p. 25.

8. This story is told comprehensively in Hundley's *The Great Thirst.*

9. Waterman, "Addressing California's Uncertain Water Future by Coordinating Long-Term Land Use and Water Planning," pp. 129–32, 162–64; *Planning and Conservation League v. Dep't of Water Resources,* 83 Cal. App. 4th 892

(2000); *Santa Clarita Organization for Planning the Environment (SCOPE) v. County of Los Angeles*, 106 Cal. App. 4th 715 (2003). SB 60 (1999) required that MWD annually report to the state legislature on progress in achieving the goals of cost-effective conservation, recycling, and groundwater recharge.

10. Interview with Ron Gastelum; *California Public Resources Code*, Sects. 21000–21178; *Friends of Mammoth v. Board of Supervisors*, 8 Cal. 3d 247 (1972); *Cal. Statutes* (1983) 3555; *California Water Code*, Sects. 10610–10656; James P. Morris, "Who Controls the Waters? Incorporating Environmental and Social Values in Water Resources Planning," *Hastings West-Northwest Journal of Environmental Law and Policy*, 6 (Winter–Spring 2000), pp. 133–35.

11. Waterman, "Addressing California's Uncertain Water Future by Coordinating Long-Term Land Use and Water Planning," pp. 129–33; Johnson and Loux, *Water and Land Use*, pp. 237–48.

12. Daniel M. Rodrigo et al., "Integrated Resources Planning and Reliability Analysis: A Case Study of the Metropolitan Water District of Southern California," *Advances in the Economics of Environmental Resources*, 1 (1996), pp. 49–58; Morris, "Who Controls the Waters?"; Johnson and Loux, *Water and Land Use*, pp. 95–96.

13. "Water Plan," *City News Service* (Los Angeles), July 13, 2004, p. 1.

14. MWDSC, *Southern California's Integrated Water Resources Plan*, Draft Report No. 1107, vol. 1, E1–E4 (December 1995), pp. 1–7.

15. MWDSC, *Goals and Objectives* (Los Angeles: MWDSC, 1992); MWDSC, *Southern California's Integrated Water Resources Plan*, 1, pp. 1–7, 3–2; "Pro-Active Management of Future Risk: Integrated Resource Planning," *Water Strategist*, 9:2 (Summer 1995); Ronald R. Gastelum, "Written Statement," Before U.S. House of Representatives, Transportation and Infrastructure Committee, Subcommittee on Water Resources and Environment, Hearing, "Water: Is It the 'Oil' of the 21st Century?" May 22, 2003, http://www.house.gov/transportation/water/05-22-03/gastelum.html.

16. Robert Gottlieb and Margaret FitzSimmons, *Thirst for Growth: Water Agencies as Hidden Government in California* (Tucson: University of Arizona Press, 1991), pp. 11–15; MWDSC, Water Planning, Quality and Resource Committee Meeting, July 13, 2004 (Los Angeles: MWDSC, 1992); MWDSC, *Integrated Water Resources Plan 2003 Update* (Los Angeles: MWDSC, May 2004), p. 21, http://www.mwdh2o.com/mwdh2o/pdf/irp_01.pdf; Dennis E. O'Connor, *The Governance of the Metropolitan Water District of Southern California: An Overview of the Issues* (Sacramento: California Research Bureau, August 1998), pp. 5–17, http://www.library.ca.gov.

17. MWDSC, *Integrated Water Resources Plan 2003 Update*, pp. 15–16, 18, 22–23.

18. MWDSC, *Annual Progress Report to the California State Legislature: Snapshots of the Past . . . Portrait of a New Reality; Achievements in Conservation, Recycling and Groundwater Recharge* (Los Angeles: MWDSC, February 2004), p. 35, http://mwdh2o.com/mwdh2o/pages/yourwater/SB60/sb60_main.html; MWDSC, *Integrated Water Resources Plan 2003 Update*, p. 26; Johnson and Loux, *Water and Land Use*, pp. 41–2, 249–66; Peter H. Gleick, Dana Haasz, and Gary Wolff, "Urban Water Conservation: A Case Study of Residential Water Use in California," in Gleick et al., *The World's Water, 2004–2005* (Washington, DC: Island Press, 2004), pp. 105–26.

19. Sandra Postel, *Last Oasis: Facing Water Scarcity* (New York: W. W. Norton, 1992), pp. 141–42; Martha Davis, "Stepping Outside the Box: Water in Southern California," speech at UCLA Environment Symposium, March 3, 1998; MWDSC, *Integrated Water Resources Plan: 2003 Update*, Table A1-1; Gleick, "A Soft Path," pp. 189, 191; Gleick, Haasz, and Wolff, "Urban Water Conservation: A Case Study of Residential Water Use in California," pp. 105–26; Gleick, Srinivasan, Henges-Jeck, and Wolff, "Urban Water Conservation: A Case Study of Commercial and Industrial Water Use in California," in *The World's Water, 2004–2005*, pp. 153–54.

20. MWDSC, *Integrated Water Resources Plan 2003 Update*, p. 31.

21. MWDSC, *Integrated Water Resources Plan 2003 Update*, pp. 8, 26–30; MWDSC, *Annual Progress Report to the California State Legislature*, pp. 11, 22; Kevin L. Wattier, "Seawater Desalination Concerns and Benefits," presentation to the Southern California Association of Governments, December 11, 2003.

22. Interview with Ron Gastelum; MWDSC, *Integrated Water Resources Plan 2003 Update*, pp. 32–34, 36, 44, 46–47, 50–51; Johnson and Loux, *Water and Land Use*, p. 138.

23. MWDSC, *Integrated Water Resources Plan 2003 Update*, pp. 60–61; interview with Ron Gastelum; interview with Jerry Gewe.

24. Gastelum, "Written Statement," Before U.S. Congress, Transportation and Infrastructure Committee, Subcommittee on Water Resources and Environment, May 22, 2003; "Water Plan," *City News Service* (Los Angeles), July 13, 2004.

25. Gastelum interview; "Ron Gastelum's MWD Exit Interview: Adequate Water Supply Predicted," *Metro Investment Report*, 12:3 (November 2004), pp. 1, 12, 13, 16; MWDSC, *Integrated Water Resources Plan 2003 Update*, pp. 39–43; Michael Gardner, "Drought Creates a River of Doubt," *San Diego Union-Tribune*, April 25, 2004, p. A3. Some believe that MWD accepted a Colorado River supply reduction because of the likelihood of having to provide more water to Arizona than would be gained from the surplus under the provisions of the Interim Surplus Plan.

26. Interview with Ron Gastelum.

27. MWDSC, *Integrated Water Resources Plan 2003 Update*, pp. 39–44.

28. MWDSC, *Integrated Water Resources Plan 2003 Update*, pp. 10, 60, 99; San Diego County Water Authority (SDCWA), Water Policy Committee, "Agenda for January 29, 2004," p. 8, http://www.sdcwa.org/board/documents/2004_01_29/WP.pdf; Michael Gardner, "2 Water Plans Aim to Quell Feuding," *San Diego Union-Tribune*, June 5, 2004, p. A1.

29. Gardner, "Drought Creates a River of Doubt," p. A3.

30. Gardner, "Drought Creates a River of Doubt," p. A3; Gardner, "2 Water Plans Aim to Quell Feuding," p. A1.

31. MWDSC, *Integrated Water Resources Plan 2003 Update*, pp. 23, 37, 43, 53–55, 66, 95–96, 101–2; "MWD Water," *City News Service* (Los Angeles), October 12, 2004; Gardner, "Drought Creates a River of Doubt," p. A3.

32. MWDSC, *Integrated Water Resources Plan 2003 Update*, pp. 24, 36, 60, 64; MWDSC, *Report on Metropolitan's Water Supplies* (Los Angeles: MWDSC, March 25, 2003), p. 14, http://mwdh20.com/mwdh2o/pdf/sb221/sb221.pdf.

33. MWDSC, *Integrated Water Resources Plan 2003 Update*, pp. 24, 60; California, Office of Environmental Health Hazard Assessment, "Public Health Goals," http://www.oehha.ca.gov/water/phg/perchphg31204.html; Janet Wilson, "Toxic Tailings May Be Hauled Off," *Los Angeles Times*, April 7, 2005, p. A12; Timothy F. Brick, "Water Quality: Are We Making the Grade," MWDSC, http://mwdh20.com/mwdh2o/pages/news/features/11%5F01/waterquality01.htm.

34. MWDSC, "Commitment to Water Quality: Tighter Security and Persistent Monitoring," in *Annual Water Quality Report for 2003* (Los Angeles: MWDSC, 2003), http://mwdh20.com/mwdh2o/pages/yourwater/2003%5Freport/protect%5F02.html; MWSDC, "Drinking Water and Your Health," in idem; MWDSC, "Ozone Technology Application," in idem; MWDSC, "Statewide Activities," in idem; MWDSC, "Water Quality Standards," in idem; MWDSC, "Investments to Protect, Ensure Water Quality Drive First Increase in Cost of Treated Water in Seven Years," press release, March 11, 2003; Claudia Copeland and Betsy Cody, "Terrorism: Water Supply Infrastructure," in Ervin L. Clarke, ed., *Water Resources: Issues and Perspectives* (New York: Nova Science Publishers, 2002), pp. 1–6.

35. Interview with Ron Gastelum; MWDSC, *Annual Progress Report to the California State Legislature*, p. 30; California Water Code 10634 (2003); Waterman, "Addressing California's Uncertain Water Future by Coordinating Long-Term Land Use and Water Planning," p. 132; Ken Farfsing, "Congressional Statement," Before U.S. House of Representatives, Transportation and Infrastructure Committee, Subcommittee on Water Resources and Environment, June 19, 2003, pp. 1–9.

36. "Water Testing and Treatment Reflect the Times," *R&D Magazine*, 46:5 (May 2004), p. 52.

37. "Santa Margarita GM John Schatz Elaborates on So Cal Regional Water Issues," Metro *Investment Report*, 12:3 (November 2004), pp. 9, 18.

38. MWDSC, *Report on Metropolitan's Water Supplies*, p. 2.

39. City of Los Angeles, Department of Water and Power (LADWP), *Urban Water Management Plan: Fiscal Year 2003–2004 Annual Update*, pp. 4, 6–10, 14, http://ladwp.com. Los Angeles's supplies from MWD during normal and dry years primarily come from the State Water Project to better fit LADWP's system hydraulics and reduce treatment costs.

40. LADWP Water Service Organization, *2003 to 2008 Business Plan* (Los Angeles: LADWP, 2003); Robert V. Phillips and Kenneth W. Downey, "Secession: The Next Great Water War," *Los Angeles Times*, September 15, 2002, p. M3.

41. Interview with Mike Madigan, 2005.

42. Tony Perry, "San Diego Aims to Cut Reliance on L.A. Water," *Los Angeles Times*, June 25, 2004, p. B1; SDCWA, *San Diego County Water Authority 2004 Annual Supply Report* (San Diego: SDCWA, June 2004), p. 3, http://www.sdcwa.org/news/pdf/WaterSupplyReport2004.pdf.

43. Douglas Jehl, "Alchemy or Salvation? Desalting the Sea," in McDonald and Jehl, eds., *Whose Water Is It?* pp. 199–211; Brian Baker, "Stubborn Thirst," *Utility Week*, April 13, 2003, p. 22; SDCWA, "Minutes of the Formal Board of Directors Meeting," October 23, 2003, p. 3; "Strains Develop in Desal Plant Partnership," editorial, *San Diego Union-Tribune,* January 28, 2004, p. B4; Gig Conaughton, "Simmering Water Rate Dispute Added to Desalination Story," *North County Times*, July 31, 2004, p. 1; Bud Pocklington, "Moving Forward on Seawater Desalination," news release, SDCWA, August 20, 2004, http://www.sdcwa.org/clips/2004/08aug/082004/082004movingforward.html.

44. Mike Lee, "Treatment Site Trickles into Service," *San Diego Union-Tribune*, February 21, 2005, p. A1; Amy Oakes, "New Facility to Process Water Close to Approval," *San Diego Union-Tribune*, February 21, 2005, p. A14.

45. Inland Empire Utilities Agency (IEUA), 2003 *Annual Report*, pp. 9, 13, http://www.ieua.org/Home/Docs/Reports/Annual%20Report%202003.pdf; Municipal Water District of Orange County, *2001 Strategic Plan*, pp. 2, 7–8, http://www.mwdoc.com/board_of_dirs/2001final-strategic-plan.pdf; Zema Mehta, "O.C. Sees Water Era Ending," *Los Angeles Times*, September 29, 2002, p. B1.

46. Paul Rosta, "Long Dry Spell Taxes Utilities in the West," *Water Management*, 253:3 (July 19, 2004), p. 10; "Sustainable Solutions to Water Scarcity," *Water & Waste Water International*, 17:5 (October 2002), p. 42; Municipal Water District of Orange County, *2001 Strategic Plan*, pp. 2, 7–8, http://www

.mwdoc.com/board_of_dirs/2001final-strategic-plan.pdf; Zema Mehta, "O.C. Sees Water Era Ending"; Minaya, "Orange County: O.C. to Be Water Bank for MWD," p. B3; "Santa Margarita GM John Schatz Elaborates on So Cal Regional Water Issues," pp. 9, 18. Under MWD's new rate structure, third-party transfers are permitted at a wheeling cost the same as what MWD charges itself for transportation of water.

47. Michael Parfit, "Water: A Portrait in Words and Pictures," *National Geographic Magazine Special Edition*, 184: 5A, November 1993, pp. 5–17.

48. Gig Conaughton "Simmering Water Rate Dispute Added to Desalination Story."

49. Other regional authorities have faced similar representational dilemmas. Consider the Port Authority of New York/New Jersey. The city of New York initially thought that it should be directly represented on the board, but the mayor misplayed his hand. Only gubernatorial state appointees were installed. If population or wealth had been the key criteria, then New York State could outvote New Jersey by 2 to 1 or more. See Jameson W. Doig, *Empire on the Hudson: Entrepreneurial Vision and Political Power at the Port of New York Authority* (New York: Columbia University Press, 2001).

50. Dennis O'Connor, *The Governance of the Metropolitan Water District of Southern California: An Overview of the Issues* (Sacramento: California Research Bureau, August 1998), pp. 5–17; O'Connor, *The Governance of the Metropolitan Water District of Southern California: Options for Change* (Sacramento: California Research Bureau, December 1998), pp. 7, 10, http://www.library.ca.gov.

51. O'Connor, *An Overview of the Issues*, pp. 37, 39, 45–48; O'Connor, *Options for Change*, pp. 10–11; "Water District Change Overdue," editorial, *Los Angeles Times*, May 30, 2000, p. B6; "Water Rates," City News Service (Los Angeles), January 9, 2001; "Metropolitan Water to Maintain Rates for Fifth Year," *Water Tech Daily News*, January 11, 2001, http:/www.watertechonline.com.

52. "Ron Gastelum's MWD Exit Interview: Adequate Water Supply Predicted," p. 1; O'Connor, *Options for Change*, pp. 23–25; Thair Peterson, "Strategic Plan: Building a Platform for Tomorrow," *Aqueduct Magazine* (March 2001), http://www.mwdh2o.com/Aqueduct/march2001/strategic.htm.

53. Steven P. Erie and Pascale Joassart-Marcelli, "New Battlegrounds in the L.A. vs. San Diego Water War," *Los Angeles Times*, January 30, 2000, p. M6; O'Connor, *An Overview of the Issues*, pp. 49–50; O'Connor, *Options for Change*, pp. 21, 33–42.

54. O'Connor, *Options for Change*, pp. 5, 22; Tony Perry, "The State: Tensions Rise over Bill to Alter Water Delivery Policy," *Los Angeles Times*, May 6, 2001, p. B8; Thair Peterson, "Strategic Plan: Building a Platform for Tomorrow"; Katie Cooper, "New MWD Policy May Trim Water Prices by 10%: Ventura County

Expected to Benefit," *Los Angeles Times*, May 17, 2000, p. A9; James Flanigan, "MWD Restructures Rates, Regulations on Water Supplies," *Los Angeles Times*, December 13, 2000, p. C2; Flanigan, "Creating a Free-Flowing Market to Buy, Sell Water," *Los Angeles Times*, October 24, 2001, p. C1.

55. Cooper, "New MWD Policy May Trim Water Prices by 10%"; "MWD Rates," *City News Service* (Los Angeles), March 9, 2004.

56. Tony Perry, "Appeals Court Ruling a Victory for MWD," *Los Angeles Times*, May 31, 2000, p. A3; SDCWA, "Preferential Rights," October 2001; Perry, "San Diego Aims to Cut Reliance on L.A. Water," *Los Angeles Times*, June 25, 2004, p. B1; SDCWA, *San Diego County Water Authority 2004 Annual Supply Report* (San Diego: SDCWA, June 2004), p. 3, http://www.sdcwa .org/news/pdf/WaterSupplyReport2004.pdf; SDCWA, "Minutes of the Formal Board of Directors' Meeting," February 26, 2004, http://www .sdcwa.org/board/minutes/2004_02_26.phtml.

57. Jason Felch, "MWD Taps Ex-Mayor to Lead Board," *Los Angeles Times*, October 13, 2004, p. B3; Jose Luis Jiménez, "S.D. Gains Ally at L.A. Water Agency; Official Vows to Improve Ties to Local Authority," *San Diego Union-Tribune*, March 15, 2005, pp. B1, B3.

58. Jiménez, "S.D. Gains Ally at L.A. Water Agency," p. B1; Anna Gorman, "MWD Names Executive Officer," *Los Angeles Times*, April 2, 2005, p. B3.

59. Gottlieb and FitzSimmons, *Thirst for Growth*, p. 217.

60. Gleick, "A Soft Path," p. 190.

61. Peter H. Gleick, "The Millennium Development Goals for Water: Crucial Objectives, Inadequate Commitments," in Gleick et al., *The World's Water, 2004–2005*, pp. 1–5; Siyan Malomo and Sandra M. E. Wint, *Groundwater Vulnerability in Developing Commonwealth Countries* (London: Science and Technology Division, Commonwealth Secretariat, July 2003), pp. vi, xi.

62. Organisation for Economic Co-Operation and Development, *Social Issues in the Provision and Pricing of Water Services* (Paris: OECD, 2003), pp. 121–22, 130; Nicholas Spulber and Asghar Sabbaghi, *Economics of Water Resources: From Regulation to Privatization* (Boston: Kluwer Academic, 1998), pp. 228–39; Meena Palaniappan, Peter H. Gleick, Catherine Hunt, Veena Srinivasan, "Water Privatization Principles and Practices," in Gleick et al., *The World's Water, 2004–2005*, pp. 63–64; Neil S. Grigg, *Water Resources Management: Principles, Regulations, and Cases* (New York: McGraw Hill, 1996), p. 210.

63. Palaniappan et al., "Water Privatization Principles and Practices," p. 63–64; Grigg, *Water Resources Management*, p. 210.

64. OECD, *Social Issues in the Provision and Pricing of Water Services*, pp. 115–17; Spulber and Sabbaghi, *Economics of Water Resources*, p. 240; Palaniappan et al., "Water Privatization Principles and Practices," p. 60; Grigg,

Water Resources Management, p. 212; United Nations, Economic and Social Commission for Asia and the Pacific (UNESCAP), *Guidelines on Water and Sustainable Development: Principles and Policy Options* (New York: United Nations, 1997), pp. 22, 33; Harald D. Fredriksen, *Water Resources Institutions* (Washington, DC: The World Bank, 1992), p. 33; Y. Takahasi, "Water Management in Japan after World War II," in Asit K. Biswas, Mohammed Jellali, and Glenn E. Stout, eds., *Water for Sustainable Development in the Twenty-First Century* (Delhi: Oxford University Press, 1993), pp. 189–98; Marq de Villers, "Three Rivers," in McDonald and Jehl, eds., *Whose Water Is It?* p. 54; Weilu Wang, "Water Management in the People's Republic of China," in Manas Chatterji, Saul Arlosoroff, and Gauri Guha, eds., *Conflict Management of Water Resources* (London: Ashgate, 2002), pp. 88–115.

65. UNESCAP, *Guidelines on Water and Sustainable Development*, pp. 1, 22, 36–37, 54, 63; UNESCAP, *Sustainable Development of Water Resources in Asia and the Pacific: An Overview* (New York: United Nations, 1997), pp. 8–12; Fredriksen, *Water Resources Institutions*, pp. 31, 33; Diane Raines Ward, *Water Wars: Drought, Flood, Folly, and the Politics of Thirst* (New York: Riverhead Press, 2002), pp. 31, 34, 214–15; OECD, *Social Issues in the Provision and Pricing of Water Services*, pp. 125, 128, 131; Johnson and Loux, *Water and Land Use*, pp. 45–46, 69; Grigg, *Water Resources Management*, p. 444; Peter Rogers, *America's Water: Federal Roles and Responsibilities* (Cambridge, MA: MIT Press, 1993), p. 15.

66. Andrew A. Dzurik, *Water Resources Planning* (London: Rowman and Littlefield, 1990), pp. 71–73; Grigg, *Water Resources Management*, p. 442; Rogers, *America's Water*, p. 15.

67. UNESCAP, *Guidelines on Water and Sustainable Development*, pp. 1, 16–17; Grigg, *Water Resources Management*, p. 443; "Santa Margarita GM John Schatz Elaborates on So Cal Regional Water Issues," pp. 9, 18; David H. Getches, "Constraints of Law and Policy on the Management of Western Water," in William M. Lewis Jr., ed., *Water and Climate in the Western United States* (Boulder: University of Colorado Press, 2003), p. 214. Stegner is quoted in Ward, *Water Wars*, p. 123.

68. UNESCAP, *Guidelines on Water and Sustainable Development*, p. 37; Fredriksen, *Water Resources Institutions*, p. 21.

69. Interview with Duane Georgeson, former MWDSC assistant general manager, 2005.

70. Gottlieb and FitzSimmons, *Thirst for Growth*, p. 212; Grigg, *Water Resources Management*, p. 443.

71. Interview with Carl Boronkay, 2005; Malin Falkenmark and Gunnar Lindh, "Water and Economic Development," in Peter H. Gleick, ed., *Water in*

Crisis: A Guide to the World's Fresh Water Resources (New York: Oxford University Press, 1993), p. 87; Morris, "Who Controls the Waters? Incorporating Environmental and Social Values in Water Resources Planning," pp. 152–53; Dennis Piarges, "Sustainability as an Evolving Process," *Futures*, 26 (1994), p. 197; David Lewis Feldman, *Water Resources Management: In Search of an Environmental Ethic* (Baltimore: Johns Hopkins University Press, 1991), pp. 2–3.

72. Gottlieb and FitzSimmons, *Thirst for Growth*, pp. 212–17; Rodrigo et al., "Integrated Resources Planning and Reliability Analysis," p. 71; Johnson and Loux, *Water and Land Use*, pp. 59, 66; John Carver and Miriam Mayhew Carter, *Reinventing Your Board: A Step-by-Step Guide to Implementing Policy Governance* (San Francisco: Jossey-Bass, 1997), chapter 7; O'Connor, *The Governance of the Metropolitan Water District of Southern California: Options for Change*, p. 14.

73. William L. Kahrl, *Water and Power* (Berkeley: University of California, 1982), p. 1.

74. Interview with Ron Gastelum.

Index

Boldface page numbers indicate material in tables or figures.

Nadeau, Remi, 36
NAFTA, 23
Napolitano, Grace, 166
National Association of Water Companies, 175
National Audubon Society, 151
National City, 131
National Environmental Protection Act (NEPA), 242. *See also* Environmental Protection Agency (EPA)
National Oceanic and Atmospheric Administration (NOAA), 216
National Water Commission, 180
Native Americans, **11**, 116, 219
Natomas Central Mutual Water Company, 195–196
Natural Resources Defense Council, 195
The Nature Conservancy, 165, 187
Navajo Generating Station, 217
NDMA, 234
Nebraska, 20, 180
NEPA, 242
Nevada: Colorado River and, 19, 138, 147; Lake Mead (*see* Mead, Lake); Miller on MWD/SNWA, 141; population of, 213, **214**; reservoirs in, **217**; SNWA, 141, 250
New Almaden mine, 232
New Frontier, 43
New Idna mine, 232
New Jersey, 175, 333*n*49
New Mexico, 19, 20, **214**, **217**
New Orleans' Sewage and Water Board, 175–176
Newport Beach, **11**
New York (state), 20, 174, 333*n*49
New York Board of Water Commissioners, 174
New York Port Authority, 333*n*49
Nichols, Mary, 160
Nickel, George, 187

Nile River, 23
nitrates, 235
nitrogen, total, 251
n-nitrosodimethylamine (NDMA), 234
NOAA, 216
Nordskog, Andrae, 42, 46
Norman, Harvey Van, 38
North American Free Trade Agreement (NAFTA), 23
North American Water and Power Alliance, 181–182
North Carolina, 19
North County Times, 255
Northern California Water Association, 193
Norton, Gale, 147
Norwalk, 115
nuts, 223

Oakland Tribune, 158
Oceanside, **11**, 131
Office of Environmental Health Hazard Assessment, 233, 250
Ogallala Aquifer, 20, 175
Oklahoma, 20
Ontario, **11**, 47, 52, 102
"Open Channel Isolated Facility" option, 156–157, 159
Orange (city), 268*n*12
Orange County: Anaheim, 10, **11**, **12**, 268*n*12; Berrenda Mesa Water District and, 186; CALFED lawsuit, 161; cost-of service for, 65–70, 76–77, 82, 286*n*31; Fullerton, **11**, **12**, 268*n*12; groundwater in, 254–255; and MWDOC (*see* MWDOC); Orange County Water District, 255; population of, 56, 76, 209; Santa Ana, 10, **11**, **12**, 268*n*12; Santa Margarita Water District, 195, 255; suburbanization of, 58

121, 144–152, 254; Ralph M. Parsons Company and, 182; rates, 119, 128, 129, 131, 254; Regional Facility Master Plan, 128; Salton Sea and, 119–120, 144–145; on San Vicente Dam, 254; storage facilities, 116, 128; subsidies and, 63–69, 77–80, 259, 285n29; on SWP capital costs, 284n21; 2020 Plan of, 253; Water Banking Authority and, 139; water delivery to, 10, **12**, 99–100, 283n10; Western Farms and, 109–110; wheeling charges for, 110–111, 114–116

San Diego Daily Transcript, 126

San Diego Gas and Electric Company (SDG&E), 184, 202

San Diego Union-Tribune: on the Bass brothers, 48; on deregulation, 117; on MWD, 48, 107, 116; on MWD rates, 248; on preferential rights, 121; on Salton Sea, 119; SDCWA and, 107; on water transfers, 48, 107

San Fernando (city), 10, **12**, 62

San Fernando Valley: annexation of, 34; Owens Valley and, 40; real-estate speculation in, 36–38; San Fernando Mission Land Company, 35; secession initiative by, 253; VOCs in, 234

San Francisco, 41, 155, 191

San Francisco Bay, **93**; CALFED (*see* CALFED Bay-Delta Program); CVP and, 160; earthquakes and, 219; global warming and, 224–225; Peripheral Canal and, 153; Proposition 50 and, 164

San Francisco Bay Area Council, 191

San Gabriel Valley, 234–235

San Gabriel Valley MWD, Upper, **11**, **12**

San Joaquin County, 190

San Joaquin Delta, **93**; agricultural water from, 154–157; bond issues for, 155–156; CALFED (*see* CALFED Bay-Delta Program); CVP and, 160; DWR and, 136; earthquakes and, 219; endangered species, protection of, 227; 4.4 Plan and, 167; global warming and, 224–225; Peripheral Canal and, 136, 153; Proposition 13 and, 155, 159; Proposition 50 and, 164; San Francisco and, 155; water transfers from, 48, 135–136, 154

San Joaquin River, 164, 195, 197, 201

San Joaquin Valley: Friant Water Users Authority, 164, 194–195, 197; groundwater in, 236; Kern County water transfers and, 185–187; Water Transfer Clearinghouse in, 192; wildlife habitat in, 166, 190, 227

San Luis Rey Mission, 116

San Marcos, 254

San Marino, 10, **11**, **12**, 268n12

Santa Ana, 10, **11**, **12**, 268n12

Santa Clara County, 236

Santa Margarita Water District, 195, 255

Santa Monica: on blended rate, 139; Gottlieb and, 49; groundwater in, 235; map of, **11**; in MWD, **12**, 268n12; population of, **12**; water delivery to, **12**

Santa Rosa Plateau Ecological Reserve, 187

San Vicente Dam/Reservoir, **11**, 254

SARS, 252

Saudi Arabia, 181